Key Concepts in
Counselling
and Psychotherapy

Key Concepts in Counselling and Psychotherapy

A critical A-Z guide to theory

Vicki Smith, Patrizia Collard, Paula Nicolson and Rowan Bayne

 Open University Press

Open University Press
McGraw-Hill Education
McGraw-Hill House
Shoppenhangers Road
Maidenhead
Berkshire
England
SL6 2QL

email: enquiries@openup.co.uk
world wide web: www.openup.co.uk

and Two Penn Plaza, New York, NY 10121-2289, USA

First published 2012

A catalogue record of this book is available from the British Library

ISBN-13: 978-0-33-524221-4 (pb)
ISBN-10: 0-33-524221-9 (pb)
eISBN-13: 978-0-33-524222-1

Library of Congress Cataloging-in-Publication Data
CIP data applied for

Typesetting and e-book compilations by
RefineCatch Limited, Bungay, Suffolk
Printed in the UK by Bell & Bain Ltd, Glasgow

Fictitious names of companies, products, people, characters and/or data that may be used herein (in case studies or in examples) are not intended to represent any real individual, company, product or event.

MIX
Paper from
responsible sources
FSC® C007785

The *McGraw·Hill* Companies

Contents

About the authors   xi
Acknowledgements   xiii
Introduction   1

A

Acceptance commitment therapy   5
Adlerian therapy   7
Anxiety   8
Anxiety, existential   10
Archetypes   11
Assertiveness   13
Attachment theory   14

B

Basic assumption groups   17
Beck, Aaron T. (1921–)   21
Behaviour therapy (BT)   23
Being mindful   26
Berne, Eric (1910–1970)   28
Bibliotherapy   29
Bion, Wilfred R. (1897–1979)   31
Blind eye   34
Boundaries   39
Brief therapy   42

C

Catharsis   45
Client feedback, collecting   46
Cognitive analytic therapy (CAT)   47
Cognitive behavioural therapy (CBT)   49
Cognitive distortions (CD)   52

Collaborative empiricism   54
Collective unconscious   55
Collectivism – individualism dimension   57
Compassionate mind training   58
Conditions of worth   61
Congruence   62
Constructivism   64
Container/contained   65
Core beliefs (CB)   68
Core conditions   70
Counter-transference   72

D

Death, fear of   75
Defence mechanisms   76
Denial   78
Depressive position   79
Dialectical behaviour therapy (DBT)   80
Displacement   83
Drama triangle, the   84
Dream analysis   85
Dynamic unconscious   87

E

Egan's skilled helper model   89
Ellis, Albert (1913–2007)   92
Empathy   95
Erikson, Erik (1902–1994)   98
Eriksonian analysis   99
Ethical concepts   100
Existential counselling   103
Eye movement desensitization and reprocessing (EMDR)   107

F

Feminist counselling   111
Free association   114
Freud, Sigmund (1856–1939)   116
Freudian analysis   121

G

Games   125
Gestalt therapy   126
Goal consensus   128
Groups   129

H

Humanistic approaches   135

I

Imagery, guided   137
Immediacy   139
Individuation   141
Integrative models   143
Interpretation   146
Introjection   147
Irrational beliefs (IBs)   148

J

Jung, Carl (1875–1961)   151

K

Kabat-Zinn, Jon (1944–)   153
Klein, Melanie (1882–1960)   154
Kleinian analysis   158

L

Lazarus, Arnold A. (1932–)   161
Life scripts   164
Life traps   165
Locus of evaluation   168
Logotherapy   169

M

Mindfulness-based cognitive behavioural coaching (MBCBC)   173
Mindfulness-based cognitive coaching (MBCC)   175

Mindfulness-based cognitive therapy (MBCT)   177
Mindfulness-based stress reduction (MBSR)   179
Motivational interviewing (MI)   181
Multicultural counselling   185
Multimodal therapy (MMT)   187

N

Narcissism   189
Narrative therapy   190
Negation and disavowal   193
Negative automatic thoughts   195
Neuro linguistic programming (NLP)   198

O

Object relations theory   201
Oedipus complex   203
Open systems theory   209
Organismic valuing process (OVP)   212
Organizational dynamics   213

P

Paranoid-schizoid position   219
Paraphrasing   220
Perls, Fritz (1893–1970)   222
Person-centred counselling   224
Personal construct therapy   225
Personality   228
Phenomenology   230
Positive psychology (PP)   232
Preferences   234
Projection   236
Projective identification   237
Psychic prison   239
Psychoanalysis   240
Psychodynamic counselling   243
Psychosexual development   244
Psychosocial development   247

Q

Questions   251

R

Rational emotive behaviour therapy (REBT)   255
Rationalization   257
Relational depth   258
Repression   259
Resistance   260
Rogers, Carl (1902–1987)   261
Ruptures in the therapeutic alliance   264

S

Schema therapy   267
Seduction   268
Self   271
Self-acceptance   273
Self-actualization   274
Self-concept   277
Self-disclosure   278
Social learning theory   281
Socratic dialogue   282
Splitting   284
Stages of change   286
Strengths   287
Structural model of the mind   288
Sublimation   291
Systemic therapies   292

T

Therapeutic relationship, the   297
Transactional analysis (TA)   299
Transference   302
Transitional objects   304

U

Unconditional positive regard   307

V

Values   311

W

Winnicott, D.W. (1896–1971)   313

Y

Yalom, Irvin (1931–)   315

Index   317

About the authors

Vicki Smith is Senior Lecturer in Counselling Studies at the University of Huddersfield. She has previously worked with young people as a counsellor and careers counsellor as well as in training and consultancy roles. Her present research focuses on the impact of the student/tutor alliance on the quality of the learning experience.

Dr Patrizia Collard is an international Mindfulness Educator, Writer, Psychotherapist and Coach in private practice and Senior Lecturer for Integrative Psychotherapy (Department of Psychology) at the University of East London. She has worked and lived in Vienna, Wales, England, Hong Kong and China and taught in Austria, the UK, the Greece, Spain and Slovenia.

Paula Nicolson is Emeritus Professor of Social Health Psychology at the University of London (Royal Holloway). She is now working as a freelance organizational consultant using psychodynamic and systemic approaches and completing a postgraduate diploma in psychodynamic couple counselling and psychotherapy. She is the author of numerous books and articles.

Rowan Bayne is Emeritus Professor of Psychology and Counselling at the University of East London where he was a core tutor on counselling and psychotherapy courses for over 30 years. He has also run courses for many major organizations such as British Rail, the BBC, the City of London and Warwick University and has written several books on personality and counselling.

Acknowledgements

Vicki would like to thank Paul for his support during the writing of this book, particularly in the latter stages when the pressure was on! Also thanks to Rowan who was always willing to discuss issues as they arose and to offer suggestions based on his wealth of experience.

Patrizia would like to thank Bernhard, my rock and Dan and Toby, my lights. Many heartfelt thanks to Vicki Smith for her patience, encouragement and support.

Paula would like to acknowledge the continued inspiration and support of colleagues and friends from 'D10' at the Tavistock Clinic as well as from Derry and Kate Nicolson and Malachi and Azriel Annon-Nicolson.

Rowan would like to thank Katherine Bayne and my colleagues and students very warmly. You have contributed so much to my understanding and enjoyment of applied personality theory and counselling.

All the authors would like to say a big thank you to Monika Lee, Richard Townrow, Bryony Skelton and Claire Munce at McGraw-Hill for their support during the writing and publication of this book. They were always there to answer queries and to help us remain focused, particularly during the more demanding phases of the writing process.

Introduction

The aim of this book

The principal aim of this book is to provide a concise, user-friendly introduction to some of the main ideas in counselling and psychotherapy. It is likely to be most suitable for students on undergraduate courses, those embarking on training courses and for practitioners wanting to refresh themselves about certain aspects relevant to their work. Our intention is that you will be able to dip into the book in order to obtain some accessible, relatively brief but, hopefully, insightful information about a particular concept, whether it is a theoretical perspective or term, a central technique or a leading figure in the counselling or psychotherapy field.

We are not setting out to provide a comprehensive handbook on counselling and psychotherapy as there are a number of extremely valuable ones available already. Nor are we aiming to offer a practical guide covering elements relevant to practice in a 'how to' type format. Although some important techniques are included they have mainly been selected in order to elucidate a par-ticular theoretical standpoint rather than to clarify how they may be used in practice.

Choice and focus of concepts

Inevitably the range of concepts we have selected will appear more comprehensive to some readers than others, and not everyone will agree with our choices. Although we accept this as inevitable, we have aimed to provide a broad canvas with particular focus on the main theoretical schools of cognitive-behavioural therapy (CBT), psychoanalysis and psychodynamic therapy, humanistic perspectives and eclectic and integrative approaches. As CBT is arguably a predominantly technique-based therapy we have placed more emphasis here on techniques than on some of the other more theory-based therapies. The recent growth in, and popularity of, CBT and mindfulness-based therapies has led us to include a number of closely linked, but nevertheless distinct, approaches and related techniques. We acknowledge that there will be some unavoidable bias in our choice of concepts based on our own interests and areas of expertise, but have also worked hard to select a range of subjects which cover a broad span and provide an appropriate balance for those wanting to gain an overview of the main concepts.

Each entry is designed to provide a relatively succinct overview of the concept, but with sufficient detail to enable you to develop an initial understanding of the topic. The entries are intended to provide a critical perspective and to include some comments on the role or relevance of research where appropriate.

The authors

Each author wrote on our own choice of key concepts and generally within our specialisms: Patrizia on CBT and mindfulness (which is becoming an orientation in its own right), Paula on psychodynamic/psychoanalytic therapy and Vicki and Rowan mainly on humanistic/existential and integrative/eclectic approaches.

The relevance of a range of counselling theories

Recent reviews of research on counselling outcome by Cooper (2008), Duncan et al. (2010) and Norcross and Wampold (2011) have concluded that some of the major common factors in effective counselling are now both clear and well supported by research, especially the relationship between counsellor and client and client readiness to change. For example Norcross and Wampold (2011) refer to empathy and collecting client feedback as 'demonstrably effective'; goal consensus, collaboration and positive regard as 'probably effective'; and congruence, repairing alliance ruptures and managing countertransference as 'promising' (p. 98). Further promising elements include adapting the therapy relationship to each client and similarity between the therapist's and the client's views of therapy (and reality).

It is striking that all these factors (including countertransference, which is readily defined in other terms) transcend all the major theories of counselling and psychotherapy except integrative/eclectic. It could therefore be argued that the other theories of counselling are redundant! However, there are least three reasons why all the major theories remain important.

First, therapists find it helpful to know, or know of, others who use the same concepts as they do and thus who think about therapy in broadly the same way. It seems likely that clients also respond to the similarity of their own and their therapist's views of counselling. For example, each theory provides a rationale to offer clients about choice of strategy or 'mechanism' of change.

Second, finding a theory that 'fits' you, or developing your own variation of it – one that you find coherent and practical – may be related to greater therapeutic effectiveness. Possible explanations are greater confidence, enthusiasm and authenticity.

Third, each theory – and concept – may be most useful for a particular client, problem or stage of counselling. If so, the more concepts available to a counsellor the better, though clearly there are practical limits to such versatility.

Therapists therefore need a variety of concepts from which to create their own model and the *key* concepts for each of us are likely to be those which we find most useful in practice. Choice of concepts to try out and adopt or discard may also be influenced by our philosophy, reading and discussion, research findings, training, supervision and experience of being a client.

Some of these ideas are discussed further in sections of the book.

A–Z format

This format tends to lend itself to a book of this type where a specific concept or idea can be found easily, and the cross-referencing (terms in **bold** type) enables related topics to be located with equal ease. Each section includes suggested annotated further reading so that you can explore areas of interest in greater depth.

Notes on terminology

There is an ongoing debate as to the nature and degree of distinction between counselling and psychotherapy, with some authors declaring they have far more similarities than differences (Feltham 2012) and others specifying the distinction to centre around counselling seeing the person within their social context and not imposing one theoretical model on the client (McLeod 2009). We tend to agree with Feltham, considering there to be a lot of overlap and little convincing difference between the two terms, particularly in terms of impact on the therapy itself. We therefore use the terms 'counselling' and 'psychotherapy' interchangeably. The same applies to the terms 'counsellor' and 'therapist'.

Feedback to authors

We would welcome any feedback you would like to give us about this book whether positive or constructively negative! Please forward any comments to us via the publishers.

References

Cooper, M. (2008) *Essential Research Findings in Counselling and Psychotherapy: The Facts are Friendly*. London: Sage.

Duncan, B.L., Miller, S.D., Wampold, B.E. and Hubble, M.A. (eds) (2010) *The Heart and Soul of Change: Delivering What Works in Therapy*, 2nd edn. Washington, DC: APA.

Feltham, C. (2012) What are counselling and psychotherapy? In C. Feltham and I. Horton (eds) *The SAGE Handbook of Counselling and Psychotherapy*, 3rd edn. London: Sage.

McLeod, J. (2009) *An Introduction to Counselling*. Maidenhead: Open University Press.

Norcross, J.C. and Wampold, B.E. (2011) Evidence-based therapy relationships: research conclusions and clinical practices. *Psychotherapy*, 46: 98–102.

A

Acceptance and commitment therapy

See also: behaviour therapy; cognitive behavioural therapy; dialectical behaviour therapy; mindfulness-based cognitive therapy

> To the relief of human suffering using methods that have been shown to work.
>
> (Autismindex.com)

How does the very nature of being human and using language lead to psychological distress? How can a person commit to living an adventurous and purposeful life from this moment onwards, despite suffering from emotional or physical pain? Acceptance and commitment therapy (ACT) was developed within a coherent theoretical and philosophical framework and thus differs from other CBT approaches. It is based on relational frame theory, an approach that investigates how the human mind functions. It belongs to the approaches of psychotherapy that are considered to be 'the third wave in cognitive and behavioural psychotherapy'.

While CBT focuses mainly on empiricism (randomized control trials and other studies), Stephen Hayes and co-workers believed that this was not enough for psychological science to progress. He stated that there had to be a synergy between empiricism, theory and observation. 'The ultimate purpose of theory and philosophy is to guide the behaviour of the therapist through new territory' (Hayes et al. 1999).

Thus ACT is unique in combining the above and using acceptance, mindfulness, commitment and behaviour interventions to increase psychological flexibility. Psychological flexibility means being in touch with the present moment fully and on purpose, and changing, or persisting with, behaviour in the service of chosen principles.

Acceptance and commitment therapy (ACT) is an active psycho-educational application of mindfulness, employing metaphors to communicate the multifaceted concept of mindfulness, as well as using cognitive behavioural exercises and homework to apply mindfulness to very specific case formulations (e.g. very specifically avoided private events, automatic evaluative thinking or avoidant behaviours). ACT is suited to one-on-one therapy but can also be applied to groups.

Research shows that ACT has better outcomes in decreasing the believ-ability of depressogenic thoughts vis-à-vis CBT and also scores higher in pain management.

Hayes, the founder of ACT, started his studies in the 1960s with a partic-ular interest in behaviour analysis, but was also drawn to Eastern philosophy. He has published well over 400 scientific papers and over 30 books, and as he is a co-author of the majority of publications it is somewhat difficult to obtain absolutely neutral discussions of this model. Currently, traditional CBT has a much larger base of research that supports its validity than ACT, and ACT proponents mostly acknowledge this. ACT also focuses largely on addressing verbal barriers and can thus only be effective for clients who do not have skills deficits in using and understanding language.

ACT is intellectually deep and complex and works with focusing on 'Six Core Processes': acceptance, cognitive diffusion, being in the present, self as perspective, values and committed action.

In their book *Get Out of Your Mind and Into Your Life*, Hayes and Smith (2005) state: 'ACT is not about fighting your pain; it's about developing a will-ingness to embrace every experience life has to offer. It's not about resisting your emotions; it's about feeling them completely . . . [and choosing] . . . what matters to you most.'

References

Hayes, S.C., Strosahl, K. and Wilson, K.G. (1999) *Acceptance and Commitment Therapy: An experiential approach to behavior change*. New York: Guilford Press.
Hayes, S. and Smith, S. (2005) *Get Out of Your Mind and Into Your Life*. Oakland, CA: Harbinger.

Annotated further reading

Hayes, S. and Smith, S. (2005) *Get Out of Your Mind and Into Your Life*. Oakland, CA: Harbinger.

This is the most accessible self-help book on ACT. It contains humour, compassion, insight and wisdom and shows how we can often turn painful emotions around through paradoxical interventions.

Kazantzis, N., Reinecke, M.A. and Freeman, A. (2010) *Cognitive and Behavioural Theories in Clinical Practice*. New York: Guilford Press.

This recent publication contains in-depth chapters on the rich approaches that CBT contains. Leading experts come together and describe with insight how each approach differs from the other. Recent research is given a prominent place.

Adlerian therapy

Alfred Adler was born in Vienna in 1870 and died in 1937 in Aberdeen during a lecture tour. Not only had he warned fellow Austrians of Jewish origin to leave Austria promptly long before Hitler's move to annex but he also predicted the Second World War. He was the only member of the Vienna Psychoanalytical Association who was a member of the Social Democratic Party of Austria. He gave talks about the 'psychology of Marxism' which was yet another reason for Freud to reject him further. Adler saw our human existence in its wholeness and developed a therapy that treated body, soul and mind and thus he can be seen as one of the pioneers for psychosomatic treatment approaches.

He is best known for the creation of the 'inferiority complex'. The main theory of his Individual Psychotherapy is based on the inferiority complex of the child. His best known publication in 1912, *About the Nervous Personality*, discusses this notion in depth.

He was convinced that each individual had the capacity to actively lead and create their own life and the strength to make their own decisions. Adlerian therapy intends to teach, inform and create hope in the client, in order to help the client fix basic mistakes in their personal logic. The therapist collaborates with the client to achieve the desired outcome. Adler's characteristic concept is how an individual feels towards and is aware of being part of human society. How the client perceives him/herself in this society can cause disturbances in personality and interventions are employed in the therapeutic sessions to decrease them.

Childhood experiences are not, as such, important in themselves. However, how we view them and our past is of significance as this will have an effect on our current perceptions of ourselves. He measures mental health by the extent to which we can create wholesome relationships with others and to what degree we can show and apply compassion towards fellow human beings. He seems to say that contentment and success are mostly linked to social 'connectedness'.

One of his favourite examples of creating change in one's own life is the story of Demosthenes, who had a severe speech impediment. His inferiority complex led him to practise speaking while standing near the roaring sea. Thus compensating for his lack of ability, he eventually became the best known orator of antiquity.

Adler thinks that encouragement is the most powerful method of shifting a person's lack of confidence and courage. Clients learn to understand that only they themselves have the power to transform their life and act differently. Adlerian therapy emphasizes a positive view of human nature and that we are in command of our own fate and not a victim.

The therapist will look at family history only in so far as this information will help the client set goals. These goals may be very pragmatic and 'useful', such as becoming a better parent, spouse or giving up an addiction. In common with CBT the therapist at times suggests home practice to reach the set goals more swiftly. Adler was a true educator. He viewed people as socially rooted beings who, however, had the choice of their own free will. He never saw a client just as a victim. Adler was highly influential in reforming education in Vienna and held hundreds of lectures for teaching professionals. He wanted not only to heal but also to prevent mental illness.

Annotated further reading

Carlson, J., Watts, R. and Maniacci, M. (2005) *Adlerian Therapy: Theory and Practice*. Washington: APA.

This book is an introduction to Adler's influential and unique approach to psychotherapy. Starting from the principle that human behaviour is goal-oriented and socially embedded, his therapy is a brief psycho-educational approach that emphasizes understanding individuals' characteristic ways of living life – their lifestyle – before working towards change. The book describes the relevance of Adlerian therapy today by illustrating how Adler's ideas have influenced current practice and pointing out the short-term nature of its interventions. The authors also point out the application of Adlerian therapy in practice with individuals, couples, families and groups, as well as in educational settings.

Anxiety

See also: cognitive behavioural therapy; schema therapy

Worry is the cognitive process during anxiety that aims to prepare an individual for future threat (Barlow 1988). Anxiety tends to affect the body and the mind, exhibiting a multitude of symptoms such as tension, heart palpitations and raised or irregular heart beat, fast breathing and hyperventilation, feelings of sickness, an upset digestive and urinary system and aches and pains particularly in the head, neck and back area. Emotionally, anxiety brings on a sense of dread and fear of fainting or even dying. What keeps anxiety going however can be extremely unhelpful thought patterns that the anxious person tends to engage in and habituate to.

A CBT interpretation for why anxiety continues would be the tendency to mentally over-worry (fixating on danger), i.e. engage in ruminations about what could possibly go wrong and how this may forever affect your life. The topic of 'danger' would be apparent in the content of anxious schemas (assumptions and beliefs) and even in the content of negative automatic thoughts. The predominance of danger-related thinking would be like an ongoing stream of worry-thoughts in your awareness.

However, a psychoanalyst would argue that repressed conflicts were the cause for your worry. You may have found it impossible to share fearful thoughts with significant elders during your childhood. This pattern may have never stopped and may still be occurring in adult life and adult relationships. Thus it would be your way of being and understanding life.

From a medical perspective you may have an overactive adrenal gland or even a tumour on an adrenal which causes your body to be imbalanced when it comes to body chemistry. This again may have been caused by a genetic flaw or by the habit of worrying which may have pushed your adrenal glands into overdrive. Of course there may even be a neurological abnormality in the brain that may cause 'over firing' in the amygdale.

Consuming stimulants like amphetamines, alcohol, marijuana and even coffee can cause anxious or out-of-control feelings. Very low levels of blood sugar can also cause symptoms of anxiety (hypoglycaemia). There is also a heart condition called 'mitral valve prolapse' which has been associated with panic attacks.

Treatment from the CBT perspective would focus on how to reduce the predominance of danger-related thoughts in the stream of consciousness. The treatment would also include making the client aware of the overestimation of danger and the underestimation of abilities and skills to deal with it.

Burns (1990) claims that people suffering from anxiety or panic disorder 'nearly always have unexpressed negative feelings about some problem in their lives and may not even be aware of this'. Two categories seem particularly often denied: anger and unexpressed desire.

References

Barlow, D.H. (1988) *Anxiety and its Disorders: The Nature and Treatment of Anxiety and Panic*. New York: Guilford Press.

Burns, D. (1990) *The Feeling Good Handbook*. New York: Plume.

Annotated further reading

Burns, D. (1990) *The Feeling Good Handbook*. New York: Plume.

The subtitle to this excellent self-help book is 'The new mood therapy' and is rich with insight and powerful techniques to help the

reader deal with destructive emotions. It is equally helpful to any therapist as it includes chapters on psychiatric drugs and how to make
therapy successful.

Anxiety, existential

See also: death, fear of; existential counselling

We feel existential anxiety or angst when we see life as meaningless, confront
our own mortality, accept that we're free (in Sartre's phrase 'condemned to
freedom') or that we are ultimately alone. Usually this is a terrifying and deeply
disturbing experience. Sartre suggested anguish, forlornness and despair as
characterizing it but – and this is a central point – saw it as a potentially very
positive experience.

The following example of angst as positive is based on Yalom (1980). He
described a mother seeing her youngest child leave home. She has longed for
this day. Freedom! Yet she's very upset; she sobs and shudders and becomes
anxious. She goes to see a counsellor who offers her a new perspective: that of
course she's anxious; it's 'empty nest syndrome' and she'll feel much more
positive if she does something like finding work, taking an assertiveness
training or other adult education course or tries taking a mild sedative. She
chooses a new activity and her anxiety eases.

Yalom sees her choice and the counsellor's approach as a 'missed opportunity'. From an existential point of view he would rather she 'nursed the shudder
rather than anaesthetize it': what did her shudder mean? What terrified her
about freedom? Approaching her anxiety in this way, he argued, is more likely
to lead to a richer appreciation of life and a more authentic way of being.

It may also lead to a sense of surprise that we exist at all. For existential
therapists and philosophers this is a terrifying thing to really understand but it
is also awakening. Moreover, in their view our angst is likely to diminish as we
feel more fulfilled and confident through the choices we make after this
realization.

References

Spinelli, E. (2007) *Practising Existential Psychotherapy: The Relational World*. London:
    Sage.
van Deurzen, E. (2009) *Everyday Mysteries: Existential Dimensions of Psychotherapy*,
    2nd edn. London: Routledge.

van Deurzen, E. (2010) *Skills in Existential Counselling and Psychotherapy*. London: Sage.

Yalom, I. (1980) *Existential Psychotherapy*. New York: Basic Books.

Annotated further reading

Funder, D. (2011) *The Personality Puzzle*, 5th edn. New York: W. W. Norton.

The clearest and most engaging short (10 pages) review and commentary on existential thinking that I've found. As he says, 'This is pretty stern stuff' (p. 480), meaning emotionally, I think. However, many of the original existential philosophers are also particularly hard to try and understand intellectually. Of specialized texts, all clearly written, I recommend Yalom (1980), van Deurzen (2009, 2010) and Spinelli (2007) (see the References above).

Archetypes

See also: life scripts; collective unconscious

An archetype can be defined as 'an internal mental model of a typical generic story character to which an observer might resonate emotionally' (Faber and Mayer 2009: 397). While this definition is accurate and useful, it does not capture the daring and power of Jung's concept and it deliberately excludes the central mystical aspect of archetypes: the idea that when a person or event arouses an archetype in you it then takes over and has you in its grip. For example, when faced with a situation that does not suit you, you might be seized by the archetype of the Warrior (who fights or persists) or the Wanderer (who leaves).

Jung proposed that these patterns of energy or roles lie waiting in the depths of our personalities, in what he called the 'collective unconscious'. He saw them as similar to instincts in other animals – genetically programmed ways of behaving which are activated by certain recurring situations such as fighting or becoming a mother. Pearson and Marr (2007) focus on 12 such archetypes: Innocent, Orphan, Warrior, Care-giver, Seeker, Lover, Creator, Destroyer, Ruler, Magician, Sage and Jester. All have both positive and negative aspects, for example the Innocent is described as trusting others but sometimes too much, and relying on others, again perhaps too much.

If the idea of archetypes is valid then awareness of our particular archetype or archetypes at this point in our lives gives us more choice and the possibility of harnessing its power rather than being controlled by it. It would also be an element in Figure 1 in the section on **self**. However, I do not think it deserves this level of recognition because the evidence for archetypes is open to the same alternative and similar interpretation – that they are major universal themes of human existence expressed in dreams, myths, stories and books – as the concept of the collective unconscious.

However, archetypes may have some value as narratives, scripts or stories. Faber and Mayer (2009) proposed a new theory of archetypes and tested their reasoning that 'if archetypes exist . . . these affective schemas or mental models can be identified in the popular music, movies, television, literature and classic art of today' (p. 310). They did find such relationships, and interpreted them as 'surprising new evidence for the possible existence of dominant archetypal themes in our lives' (p. 320). For example, Carers tend to enjoy romantic movies and fashion books and Strivers tend to enjoy action movies, sports TV and books about spies. The authors speculate that archetypal themes will also predict social behaviour, complementing and adding to the predictions from personality traits and from social roles. Further, such themes may be useful in designing more effective advertising and health messages as well as in therapy.

Faber and Mayer (2009) list the music tracks used as part of their measure of archetypes. You may like to think of your favourite tracks and what they may say about you. Examples are 'Paranoid android' (by Radiohead, of course!) representing the archetypal theme of the Sage, 'Angel of death' (Slayer), the Shadow and 'It's oh so quiet' (Bjork), The Innocent.

References

Faber, M.A. and Mayer, J.D. (2009) Resonance to archetypes in media: there's some accounting for taste. *Journal of Research in Personality*, 43: 307–22.

Pearson, C.S. and Marr, H.K. (2007) *What Story Are you Living?* Gainsville, FL: Centre for Applications for Psychological Type.

Annotated further reading

Faber, M.A. and Mayer, J.D. (2009) Resonance to archetypes in media: there's some accounting for taste. *Journal of Research in Personality*, 43: 307–22.

This paper reviewed ideas about archetypes, including various schemes for describing them, developed a new theory and measure, the Rich Culture Archetype Scale and reported a test of its validity.

Pearson, C.S. and Marr, H.K. (2007) *What Story Are you Living?* Gainsville, FL: Centre for Applications for Psychological Type.

An evocative title and a systematic and detailed approach to (in the authors' view) discovering which of 12 archetypes are the most influential in various ways in one's own life and stage of life. The reader decides, not an expert interpreter. They too have developed a questionnaire: the Pearson-Marr Archetype Indicator.

Assertiveness

See also: self; self-actualization

Assertiveness is one of many concepts in counselling (including of course counselling itself) which are used in various and sometimes contradictory ways. It is usefully defined as 'expressing and acting on your rights as a person, while respecting the same rights in other people'. This definition excludes such meanings as getting your own way or being forceful, noticeable, blunt, dramatic or aggressive.

Assertiveness training is often seen as a behavioural technique but is also consistent with the humanistic-existential approach. Indeed, it is self-actualization in action and at its heart is a fundamental existential question: shall I do what *I* want to do or what *others* want me to do? Assertiveness training can emphasize behaviour, e.g. role-plays with coaching, or self-awareness, e.g. what is it about saying 'no' to this person and this request which is troubling me, or which seems impossible, or both?

'Coaching' may sound as if there is one right way to be assertive or as if there is an ideal of being assertive at all times. Neither presumption is true. Skilful assertiveness is individual and authentic rather than mechanical and following a formula, and one assertive right is *not* to be assertive.

An example of an assertive right is: 'I have the right to say "No" without feeling guilty'. Consistent with the definition above, others too have the right to say 'No' without feeling guilty and their right to do so should accordingly be accepted by the person they've said no to. The rights – and typically 10–12 are listed with considerable overlap between lists – are quite provocative in abstract form, but really come to life in relation to a specific situation.

There has been very little research on assertiveness since the Rakos (1991) review of several hundred studies. His judgement that it remains 'entrenched as a mainstream behavioural intervention . . . quite effective when used appropriately' (Rakos 1991: xi) still holds.

Reference

Rakos, R.F.T. (1991) *Assertive Behaviour: Theory, Research and Training*. London: Routledge.

Annotated further reading

Dickson, A. (1987) *A Woman in Your Own Right: Assertiveness and You*. London: Quartet.

The best practical guide to assertive skills (and because 'interpersonal problems' are timeless, still highly relevant) – and in print!

Nicolson, P. and Bayne, R. (in press) *Psychology for Social Work Theory and Practice*, 4th edn. Basingstoke: Palgrave Macmillan.

Practical guidelines on the main assertive skills discussed by Dickson: saying no, making requests, giving and receiving compliments and giving and receiving criticism.

Attachment theory

See also: psychoanalysis; object relations theory

The key figure associated with attachment theory is John Bowlby (1907–1990) whose ideas around attachment have become increasingly influential in recent years. Bowlby asserted that human beings possess a basic need to form attachments with other people and that problems arise if they experience difficulties in forming secure attachments. Such difficulties tend to result if relationships with parents or carers have in some way been disrupted during childhood. Possible causes of disruption might include loss of a parent through death or separation, or lack of consistent care due to mental illness or drug or alcohol abuse.

If a child experiences what Bowlby termed a 'secure base' from parents or care-givers, they will be better able to establish intimate relationships later on. If care-giving is unpredictable or absent, the individual will find it much harder to trust others and will find it more difficult to establish close, satisfying relationships as an adult.

Attachment theory is closely linked to psychoanalytic theory and shares the belief that experiences in early childhood have an important influence on development and behaviour in later life. However, Bowlby considered that Freud had placed too much emphasis on childhood fantasies at the expense of actual events. More specifically this theory draws on Klein's object relations theory, which supports the idea that the personality is shaped by early attachment experiences. However, Bowlby placed greater emphasis on the effect of actual events on the individual's psyche than did Freud or Klein whose focus was more on childhood fantasies.

Building on Bowlby's ideas, Mary Ainsworth (Ainsworth et al. 1978) outlined four different types of attachment, three of which can be problematic for the individual later in life. These are: secure attachment, where a child clearly misses the parent when they leave and looks to re-establish contact when they return; insecure-avoidant attachment, where the child appears not to miss the parent and avoids them when they come back; insecure-ambivalent, where the child shows signs of great distress/anger on being left and finds it hard to settle on the parent's return; and insecure-disoriented, where the infant displays rigid patterns of behaviour. These infant behaviours were shown to be in response to the behaviour of the parent, so that secure infants were treated sensitively with their emotional needs being met, whereas insecure children were either rejected or treated insensitively or inconsistently (McLeod 2009).

Attachment styles are thought to have a particularly strong impact when an individual suffers the loss of an attachment figure, such as a parent or a spouse. They are then likely to respond in a way which reflects the attachment style developed during childhood. As a result, people with secure attachment styles are likely to cope more effectively with bereavement and loss than those with insecure attachment styles.

In terms of the application of this theory in therapeutic practice, it provides a way of understanding why clients relate to others in certain ways. Therapists also need to be mindful of how their own attachment styles might impact on clients. It is important for therapists to be aware of their role as an attachment figure and to aim to provide the 'secure base' which many clients lacked as children and from which they can explore painful issues.

Fonagy (2001) summarizes some of the recent research on attachment theory and outlines a number of criticisms which include the following: insufficient consideration is given to the fact that different children may perceive similar parental or carer behaviour in different ways due to their inevitably different perceptions of reality; developmental aspects of attachment theory are limited, and the categories of secure and insecure attachment could be seen as overly simplistic in that security and insecurity is present to some degree in everyone.

References

Ainsworth, M.D.S., Blehar, M.C., Waters, E. and Wall, S. (1978) *Patterns of Attachment: A Psychological Study of the Strange Situation*. Hillsdale, NJ: Erlbaum.

Fonagy, P. (2001) *Attachment Theory and Psychoanalysis*. New York: Other Press Llc.

McLeod, J. (2009) *An Introduction to Counselling*, 4th edn. Maidenhead: Open University Press.

Annotated further reading

Bowlby, J. (2005) *The Making and Breaking of Relational Bonds*. Abingdon: Taylor and Francis.

This book gathers together essays and lectures by Bowlby written over a 20-year period. Bowlby writes in a clear and very approachable way and this book is an excellent introduction to his ideas as well as a practical guide to the relevance of his ideas in practice.

Holmes, J. (2001) *The Search for a Secure Base: Attachment Theory and Psychotherapy*. Hove: Psychology Press.

This is an informative book which focuses on applying attachment theory to psychotherapy practice.

B

Basic assumption groups

See also: Bion, Wilfred R. ; groups

Bion's observations of group processes suggested that groups comprise members with their own individual identity and motivations but for each there is also a 'group self', a view that differs from that of Freud (discussed in the entry on 'groups') (Freud 1921). Grotstein describes Bion's approach as that just as each person can be considered as a group of sub-personalities, so each group can be thought of as an individual as well as a group (Grotstein 2007: 190). Groups are formed for a specific *task* and when unified for that purpose, it is a 'work group'. However, over time disruption takes place or there is resistance to maintaining the unity of the group effort. These sub-group resistances are known as 'basic assumption' groups. This name refers to the way in which each of these unconscious group resistances (defences) differs from the assumption of the work group. These resistances in the basic assumption groups are 'fight-flight' (baF), 'dependency' (baD) and 'pairing' (baP).

Bion's work on group dynamics, and particularly the unconscious life of a group, has been described as the equivalent for a group as Melanie Klein's 'defence mechanisms' are for an individual (Gould 1997). As with Freud and Klein, Bion's work on groups survives and has been developed by contemporary group analysts and group theorists (Lipgar 2011). This has not been without criticism, one of which, relevant here, is that Lipgar quotes Eisold (2005) who says that Bion's theory of basic assumption groups was not intersubjective enough and that Bion was unaware of how his own subjectivity impacted upon the phenomena he observed and reported. However, neither Lipgar nor Grotstein (2007) read Bion in that way, both considering that he was very much aware of the influence of the 'social'. What is worth taking from this debate is that both positively and negatively there are different ways to 'read' Bion's work, which is of itself complex.

Bion's identification of basic assumption groups which were unconscious and 'anti task' 'gave coherence to seemingly disparate and conflicting bits of individual behaviour. Seen through the right lens, group members coordinated their behaviour "as if" they held enough common beliefs, or basic assumptions' (Eisold 2005: 3). In other words there appeared to be an unconscious process that bound group members together, which while it was active, prevented the group's focus on the primary task (the work group) – the purpose of the group meeting.

The basic assumptions are driven by emotion, such as anxiety, fear, hate and love, rather than intellect. Common to all basic assumption groups is that they are 'instantaneous, inevitable, and instinctive . . . in contrast with work-group function basic-assumption activity makes no demands on the individual for a capacity to co-operate but depends on the individual's possession of what I call valency' (Bion 1961/1986: 153).

Ba 'fight-flight'

Fight-flight refers to a method of protecting the group's survival that was either open passive or aggressive rebellion against the progress of the work group. The group would either fight against or fly from the task (and possibly the leader or therapist). This relates to Klein's paranoid-schizoid position (Gould 1997).

Ba 'dependency'

Dependency means dependency on the leader or 'when all individuals in the group look to myself as a person with whom each has an exclusive relation-ship' (Bion 1961/1986: 119). Within this mode there is little connection between the members themselves and there is a 'mass inertia' (p. 119). Bion means that this is a 'pathological' dependency during which the sub-group brushes aside its sense of co-operative responsibility of working towards a commonly agreed task and goal, projecting it onto the group generally or the group leader. This links to Klein's depressive position (Gould 1997).

Ba 'pairing'

In this phase of basic assumption consciousness two or more members develop phantasies of sexual liaison with the associated assumption that the group is hopeful that a messianic leader can be born. This state occurs through the pairing of two leaders who will produce a future leader (who may be a saviour but is sometimes an anti-Christ). Bion suggests that sometimes when a baD refers to the authority of a past leader it is near to the baP that refers to the authority of a future one. Grotstein (2007) identifies this as the most compli-cated of the three states, which is potentially equivalent to an individual's sexualized transference to the analyst as a defence against the feelings of pain and humiliation of dependency feelings. The feeling that a 'messiah' will be produced is more complicated still and may, as Gould suggests, relate to Klein's version of the Oedipus Complex (1997).

The group leader plays an important part in all of this and is the point towards which the group projections are aimed. This also relates to maternal reverie (see entry for container/contained) which Bion developed subsequently (Grotstein 2007).

Bettelheim – 'safety in the mass' (baD to baF)

One real life, but very vivid example is one described by Bruno Bettelheim, a prisoner at Dachau and later Buchenwald concentration camps in the Second World War, who provided detailed observations about this experience on himself, his fellow prisoners and the guards. The regime, particularly at Buchenwald, used 'the group' to ensure conformity in that if anyone transgressed the harsh rules in any way, the group they worked and lived with was also punished. There would therefore be an emotional and unconscious dependence on the strict regime which could be represented as baD as each of the group members related to the 'leader' (or at least the person in command) as if they had an individual relationship with them – in this case one of fear/obedience.

One cold winter night during a snowstorm all the starving prisoners were forced to stand to attention without overcoats, after a long day's work. 'The purpose was to motivate all inmates to prevent anyone from trying to escape since they knew they would have to suffer for it. Roll call did not end until the fugitives were found. In this particular instance the prisoners were threatened with having to stand all through the night' (Bettelheim 1979: 137). After more than 20 prisoners had died of exposure that night 'the discipline broke down'. Normally no one resisted any of the barbarism as they were completely subjugated to the rule of terror. However:

> Being exposed to the weather was a terrible torture; to see one's friends die without being able to help, and to stand a good chance of dying too, created a situation which obviously the prisoner as an individual could not meet successfully. Therefore, the individual as such had to disappear in the mass. Threats by the guards became ineffective because the mental attitude of most prisoners was now changed.
>
> (p. 137)

Bettelheim considered here that individuals were no longer fearing for themselves and protecting *themselves* in order to survive. They had become 'depersonalized'. It was '. . . as if giving up individual existence and becoming part of a mass seemed in some way to offer better chances for survival, if not for the person, at least for the group' (p. 137). This description and analysis of the behaviour by Bettelheim himself as witness shows the *instinctive* shift from the baD to a baF group. Among many interesting things in this case is that the baF served a particularly important purpose of resistance. Tragically, although unsurprisingly, once the 'crisis' ended so did this unconscious experience and prisoners returned to a conscious and unconscious compliance.

References

Bettelheim, B. (1979) *The Informed Heart: Autonomy in a Mass Age*. New York: Avon Books.

Bion, W.R. (1961/1986) *Experiences in Groups, and Other Papers*. London: Tavistock.

Eisold, K. (2005) Using Bion. *Psychoanalytic Psychology*, 22: 357–69.

Freud, S. (1921) *Group Psychology and the Analysis of the Ego* (Vol. S.E.13 1955). London: Hogarth Press.

Gould, L.J. (1997) Correspondences between Bion's basic assumption theory and Klein's developmental positions: an outline. *Free Associations*, 7: 15–30.

Grotstein, J.S. (2007) *A Beam of Intense Darkness*. London: Karnac.

Lipgar, R. (2011) Learning from Bion's legacy to groups. In C. Mawson (ed.) *Bion Today*. London: Routledge.

Annotated further reading

These suggestions are also relevant for the entry 'Bion, Wilfred'.

Bion, W.R. (1961/1986) *Experiences in Groups, and Other Papers*. London: Tavistock.

Originally a collection of his papers, this has been reissued many times and is a compelling read too, although I think it is better understood in its richness and insights after reading more general accounts of his work on basic assumption groups.

Grotstein, J.S. (2007) *A Beam of Intense Darkness*. London: Karnac.

James Grotstein who was analysed by Bion, has written a comprehensive and readable account of all of his work with a chapter on Bion's contribution to the study of groups.

Mawson, C. (2011) *Bion Today*. London: Routledge.

This edited collection by Chris Mawson has contemporary appreciations and critiques of the entire works of Bion but for this entry, Section 5 on 'group mentality' is particularly relevant and interesting.

Beck, Aaron T. (1921–)

See also: cognitive behavioural therapy; mindfulness-based cognitive therapy

Beck is an American psychiatrist and psychotherapist who is Professor Emeritus of Psychiatry at the University of Pennsylvania. Beck is not only well known as the originator of cognitive therapy (CT), but also for devising important measures for the validity of therapeutic interventions, such as the widely used Beck Depression Inventory (BDI), Beck Hopelessness Scale, and Beck Anxiety Inventory (BAI). He is the President Emeritus of the Beck Institute for Cognitive Therapy and Research and the Honorary President of the Academy of Cognitive Therapy.

Beck was born in Providence, Rhode Island on 18 July 1921, the youngest of four siblings. Beck's parents were Jewish immigrants who came over to America from Russia. Beck claims his need for control was a mindset he needed to develop in order to cope with his mother's depression. Beck taught himself how to work through his fears and problems after a near fatal illness from an infection. This experience was instrumental for the development of his theory and various therapeutic interventions over the years.

Beck attended Brown University, graduating *magna cum laude* in 1942 and received his MD at Yale Medical School in 1946.

Beck started to develop cognitive therapy in the early 1960s as a psychiatrist at the University of Pennsylvania. Previously he had studied and practised psychoanalysis. He became more and more convinced that suicidal, depressed patients did not benefit from the aforementioned approach but rather that in many cases they got worse. He designed and carried out numerous experiments and found a new theory for the onset and relapse of depression. He believed that it was triggered and continued due to negative views towards the world, the future, others and the self.

Beck and his colleagues have researched the efficacy of CT which soon became the preferred treatment tool for conditions like depression, anxiety, addiction, bipolar, eating disorders, personality disorders and many others. He has also devised an approach for treating schizophrenia, borderline personality disorder and people who have repeatedly attempted suicide. He has been named one of the 'Americans in history who shaped the face of American psychiatry' and one of the 'five most influential psychotherapists of all time'.

Currently he is involved in numerous research studies at Penn, and conducts several case conferences at the Beck Institute for area psychiatric residents, graduate students and mental health professionals. He was also elected a fellow of the American Academy of Arts and Sciences in 2007.

Beck was rejected by the American Psychoanalytic Institute on his application, citing 'on the grounds that his mere desire to conduct scientific studies signalled that he'd been improperly analyzed', a decision that still makes him angry.

Cognitive therapy helps clients overcome difficulties by identifying and changing dysfunctional thinking, behaviour and emotional responses. This involves helping them to develop skills for modifying beliefs, identifying distorted thinking, relating to others in different ways and changing behaviours.

Criticisms of CT claim that:

1 its focus is on immediate symptom relief and it disregards personality restructuring;
2 its approach is shallow and mechanistic;
3 the therapeutic relationship is irrelevant; and
4 emotions are of minimal importance.

However, careful examination of the methods used in cognitive therapy begin to illuminate misdirection of these criticisms. Indeed, these criticisms represent a misunderstanding of cognitive psychotherapy as a whole. Beck had indeed emphasized in his first publication *CT for Depression* (see cognitive behavioural therapy) that desirable characteristics of the therapists would include warmth, accurate empathy and genuineness.

In 2005 Beck met the Dalai Lama at the 5th International Congress of Cognitive Psychotherapy in Gothenburg, Sweden. In the opening ceremony 'Meeting of Minds' he discussed the similarities of Buddhist psychology with CBT by conversing with his Holiness the 14th Dalai Lama. It was an amazing feast for the mind and what stood out was that both representatives of their 'lineage' had a common goal: to reduce the suffering of human beings.

Annotated further reading

Beck, J.S. Questions and answers about cognitive therapy. *About Cognitive Therapy*. Beck Institute for Cognitive Therapy and Research (accessed 21 November 2008).

Book of Members, 1780–2010: Chapter B. American Academy of Arts and Sciences (accessed 29 May 2011).

http://psychcentral.com/blog/archives/2009/09/02/a-profile-of-aaron-beck/ World of Psychology, a profile of Aaron Beck, is a wonderful and clear introduction to the man who is best known for pioneering the use of CBT and revolutionizing psychotherapy by turning toward science to validate its efficacy.

http://www.academyofct.org/Library/InfoManage/Guide.asp?FolderID=10 01&SessionID={2AD1D69F-8B25-4717-9660-B5BE25D26C52}   (accessed 26 July 2011).

http://www.beckinstitute.org/ (accessed 26 July 2011).

http://www.beckinstitute.org/Library/InfoManage/Guide.asp?Folder ID=196&SessionID={A5A90C2B-35D2-472D-A6A4-8561DC4D999E} &SP=2 (accessed 26 July 2011).

http://www.psychologistanywhereanytime.com/famous_psychologist_ and_psychologists/psychologist_famous_aaron_beck.htm (accessed 26 July 2011).

Sloan, G. (1997) *British Journal of Community Nursing*, 2(10): 460–5.
Smith, D.B. (2009) The Doctor Is IN, *The American Scholar* (Phi Beta Kappa Society).
Talbott, J.A. (2002) Dix Personalité Qui Ont Changé le Visage de la Psychiatric Américaine. *L'Information Psychiatrique*, 78(7): 667–75.

Behaviour therapy (BT)

See also: cognitive behavioural therapy; multimodal therapy

This therapeutic approach was developed in the early twentieth century. Its theory and practice originally derived from clinical and laboratory-based research. It is underpinned by the theories of social learning and conditioning. The question 'how do humans achieve and retain learning?' was the central focus of BT. Eventually techniques were developed based on empirical research, which achieved actual change in patient's mental problems.

Historically, there are a number of sources that are said to have influenced the advancement of BT. To mention but a few: Anna Freud apparently wrote about struggling with a phobia, which she saw as a repression of a traumatic event and which was 'cured' by systematic desensitization, when she attended college; Locke (1693) used graded exposure to reduce fear in children and Da Silva found in the 1980s that behavioural interventions had been written about in Buddhist scriptures: techniques such as relaxation, imaginal and real exposure, for example. Other scientists that were very influential in the early stages of BT were Pavlov, Skinner, Eysenck, Wolpe, Marks, Bandura with theories on self-efficacy and social learning and Seligman with 'learned helplessness'.

Marks was the leading and renowned research psychiatrist and head of the Maudsley Hospital (Institute of Psychiatry) where a lot of research was happening in the 1960s and 1970s. Some key techniques were born there, such as exposure and response prevention. He was also the first to train nurses in behaviour therapy and thereby created a 'multiprofessional' body of people who were qualified to administer this therapy.

BT rests on a number of theoretical assumptions, but considers concepts such as 'mind' and 'ego' as unscientific and of no help in solving behaviours that have got out of control (phobias, OCD, PTSD, etc.). They do however include 'thoughts' and 'sensations' in their therapeutic assessment and work, since they can be experienced as 'natural events', rather than 'mysterious notions' (Richards 2007: 331). 'Behaviourists strongly believe that any natural event arises from other natural events, not from mysterious notions of personality or ego, for example' (Richards 2007: 331).

So the client is not seen as an anxious person or suffering from anxiety by a BT therapist; rather they are looking for anxious behaviour, such as avoiding going out, for example to parties, being unassertive, having panic attacks, etc. The client's past is only relevant in as far as it informs us of how it may be having an effect on present-day behaviours, and thus disturbing the well-being of the client in the 'here and now'. Habituation to the 'feared object' may go back a long time and in the present BT tries to find ways of reducing the triggered anxiety response by a number of different interventions. Only interventions that have been scrutinized and are based on sound scientific evidence are applied.

The change which the therapist endeavours to help create and which eventually leads to desensitization and a new way of living can however only be achieved by working collaboratively and by negotiation with the client. Thus BT typically begins with an in-depth assessment to gather information. The therapist analyses the behaviours of the patient that cause stress, reduce the patient's quality of life, or otherwise have a negative impact on the life of the patient. Once this analysis is complete, the therapist chooses appropriate treatment techniques and regularly reviews and evaluates progress. The client needs to trust the therapist's knowledge and experience in order to find the strength to engage in aversive and sometimes highly anxiety-provoking prolonged exposures. It is crucial that the client continues what has been rehearsed (maybe only by imagery techniques) in session and puts it into practice throughout the time between sessions.

Effective team work (collaboration) is an absolute necessity, so that clients learn to change. They need to accept a certain amount of discomfort regularly and repeatedly. Furthermore they have to be prepared to engage in home practice and patiently work towards reaching a new normalized type of conditioning. It is also of great importance to agree together on the specific goals the client is working towards. BT does not 'do things to people' but rather clients 'do things with behavioural techniques' (Richards 2007: 337).

Fear will only shift if the client learns to accept and be with the discomfort for a sufficient length of time repeatedly. In this way, old neuro-pathways will be overwritten and replaced by new, healthy and helpful ways of behaving and thinking.

BT is an 'outside in' approach; by changing the behaviour, the thinking about it will also change. The treatment works through a hierarchy of avoided behaviours which the client has compiled as a list. The 'easiest' (least anxiety provoking one) is usually tackled first and gradually one works through the items step by step. The use of a self-monitoring diary is recommended.

Apart from exposure, treatments can include assertiveness training, desensitization, environment modification and relaxation training. Other commonly used techniques include positive reinforcement, modelling, and social skills training.

BT is very helpful for the treatment of depression, where often 'activity scheduling' and behaviour activation (BA) are the first line of action before starting with any cognitive intervention. At one of the recent BABCP (British Association of Behaviour and Cognitive Psychotherapy) conferences BA has been shown to be as effective as medication and the preparatory tools to get a client ready for cognitive restructuring. BT can often work and arrive at desired outcomes in approximately ten sessions or less.

BT will be of little use to clients who are unwilling to get actively engaged in changing their unhelpful behaviour patterns. Furthermore, we may find that a particular phobic behaviour, for example, might have resulted from an underlying psychological problem. Unless this is also treated (albeit by another approach) we may see a replacement phobia or condition within a short term of perceived treatment success. In general, it is much more common nowadays for BT to be used in conjunction with cognitive and other interventions. In short, BT has become an integrative model for lasting benefits.

References

Richards, D. (2007) Behaviour therapy. In W. Dryden (ed.) *Dryden's Handbook of Individual Therapy*, 5th edn. London: Sage.

Annotated further reading

Richards, D. (2007) Behaviour therapy. In W. Dryden (ed.) *Dryden's Handbook of Individual Therapy*, 5th edn. London: Sage.

This is an excellent in-depth chapter on BT, not only describing its origins and roots, but also its theoretical underpinning, philosophical background and application.

Being mindful

See also: Kabat-Zinn, Jon; mindfulness-based cognitive therapy; mindfulness-based stress reduction; mindfulness based cognitive behavioural coaching;

For most of our lives we tend to be switched on in 'mindless action' which could be described as 'auto-pilot'. Reasons for this are most probably linked to how we initially learn and make the huge amount of information and interactions we need for survival accessible to us. Langer (1989) refers to causes for 'mindlessness': 'repetition, premature cognitive commitment, belief in limited resources, . . . education for outcome . . . The grooves of mindlessness run deep' (Langer 1989: 42). When, however, we endeavour to enter into each moment, on purpose and non-judgementally and thus be truly present, mindfulness enables us to take each moment as a unique event in our life experience. We can choose to respond and be creative rather than merely reactive. Mindfulness can thus help us to feel more empathic, reflective and in control, and less confined and exhausted. It supports us to overcome the separation between the self and the world and connects us with being alive and life as a whole.

In psychotherapeutic work 'being mindful' increases awareness and presence (for the therapist and the client) and, as a life-skill, 'being mindful' is taught in therapeutic approaches such as MBCT, MBSR, ACT, DBT, MBCC and others. Research shows it to be a non-pharmacological means of dealing with anxiety, depression, chronic pain, stress, addiction, suicidality, etc. (Baer 2003).

By residing more frequently in the present moment, application of mindfulness can lead us to see both the inner and outer aspects of reality. We discover that the mind is continually chattering with commentary or judgement. By observing this, we have the choice to notice thoughts and then decide if those thoughts have value. When we are in mindful, perceptive mode we realize that 'thoughts are just thoughts' – the thoughts themselves have no weight. We can choose to release any thought that may cause inner turmoil or destructive actions. By closely observing our inner reality, we may find that contentment and joy are rarely brought about by a change in outer circumstances, but rather by releasing attachment to thoughts of expectations for the future or ruminating about the past.

A practical example for mindful action would be to be truly present when eating a meal. Not only would the process of eating slow down, but equally our sensory perceptions like smell, taste, touch and vision would enhance the depth of the experience.

References

Baer, R. (2003) Mindfulness training as a clinical intervention: a conceptual and empirical review. *Clinical Psychology: Science and Practice*, 10(2): 125–43.

Langer, E. (1989) *Mindfulness*. Cambridge, MA: Perseus Publishing.

Annotated further reading

Baer, R. (2003) Mindfulness training as a clinical intervention: a conceptual and empirical review. *Clinical Psychology: Science and Practice*, 10(2): 125–43.

A sound scientific paper reviewing conceptual approaches to mindfulness and empirical research on the usefulness of mindfulness-based interventions in the treatment of a variety of problematic conditions such as stress, pain, anxiety, depressive relapse and disordered eating.

Baer, R. (2006) *Mindfulness-Based Treatment Approaches: Clinician's Guide to Evidence Base and Applications*. London: Academic Press.

Baer provides a comprehensive introduction to the main mindfulness-based treatments including mindfulness-based stress reduction (MBSR), mindfulness-based cognitive therapy (MBCT), dialectical behaviour therapy (DBT) and acceptance and commitment therapy (ACT). She looks at the conceptual foundation, implementation and evidence base of these methods including theoretical and empirical research, and also case study illustrations of how they are implemented in real life.

Langer, E. (1989) *Mindfulness*. Cambridge, MA: Perseus Publishing.

Langer writes in an interesting, engaging and scientific way about mindfulness and mindlessness, and the benefits/consequences of each. She uses research studies to demonstrate the effectiveness of mindfulness in helping all people, young and old alike, in becoming more effective, creative and healthy.

Siegel, R. (2010) *The Mindfulness Solution*. New York: The Guildford Press.

In this book Dr Ronald Siegel shows how to use mindfulness in everyday practical ways in order to build up a daily mindfulness practice. He explains how this can be beneficial in helping to increase focus, cope with difficult feelings, curb unhealthy habits, find relief from anxiety and depression and resolve stress-related pain.

Williams, M. and Penman, D. (2011) *Mindfulness: Finding Peace in a Frantic World*. London: Piatkus.

This book is based on MBCT, which was co-developed by Mark Williams of Oxford University for the reduction of depression relapse. However, this volume has been written for all of us who struggle with a lifestyle that is seemingly forcing us to live in auto-pilot mode, forgetting that life really only happens in the present moment.

Berne, Eric (1910–1970)

See also: transactional analysis

Eric Berne trained as a doctor and psychiatrist and studied psychoanalysis with Erikson at the San Francisco Psychoanalytic Institute. He worked as a psychoanalyst for many years but like many pioneers of approaches to psychotherapy found that he disagreed with some aspects of it. Stewart (1992) wrote a biography.

Berne's most famous book is *Games People Play* (1964, reissued by Penguin in 2010) but his most readable book is *Sex in Human Loving* (1970). It also works well as an introduction to key concepts in transactional analysis (TA) and is based on a series of lectures to audiences of about 600 people which overflowed into the aisles. It is easy to see why: he is an original thinker who seems compassionate (in a tough-minded way) and has clear views without being dogmatic. He also has a wry, crisp feel for language.

For example, his first chapter discusses clinical, dry words to do with sex and warm, damp ones and he deals with the problem of talking about sex 'without offending anyone' by creating new words like cuff, swerk and tunc. He writes: 'Cuff is the only word in the English language that gives the full feeling, excitement, slipperiness, and aroma of the sexual act' (p. 22).

His most useful concepts are 'games' and 'scripts', plus his general philosophy, which is humanistic in tone – he sees each person as born with the potential to work enjoyably, productively and creatively, and to benefit both themselves and society. People are 'OK' (Berne's term; Berne 1966; Stewart 2007), and we can decide our own destiny. Like many ideas in counselling, Berne's are quite simple in themselves but much more difficult to apply sensitively and skilfully.

References

Berne, E. (1964) *Games People Play*. Harmondsworth: Penguin.
Berne, E. (1966) *Principles of Group Treatment*. Oxford: Oxford University Press.
Berne, E. (1970) *Sex in Human Loving*. Harmondsworth: Penguin.

Stewart, I. (1992) *Eric Berne: Key Figures in Counselling and Psychotherapy*. London: Sage.

Stewart, I. (2007) *TA Counselling in Action*, 3rd edn. London: Sage.

Annotated further reading

Berne, E. (1970) *Sex in Human Loving*. Harmondsworth: Penguin.

This is an unjustly neglected book in which Berne is particularly clear about concepts which he and others have sometimes made unnecessarily complicated.

Bibliotherapy

See also: cognitive behavioural therapy

Bibliotherapy refers to the process and therapeutic impact of reading. Some authors include the use of films and DVDs under this heading (Bayne et al. 2008). It is an expanding area of therapeutic intervention, which is, no doubt, in part due to its being a cost-effective means of dealing with increased waiting lists. It appeals to a significant group of people who prefer to address their problems without input from a counsellor or other mental health practitioner. The most popular subjects according to Starker (1988) were assertiveness, personal growth, relationships, parenting, stress and sexuality.

McLeod (2009) outlines a number of different categories or types of books which serve this therapeutic purpose: (1) self-help manuals which focus on specific difficulties such as the areas mentioned above: these tend to include exercises and action steps and invariably approach the issue from a cognitive behavioural perspective. Individual therapists and agencies as well as publishing houses produce these types of books and leaflets; (2) books which comprise discussion of experiences and ideas rather than focusing on changing behaviour: a well-known example of this type of book is *The Road Less Traveled: A New Psychology of Love, Traditional Values and Spiritual Growth* (Scott Peck 2006); (3) autobiographical or biographical books where the reader can gain support via exploring the lives of others who have encountered similar problems and gain insight into the issues. (John Bayley's 2001 book, *Elergy for Iris*, which focuses on his experience of caring for his partner who suffered from Alzheimer's disease, is a popular example of this genre); (4) works of fiction which centre on mental health issues and which explore associated thoughts, feelings and ways of coping. (*The Bell Jar* by Sylvia Plath is a well-known example.)

Research findings

There is a significant amount of research which supports the idea that bibliotherapy is an effective form of therapeutic intervention. A study by Ogles et al. (1991, cited in McLeod 2009) found significant self-reported benefits from participants who read relevant self-help books when coping with the break-up of a relationship. Belief that the book would help resulted in greater benefits. Other studies suggest that books can be effectively combined with telephone counselling or some level of personal contact (McLeod 2009). Overall, meta-analyses such as Menchola et al. (2007, cited in McLeod 2009) tend to find that treatment by a counsellor or self-help combined with guidance from a counsellor are more effective than self-help in isolation.

Advantages

Clearly there are no side effects from bibliotherapy as compared to medication and it may be seen as a more socially acceptable intervention than either counselling or medication. It is a low cost strategy which is recommended (in the form of 'self-help materials') in the NICE (2009, 2011) guidelines for anxiety and depression.

Potential limitations

Bibliotherapy inevitably assumes that the same techniques or ideas will suit all clients, whereas much research suggests that different techniques work for different people. A huge body of research also supports the idea that the counsellor/client relationship is crucial to the effectiveness of counselling, and indeed some theoretical approaches have this relationship as the focal point of the therapeutic process. This may explain why psychodynamic counsellors were less likely to use bibliotherapy than those using other approaches (Starker 1988) and why CBT, which sees the relationship as important but not as central, is frequently used in self-help books.

Another important issue for consideration is the potentially damaging effects of using books to deal with problematic issues when there may be no one available to offer support or feedback if difficult feelings are evoked. This approach also requires a high level of self-motivation and is unlikely to be effective if users consider it to be a cheaper alternative to a face-to-face intervention.

It is also important to consider the quality of the books being read. It is essential that counsellors recommending texts ensure that they are appropriate for the individual concerned as well as demonstrating likely effectiveness.

References

Bayley, J. (2001) *Elegy for Iris*. Picador.

Bayne, R., Jinks, J., Collard, P. and Horton, I. (2008) *The Counsellor's Handbook: A Practical A–Z Guide to Integrative Counselling and Psychotherapy*, 3rd edn. Cheltenham: Nelson Thornes.

McLeod, J. (2009) *An Introduction to Counselling*, 4th edn. Maidenhead: Open University Press.

NICE (2009) Anxiety: Generalised anxiety disorder and panic disorder (with or without agoraphobia) in adults. Clinical Guideline No. 113. www.nice.org.uk (accessed 5 March 2011).

NICE (2011) Depression: the treatment and management of depression in adults. Clinical Guideline No. 90. www.nice.org.uk (accessed 5 March 2011).

Ogles, B.M., Lambert, M.J. and Craig, D.E. (1991) Comparison of self-help books for coping with loss: expectations and attributions. *Journal of Counselling Psychology*, 38: 387–93.

Scott Peck, M. (2006) *The Road Less Traveled: A New Psychology of Love, Traditional Values and Spiritual Growth*. London: Arrow.

Starker, S. (1988) Do-it-yourself therapy: the prescription of self-help books by psychologists. *Psychotherapy*, 25: 142–6.

Annotated further reading

Beinart, H., Kennedy, P. and Llewelyn, S. (eds) (2009) *Clinical Psychology in Practice*. Oxford: Blackwell Books.

Contains a useful chapter by David S.J. Hawker entitled 'Bibliotherapy and self help' which discusses how effective self-help methods are together with some of their limitations.

The BACP journals and website (as well as those of other counselling and psychotherapy professional bodies) contain regular reviews of self-help resources.

Bion, Wilfred R. (1897–1979)

See also: groups; basic assumption groups; container/contained

Bion, trained in psychiatry as well as psychoanalysis, was one of the first who worked psychoanalytically with patients in psychotic states and is credited with developing the existing projective theories (see **projection** and

projective identification) evolving new concepts around them. Mawson (2011) in the introduction to his book suggests that Bion, Melanie Klein, Herbert Rosenfeld and Hanna Segal all worked so closely together in their work with psychotic patients that it is difficult retrospectively to distinguish their exact individual contributions to the concepts of 'splitting', 'projective identification', 'unconscious phantasy' and the use of countertransference in therapy. However, clearly this group did move key concepts on beyond Freudian psychoanalysis and did much to shape the future direction, particularly of the Tavistock approach, of analysis applied to neurosis and psychosis.

Wilfred Bion was born in India in 1897 during the days of the British Raj and died in 1979 in England. He was sent to a boarding school in England at the age of 8 and lived there for most of his life until the last 12 years, which he spent in California. He left school just before his 18th birthday to join the Tank Corps and served in France during the First World War, which was an emotionally devastating experience for him but also one (alongside his unhappy childhood) that formed the beginnings of some of his ideas about psychology and psychoanalysis in particular (Bion 2005). It was while Bion was in California, towards the end of his life, that James Grotstein entered analysis with him and wrote about this experience along with a broader appreciation of Bion's work (Grotstein 2007).

Between 1962 and 1965 Bion was President of the British Psychoanalytic Society and he has been acknowledged to be one of the greatest psychoanalytic thinkers after Freud (Symington 2004: 7) and one who made a 'potent and original contribution to psychoanalysis' (Mawson 2011: 3).

Mawson credits Bion and others working in London in the 1960s with developing what he identifies as the 'contemporary Kleinian' development of psychoanalysis (p. 5). Others claim their work (particularly that of Bion) as the 'Tavistock' approach. Bion's clinical thinking revolved around notions of schematic precision but also a certain 'mysticism' is attributed to his work. Grotstein suggests that Bion 'pulled the positivistic psychoanalysis of Freud and Klein into the new, uncharted realms of uncertainty: from the strictures and prison of verbal language to a realm before and beyond language' (p. 44). However, Mawson considers that Bion's work demonstrated a clear developmental trajectory from that of Klein (as Klein's did from that of Freud).

Alpha and beta elements and functions

Bion proposed that all analytic exchanges can be interpreted, but that they might also be classified into Alpha (α) elements and Beta (β) elements. β-elements represent the earliest matrix from which thoughts can be supposed to arise – thoughts are things and things are thoughts.

α-elements represent the outcome of work done by the α-function on sense impressions. They are more abstract and make possible the use of dream thoughts (Bion 1963: 22). Thus the α-elements are the stuff of 'knowing'.

The concept of the alpha function led to that of the container/contained relationship (see entry **container/contained**).

Bion had been concerned that psychoanalytic theories were not considered to be 'scientific enough' in that, clinically, there appeared to be a reliance on theory rather than a factual account of the patient's experience and behaviour.

The Grid (Bion 1963) represented the α-function that mediates elements subject to the reality principle. It is a mathematical device consisting of a plane covered by crossed lines, which creates the image of boxes (containers) both vertically and horizontally. Bion saw these as 'thought bins' to store thoughts and emotions and to trace movement during the transformative process of psychoanalysis (Grotstein 2007). As Grotstein continues to explain the vertical axis designates progressive sophistication of *thoughts* whereas the horizontal axis represents the *thinking* act – the use the thoughts are being put to.

Bion's focus on the elements of psychoanalysis was very precise and based on meticulous observations and feelings. The first element thus was projective identification that 'if it were less it could no longer be related to projective identification at all; if it were more it would carry too great a penumbra of associations for my purpose. It is a representation of an element that could be called a dynamic relationship between container and contained' (p. 3). For example he proposed a schema of affective links L (loving), H (hating) and K (knowing) to represent emotional relationships in an attempt to make abstraction more concrete.

References

Bion, W. (2005) *The Long Weekend 1987–1919: Part of a Life*. London: Karnac.
Bion, W.R. (1963) *Elements of Psycho-Analysis*. London: William Heinemann.
Grotstein, J.S. (2007) *A Beam of Intense Darkness*. London: Karnac.
Mawson, C. (2011) *Bion Today*. London: Routledge.
Symington, N. (2004) *Narcissism: A New Theory*. London: Karnac.

Annotated further reading

Bion, W.R. (1961/1986) *Experiences in Groups, and Other Papers*. London: Tavistock.

Bion's writing is dense, rich and frequently difficult to understand over the first few readings. However, it is necessary to have some first hand knowledge of his writing in order to make sense of his supporters' and critics' assessments and developments of his work.

Bion, W. (2005) *The Long Weekend 1987–1919: Part of a Life*. London: Karnac.

This autobiography is particularly interesting in putting Bion's ideas into an emotional and temporal context. He tells of cruelty and neglect in childhood, experiences in the First World War and life as a therapist.

Grotstein, J.S. (2007) *A Beam of Intense Darkness*. London: Karnac.

Grotstein's analysis and overview help to make sense of some of Bion's more complex ideas and provide a review of applications of Bion's concepts in therapy.

Blind eye

See also: Oedipus complex

The phrase 'turning a blind eye' is a common one in everyday speech. It literally means not 'seeing' evidence of behaviour, processes or events taking place in front of our eyes. By implication this suggests that the blind eye is turned towards unpalatable information and thus likely to raise questions of morality and/or corruption in relationships and organizations. Not every individual or group who turns a blind eye is necessarily immoral or corrupt. Indeed frequently we 'choose' to ignore impending dangers to our *own* safety from threatening individuals or regimes as for example in violent interpersonal relationships (Nicolson 2010) or mass extermination of an ethnic or social group (Laquer 1982).

The Oedipus myth is credited with the origin of the concept of the 'blind eye' that has become particularly important in psychoanalytic understanding of corruption in human interrelationships. In the numerous stories about Oedipus there are literal and metaphorical examples of 'self-blinding' in that there are some things Oedipus does not want to know. Oedipus, who in the Greek myth believed he had escaped his destiny, was eventually confronted by his mother, Jocasta, who told him that he *had* killed his father and married her, *his mother*, who was also the mother of his children. Jocasta then entered the palace and hanged herself after which Oedipus, declaring that he had been *blind*, reached for the brooch that clasped his cloak and stabbed himself in his eyes. Sophocles' plays about Oedipus resonated with the Athenian audiences as a 'collective cultural memory' but there also remains a clear connection in the stories of Oedipus to the experiences of contemporary 'audiences' (Palombo 1994: 2).

When Oedipus is found out, and finds himself out (for murder and incest) he is desperate to justify his behaviour to himself. However, his overwhelming feelings of guilt and self-pity turn into self-hatred and 'most significantly he attacks his eyes which are his link to the reality he cannot bear' (Steiner 1990: 2). But there are also examples in the myth where there is a conscious knowledge of wrong-doing but unconscious collusion of a group in turning a blind eye, as with the Thebans who unconsciously collude in the rise of Oedipus to power by turning a blind eye to his killing of Laius (Palombo 1994; Pasquali 1987; Steiner 1985).

There are different levels at which we *fail* or *choose not* to see or recognize this information and below are some examples of 'turning a blind eye', and then a consideration of the levels of consciousness that are mediating between the information in the external world and the individual, group and/or society turning a blind eye.

The complexity of the processes in which individuals engage with and construct their reality is articulated here by Steiner (1985: 161) who asserts:

> In recent years it has become evident that our contact with reality is not an all or none affair . . . [and there is a situation] . . . in which we seem to have access to reality but choose to ignore it because it proves convenient to do so. I refer to this mechanism as turning a blind eye because I think this conveys the right degree of ambiguity as to how conscious or unconscious the knowledge is.

Steiner's paper makes clear that to 'see' or 'not to see' (consciously or unconsciously) represents *an action* by the individual(s) involved.

Examples of the 'blind eye'

To illustrate: Eddie Chapman, a British 'double agent' during the Second World War, worked both for the British and German Secret Service, the Abwehr (MacIntyre 2007). Most of the Abwehr were anti-Nazi including Chapman's German handler *Stephan Von Gröning*. Von Gröning's status benefitted from Chapman's (apparent) skills as a spy even though Chapman's 'exploits' against the British (including faked sabotage) were fabrications. However, 'Chapman [also] needed Von Gröning to believe him, and Von Gröning needed Chapman to succeed, forging a strange, unspoken complicity' (p. 226). The fear for the spymaster was to have an inactive agent. 'If Von Gröning suspected he was being lied to, that the entire tale of sabotage, heroism and escape was a monstrous fabrication, he said nothing and the heavy-lidded eyes chose not to see' (p. 227).

This intriguing relationship must have had both conscious and unconscious elements to it. What flies against 'logic' is that the man with the (apparent) power (Von Gröning) was prepared to place his desire for Chapman's success above the 'truth' that the 'intelligence' he was gaining was, in fact, a fiction. Was Von Gröning thus a traitor? Perhaps the (unspoken) anti-Nazi ethos of the Abwehr unconsciously engaged him (and of course Chapman) in a destructive phantasy towards Hitler? Perhaps the issue was simply that Von Gröning had initially believed and trusted Chapman, boasted of his agent's exploits so that the 'truth' that he had been betrayed (and had been totally unaware of that betrayal) was so intolerable and shameful that he colluded unconsciously with Chapman in a joint phantasy cover-up. The outcome, at the time, was that Von Gröning kept his sense of self/pride intact and Chapman kept his cover.

From a different perspective, but equally evocative of knowing and not knowing, Stan Cohen (2001) recalls his childhood epiphany in apartheid South Africa. 'Just before going to bed, I looked out of the window and saw [an old Zulu 'Night Watch Boy'] huddled over a charcoal fire, rubbing his hands to keep warm . . . As I slipped into my over-warm bed . . . I suddenly started thinking about why he was out there and I was in here' (p. ix). Cohen had an uneasy sense of something being 'deeply' wrong 'but also knowing that I could not live in a state of permanent awareness of this knowledge. Without my deliberate intention, this awareness would switch itself on or, more often off' (pp. ix–x).

After the liberation of Belsen the world was (apparently) shocked and outraged. The camp was considered the 'greatest possible abomination' (Laquer 1982) as well as 'unbelievable'. Laquer sought to find out what had been known or not known about Hitler's 'final solution'. He suggests the consequent shock of discovery was because of the psychological rejection of unacceptable information. With his spotlight on those who became victims he asked 'What is the reason for the inclination among otherwise normal, sometimes even highly intelligent, human beings to deny reality, however glaring?' (p. 3).

Knowing/not knowing takes different forms – in dyadic relationships as with Chapman and Von Gröning where both seem to *share an unspoken secret*; between an individual of one 'class' in relation to the 'other' as with Cohen and Black South Africans; and between an individual and the society, group or organization s/he lives and works in as with Jews under 'threat' of Hitler's 'final solution'.

In all three cases although different in character, to face full knowledge of what was going on between the actors/participants in these scenarios was *intolerable*.

In the first example, acknowledgement from either player would have meant the uncovering of a betrayal with potential dangers for both if the knowledge became explicit. In the second case, shame (only partly understood by the child Cohen) masked perhaps by a *disbelief* that lives could be lived in such proximity yet be so different, defended him against the anxieties accompanying the guilt (and impotence) in the face of suffering and inequalities. In the third example it was impossible for the intended victims to contemplate that the ultimate terror could possibly be true so that various Jewish communities *unconsciously colluded* to defend themselves by *refusing to think*. Later some commentators would deny the Holocaust, in part because it was 'unbelievable' but also because it demonstrated the full horror of how people could behave towards each other which is intolerable, particularly among those who were perpetrators or bystanders (Lipstadt 1994).

Defending against external reality

The psychology of turning a blind eye is difficult to disentangle. Does the phrase 'imply that we have access to reality, but choose to ignore it because it is convenient to do so'? Or 'are we vaguely aware of choosing not to look at the facts, but not quite conscious of just what it is we are evading. We know but at the same time we don't know' (Cohen 2001: 5)?

People *do* openly lie to themselves as a defence against feelings of guilt which might lead to self-hate (as for instance in the case of Oedipus), or to others to avoid retribution (as with Bernard Madoff the financier who swindled his investors or those British MPs whose questionable expenses claims were made public). These are overt, conscious denials (see entry on **defence mechanisms**).

But what of the cases outlined above where the failure to see (or failure to *want* to see) 'reality' leads to millions going to their death? In the case of the Jewish communities in Hitler's Europe, the consequences of this 'failure to see' are without parallel: 6 million were murdered.

Although highly relevant to individuals, groups, organizations and societies, the key evidence to explain the blind eye phenomenon originates from one-to-one clinical work (see entry for **negation**).

There are, as in the examples at the start of this entry, many things we cannot or do not want to see. The myth has therefore survived to be subjected to detailed and close scrutiny across psychoanalytic circles with the publication of over 300 papers (Edmunds and Ingber 1977; Steiner 1990).

References

Britton, R. (1994) The blindness of the seeing eye: inverse symmetry as a defense against reality. *Psychoanalytic Inquiry: A Topical Journal for Mental Health Professionals*, 14(3): 365–78.

Cohen, S. (2001) *States of Denial: Knowing About Atrocities and Suffering*. Cambridge: Polity.

Edmunds, L. and Ingber, R. (1977) Psychoanalytical writings on the Oedipus legend: a bibliography. *Amer Imago*, 34: 374–86.

Freud, S. (1927) *Fetishism*. London: Hogarth.

Laquer, W. (1982) *The Terrible Secret: Suppression of the Truth About Hitler's 'Final Solution'*. Harmondswoth: Penguin.

Lipstadt, D. (1994) *Denying the Holocaust: The Growing Assault on Truth and Memory*. New York: Vintage.

Long, S. (2008) *The Perverse Organisation and its Deadly Sins*. London: Karnac.

MacIntyre, B. (2007) *Agent ZigZag*. London: Bloomsbury.

Nicolson, P. (2010) *Psychology and Domestic Violence: A Critical Perspective*. London: Taylor and Francis.

Palombo, S.R. (1994) Oedipus and the Sphinx: triumph and catastrophe. *Journal of the American Psychoanalytic Association*, 42: 635–53.

Pasquali, L.T. (1987) Reflections on Oedipus in Sophocles' tragedy and in clinical practice. *International Review of Psycho-Analysis*, 14: 475–82.

Priel, B. (2001) Negation in Borges's 'The Secret Miracle'™: writing the Shoah. *International Journal of Psycho-Analysis*, 82(4): 785–94.

Rosenfeld, H. (1983) Primitive object relations and mechanisms. *International Journal of Psycho-Analysis*, 64: 261–7.

Sapochnik, C. (2003) Corruption: Oedipal configuration as social mechanism. *Organisational and Social Dynamics: An International Journal of Psychoanalytic, Systemic and Group Relations Perspectives*, 3(2): 177–90.

Steiner, J. (1985) Turning a blind eye: the cover up for Oedipus. *International Review of Psycho-Analysis*, 12: 161–72.

Steiner, J. (1990) The retreat from truth to omnipotence in Sophocles' Oedipus at Colonus. *International Review of Psycho-Analysis*, 17: 227–37.

Annotated further reading

Cohen, S. (2001) *States of Denial: Knowing About Atrocities and Suffering*. Cambridge: Polity.

This book is clearly written from a poignant personal perspective by a well-regarded scholar although the narrative seamlessly moves forward to address issues in wider society.

Laquer, W. (1982) *The Terrible Secret: Suppression of the Truth About Hitler's 'Final Solution'*. Harmondswoth: Penguin.

In Laquer's book the focus is on turning a blind eye to dangers to yourself and your community. Once again a fascinating but terrifying read making the process of 'turning a blind eye' both clear and horrifying in its extent.

MacIntyre, B. (2007) *Agent ZigZag*. London: Bloomsbury.

The examples from MacIntyre on Eddie Chapman, Stan Cohen and Walter Laquer make fascinating reading as do many case studies of corruption in organizations. In the Enron case for example, many of the employees claimed not to have known what was going on. More recently in the complex phone hacking scandal in the UK David Cameron, the Prime Minister at the time, claimed that people who worked at the *News of the World* had turned a blind eye to what others had been doing. See: http://www.dailymail.co.uk/news/article-2012505/News-World-phone-hacking-Cameron-announces-public-inquiries-Press-regulation.html (accessed 19 December 2011).

Boundaries

See also: assertiveness; games; ethical concepts; psychoanalysis; psychodynamic counselling; self-disclosure.

A boundary is a 'line', rule or principle that distinguishes between ethical and unethical ways of behaving. For example, sexual behaviour between counsellors and clients is very widely regarded in the counselling profession as breaking a boundary. This particular boundary has a strong underlying rationale: breaking it abuses clients and damages counselling's reputation, thus possible deterring potential clients.

Other boundaries may be more the result of tradition or habit, for example the 50-minute session. Some counsellors regard extending a session as a serious breach while others are more flexible, ending sessions when it feels appropriate to do so, taking such circumstances into account as whether another client is waiting or the client has a fragile sense of self or is playing a 'game'.

The term boundary can be used in a practical sense in terms of establishing expectations at the start of therapy so that the client is clear from the outset about aspects of the therapy sessions such as length of sessions, cost of the therapy and so on. The boundaries or limits of the therapy relate to a number of issues such as time (when and for how long the sessions will take place); space (where they will take place, privacy, how closely will the client and therapist sit?); information (how much will the client know about the therapist?); contact outside of the sessions (will the therapist be available for contact or not? How will accidental meetings be handled?). Clarity about these issues serves to reduce client anxiety as well as enabling the therapist to make explicit the limits of this type of relationship and of the therapy itself.

In a more abstract or metaphorical sense, a boundary can be used to define the nature of the therapeutic relationship (McLeod 2009). Perhaps unsurprisingly, it is conceptualized in different ways according to theoretical orientation and personal approach. In psychoanalysis and psychodynamic counselling boundaries are seen as particularly important.

Clear boundaries create a sense of containment such that the client feels safe enough to express deeply hidden, and often disturbing, feelings and fantasies. This sense of containment echoes an effective parenting role, although many clients will have experienced inadequate parenting. Adult responses to others are heavily influenced by childhood reactions to boundaries experienced in childhood, for example, how responsive parents were to the child when they needed attention. If the therapist can recreate a boundaried and safe environment for the client, the therapeutic work is likely to be more effective.

Another feature of psychodynamic counselling is the significance placed on the breaking of boundaries. If a client misses or is late for a session, this can be seen as having another more significant meaning in the client's unconscious world. Such acts will need to be discussed and interpreted so as to illuminate the client's unconscious motivations, which may be highly destructive. Such an intense focus on these types of incident can be seen as excessive by therapists from other theoretical orientations.

The humanistic tradition tends to place far less emphasis on the concept of boundaries, instead favouring the idea of authentic contact. Some person-centred counsellors would not see a problem in extending sessions, having contact between sessions or allowing physical contact such as hugging or non-sexual touching. Such behaviour might be perceived as a violation of boundaries and as such unethical by some psychodynamic counsellors.

Other approaches have a different slant on the idea of boundary. For example, gestalt therapy conceptualizes different types of 'contact boundary' or style. The focus here is on the relationship between the individual and their circumstances, with people connecting (or not) to their surroundings (including other people) in more or less effective ways. For example, someone may struggle to express feelings appropriately resulting in either expressions of uncontrollable anger or an inability to express it, often with resulting somatic symptoms when the anger is held inside. Both types of behaviour can cause problems for the individual. (See Dryden 2002 for more detail.)

A distinction is sometimes made between boundary crossings and boundary violations (McLeod 2009). Boundary violations on the part of the client will often need to be discussed in the therapy and may provide a useful insight into the client's internal world. Violations by therapists can involve exploitation of the client, such as engaging in a sexual relationship or coercing the client to behave in certain ways. However, while some forms of therapist behaviour are almost universally regarded as unethical (such as having a sexual relationship with the client), others are viewed differently depending on the therapist's theoretical perspective (e.g. the use of touch).

Generally, being clear about boundaries and implementing them assertively can help create a framework in which clients develop trust in their counsellor and in the process of counselling. They can also help protect therapists from burnout. For example a more literal and specific boundary is the space between sessions for different clients. It may help if the counsellor can bring a sense of closure for one session and allow some space to prepare for the next: breathing or mindfulness exercises or running up a flight of stairs are some ways of doing this. More generally, boundaries which are about the nature of the relationship, e.g. between friendship and counselling and not being available for clients at any time, can be healthy for both counsellors and clients.

Research in this area (Hartman 1997, in McLeod 2009) suggests that different people have different boundary needs, so that one approach to boundaries will not suit everyone. It could be argued, therefore, that it may be necessary to adapt one's approach to boundaries to suit different clients, although most therapists will not wish to move too far away from their own philosophical perspective on the use of boundaries.

References

Dryden, W. (ed.) (2002) *Handbook of Individual Therapy*, 4th edn. London: Sage.
McLeod, J. (2009) *An Introduction to Counselling*, 4th edn. Maidenhead: Open University Press.

Annotated further reading

Bayne, R., Jinks, G., Collard, P. and Horton, I. (2008) *The Counsellor's Handbook. A Practical A–Z Guide to Integrative Counselling and Psychotherapy*, 3rd edn. Cheltenham: Nelson Thornes.
Bond, T. (2010) *Standards and Ethics for Counselling in Action*, 2nd edn. London: Sage.

Both these books discuss a wide range of ethical issues, often involving boundaries, the first briefly, the second in detail.

Davies, M. (2007) *Boundaries in Counselling and Psychotherapy*. Twickenham: Athena Press.

This is a concise and easy-to-read introduction to the concept of boundary in the context of the main theoretical approaches to counselling and psychotherapy.

Brief therapy

See also: cognitive behavioural therapy

Feltham and Dryden (2006) define brief counselling as lasting between one and twenty sessions. Having said this, many voluntary and statutory counselling agencies offer a maximum of between six to eight sessions. The terms brief counselling and time-limited counselling are often used interchangeably, although the former does not generally state the number of sessions or the ending date.

Brief counselling is a relatively new phenomenon which emerged alongside a range of new therapies such as gestalt and transactional analysis in the 1960s and 1970s. In the 1980s cognitive behavioural and solution-focused therapies, which tended to have a relatively short-term focus, became increasingly popular. All three major theoretical orientations (psychodynamic, cognitive behavioural and person-centred) have developed ways of working in a brief and focused way. Part of this move towards shorter-term work was based on research suggesting that many people did not need long-term therapy to derive benefit, together with a drive towards making therapy more accessible to a wider population. Long-term therapy is not available via the NHS (or its equivalents in other countries), nor is it recognized by private insurance companies. It is generally very expensive and inaccessible to most.

Who is it suitable for?

This type of therapy is generally considered suitable for people undergoing life crises such as bereavement or trauma or mild anxiety and depression. Clients need to be functioning fairly well, reasonably articulate and able to discuss their problems. According to Budman and Gurman (1989 in Feltham and Dryden 2006) they need to be experiencing 'interpersonal-developmental-existential' problems. It is not suitable for people with chronic problems such as personality disorders, drug and alcohol addictions and other serious mental health problems.

A shift in values in order to offer short-term counselling?

Counsellors offering this type of counselling tend to possess rather different underlying values to those offering a longer-term approach. McLeod (2009) presents some of the differences presented by Budman and Gurman (1989), the essentials of which will be presented here. Short-term counsellors tend to be more pragmatic in that they do not so much believe in a 'cure' as in helping the client to access their strengths and resources in order to change a specific problematic situation or problem. They accept that changes may occur after the counselling has ended and that being in the world is more important than being in therapy. Counsellors contemplating working in this way need to consider whether their values would sit easily with this type of approach.

Short-term counselling also involves a different way of working, at least in some respects. As a result, counsellors need to undergo specific training in this type of counselling. The initial assessment process needs to consider whether a client will benefit from this approach. If not, referral mechanisms should be in place for those who would benefit from longer-term work. Both client and counsellor will need to be actively involved in the counselling, so that clients may need to undertake homework tasks and counsellors will need to adopt a proactive stance, suggesting new perspectives and activities to try out. Sessions need to have a specific focus; indeed the work as a whole needs to be problem-focused with clearly specified goals and objectives and a well defined structure. The ending needs to emphasize what has been gained from the sessions, which can be used on an ongoing basis after the counselling ends.

Research evidence

There is a substantial body of research which suggests that brief counselling is as effective as long-term work (see McLeod 2009 for more detail). Howard et al. (1986 in McLeod 2009) found that most counselling takes place within a limited number of sessions and that clients tend to benefit most from the early sessions. Barkham and Shapiro (1989) used what they termed a 'two-plus-one' model which comprised two sessions set at a week apart, followed by a follow-up session after three months. In another study, Barkham and Shapiro (1990) found that sixty per cent of participants benefitted significantly from the sessions. One of the key issues seems to be the importance of giving clients some choice as to the number of sessions they receive and conveying positive expectations about what can be achieved in a limited amount of time.

Possible limitations

Brief counselling is sometimes criticized as a 'quick fix' which may alleviate symptoms rather than uncovering and working through the causes of distress. Feltham (2010) states that it may take some clients more than a few sessions to build up a sufficiently trusting relationship with the counsellor before they can begin to disclose difficult issues or get in touch with repressed material. Clients who may be at risk of relapse are unlikely to benefit from counselling of short duration (Feltham 2010).

References

Barkham, M. and Shapiro, D.A. (1989) Towards resolving the problem of waiting lists: psychotherapy in two-plus-one sessions. *Clinical Psychology Forum*, 23: 15–18.

Barkham, M. and Shapiro, D.A. (1990) Brief psychotherapeutic interventions for job related distress: a pilot study of prescriptive and exploratory therapy. *Counselling Psychology Quarterly*, 23: 133–47.

Feltham, C. (2010) *Critical Thinking in Counselling and Psychotherapy*. London: Sage.

Feltham, C. and Dryden, W. (2006) *Brief Counselling: A Practical Integrative Approach*, 2nd edn. Maidenhead: Open University Press.

McLeod, J. (2009) *An Introduction to Counselling*. Maidenhead: Open University Press.

Annotated further reading

Feltham, C. and Dryden, W. (2006) *Brief Counselling: A Practical Integrative Approach*, 2nd edn. Maidenhead: Open University Press.

This book adopts a hands-on approach and includes guidelines for practice. It also includes examples of how counsellors from different theoretical perspectives might engage in brief therapeutic work.

Mander, G. (2000) *A Psychodynamic Approach to Brief Therapy*. London: Sage.

This is a practical introduction to brief, short-term and time-limited therapy from a particular perspective.

C

Catharsis

See also: anxiety, existential; empathy

Catharsis or venting is the idea that expressing emotions is healing in itself, as in the expressions 'getting it off your chest' and 'not keeping it bottled up'. It suggests that emotions can build up inside us like a fluid and that it's helpful to pour them out. This may be true for some people and emotional avoidance (though perhaps short-term) may be the best way to cope for others. Generally though an alternative view is more valid and discussed well by Kennedy-Moore and Watson (1999) and Yalom (2001).

Kennedy-Moore and Watson argue that research in social psychology shows that when emotions are vented there can be a sense of relief but that the emotion then tends to return and sometimes with greater intensity. Instead they suggest that emotional expression should be explicitly accompanied by trying to clarify and make sense of those emotions. Yalom takes the same position: 'you encourage acts of emotional expression but you always follow with reflection upon the emotions expressed' (p. 164).

Earlier in the same book Yalom stated the same principle more formally: 'effective therapy consists of an alternating sequence: *evocation and experiencing* of affect followed by *analysis and integration* of affect' (p. 71, original italics). He also commented on a key practical aspect of this strategy: 'How long one waits until one initiates an analysis of the affective event is a function of clinical experience' (p. 71) – not so helpful! Kennedy-Moore and Watson are more specific when they suggest that a client who is 'flooding' – caught up in an emotion for several minutes or longer – should be offered distraction techniques like counting backwards in sevens from 300 or breathing slowly and deeply to help them regain enough composure to reflect.

References

Kennedy-Moore, E. and Watson, J.C. (1999) *Expressing Emotion: Myths, Realities and Therapeutic Strategies*. London: Guildford Press.

Yalom, I.D. (2001) *The Gift of Therapy: Reflections on Being a Therapist*. London: Piatkus.

Client feedback, collecting

See also: collaborative empiricism; goal consensus; integrative models; the therapeutic relationship

The idea that systematically and frequently collecting (and using) client feedback is a major aspect of developing a therapeutic relationship has only recently become prominent in the counselling literature (Duncan et al. 2010; Lambert and Shimokawa 2011). For example, in the second edition of a classic book, Duncan et al. (2010) go so far as to say that 'Using formal client feedback to inform, guide and evaluate treatment is the strongest recommendation coming from this volume' (p. 424).

Similarly, Lambert and Shimokawa, on the basis of a meta-analysis of research on two methods of collecting client feedback concluded that clinicians should 'seriously consider making formal methods of collecting client feedback a routine part of their daily practice' (2011: 72). However, they also noted that so far there are only a small number of studies on the effects of collecting client feedback, that they rely on self-report measures, and that only two methods of collecting feedback were considered by them.

Two possible explanations for the benefits of using client feedback are that it can correct therapists' tendency to be too optimistic about their clients' progress, and that, used well, it communicates both respect and taking a collaborative approach. It may also help to alleviate the stress for counsellors of clients who leave counselling without warning their counsellors (Bayne et al. 2008).

References

Bayne, R., Jinks, G., Collard, P. and Horton, I. (2008) *The Counsellor's Handbook: A Practical A–Z Guide to Integrative Counselling and Psychotherapy*, 3rd edn. Cheltenham: Nelson Thornes.

Duncan, B.L., Miller, S.D., Wampold, B.E. and Hubble, M.A. (eds) (2010) *The Heart and Soul of Change: Delivering What Works in Therapy*, 2nd edn. Washington, DC: APA.

Lambert, M.J. and Shimokawa, K. (2011) Collecting client feedback. *Psychotherapy*, 46: 72–9.

Annotated further reading

Duncan, B.L., Miller, S.D., Wampold, B.E. and Hubble, M.A. (eds) (2010) *The Heart and Soul of Change: Delivering What Works in Therapy*, 2nd edn. Washington, DC: APA.

The subtitle of the classic first edition was '*What works in therapy*'. The change in emphasis in the subtitle of the second edition accurately reflects the progress made in the intervening 11 years.

Cognitive analytic therapy (CAT)

See also: personal construct therapy

On becoming head of an inner-city psychotherapy department, Anthony Ryle experienced the need to develop a form of therapy which was cheaper, less time-consuming and easier to audit and evaluate than other psycho-dynamic approaches. He developed CAT, a new hybrid of therapy, which is usually offered for between 4 and 24 sessions – 16 on average – lending itself to brief yet psychologically deep interventions and treatment. In the late 1980s a governing body, the Association of Cognitive Analytic Therapy (ACAT) was formed, to advise members on training and supervision. CAT has been subject to research and evaluation since the very beginning, yet the volume of research is still relatively limited, due to not having an academic research site. Nevertheless one RCT was published in 2008 (Channen et al.).

CAT has a time-limited focus, and integrates ideas from psychoanalytic and cognitive therapy, personal construct theory and other schools. This variety of sources creates a great diversity of approach. In brief, CAT uses concepts of conflict, defence, object relations and counter transference from psychoanalysis; as well as exploring unacknowledged or unconscious factors, the therapist–client relationship is understood and used as a 'training ground'. The framework, the therapeutic planning and the change-measurement techniques derive from the cognitive source, as does the idea of teaching patients self-observation of moods, thoughts, behaviours and symptoms. From Kelly's personal construct theory Ryle 'imported' the focus on how people make sense of their world ('man as scientist') and construct their own reality. Thus CAT is an integrative approach, which has developed a solid body of theory with an exceptional understanding of personality and development. It emphasizes the interplay between mental processes, feelings, actions and consequences.

CAT intends to help clients discover their expectations of life and what change is needed to get to their goals. Many psychological problems can benefit from CAT treatment, such as depression, anxiety, eating disorders, personal and relationship problems. It has also been used for treating borderline personality disorder, rehabilitation of offenders, and for treating poor self-care among diabetics. CAT is used for individual psychotherapy, but can be effective for couples, families and groups too. The therapist works with the client to find out how certain problems arose in the past and why certain life skills and modes of behaviour that may have worked in the past are no longer useful now. One is guided to an understanding of how problems arose originally, and how they may become even harder to bear now due to dysfunctional coping patterns. These patterns tend to be enacted in the therapeutic relationship, and it is working through these re-enactments (and avoiding collusion with the problematic elements) which is at the heart of effective CAT therapy. The therapist helps the client discover his own strengths and resources, and plans are developed collaboratively to create change. The work is active, shared, psycho-educational and user friendly. Insights are recorded and become tools for use within, outside and beyond the structure of therapy. Self-awareness is perhaps the one most desired outcome, which can assist the client to help themselves and feel less trapped in unhelpful life patterns.

The three-letter name (CAT) matches the three Rs of therapy: reformulation, recognition and revision. The reformulation is one of the key tasks in CAT and it is recorded on paper in diagrammatic or letter format. The therapist shares his insights with the client by re-telling the client's history and describes current damaging actions.

This reformulation is used throughout therapy as a basis for patient homework designed for speedy recognition. In addition, at cessation of therapy both the therapist and client write 'goodbye' letters, reviewing what has been achieved.

CAT is most certainly going to continue developing as a theory-based treatment, compared to atheoretical treatments such as CBT. Thus CAT will always be more suitable for treating complex, multilayered client profiles. The tendency in our quick-fix lifestyle points not only towards obtaining funding for approaches that may be able to cure or help out with specific problems such as a simple phobia, but in the same vein there are fewer and fewer clients prepared to work through multiple issues and invest longer-term commitment that the CAT approach undoubtedly would require.

References

Channen, A.M., Jackson, H.J., McCutcheon, L.K. et al. (2008) Early intervention for adolescents with borderline personality disorder using cognitive analytic therapy: randomised controlled trial. *British Journal of Psychiatry*, 193: 477–84.

Annotated further reading

Palmer, S.T. and Woolfe, R. (2000) *Integrative and Eclectic Counselling and Psychotherapy*. London: Sage.

This book contains 19 short yet in-depth chapters on different ways of integration in the therapeutic context. Fluently written, it enables therapists to increase the potential repertoire in an eclectic practice.

Ryle, A. and Kerr, I. (2002) *Introducing CAT: Principles and Practice*. Chichester: Wiley.

This book gives the reader a basic introduction to the principles and practices of the evolving CAT model of psychotherapy.

Cognitive behavioural therapy (CBT)

See also: mindfulness-based cognitive therapy; rational emotive behaviour therapy; multimodal therapy; Socratic dialogue

Cognitive behavioural therapy has been widely researched and refers to more than 20 differing approaches (rational emotive behaviour therapy, cognitive analytic therapy, multimodal therapy, mindfulness-based cognitive therapy, acceptance commitment therapy, dialectical behaviour therapy, etc.). It is firmly rooted in research and based on numerous studies carried out since the 1950s. Thus it has gained more and more respectability and is one of the most highly recommended talking therapies by the National Institute for Health and Clinical Excellence (NICE).

Aaron Beck (MD), a psychiatrist and 'founding father' of this cognitive therapy, had been frustrated with his attempts to treat depressed patients by using psychoanalytical therapy in the 1960s. He concluded that the notion and motto of the analytical approach that 'patients need to suffer' (Beck et al. 1979, Preface) was simply unnecessary and even damaging at times. Having applied psychoanalysis to patients, sometimes for more than six years, without noticing 'striking' improvements, he became rather disillusioned, particularly as some of them even responded adversely to analysis.

Beck's definition of cognitive therapy is: 'an active, directive, time-limited, structured approach used to treat a variety of psychiatric disorders (for example, depression, anxiety, phobias, pain, etc.)' (Beck et al. 1979: 3). The therapeutic relationship is constructed partly on the core conditions of counselling (Rogers): empathy, genuineness, respect, warmth and unconditional positive regard. However, Beck argued (Beck et al. 1979) that these characteristics alone were not sufficient to produce an optimum therapeutic effect. He suggested that therapist and client work as a team in the problem-solving process. The counselling relationship in itself could at times also become an intervention tool with clients whose core beliefs (particularly in respect of trust and other relationship issues) needed challenging.

CBT practice is open and explicit about what is going on. The approach is active-directive, but not imposing. Two-way feedback is encouraged at any time. Goals for change are identified and agreed upon. The approach is time limited (on average one to four months; longer however for chronic cases). Therapist's mistakes are admitted and clients can suggest solutions when therapy gets stuck. The client is trained to become a self-therapist.

CBT mainly focuses on the 'here and now' and intends for the therapist to accompany the client towards her chosen goals. This means that CBT counselling is *client driven* and thus the client chooses what they wish to work on throughout the whole therapy. Goals and strategies are developed together and therapeutic change happens in session just as much as it does through the home practices the client is recommended to carry out between sessions. For this purpose the client is often provided with 'bibliotherapy' (hand-outs, recommended reading, etc.) and is also advised to use a notebook in which to record insights from sessions, home practice exercises and 'hot events' clients may want to bring to the next session and work through with the therapist.

During treatment sessions the client's problems are uncovered (thus assessment is ongoing throughout the therapeutic period) through collaborative conversations. CBT examines the meanings that the individual assigns to events in order to understand their emotional and behavioural reactions to these events. Furthermore it is established how these problems affect not only the client's thoughts and emotions but also their physical health, relationships and their daily functioning in general. A treatment plan is generated early on in therapy but is constantly reviewed and expanded and a specific time frame is adhered to.

NICE guidelines recommend CBT for many mental health problems and in general therapy takes place over 12 to 16 sessions. When the client feels ready to move out of therapy and 'walk alone', usually follow-up sessions are booked in to observe how the client is getting on and to fine tune some newly learned skills.

CBT has at times been called 'quick fix' or 'therapy without a heart'. Indeed the approach may lend itself to therapists who like to work primarily cognitively and by using forms and questionnaires. Some may even fail to create a heartfelt therapeutic relationship. Furthermore due to the relatively short treatment time, CBT is sometimes expected 'to perform miracles', when more time would provide the space to work through deeper layers of automatic thoughts, assumptions and schemas. Private health insurers often expect a successful treatment outcome in six to eight sessions, which can put strain on the therapist and client.

In 2005 Lord R. Layard proposed greater funding for mental health treatment. He recommended the development of 250 new mental health centres specializing in offering short-term CBT as the treatment of choice. His position may indeed threaten other schools of thought such as psychoanalytic, humanistic or systemic therapies. On the one hand CBT research evidence might at times have been construed by 'cherry-picking' suitable clients and ignoring relapse cases of clients formerly treated with CBT. On the other hand Layard's one-sided argument may indeed spur on psychoanalytic and humanistic researchers to prove that long-term work may indeed not only be an alternative but a necessity for certain disorders such as anorexia nervosa, for example, or for clients who simply respond better to a different therapeutic approach. We may indeed ask ourselves what price we will have to pay long-term if we focus on symptoms reduction only, and not on what caused them in the first place. On the other hand, however, no human being will ever reach the status of flawless functionality and ongoing happiness, even if they invest in long-term therapy. The ancient Greek word 'Therapia' means 'to walk on a path together' and there will always be long stretches of life that we all have to walk alone.

References

Beck, A., Rush, A.J., Shaw, B.F. and Emery, G. (1979) *Cognitive Therapy of Depression*. New York: Guilford Press.

Annotated further reading

Beck, A., Rush, A.J., Shaw, B.F. and Emery, G. (1979) *Cognitive Therapy of Depression*. New York: Guilford Press.

This is a later version of the first publication on CT by Aaron Beck. It offers a complete guide to the theory, research and clinical use of CT.

Briers, S. (2009) *Brilliant Cognitive Behavioural Therapy*. Harlow: Pearson.

This volume is a wonderful and enjoyable read with lots of insight, practical examples and step-by-step strategies used in CBT.

Feltham, C. (2007) Individual therapy in context. In W. Dryden *Handbook of Psychotherapy*. London: Sage.

In this chapter Feltham focuses on the development of psychotherapy and counselling. He refers to the numerous types and roots of various therapies and emphasizes on page 22 that due to 'CBT favouritism' psychodynamic and person-centred approaches have felt spurred on to engage in more research-based publications to prove validity of their own approaches.

Neenan, M. and Dryden, W. (2000) *Essential Cognitive Therapy*. London: Whurr.

This book gives a brief and eloquent introduction to the use and key elements of CBT. It also looks at possible difficulties clients may experience when entering this form of therapy.

Cognitive distortions (CD)

See also: cognitive behavioural therapy; Beck, Aaron T.

Cognitive distortions are irrational thoughts that are identified in cognitive therapy and tend to perpetuate certain psychological disorders. Aaron Beck (1976) first proposed the theory of cognitive distortions. To improve mood and discourage depression and chronic anxiety, CBT suggests the need to eliminate these distortions and negative thoughts. The process of refuting these distortions is called 'cognitive restructuring', which has a goal of replacing one's irrational, counter-factual beliefs with more accurate and beneficial ones.

Cognitive distortions are also considered logical fallacies, for example, thinking of things in absolute terms, also known as all-or-nothing thinking. This type of thinking error can contribute to depression. Other examples include overgeneralization, magnification, labelling and personalization. In regards to sex offenders for example, offences may be initiated and 'acceptable' by cognitive distortions of the sex offender, such as minimization of the abuse, victim blaming and excuses (Ward et al. 1995). Overgeneralization is when a person comes to a general conclusion based on a single piece of evidence. If something bad happens once, we expect it to happen over and over again. A person may see a single, unpleasant event as a never-ending pattern of defeat (http://psychcentral.com/lib/2009/15-common-cognitive-distortions/).

People can also jump to conclusions, such as being able to determine how people are feeling toward us (mind reading). For example, a person may conclude that someone is reacting negatively toward them and not actually bother to find out if they are correct. Another example of a CD is to anticipate that things will turn out badly, and therefore feel convinced that the prediction is already an established fact.

Magnification is when you exaggerate the importance of things, like making a mistake or being late. There is also minimization, which is when you shrink things until they appear tiny, for example your own desirable qualities. CD have popularized various idioms such as 'make a mountain out of a molehill'. In depressed clients, often the positive characteristics of *other people* are exaggerated and negative characteristics are understated. There is one subtype of magnification, known as catastrophizing. This is focusing on the worst possible outcome, however unlikely, or thinking that a situation is unbearable or impossible when it is really just uncomfortable.

Disqualifying the positive occurs when one de-emphasizes positive experiences for arbitrary reasons. This is also known as special pleading. For example, 'I'm not relying on faith in small probabilities here. These are slot machines, not roulette wheels. They are different.' With this, what is said is unverifiable, because it is too remote and impossible to define clearly.

Cognitive distortions have also been linked with eating disorders (http://www.anorexia-reflections.com/cognitive-distortions.html). For example, with black and white thinking, it can make people with an eating disorder think, 'I'll lose my mind if I don't count every calorie', or 'I will only feel good when I consume low-fat, diet foods'. Cognitive restructuring is usually part of the required treatment to help treat eating disorders.

Narcissistic rage is linked with cognitive distortions as well. This is directed towards the person that the narcissist feels has insulted them; to other people the rage is incoherent and unjust. This rage impairs their cognition (stress chemicals like cortisol are released and impair brain function), therefore impairing their judgement. During the rage they are prone to shouting, fact distortion and making groundless accusations (Golomb 1992).

References

Beck, A.T. (1976) *Cognitive Therapy and the Emotional Disorders*. Boston: Penguin.

Golomb, E. (1992) *Trapped in the Mirror: Adult Children of Narcissists in their Struggle for Self*. New York: HarperCollins.

Ward, T., Hudson, S.M. and Marshall, W.L. (1995) Cognitive distortions and affective deficits in sex offenders: a cognitive deconstructionist interpretation. *Sexual Abuse: A Journal of Research and Treatment,* 7(1): 67–83.

Annotated further reading

Beck, A. (1976) *Cognitive Therapy and the Emotional Disorders*. Boston: Penguin.

This book is another must for understanding CBT and many important treatment aspects, as well as theory and application.

Collaborative empiricism

See also: cognitive behavioural therapy; negative automatic thoughts

The concept of collaborative empiricism is a major focus in practising cognitive behavioural therapy. Interventions and thus treatment are not solely designed by the therapist. The client and practitioner work as a team and decide in cooperation which treatment may be most suitable in this particular case.

Throughout the sessions, the therapist works with the client and gathers detailed information about how the client thinks and which typical thinking errors (thoughts that cause the client to suffer) he engages in. Similarly emotions, imagery and behaviours that lead to dissatisfaction and an unsatisfactory life experience are collected. All of the above data serves to understand the particular problem 'cocktail' of this individual and is therefore used to create a personal treatment plan.

Collaborative empiricism has a paramount importance when the focus of treatment shifts from assessment to intervention. Many cognitive-behavioural techniques are based on first-hand observation and 'behavioural experiments' to check the range of NATs (negative automatic thoughts), dysfunctional beliefs and unhelpful behaviours and to experiment with more beneficial alternatives. Rather than relying on the therapist's knowledge, insights or reasoning, CBT assumes that experiential examination by the client himself is the most dependable way for him to bring about effective change.

The therapist conveys repeatedly to the client that the client's views are taken very seriously. An important distinction is made between the respect shown towards the individual as a person and perhaps a non-acceptance of some behaviours he engages in.

The client is encouraged to view his experiences and personal constructs as a hypothesis about life, rather than an unchangeable, indisputable fact. By engaging in new ways of behaving or thinking, initially merely as an experiment, he may then conclude that he wishes to adopt new strategies in future. 'A key element of collaboration is compromise' (Beck et al. 1993: 69). 'Through the process of Collaborative Empiricism, clients can learn to become "personal scientists"' (Neenan and Dryden 2001: 11) and thus eventually their own therapist. Collaborative empiricism is not simply an intervention used to replace the client's irrational or unhelpful beliefs, but rather a way to develop skills in objective thinking. Working together, therapist and client create new and more adaptive views of the client's problems and options. This intervention depends on a trusting relationship where the client is guided by the therapist. It also benefits greatly from high client motivation, when the former is required to carry out behavioural experiments on his/her own, for example. Unless the team is working harmoniously, this intervention will not result in beneficial outcomes.

References

Beck, A.T., Wright, F.D., Newman, C.F. and Liese, B.S. (1993) *Cognitive Therapy of Substance Abuse*. London: Guilford Press.

Neenan, M. and Dryden, W. (2001) *Essential Cognitive Therapy*. London: Whurr Publishers.

Annotated further reading:

Beck, A.T., Wright, F.D., Newman, C.F. and Liese, B.S. (1993) *Cognitive Therapy of Substance Abuse*. London: Guilford Press.

Considered to be one of the best publications of the 'man who started it all' is expanded from the original *Cognitive Therapy of Depression* and applies CBT to addiction with 'strong theoretical grounding and great clinical acumen' (recommended by Mark Galanter, Professor of Psychiatry). This comprehensive and accessible volume clearly describes the cognitive model of addiction, the proper approach to case formulation and the therapeutic relationship, and the structure of the therapy sessions. It informs the reader how to educate clients in the treatment model (teach them to be their own therapist) and how to manage their cravings and urges for drugs and alcohol. Important cognitive and behavioural strategies and techniques are discussed in detail, as is the management of severe crises and persistent problems in patients' lives. Methods for understanding and working with this type of client who present associated problems of depression, anxiety, low frustration tolerance, anger, and personality disorders are focused in detail. Significant issues such as the prevention and management of relapse are also included.

Neenan, M. and Dryden, W. (2001) *Essential Cognitive Therapy*. London: Whurr Publishers.

This is a very readable basic introduction to the understanding and application of CBT.

Collective unconscious

See also: archetypes; Jung, Carl; dynamic unconscious

Like Freud, Jung emphasized unconscious causes of behaviour in the dynamic sense of unconscious: powerful forces pressing for expression and shaping our lives. However, he distinguished two parts in his version of this concept: the personal, which contains repressed individual memories, and the collective, which contains ancestral memories of the shared experiences and wisdom of all generations of humankind.

Jung came to this idea through his extensive reading of philosophical, religious and mystical texts in a wide range of cultures. Some interpreters of Jung and perhaps Jung himself see it as a reality, like a house or an ocean. For example Jung wrote that archetypes, which are the main elements of the collective unconscious, 'are not mere objects of the mind but are also autonomous factors' (1969: 469). Ocean is a good image for the collective unconscious with its mysterious depths and exotic creatures.

The idea of a collective unconscious may make some sense from an evolutionary perspective. Our brains have evolved in the face of common threats and tasks and the archetypes are generally understood as universal themes of human experience over time and cultures, as revealed in art, literature, dreams, visions, myths, fairy tales and films. Jungian therapists traditionally analyse dreams in particular in great depth and it may be that their clients/patients feel encouraged to have appropriate dreams. Examples of archetypes are Hero, Earth Mother, Trickster and Sage.

The evidence for the collective unconscious is the themes (archetypes) already mentioned, which can be explained by universal experiences in themselves, paranormal phenomena and what Jung called 'synchronicity'. Synchronicity is when two things occur together in what seems an uncanny way. An everyday example is thinking of somebody, the phone rings and it's them. Eerie! There are two kinds of explanations for synchronicity and, as for the concept of the collective unconscious, one explanation is mysterious and awesome, and the other rational (and also awesome in its way). The rational explanation is that with so many things happening at any one moment co-incidences are inevitable. Moreover, we naturally search for meaning, remember the confirming events and forget, for instance, all the times we thought of someone and the phone didn't ring. We find patterns where there aren't any and misinterpret them as meaningful.

Neher (1996) suggested five other reasons for the appeal of concepts like the collective unconscious and archetypes. They provide:

1   a comforting perspective, especially on disturbing dreams and fantasies;
2   an avenue to personal insights, making sense of aspects of ourselves which seem strange, e.g. using the Anima, which is Jung's name for the archetype representing our feminine side, to explain, or appear to explain, non-masculine behaviour or desires in a masculine man;
3   a quasi-spiritual approach, for people who are attracted by transcendental or paranormal phenomena;
4   the promise of a shared relatedness, perhaps to ease existential aloneness;

5   a 'handy framework' for the easy understanding of behaviour, though
    as Neher says, the important question is 'What is valid?' not 'What is
    easy?'.

Reference

Jung, C.G. (1969) *Psychology and Religion: West and East*, 2nd edn. Princeton, NJ:
    Princeton University Press.

Annotated further reading

Neher, A. (1996) Jung's theory of archetypes: a critique. *Journal of Humanistic
Psychology*, 36: 61–91.

Well-informed and well-argued critique of the collective unconscious
as well as archetypes when many writers about Jung or personality and
counselling either accept Jung's ideas uncritically, dismiss them,
mention them in passing or ignore them.

Collectivism – individualism dimension

See also: multicultural counselling; narrative therapy; feminist counselling

Collectivism and individualism are two very different ways of understanding
the world and of conceptualizing the self. Collectivism is the principle or practice of giving the group, whether it is family, clan or society, priority over each
individual in it. It can involve sacrificing oneself for the good of the group.
Individualism, on the other hand, advocates the rights and independent action
of the individual. It promotes the individual over and above the group. These
concepts are important in counselling and psychotherapy because most counselling theories have been developed in western cultures which assume an
individualistic standpoint and adherence to values such as autonomy and self-
reliance. Such values are alien in many non-western cultures where the self
exists only in relation to others. Decisions are usually made based on the values
and needs of the family or other social group. For example, Chinese philoso-
phies view the self as inseparable from the natural world.

    As a result of this different perspective, traditional counselling models
such as the psychodynamic and humanistic models as well as cognitive
behaviour therapy and the existential approach, can be experienced as alien by
clients from non-western cultures. For example, many person-centred concepts

such as self-actualization or internal locus of evaluation may hold little meaning for someone who regards duty and honour as core values.

As the goal of most therapy is change at the individual level, therapists need to be aware of, and take into account, other perspectives on the self. Traditional models may be inappropriate and the therapist may need to consider using therapeutic techniques from other cultures or drawing on western models which allow for a more collectivist standpoint such as narrative or feminist therapy (McLeod 2009). The section on multi-cultural counselling discusses issues associated with working with non-western client groups in more detail.

Reference

McLeod, J. (2009) *An Introduction to Counselling*, 4th edn. Maidenhead: Open University Press.

Annotated further reading

Palmer, S. (ed.) (2002) *Multicultural Counselling: A Reader*. London: Sage.

A useful introduction to some of the main issues.

Pederson, P. (2008) *Counselling Across Cultures*, 6th edn. London: Sage.

This book contains a clear discussion of this particular cultural dimension together with a range of others. There is also information about the central aspects of different collective cultures.

Compassionate mind training

Compassion is an important skill, which adds to mindfulness the ability to 'love what is' and to see oneself as if we were a beautiful diamond, which needs just a little polishing here and there. If one can learn to truly accept oneself with compassion it may be much easier to be present in the 'here and now', and not be drawn back to old fears, guilt or worries about future goals.

William Bloom (a holistic teacher and author) put it like this in his public newsletter:

> This debate between love and enlightenment can be portrayed as the major difference between the spiritualities of east and west. In the west, there is the Love taught by Christ. In the east, the Enlightenment taught by Buddha.

This polarisation is an interesting and provocative perspective, but of course it is an overgeneralisation. Christ, for example, challenged us to be awake and fully alive, just as Buddha taught compassion and love in action.

I have learnt that I need to pause and clarify what I mean. By Love I do not mean sentimentality. I mean heartfelt, meticulous caring attention, goodwill, generosity of spirit, and the infinite and mysterious power of benevolent universal energy that ultimately penetrates everything.

By Enlightenment, I do not mean a cold frigid detachment. I mean the ability to be fully mindful and awake, and have a continuous compassionate awareness of all life and Beings.

One way of traditionally practising for 'opening up' to loving kindness is a meditation (Metta-Meditation) that uses the following phrases:

'May I be safe and protected.'

'May I be peaceful.'

'May I live with Ease and with Kindness.'

These words can be adapted and changed to what works better for the individual. The practice can help with being able to deal with difficult interpersonal situations with more ease and lightness.

When we have genuine self-love we can tap into our true goodness, see the gifts we've been given and then experience the joy of sharing them with others. Instead of being overwhelmed by destructive emotions (sadness, anger, anxiety, fear, etc.), we learn to accept them and work around them.

In Martin Seligman's 2003 book, *Authentic Happiness*, the author's main point is that rather than mistakenly thinking acquiring will fulfil us, a deeper happiness comes from *understanding our strengths* and enjoying sharing them with the world in an altruistic way. Preparing to do this we intend to learn not only to accept ourselves but also fully appreciate who we are.

In the 'Awakening Joy' course (www.awakeningjoy.info) a trainer shared the following story:

> I was sitting on the 1979 Fall Retreat in Massachusetts when His Holiness, the Dalai Lama came to visit. Someone asked him for advice on working with unworthiness. It took some time for him to understand the concept but when he finally did, he looked straight at the questioner and very emphatically said, 'You're wrong! You're absolutely wrong!' He went on to point out that seeing yourself as unworthy is missing the point that you are a perfect expression of life and have the same True Nature (Divine Spirit, one could say) as every other living being.

At a conference in June 2005 in Gothenburg entitled 'Making sense of the 21st century', the Dalai Lama was asked by Aaron Beck a similar question; something like how one could learn to improve one's self-esteem. He still found it very difficult to make sense of the question and his answer was hardly different from what was shared above.

In a famous teaching the Buddha was supposed to have said that we could search the whole world over and not find anyone more deserving of love than ourselves.

The 'science of love' has created an interest in research and a large number of studies are presently in progress showing how to encourage and nurture the best in human nature (Boyce 2010). What, if any, drawbacks are there in implementing compassionate mind practices into a twenty-first-century life? There is no research available discussing this topic. However, it proves for many a goal that would require them to give up the 'wants of the world', at least to some extent. Learning to listen to yourself, to your inner guidance and limitations, working with a win-win attitude towards all Beings, and wishing peace and safety even to those whom you consider your enemies or who have harmed you, is often too much to chew for an individual. And it is this deeply ingrained belief in the 'Self' and in 'what we deserve' that will prevent many from engaging in CMT.

References

Boyce, B. (2010) The science of love. *Shambala Sun*, 18(5): 77–81.
Seligman, M.E.P. (2003) *Authentic Happiness: Using the New Positive Psychology to Realise Your Potential for Lasting Fulfilment*. London: Nicholas Brealey Publishing.

Annotated further reading

Germer, C. (2009) *The Mindful Path to Self-Compassion*. New York: Guilford Press.

A wonderful introduction to helping oneself experiment with and experience the power of self-compassion. There is theory and application available, so it will suit many different readers.

Gilbert, P. (2009) *The Compassionate Mind: A New Approach to Life's Challenges*. London: Constable & Robinson.

Paul Gilbert confronts our capacity for cruelty in this book. He looks at Hitler, Stalin, Sadam Hussein and others to pose the question of how these leaders could never have performed killings of such magnitude had there not been an attitude of cruelty and submission too among all those who helped them to achieve such atrocities.

Conditions of worth

See also: person-centred counselling; self-concept; self-actualization; core conditions; locus of evaluation; the therapeutic relationship

As McLeod (2009) puts it, 'conditions of worth' comprise the entire model of child development put forward by the person-centred approach to counselling. This stands in contrast to the psychodynamic approach, which espouses a series of developmental stages which need to be negotiated. The basic premise is that love or approval from parents or carers can be unconditional or conditional on the child behaving in a certain way. If conditional, the child – who needs this love and approval – begins to define themselves according to the values of these significant others rather than their own. For example, 'I will love you if you will be quiet and conforming'. Their sense of themselves starts to be understood by these initially alien values and beliefs which are gradually internalized and which they start to use to cope with experience. This almost inevitably leads to the development of a negative self-concept due to the fact that they cannot meet the demanding expectations of others and because they become increasingly separated from their own inner wisdom.

There is no requirement in person-centred counselling to focus on particular childhood incidents or processes which may have given rise to the development of these conditions of worth, but the client is free to do so if they think this would be helpful. As McLeod (2009) points out, this theory conceptualizes internalized values and concept of self rather than internalized images of real people.

The concept of conditions of worth could be seen as a rather simplistic model of child development as compared to the much more complex one espoused by the psychoanalytic tradition. The underlying assumption that all negative traits stem from messages received from parents or carers rather than a combination of genetic and environmental factors may be regarded as suspect. It is also highly debatable as to whether such traits can be worked through and eliminated through the process of counselling (Feltham 2010).

References

Feltham, C. (2010) *Critical Thinking in Counselling and Psychotherapy*. London: Sage.
McLeod, J. (2009) *An Introduction to Counselling*, 4th edn. Maidenhead: Open University Press.

Annotated further reading

Cooper, M., O'Hara, M., Schmid, P.F. and Wyatt, G. (eds) (2007) *The Handbook of Person Centred Counselling and Psychotherapy*. Ross-on-Wye: PCCS Books.

This is an excellent, comprehensive overview of theory and practice.

Mearns, D. and Thorne, B. (2007) *Person-centred Counselling in Action*, 3rd edn. London: Sage.

This is highly recommended for showing how the key concepts apply to practice.

Congruence

See also: empathy; unconditional positive regard; core conditions; person-centred counselling; Rogers, Carl

Congruence can be defined as being genuine, or not putting up a professional façade. It is one of the three main core conditions (the others being 'unconditional positive regard' and 'empathic understanding') which Carl Rogers identified as being crucial to therapeutic personality change. Mearns and Thorne (2007: 75) define it as 'the state of being of the counsellor when her outward responses to the client consistently match the inner feelings and sensations that she has in relation to the client'. In other words, if the therapist is to be regarded as trustworthy it is important that what she says and does in relation to the client reflects what she really thinks and feels about them. If the client detects a lack of congruence, it will be more difficult for them to be genuine themselves.

It is the person-centred approach which places most emphasis on congruence or authenticity. The therapist needs to come across as a real human being with strengths and weaknesses and someone who feels some real emotional involvement with the client. According to Casemore (2006) congruence or authenticity has two elements in contemporary person-centred therapy. These are 'internal congruence' and 'appropriate transparency' (p. 52). Internal congruence is about there being a match between how the therapist is feeling and how they are behaving. Transparency relates more to whether the therapist shares or shows their feelings, either verbally or otherwise.

A common question asked by students working to understand this concept is whether the therapist needs to share whatever pops into their head! This is certainly best avoided. What is important is that the therapist needs to be able to decide what it is appropriate to communicate and when and how to do this. A good rule of thumb would be those thoughts and feelings which are consistently experienced or, according to Thorne (2002), seem to be preventing the other core qualities being expressed.

There is no doubt that being genuine in a therapeutic relationship is no mean feat! The therapist needs to be able to be in touch with their own thoughts and feelings as they come and go, while at the same time responding appropriately to the client and deciding what it is and is not appropriate to share with them. This places a great deal of emphasis on the therapist's relational abilities.

In terms of the research evidence, as Cooper (2008) points out, it is difficult to distinguish between concepts such as 'genuineness', 'giving feedback' and 'self-disclosure'. A review of the research (Orlinsky et al. 2004 in Cooper 2008) found that only 38 per cent of results showed a significant positive relationship between congruence and effective therapeutic outcomes, although this was higher when only clients' and therapists' (and not observers') ratings were used. Also, congruence is not often selected when clients are asked about the most important aspects of their therapy (Burckell and Goldfried 2006 in Cooper 2008). This may be because this quality is taken for granted, or some clients may actually prefer therapists who are more formal and professional, believing them to be more competent (Cooper 2008).

References

Casemore, P. (2006) *Person-centred Counselling in a Nutshell*. London: Sage.

Cooper, M. (2008) *Essential Research Findings in Counselling and Psychotherapy: The Facts are Friendly*. London: Sage.

Mearns, D. and Thorne, B. (2007) *Person-centred Counselling in Action*, 3rd edn. London: Sage.

Thorne, B. (2002) Person-centred therapy. In W. Dryden (ed.) *Handbook of Individual Therapy*, 4th edn. London: Sage.

Annotated further reading

Casemore, R. (2006) *Person-centred Counselling in a Nutshell*. London: Sage.

A succinct guide to person-centred theoretical concepts and to the counselling relationship.

Cooper, M., O'Hara, M., Schmid, P.F. and Wyatt, G. (eds) (2007) *The Handbook of Person Centred Counselling and Psychotherapy*. Ross-on-Wye: PCCS Books.

An excellent, comprehensive overview of theory and practice.

Constructivism

See also: personal construct therapy

Constructivism is a philosophical theory which argues that humans generate knowledge and meaning from an interaction between their experiences and their ideas. In the past, for example, children's play may have seemed aimless and of little importance. Jean Piaget, however, a French-speaking Swiss developmental psychologist and philosopher, thought differently. He saw play as an important part of the learner's cognitive development and he provided scientific evidence for his views. Constructivist theories spread and became influential throughout much of the non-formal learning sector. The 'Investigate Centre' at the Natural History Museum in London provides a good example of constructivist learning. There, visitors are encouraged to explore a collection of real natural history specimens, to help them make discoveries for themselves by practising some scientific skills.

Piaget, who initially formalized the idea of constructivism, suggested that through processes of accommodation and assimilation, individual people construct new knowledge from their experiences. For example, when people assimilate, they incorporate the new experience into an already existing framework without changing that framework. The individual experiences are aligned with their internal representations of the world, but it is also possible that they may not notice these events, or may decide that they are unimportant as information about the world. But when people accommodate, which is the process of reframing one's mental representation of the external world to fit new experiences in, they may feel as if 'failure' leads to learning: when we act on expectations that the world operates and if it violates our expectations, we 'fail', but then we learn from the experience, and reframe the model of the way the world works and thus enrich our understanding.

Constructivism as a theory describes how learning happens, whether it is learning by reading instructions or by using our own experience. In both cases however, we learn by constructing knowledge out of our experience.

Social constructivism relies on the learner being a unique individual with a unique background and needs. Each learner is also seen as complex and multidimensional. The background and the culture of the learner are very important, as they encourage the learner to arrive at their version of the truth. Language, logic and mathematical systems are inherited by the learner as a member of a particular culture, and they are learned throughout the learner's life. Without the social interaction with other people who may be more knowledgeable, it may be impossible to acquire social meaning of the important symbol systems and how to utilize them properly. Young children learn and develop their abilities by interacting with other children, adults and the physical world around them.

It can also be said that the responsibility should fall upon the learner to learn by oneself, as social constructivism encourages us to be more active and more involved in the learning process. This is a radically different viewpoint from the traditional notion where the responsibility of learning stays with instructors or teachers to teach, and the learner is in a passive and more receptive role.

Another vital aspect of constructivism is the motivation of the learner. Getting motivation to learn relies on the learner's confidence in their potential for learning. Since adults have many more experiences and previously existing neurological structures than children do, methods must take account of differences in learning.

In summary constructivism is a general approach to understanding people, conceptualizing psychological distress and fostering human change.

Annotated further reading

Segal, L. (2001) *The Dream of Reality: Heinz von Foerster's Constructivism*. New York: Springer.

This is a highly engaging account of Foerster's theory of life, which defies realism as we have understood it so far. He proposed that there were no objective truths, facts, or even consciousness. In fact, all we believe in was purely constructed by language and thought. Segal recounts the ideas of Foerster, who asked whether we actually discovered the world or rather created it.

Constructivism is not only important to cognitive science but Segal argues these ideas are of great significance to us all for: 'grasping the limits of our own understanding, can free us to live more creative and meaningful personal and professional lives'.

Container/contained

See also: Bion, Wilfred R.

The concept of container/contained is central to the work of Wilfred Bion representing one of his most important contributions to clinical psychoanalysis and theory, and perhaps therefore the contribution for which he is best known. Bion theorized this concept as a fundamental intersubjective experience of emotional communication between an infant and her mother and thus between the analysand and analyst (Grotstein 2007). Bion's initial presentation of this theory was (typically) complex and involved the use of the symbols for woman and man designating the container/woman and contained/man which Grotstein suggests might be because Bion believed that the breast, vagina and penis represented 'linking organs' between objects and the challenge of the primal scene that the infant must confront (Grotstein 2007: 155).

To make sense of this important function more simply however, the idea of 'maternal reverie' needs to be introduced and described.

Maternal reverie

At the beginning of its life, the baby does not have access to a thought/thinking (i.e. α elements, see **Bion, Wilfred R.**) because their mental apparatus is not mature enough to 'metabolize' and integrate these very first mental or proto-mental materials. Bion has described this as having thoughts without a thinker (Grotstein 2007). These primitive experiences are the beta (β) elements (see **Bion, Wilfred R.**), which correspond to extremely archaic bodily feelings; to emotional states linked to the infant's very earliest sensory and relational experiences, which the infant cannot utilize as such. The baby therefore has to divert these feelings through an 'Other', which in this case is the maternal object (see **object relations**) (Bion 1962; 1963; 1967).

The infant projects (see **projection**) these beta elements into the psyche of its mother (or maternal object) who lends the infant their own 'thought-thinking apparatus' to reshape, detoxify and transform the beta elements into alpha elements. This material can then be assimilated by the infant and integrated into its own mental functioning. This transformation is due to the alpha function of the mother's psyche, or capacity for maternal reverie, which thus takes away the overwhelming toxicity of the beta elements produced and felt by the infant (or by the patient).

The positive container object

The ability to detoxify and make the infant's emotions and primitive feelings knowable and tolerable requires the mother/maternal object/analyst to have certain qualities that support the containing function.

The mother/maternal object/analyst, who is able to engage in maternal reverie, acts as a positive container object with the capacity for reverie: she absorbs; sorts out (triages, prioritizes); detoxifies; transduces the beta elements from infinity to finiteness; reflects upon these projected emotional communications; allows them to incubate within her; and at the same time allows them to resonate with her own emotions and conscious and unconscious experiences thus giving some coherence to the projected communication. In the meantime the infant's original beta elements (proto-emotions) have become transformed into alpha elements suitable for mentalization. The maternal object then appropriately responds to or 'informs' the infant (interprets) what he/she is feeling. The maternal object may withhold the interpretation until a future time. Thus in the therapeutic context the analysand will tell or demonstrate a proto-emotion to the analyst who, like the maternal object for the infant, absorbs, detoxifies and returns the feeling in a form that the analysand can bear and can subsequently work with.

It is important to remember that Bion talked about the possibility of the maternal object as both a negative and a positive container although the subsequent emphasis among psychoanalytic thinkers has been upon thinking about the analyst as the positive container. This also connects with the outcome research indicating that the qualities of the therapist/analyst are the most important indicators of successful outcome.

Alternation of container/contained

While it is generally described as a relationship in which the infant or analysand projects the primitive emotions and feelings onto the maternal object or analyst, it has been proposed that there is a likelihood and clinical evidence that the process can proceed both ways and on more than one level. While the analyst is working – listening to the patient, trying to understand the unconscious communications and interpret them – s/he is the container. However, after the interpretation the analysand becomes the container for a while as s/he tries to make sense of the interpretation and make the response bearable for the analyst (and his/her self). However, it is here that the analysand might operate as a negative container and respond to the interpretation in a toxic way.

References

Bion, W.R. (1962) *Learning from Experience*. London: Heinemann Medical.
Bion, W.R. (1963) *Elements of Psycho-Analysis*. London: William Heinemann.
Bion, W.R. (1967) *Second Thoughts: Selected Papers on Psycho-analysis*. New York: Aronson.
Grotstein, J.S. (2007) *A Beam of Intense Darkness*. London: Karnac.

Annotated further reading

Grotstein, J.S. (2007) *A Beam of Intense Darkness*. London: Karnac.

Grotstein is probably the best source for the reader new to psychoanalysis and particularly those new to Bion.

Core beliefs (CB)

See also: cognitive behavioural therapy; rational emotive behaviour therapy; schema therapy; life traps

Beck and others differentiate between core and conditional beliefs. Core beliefs are definitely not actual thoughts, which are cumbersome to identify and to challenge. A core belief is an unconditional assumption about self, others or the world as a whole. Mental agreements need to be identified to try and change those CBs, and they usually come in bundles. The way to identify them is to use various clues to get to the deepest neuropathways of the unconscious. If we look at the example of fear of public speaking, we can deduct that this in itself is not a CB, but rather an emotional reaction to a belief. In anxiety disorder or depression CBs often remain deactivated until a critical incident brings them to life.

Core beliefs are often associated with what other people think of us, and triggers can be situations where we feel outside of our comfort zone, like asking people out on a date, asking for something we want or having to give a speech to a large audience. We need to follow the emotion that comes up in the given situation to find the CB behind it, rather like finding evidence to solve a crime.

If, for example after having given a speech, someone pointed out to you that they thought of you as 'a fool' and you know it definitely not to be a valid statement, even if the other person laughed at you, you would know that they have a problem with perception and not believe yourself to be a fool. Thus we can conclude that what people think of us does not necessarily hurt us at all if it is purely a perception problem of the other. This would give us immunity from their opinion. Therefore, we would only be deeply hurt if we actually believed we were 'a fool', and this belief then is the real cause of our emotional pain. So in the end, it is not so much about what others think, but the experience of the fear of the emotional pain that results from believing those negative thoughts/statements about ourselves.

To identify our CBs, we have to look beyond the thoughts we think. The way the CBs begin and then stretch out into false beliefs could be seen as follows:

First core belief: If someone else believes we are a fool then it is true.
Second core belief: We believe we are an absolute fool.
Third belief is a corollary of the second: if someone believes we are smart then we are smart. This means that whatever someone believes about us is what we are.
Fourth false belief is that what other people think of us can somehow hurt us emotionally. This false assumption is what the mind uses to generate fear of emotional pain. It is not true because thoughts in another person's head

don't determine our emotions. What we believe about ourselves determines how we feel.

The fifth false belief is that we can accurately read other people's minds and know what they think about us.

The way we change CBs is first to realize how far removed from reality the above statements really are, as, for example, it is rather impossible to read accurately other people's minds, and from that one thing alone you can start to identify the whole set of arguments and discover they don't really hold that much power over you. You can even just see them as links in a chain, and if you break just one link in the chain then CBs all lose power.

So to really root out a CB would necessitate the willingness to stop believing it. The problem is developing the awareness to identify those beliefs. You need to change your point of view in order to change a CB. If, for example, we judge the beliefs we happen to find in our awareness, or judge ourselves for having them, they tend to get further engraved. We then also tend to create and believe a judgement story about our beliefs. When this happens we have built a layer of story and beliefs on top of the existing core belief. Therefore the point of view to adopt is best free of judgement about the core beliefs we have identified. Changing core beliefs is not easy because all new cognitive input gets filtered through the underlying core beliefs.

In summary it is an ongoing challenge to really track down and replace those very early schemas or thinking/believing pathways. Working through them requires enormous commitment by the client and great insight by the therapist.

Annotated further reading

http://www.pathwaytohappiness.com/writings_falsebeliefs.htm

> 'Changing core beliefs is most easily done by first establishing a new emotional base and then making step changes to our point of view. Recovering personal will power will make this process move faster.'

Moorey, S. (2007) Cognitive therapy. In W. Dryden (ed.) *Dryden's Handbook of Individual Therapy*. London: Sage.

> This is a very good introduction to cognitive therapy and practice. It also offers a very in-depth list for further reading.
>
> The internet has a huge number of core belief worksheets and therapeutic offers, even whole approaches of therapy that make 'rooting out core beliefs' into their one major intervention.

Core conditions

See also: Rogers, Carl; person-centred counselling; empathy; unconditional positive regard; congruence; the therapeutic relationship

Initially termed the 'necessary and sufficient conditions of therapeutic personality change' (Rogers 1957: 95), these 'conditions' or qualities were first identified by Carl Rogers while developing his person-centred approach to counselling. Although Rogers originally specified six characteristics, three of these have become particularly associated with this theoretical approach. These are: congruence (or genuineness), empathic understanding (or empathy) and unconditional positive regard (or acceptance).

Rogers first referred to his work as 'relationship therapy' (Feltham and Horton 2006) and what became known as the 'core conditions' model is indeed a model of the therapeutic relationship. Rogers thought that people entering counselling with emotional problems would have experienced relationships in which they were not accepted or properly understood. In order to change, these clients needed to experience a relationship in which they felt fully accepted and valued (McLeod 2009). Rogers believed that in order for therapy to be effective, the counsellor needed to hold certain attitudes – or conditions – and must effectively communicate these to the client on an ongoing basis. The process of change in the client is conceptualized as a greater openness to experience, a greater trust in their own thoughts and feelings and less dependence on the judgements of others. As the client experiences empathic understanding of their difficult thoughts and feelings from the counsellor, they develop a greater empathic understanding of those thoughts and feelings themselves; as they encounter acceptance of themselves and whatever they are struggling with from someone else, so they slowly develop a greater acceptance of themselves; and as they experience genuineness in another, so they develop the capacity to be more open and genuine themselves.

That Rogers argued that these conditions were sufficient in themselves and that no specific skills or techniques were needed on the part of the counsellor was a major departure from the leading approaches of the time (namely psychoanalysis, which regarded interpretation as essential and behaviourism, which used techniques for bringing about behaviour change).

Because the focus is on counsellors possessing certain attitudes, it can be argued that there is a strong need for them to engage in extensive and ongoing self-development in order to effectively embody the core conditions. Indeed Thorne (2002) asserts that person-centred counselling puts the most demands of any approach on the counsellor because they are required to demonstrate attitudes which are very difficult to achieve.

Research evidence

A substantial amount of research has been done both by Rogers himself and others. In 1957 Rogers and his colleagues conducted a major research study aimed partly at testing the validity of the core conditions with hospitalized schizophrenic patients. The findings suggested that this approach was not particularly effective with this sort of client. In other words, as Rogers himself indicated, the client needs to be capable of establishing basic psychological contact with other human beings in order for the counselling to be effective.

Most research into the core conditions supports the idea that they are necessary for effective therapy in general. Cooper (2008) draws together the existing research evidence into the three separate conditions, concluding that empathy is a 'demonstrably effective' element of the therapeutic relationship and that unconditional positive regard and congruence are each a 'promising and probably effective element of the relationship' (Steering Committee 2002 in Cooper 2008). However, the research is less clear cut in support of the core conditions being sufficient in themselves to ensure positive outcomes.

References

Cooper, M. (2008) *Essential Research Findings in Counselling and Psychotherapy: The Facts are Friendly*. London: Sage.

Feltham, C. and Horton, I. (eds) (2006) *The SAGE Handbook of Counselling and Psychotherapy*, 2nd edn. London: Sage.

McLeod, J. (2009) *An Introduction to Counselling*. Maidenhead: Open University Press.

Rogers, C.R. (1957) The necessary and sufficient conditions of therapeutic personality change. *Journal of Consulting Psychology*, 21: 95–103.

Thorne, B. (2002) Person-centred Therapy. In W. Dryden (ed.) (2002) *Handbook of Individual Therapy*, 4th edn. London: Sage.

Annotated further reading

Casemore, R. (2006) *Person-centred Counselling in a Nutshell*. London: Sage.

A succinct guide to person-centred theoretical concepts and to the counselling relationship.

Cooper, M., O'Hara, M., Schmid, P.F. and Wyatt, G. (eds) (2007) *The Handbook of Person Centred Counselling and Psychotherapy*. Ross-on-Wye: PCCS Books.

An excellent, comprehensive overview of theory and practice.

Counter-transference

See also: transference; psychodynamic counselling; psychoanalysis; Freudian analysis; dynamic unconscious

Whereas transference refers to the feelings a client originally experienced towards important childhood figures being transferred onto the therapist, counter-transference concerns the therapist's emotional responses to the client. The original Freudian view was that counter-transference was something that interfered with the therapy in that it resulted from the therapist's unresolved conflicts which the therapist had not properly worked through. In a sense these were therapist blind spots and were best avoided. For example, a therapist might have an unconscious need to feel important and needed and might therefore encourage clients to remain dependent on them rather than help them to develop their own resources and sense of personal responsibility.

A rather different perspective is that counter-transference can provide an insight into the client's characteristic way of relating to others. If the therapist is able to get in touch with their reactions to the client, this can provide clues to the client's inner world and how others might react to them. As Heimann (1950, in McLeod 2009: 99) puts it: 'The analyst's unconscious understands that of the patient. This rapport on a deep level comes to the surface in the form of feelings the analyst notes in response to (the) patient.' For example, a client may be experienced by the therapist as incredibly boring and tedious to listen to. While this may sometimes reflect an unresolved issue in the therapist, it may suggest a common response to the client, resulting perhaps from their inability to really engage with others at a deep emotional level.

It is now widely acknowledged that counter-transference, like transference, features in all relationships and, as such, many therapists from other theoretical perspectives acknowledge its existence in therapy. According to Dryden (2002) even cognitive behavioural therapy training now focuses on these processes!

Considering these somewhat different definitions, and assuming that both have some validity, it can be difficult to identify which one is pertinent at a particular point in the therapy. There is always the danger that a therapist might assume that their own unresolved issue is, instead, an issue for the client which they are picking up in the counter-transference. For this reason, it is crucial that therapists are skilled at engaging in accurate self-reflection, or internal supervision, as well as having regular external supervision, in order to explore this issue in depth.

A research study by Hayes et al. (1998, in Cooper, 2008) found that counter-transference was identified in about 80 per cent of sessions. However, other studies suggest that therapists with a greater awareness of their feelings or more 'integrated' personalities experience fewer counter-transference reactions (Hayes and Gelso 2001, in Cooper 2008). This would seem to confirm the more negative aspects of this process.

A number of studies (Cooper 2008) suggest that those therapists who manage their counter-transference feelings effectively are more likely to see better outcomes for their clients. However, there is not very much empirical evidence to support this finding.

Nevertheless, and particularly as a result of the proliferation of eclectic and integrative perspectives, an awareness of the possible impact of counter-transference feelings is regarded as important by contemporary therapists from many different perspectives.

References

Cooper, M. (2008) *Essential Research Findings in Counselling and Psychotherapy: The Facts Are Friendly*. London: Sage.

Dryden, W. (2002) *Handbook of Individual Therapy*, 4th edn. London: Sage.

McLeod, J. (2009) *An Introduction to Counselling*. Maidenhead: Open University Press.

Annotated further reading

Jacobs, M. (2010) *Psychodynamic Counselling in Action*, 4th edn. London: Sage.

Jacobs looks at aspects of theory, including counter-transference, as it occurs in practice.

D

Death, fear of

See also: anxiety, existential; self; Yalom, Irvin

Fear of the inevitability of death is one of four existential 'givens' – profoundly significant realities of life – proposed by Yalom (e.g. 1989). The other givens are freedom (personal responsibility for our choices), ultimate aloneness and meaninglessness. All are seen as very bleak and disturbing on the one hand and hopeful and enlightening on the other. Yalom goes so far as to state that 'Death is a visitor in every course of therapy' (2001: 124).

The givens are not just esoteric or occasional concerns but, it has been suggested, a major influence on everyday behaviour (Jones 2008). For example, Hansen et al. (2010) compared the effects on smoking of two warnings on packets of cigarettes: 'Smokers die earlier' and 'Smoking makes you unattractive'. Smokers who described smoking as important to their self-esteem reported a more *positive* attitude towards smoking after seeing the death warning. This apparently counterintuitive finding was predicted by a theory about fear of death's inevitability called 'terror management theory' (TMT). TMT proposes that cultural worldviews, e.g. a national identity or belief in a just world, protect us psychologically from thoughts about our mortality, and a substantial body of research since the 1980s supports this view; for example Schimel et al. (2007) found that weakening cultural worldviews increases awareness of death, and argued that death is 'the worm at the core of human pretensions to happiness' (p. 789).

That's the bleak aspect! A literary example (though bleak for the person concerned) suggests the hopeful aspect.

In Tolstoy's short story *The Death of Ivan Illych*, Illych realizes as he is dying that he thinks of everyone in superficial, contractual terms: he becomes acutely aware of his wasted life and the absence in it of love, intimacy and enthusiasm. He does not know anyone nor they him.

> It occurs to him that what had appeared utterly impossible before – that he had not lived his life as he should have done – might after all be true. It strikes him that those scarcely detected inclinations of his to fight against what the most highly placed people regarded as good, those scarcely noticeable impulses which he had immediately suppressed, might have been the real thing and all the rest false.

The implication then is that acceptance of one's own death as final enriches and transforms everyday life. In particular, it increases a sense of what matters and what is trivial and makes appreciation of the present stronger. Conversely, if we see life as stretching out endlessly, or don't think about it fully, we are more likely to lead a relatively unfilled, inauthentic life.

References

Hansen, J., Winzeler, S. and Topolinski, S. (2010) When fear of death makes you smoke: a terror management perspective on the effectiveness of cigarette on-pack warnings. *Journal of Experimental Social Psychology*, 46(1): 226–8.

Jones, D. (2008) Running to catch the sun. *The Psychologist*, 21(7): 580–3.

Schimel, J., Hayes, J., Williams, T. and Jahrig, J. (2007) Is death really the worm at the core? Converging evidence that worldview threat increases death – thought accessibility. *Journal of Personality and Social Psychology*, 92(5): 789–803.

Yalom, I.D. (1989) *Love's Executioner and Other Tales of Psychotherapy*. London: Penguin.

Yalom, I.D. (2001) *The Gift of Therapy*. London: Piatkus.

Annotated further reading

Vess, M., Routledge, C., Landan, M.J. and Arndt, J. (2009) The dynamics of death and meaning: the effects of death – relevant cognition and personal need for structure on perceptions of meaning in life. *Journal of Personality and Social Psychology*, 97(4): 728–44.

Some preliminary studies of individual differences in the effects of increase 'mortality salience' – reminder of one's death – and sense of meaning.

Yalom, I.D. (2001) *The Gift of Therapy*. London: Piatkus.

Brief discussions of why it's desirable to talk about death in therapy and why it's avoided (pp. 124–5), and how to talk about it (pp. 129–32).

Defence mechanisms

See also: Freud, Sigmund; negation and disavowal; projection; projective identification; psychosocial development; splitting; structural model of the mind; sublimation

The phrase 'defence mechanism' was Freud's term for unconscious strategies for reducing anxiety. Because these mechanisms are unconscious they involve some self-deception, but they are also quite normal, and part of everyone's experience.

The ego is the (mainly) conscious part of the mind that manages the relationship between the conscious and unconscious. The id and superego are unconscious. These parts of the psyche are seen in all psychoanalytic theories as being in conflict, and the result of this conflict is **anxiety**. Most people experience anxiety that can be directly handled by the ego. However, some anxieties have their origins in primitive preverbal life. These are related to seeking sensuality/pleasure as well as anxieties about annihilation.

Such unspeakable anxieties are also emotionally and consciously intolerable and thus there is a conflict between the ego that is managing everyday life and the sense of a person's identity. These anxieties might emerge into consciousness at any time, perhaps when someone faces a particularly stressful and emotionally resonant situation. Defence mechanisms therefore are a normal and desirable part of life and without psychological defences in place we would be overcome with anxieties and guilt and would become, largely, unable to function. However if, for whatever reason, these unconscious defences are too great, blocking necessary information from consciousness, then energy and creativity will also be blocked. Psychoanalysis aims to release creative energy through recognition of the source of anxieties that can then be put into proportion, linked to external reality and made more bearable.

The defence mechanism can take the form of **repression, denial, rationalization** and **projection**. **Resistance** to psychoanalysis is a further more complex process of defence of the ego. As is discussed in several other entries dealing with psychoanalytic concepts, the conflict between 'knowing' and 'not knowing' is a major source of anxiety in the human psyche and the relationship between the conscious/unconscious mediated through defence mechanisms is the means by which the psyche attempts to survive these contradictions.

References

Billig, M. (2006) A psychoanalytic discursive psychology: from consciousness to unconsciousness. *Discourse Studies*, 8(1): 17–24.

Brennan, T. (1992) *The Interpretation of the Flesh: Freud and Femininity*. London: Routledge.

Craib, I. (2001) *Psychoanalysis: A Critical Introduction*. Cambridge: Polity.

Fonagy, P. (1999) Memory and therapeutic action. *International Journal of Psycho-Analysis*, 80: 215–23.

Gay, P. (1995) *The Freud Reader*. London: Vintage.

Hinshelwood, R. (1991) *A Dictionary of Kleinian Thought*. London: Free Association Books.

Hinshelwood, R. (1997) Primitive mental processes: psychoanalysis and the ethics of integration. *Philosophy, Psychiatry and Psychology*, 4(2): 121–43.

Klein, M. (1946) Notes on some schizoid mechanisms. In H. Segal (ed.) *Envy and Gratitude and Other Works 1946–1963*. London: Virago.

Wright, E. (1992) *Feminism and Psychoanalysis: A Critical Dictionary*. Oxford: Blackwell.

Zaretsky, E. (2000) Charisma or rationalization? Domesticity and psychoanalysis in the United States in the 1950s. *Critical Inquiry*, 26(2): 328–54.

Annotated further reading

Craib, I. (2001) *Psychoanalysis: A Critical Introduction*. Cambridge: Polity.

> Craib provides a clear and easily understood overview of Freudian and Kleinian perspectives on defences.

Gay, P. (1995) *The Freud Reader*. London: Vintage.

> Gay provides key extracts from Freud's writings with a brief review of important concepts in some places throughout the text. However, the extracts from Freud do require some (worthwhile) effort.

Hinshelwood, R. (1991) *A Dictionary of Kleinian Thought*. London: Free Association Books.

> Hinshelwood is particularly useful on Klein and Kleinian thought as the title suggests – it is a clear and valuable read.

Denial

Denial is a concept that most people recognize in everyday interaction. A person might deny they are ill, or deny that their organization or family is in disarray and behave as if everything is healthy when in reality and observably there are major problems (Craib 2001). Denial, originally called 'scotomatization' by Freud takes place when a piece of perception is obliterated (Hinshelwood 1991) to defend against the importance of aspects of external or internal reality.

Reaction formation is one step beyond denial (Craib 2001) whereby the feared impulse is so strong that it can only be fought by consciously embracing its opposite with all the person's psychic strength. He warns us to bear in mind that passions felt to the exclusion of all else have a reverse side and if there is no room for reflection then it is likely that this is a defence against having to face the real reason for the passionate feelings and actions.

References

Craib, I. (2001) *Psychoanalysis: A Critical Introduction*. Cambridge: Polity.
Hinshelwood, R. (1991) *A Dictionary of Kleinian Thought*. London: Free Association Books.

Annotated further reading

Craib, I. (2001) *Psychoanalysis: A Critical Introduction*. Cambridge: Polity.

This is a worthwhile read as it is comprehensive and clear with a critical perspective.

Hinshelwood, R. (1991) *A Dictionary of Kleinian Thought*. London: Free Association Books.

This is well written and an ideal introduction to all Kleinian ideas.

Depressive position

See also: Klein, Melanie; object relations theory; paranoid-schizoid position; projective identification; splitting

Klein identified the depressive position as a constellation of attitudes and phantasies that first appear when the baby is around 3 months. The tone of the baby's cry changes around then from a piercing scream to a more 'human' sound, she believed. Klein considered that the depressive position represented a major step forward in being able to tolerate waiting for attention or food rather than simply responding to primitive early pain and anxieties (Segal 1993).

Because Klein differed from Freud in the belief that there was a stage where the baby only relates to itself (see **narcissism**) she saw the baby (and later adult) as always being in relation to others (part objects as first – i.e. the nipple, and whole objects later – the mother).

Klein considered that in the depressive position we move away from the extreme belief that objects are either all good or all bad towards a more realistic mix of emotions. We integrate experience rather than split it. Therefore the concept of 'mixed' feelings towards objects arises, such as anger *and* remorse. The success of this step depends entirely upon the process of internalizing a good loving object producing an internal state of well-being. Thus anxieties and fears are *for* the object rather than *of* the object and relationships allow for greater separateness (Hinshelwood 1991).

Conflicts within the self at this stage are held by the individual and a representation of the good, caring and attentive mother are held internally as a good object and disappointment in the mother does not turn into something that is wholly bad and dangerous and damage is no longer feared as total destruction.

The baby also begins to get a sense of guilt in the depressive position realizing that the mother it loves is also the mother it attacks and some of the drama in this position is connected with feelings of guilt.

For these reasons the depressive position is not the most comfortable place to be and it frequently involves a sense of sadness (which Hinshelwood notes is not clinical depression). So in times of extreme stress and anxiety the child may try to move away from this new awareness of the world around it and move into the paranoid-schizoid position.

References

Hinshelwood, R. (1991) *A Dictionary of Kleinian Thought*. London: Free Association Books.

Segal, J. (1993) *Melanie Klein*. London: Sage.

Annotated further reading

Segal, J. (1993) *Melanie Klein*. London: Sage.

Julia Segal's book is a clear and comprehensive review of Klein's background, theory and work.

Spillius, E. (2007) *Encounters with Melanie Klein*. London: Routledge.

Spillius provides greater depth in her volume, which includes notes made by Klein for lectures as well as other unpublished material alongside the better known work.

Dialectical behaviour therapy (DBT)

See also: acceptance commitment therapy; behaviour therapy; cognitive behaviour therapy; mindfulness-based cognitive therapy

DBT was originally developed by Marsha M. Linehan, a researcher in the Department of Psychology at the University of Washington. She had originally found research rather cold, but realized that only stringent research would improve treatment options for very difficult client groups (Linehan et al. 1991). She chose to treat people with borderline personality disorder (BPD), clients who tend to self-harm, and those who are in danger of committing suicide and also suffer from extreme mood swings.

Her treatment approach combined standard cognitive-behavioural techniques for emotion regulation and reality testing with concepts of distress tolerance, acceptance, and mindful awareness largely derived from Buddhist (Zen) meditative practice. It may be the first therapy that has been demonstrated to be generally effective in treating BPD (Brody 2008).

Research has also indicated that DBT is effective in treating patients who presented varied symptoms and behaviours associated with spectrum mood disorders, including self-injury. It can also be quite effective with sexual abuse survivors and clients who are dependent on drugs (Decker and Naugle 2008).

The main purpose of DBT is for the therapist to befriend the patient. The therapist aims to accept and validate the client's feelings at any given time, while of course informing the client that some feelings and behaviours are maladaptive and unhelpful and then showing them various alternatives (Linehan and Dimeff 2001).

DBT consists of a number of major components and two specific parts of treatment. Part I refers to the one-to-one treatment aspect. The therapist and patient discuss the various issues that arise during the week, which are recorded using diary cards, and follow a treatment target hierarchy, with self-harm and suicidal behaviours taking priority. Next in priority are behaviours that are not considered to be self harmful, but are interfering with the treatment. The approach also looks at the client's quality of life and towards improving one's own life. During the whole session the therapist and the patient work towards improving life skills.

Part II is a group component in which a group of clients in treatment meet once a week for 2–3-hour sessions and learn how to use specific skills which are broken down into four modules: core mindfulness skills, interpersonal effectiveness skills, emotion regulation skills and distress tolerance skills.

DBT also emphasizes that all therapists need to attend weekly peer supervision and furthermore each therapist offers availability through telephone coaching between sessions. The therapist thus becomes part of the client's real world.

It is generally required that both components are used together, as the patient's potential suicidal urges would disrupt group sessions, for example, which are vital to teach the unique skills in context of life in a community. DBT tends to have very effective and satisfying treatment outcomes, but occasionally other skills may have to be taught additionally.

There is a general rule when it comes to certain aspects of DBT, which applies to clients and therapists alike, which states 'Any individual who misses four consecutive DBT meetings can no longer work with their pre-assigned

DBT therapist no matter how long they have been working together.' This is generally used to encourage participation, but it is argued that this rule tends to penalize patients since hospitalizations for medical purposes are not exempt. Anyone that wishes to use DBT needs to be committed and be ready and willing to share what is going on with their lives.

One tool used in DBT is 'chain analysis', which is a form of functional analysis on behaviour but with increased focus on sequential events that form the behaviour chain. It has strong roots in behavioural psychology in particular applied behaviour analysis concept of chaining. A growing body of research supports the use of behaviour chain analysis with multiple populations (Sampl et al. 2008).

DBT has grown into a very popular treatment model since its first publication. The training for therapists however is very expensive. Furthermore there are a number of gaps in DBT publications, such as research that includes male or minority clients. It continues to evolve in its application to new client populations.

References

Brody, J.E. (2008) The growing wave of teenage self-injury. *New York Times*.

Decker, S.E. and Naugle, A.E. (2008) DBT for sexual abuse survivors: current status and future directions. *Journal of Behaviour Analysis of Offender and Victim: Treatment and Prevention*, 1(4): 52–69.

http://courses.washington.edu/chile08/Linehan4.pdf

Linehan, M.M., Armstrong, H.E., Suarez, A., Allmon, D. and Heard, H.L. (1991) Cognitive-behavioral treatment of chronically parasuicidal borderline patients. *Archives of General Psychiatry*, 48: 1060–4.

Linehan, M.M. and Dimeff, L. (2001) Dialectical behavior therapy in a nutshell. *The California Psychologist*, 34: 10–13.

Sampl, S., Wakai, S., Trestman, R. and Keeney, E.M. (2008) Functional analysis of behavior in corrections: empowering inmates in skills training groups. *Journal of Behavior Analysis of Offender and Victim: Treatment and Prevention*, 1(4): 42–51.

Annotated further reading

Kazantzis, N., Reinecke, M.A. and Freeman, A. (eds) (2010) *Cognitive and Behavioral Theories in Clinical Practice*. New York: Guilford Press.

This publication contains in-depth chapters on the rich approaches that CBT contains. Leading experts come together and describe with insight how each approach differs from the other. Recent research is given a prominent place. The DBT chapter has a fascinating case study as its conclusion (pp. 232–8).

Displacement

See also: defence mechanisms; dream analysis; sublimation

Freud's work on dreams was central to his clinical work and theory development about the unconscious (Freud 1900, 1952/1989). Freud noticed that important things in the latent dream-thoughts were often represented by seemingly insignificant things in the manifest content of the dream, and vice versa. The dream itself seemed to be about one thing whereas the dream-thoughts showed it was really about something else. Freud believed that the interpretation of dream metaphors was a highly effective way into the patient's unconscious, and psychoanalysis (Freudian and other) generally takes patients' accounts of dreams to be a serious and potentially production part of the analytic process. Freud proposed that dreams were wish fulfillments although the wish fulfillment was not necessarily obvious to the person. Thus even though the defences (or censoring mechanisms) were relaxed during sleep it would still be dangerous to expose the mind to the full desires of the unconscious. Thus the dream was to protect the sleep when the defences were down (Craib 2001; Symington 1986).

During the day (not only the day before the dream) the unconscious would attach itself to objects and events that would enter the dreamer's life in a distorted or strange way with the desire appearing in disguised form. This is known as 'dream work' of which there were four types in any one dream:

1   condensation
2   displacement
3   symbolization
4   secondary revision.

Displacement focuses on the metaphor – that is the description/experience of one thing as if it were another. The aim of displacement is to hide something important and to displace it onto something seemingly trivial. It is only through analysis and working with associations that the true location of the affect can be identified (Symington 1986). Each chain of associations that emerges will be peculiar to the dreamer rather than the more popular view that there are universal symbols (Craib 2001). The dreamer's associations are able to provide an emotional map of the dream which moves the patient towards an integration between their inner world and outer reality.

Freud said that the relative importance of the dream elements (the 'psychical value' or 'cathexis') could undergo 'displacement'. The emotion associated with one idea or experience is detached from it and attached to another one.

References

Craib, I. (2001) *Psychoanalysis: A Critical Introduction.* Cambridge: Polity.

Freud, S. (1900) *The Interpretation of Dreams* (Vol. S.E. 4 1953). London: Hogarth Press.

Freud, S. (1952/1989) *On Dreams.* London: W.W. Norton and Co.

Symington, N. (1986) *The Analytic Experience: Lectures from the Tavistock.* London: Free Association Books.

Annotated further reading

http://www.freud.org.uk/education/topic/10576/subtopic/40025/

The Freud Museum in London has an educational website with accessible accounts of his work on dreams with examples including illustrations of displacement.

Freud, S. (1952/1989) *On Dreams.* London: W.W. Norton and Co.

Freud's short book about his work on dreaming is also accessible and useful for those with an interest in taking this forward.

Drama triangle, the

See also: assertiveness; games; life scripts

The drama triangle (Karpman 1968) suggests three complementary roles, called rescuer, victim and persecutor. It combines elements of both games and scripts from TA. In the Karpman drama triangle (KDT) rescuers want to be needed and seek out people who are struggling, but they may complain that they give too much help and that they're tired. Victims see themselves as helpless and powerless; they complain that they can't do anything right and may use guilt to manipulate others, especially rescuers. Persecutors attack rescuers for being too helpful and victims for being too weak. They believe and may say that it's a tough world and people need to look out for themselves.

In the KDT, these three roles are exaggerated versions of normal behaviour – there are genuine rescuers, etc. – and the players become stuck in one of them, although occasionally and dramatically switching roles. For example, a person in the rescuer role may try to help someone in the victim role and then one of them switches to persecutor. No positive changes occur before or after the switch.

To escape from a KDT, one or more of the players stops playing. They notice the excessive and recurring neediness, the blaming or putting others' needs first and take action accordingly and assertively. However, the pattern is usually deeply ingrained, can be hard to break and may recur.

Reference

Karpman, S. B. (1968) Fairy tales and script drama analysis. *TA Bulletin*, VII (26): 39–43.

Annotated further reading

There are many internet resources on the KDT, e.g. www.karpman dramatriangle.com and Stephen Karpman's own site, both still 'live' in 2011 and offering free downloads of the original article and many ideas about it, but no empirical research.

Dream analysis

See also: dynamic unconscious; interpretation; Jung, Carl; psychoanalysis; psychodynamic counselling

Freud famously described dream analysis as 'the royal road to the unconscious'. He regarded dreams as a rich source of material which would provide insights into a patient's unconscious wishes, fears and conflicts. According to Freud, dreams allowed the analyst to examine material which was at a less defended level of the personality than that available at a conscious level. Freud made a distinction between the manifest (or actual) content and the latent (or hidden) content of dreams (Howard 2006). The latent content usually related to repressed infantile sexual or aggressive urges. Jung also believed in the value of dream analysis but disagreed with Freud's focus on infant sexuality and aggression. He developed the idea that there were two types of dreams: individual dreams and collective dreams (dreams which we all experience, which are linked to the collective unconscious).

More recently, dream analysis tends not to be as prominent in psychoanalysis as it once was, though it is still seen as a means of gaining access to the unconscious mind (Lemma 2002). It is also more difficult in shorter-term work to analyse dreams in depth, although the rich material available in dreams can still be insightful. Clients may be asked to make links or associations between aspects of a dream and problematic aspects of their life, one important purpose being to understand how they relate to other significant people from the past and the present. Since Freud, there has been a shift of emphasis from the therapist's interpretations of the dream to the meanings it holds for the client.

According to Yalom (2000: 86), who trained as a psychiatrist but worked from an existential perspective, 'the most important fact about a dream is its emotion', so he would often ask the client about the predominant feelings associated with the dream. He advocated a pragmatic approach, using dream material to explore themes that have already emerged in the therapy with the aim of speeding up the therapeutic process. As dreams have many levels of meaning, it is impossible ever to analyse them completely.

This technique is not exclusively used by psychoanalysts and psychodynamic therapists. The purpose of dreams can be conceptualized in quite a different way depending on one's theoretical standpoint. For example, they can be seen as a means of creative expression or as a mechanism for maintaining mental health (Jinks 2006). From a cognitive perspective, the therapeutic work might involve the client keeping a dream diary in which they record details of their dreams. These can then be discussed in order to better understand the client's negative thoughts and negative core beliefs.

Gestalt therapists may use an active technique whereby the client identifies the main aspects of a dream and explores what these different aspects think and feel about other elements. The assumption here is that different parts of a dream represent different aspects of the dreamer. The client is thereby helped to increase their awareness of the dream's elements and how they interrelate. Another approach involves helping the client to take control over their dream by encouraging them to re-enter their dream world (Jinks 2006). By identifying the most important aspect of the dream, the client can then be encouraged to engage in dialogue with this key figure (whether person or object) and to make an ally of this figure, even if initially hostile. The intended outcome is that by confronting a problematic figure in this way, it becomes less threatening.

One of the criticisms levelled at dream analysis is that it is impossible to provide evidence that this technique actually works. Dreams which are formed in the unconscious mind are inevitably nebulous entities and their interpretation may be assumed to be accurate and to have therapeutic value simply because it seems to have meaning for the client at a specific moment in time.

References

Howard, S. (2006) *Psychodynamic Counselling in a Nutshell*. London: Sage.

Jinks, G. (2006) Specific strategies and techniques. In C. Feltham and I. Horton (eds) *The SAGE Handbook of Counselling and Psychotherapy*, 2nd edn. London: Sage.

Lemma, A. (2002) Psychodynamic therapy: the Freudian approach. In W. Dryden (ed.) *Handbook of Individual Therapy*, 4th edn. London: Sage.

Yalom, I. (2000) *Love's Executioner and Other Tales of Psychotherapy*, 2nd edn. New York: Perennial.

Annotated further reading

Jacobs, M. (2010) *Psychodynamic Counselling in Action*, 4th edn. London: Sage.

An excellent introduction to this and other psychodynamic concepts from a practical perspective.

Klein, M. (2001) *Psychodynamic Counselling Primer*. Ross-on-Wye: PCCS Books.

A concise introduction to the main concepts which is particularly suitable for those new to the subject.

Dynamic unconscious

See also: archetypes; collective unconscious

Although the idea of a dynamic unconscious is central to psychoanalytic theory, to some writers it is a myth (e.g. Spinelli 2001). Part of the problem with it is vagueness and therefore inconsistent use: writers tend to slip from one meaning to another. The first sense is dynamic unconscious, as a source of motivation, powerful forces that we're not aware of causing our behaviour, e.g. a dentist motivated to herself compassion but unconsciously by sadism. The second sense is 'unconscious' as automatic behaviour, e.g. breathing, walking, habits, thoughts and emotions, etc. Contemporary psychology recognizes that we process a lot of information out of awareness but this conception is relatively gentle (Matthews et al. 2009: 128–33).

Another problem with the idea of a dynamic unconscious is the lack of good evidence for it, though this is of course a matter of judgement. Take, for example, dreams and slips of the tongue. Both can seem to vividly illustrate dynamic unconscious forces but can they be explained more simply? Thus, dreams may be random nonsense rather than a royal road to the unconscious through unconscious wishes struggling for expression, while slips of the tongue might reflect emotions which the person is well aware of (or which are just below the surface of their awareness), or they may be a speech error which happens on this occasion to make sense (Reason 2000). The many speech errors which don't 'make sense' are quickly forgotten.

The general notion here is that coincidences happen occasionally, just by chance, because so many things happen and we are not skilled at judging probabilities. At the same time, our perceptions and memories are biased by a 'search for meaning'.

An example of research which has a Freudian 'flavour' but which does not appear to support the *dynamic* unconscious is Myers' (2000; 2009) extensive work on repressive coping. One characteristic of people with this style is to report low levels of distress when they're in stressful situations but to have substantially increased heart rates and raised blood pressure.

References

Matthews, G., Deary, I.J. and Whiteman, M.C. (2009) *Personality Traits*, 3rd edn. Cambridge: Cambridge University Press.

Myers, L.B. (2000) Deceiving others or deceiving themselves. *The Psychologist*, 13(8): 400–3.

Myers, L.B. (2009) The importance of the repressive coping style: findings from 30 years of research. *Anxiety, Stress and Coping*, 23(1): 3–17.

Reason, J. (2000) The Freudian slip revisited. *The Psychologist*, 13(12): 610–11.

Spinelli, E. (2001) *The Mirror and the Hammer: Challenges to Therapeutic Orthodoxy*. London: Continuum.

Annotated further reading

Funder, D.C. (2010) *The Personality Puzzle*, 5th edn. London: W. W. Norton and Co.

Westen, D. (1998) The scientific legacy of Sigmund Freud: Toward a psychodynamically informed psychological science. *Psychological Bulletin*, 124, 333–71.

These two sources offer balance to the above critique. Funder (2010) reviews in an open-minded and lively way some of the empirical research on the concept of 'the unconscious' (and other psycho-dynamic concepts), and he recommends Westen's paper as 'A thorough and highly readable summary of the modern research evidence that supports many of Freud's key ideas' (p. 468). These include the unconscious. Funder also states a (to me, surprising) judgement later in his book. He writes about 'Freud's fundamental argument for the existence of the unconscious . . . the one that clinched the issue for me the first time I heard it: We do things without knowing why, and have thoughts and feelings we do not understand. It's obvious that our own minds are doing things we don't know about' (p. 620).

E

Egan's skilled helper model

See also: integrative models

Born in 1930, Gerard Egan still works as Professor Emeritus of Organizational Development and Psychology at Loyola University, Chicago. He has written more than 15 books, with perhaps the best known being *The Skilled Helper: A Problem-management and Opportunity-development Approach to Helping*, now in its ninth edition.

The focus of Egan's work has been on two main areas: counselling and communication and business and management. He shifts between the roles of counsellor, coach, consultant and trainer, bearing in mind the overlap between these roles. He himself states that he regards interpersonal communication as 'one of the major enabling skills of life' (Egan 2007: x).

The main influences on Egan's work are various. His person-centred values and principles derive from Carkhuff, who was himself influenced by Carl Rogers (Egan 2007). His cognitive-behavioural stance which is clearly apparent in much of his work is based on the writings of Bandura, Beck, Ellis, Seligman and Strong (Woskett 2006b). The Skilled Helper model certainly has a strong cognitive-behavioural bias, with its emphasis on challenging distorted ways of thinking and on the importance of developing client skills. Other influences include social learning theory, cognitive dissonance theory, motivation and, more recently, positive psychology.

Key aspects of Egan's Skilled Helper model are encapsulated in the terms often used to describe it: an 'integrating framework' (Egan 2002: 37); a 'process model' and a 'shared map' (Egan 2002: 35). The term 'framework' captures the fact that it provides a structure for the helping process, but is not based on specific theoretical constructions. It is a process model in that it sees helping as a three stage process made up of a series of tasks. As a kind of shared map, it tells the helper where they are with the client and suggests which interventions might be most helpful (Egan 2002). It is shared in that it encourages the client to be an active participant in the helping process.

The stages of the model

The model consists of three stages, each of which has a specific purpose.

Stage 1 is about the *current situation* and focuses on defining and clarifying the problem or issue. The key question is 'What is going on now?'

Stage 2 centres on the *preferred scenario* which involves setting goals. A key question is 'What would I prefer things to be like?'

Stage 3 is about *action planning* and involves asking, 'How do I get things moving forward?'

Within each stage there are three tasks:

Stage 1 comprises (a) telling their *story*: encouraging the client to explore their problems and missed opportunities, but in a way that helps them to get in touch with their internal world; (b) *blind spots*: assisting the client in identifying areas they may have neglected in order to reach new perspectives on their issues; and (c) *leverage*: choosing the issue to focus on which will have most impact on changing their situation.

Stage 2 involves (a) *possibilities*: supporting the client in imagining what they want their future to be like in as detailed a way as possible. It is about creating a sense of hope; (b) *change agenda*: establishing workable goals which will enable them to make the changes they are aiming for. It is important that these goals are realistic and client led; (c) *commitment*: finding incentives which will help the client stick to their goals. Internal incentives such as feeling more positive tend to be most effective.

Stage 3 consists of: (a) *possible strategies*: coming up with possible ways of achieving what they want; (b) *best-fit strategies*: narrowing down the options to include only those which appeal to the client and are most likely to lead to the chosen outcome; (c) *plan*: organizing the strategies in time order so that they can be approached systematically.

Egan stresses the fact that action needs to be embedded in the entire process and not just the third stage. In practice this might involve helping the client to arrive at some action steps at the end of each session. However, action is not limited to behaviour change. It can involve internal shifts such as new insights or changes to thoughts or feelings. See Woskett (2006a) for more detail on the many forms action can take and on the three tasks within each stage of the model. The model advocates the use of a group of specific skills within each stage, for example paraphrasing and summarizing in stage 1 and challenging and immediacy in stage 2. (See Egan (2007) for more detail.) The final point which it is important to emphasize here is that one of the main aims of the model is to develop and maintain a strong and effective therapeutic relationship between counsellor and client. The stages and tasks of helping are designed to be closely connected to the quality of the counselling relationship.

Key principles underlying the model

Egan emphasizes the ideas espoused by positive psychology, in that he believes in focusing on clients' personal strengths as well as resources available to them in their communities. Heavily influenced by the person-centred approach to counselling, he has a strong belief in human potential and in the importance of the counsellor qualities of empathy, respect and genuineness. However, he differs from this perspective in that he does not regard these core conditions as sufficient in themselves and advocates developing client's problem-solving skills as well as developing an effective counselling relationship.

The values which Egan emphasizes include: client empowerment, empathy and consideration of the socio-cultural context in which clients live. Even if clients have limited control over their lives, Egan believes it is possible for them to make changes in the aspects of their lives where freedom exists. Part of this notion of empowerment involves the counsellor acting as a skills trainer and consultant (Woskett 2006a). In terms of empathy, it is regarded not only as a value, but also as an interpersonal communication skill (paraphrasing effectively can convey empathy). Consideration of the client's life context is referred to by Egan (1984) as a people-in-systems approach. He is critical of approaches which disregard the many environmental factors which can have a profound impact on people.

Criticisms of the model

Egan's model is sometimes regarded as prescriptive and mechanistic, which may be based on an assumption that it is a linear model which must be rigidly adhered to. In reality, a counsellor can move back and forth between stages and need only use those aspects of the model which are of value to any particular client. It is important, therefore, to learn to use the model in a flexible manner.

Another common criticism is that the model pays very little attention to the client's past experiences. In fact there is scope for discussion of the past, although Egan tends to view the purpose of this as helping the client to deal with unresolved issues affecting them in the present. Clearly this can be of use in itself and some clients do not in any case wish to revisit past experiences in any depth. However, it is fair to say that those clients wanting a psychodynamically-orientated approach to therapy with its emphasis on unconscious processes would be more likely to find it elsewhere.

Research evidence

As a framework which can be adapted and potentially used very differently by each user, it is difficult to measure the effectiveness of the Egan model via outcome research in the way that an approach using a specific set of therapeutic techniques might be. The model has, however, been developed in line with research evidence on the helping process including social learning theory and positive psychology.

References

Egan, G. (1984) People in systems: a comprehensive model for psychosocial education and training. In D. Larson (ed.) *Teaching Psychological Skills: Models for Giving Psychology Away*. Monterey, CA: Brooks/Cole.

Egan, G. (2002) *The Skilled Helper: A Problem-management and Opportunity-development Approach to Helping*, 7th edn. Pacific Grove, CA: Thompson Brooks/Cole.

Egan, G. (2007) *The Skilled Helper: A Problem-management and Opportunity-development Approach to Helping*, 8th edn. Pacific Grove, CA: Thompson Brooks/Cole.

Woskett, V. (2006a) *Egan's Skilled Helper Model: Developments and Applications in Counselling*. London: Routledge.

Woskett, V. (2006b) The skilled helper model. In C. Feltham and I. Horton (eds) (2006) *The SAGE Handbook of Counselling and Psychotherapy*, 2nd edn. London: Sage.

Annotated further reading

Egan, G. (2009) *The Skilled Helper: A Problem-management and Opportunity-development Approach to Helping*, 9th edn. Pacific Grove, CA: Brooks/Cole.

Although some find Egan's writing style a little dense, it is valuable to read about his model in his own words.

Woskett, V. (2006) *Egan's Skilled Helper Model: Developments and Applications in Counselling*. London: Routledge.

An excellent book which discusses Egan's model of helping in an accessible and insightful way.

Ellis, Albert (1913–2007)

See also: rational emotive behaviour therapy

Albert Ellis was born on 17 September 1913 in Pittsburgh, USA and died in 2007 after a long illness. He was the eldest of three children. Ellis's father was a businessman and typical of fathers of this generation in that he was not particularly emotionally available for or interested in his children. Ellis described his mother as a narcissistic yet gregarious woman, in no way closer to her children than her husband. When they eventually divorced, Ellis stated that he was surprised but not shocked about it.

As the eldest he took on the carer's role in the household. All three children had to find jobs to support the family. Albert was in poor health as a young man, one of his illnesses lasting nearly a year. However, he had a natural talent for figuring out how to make himself 'emotionally resilient'. 'In a way I was a born therapist for myself' (Palmer et al. 1995: 55).

He entered the field of clinical psychology after first finishing a degree in business studies. He began to write about the field of human sexuality, one he had developed a noted expertise in, which eventually led him to counselling in this field.

In 1942 he began his studies in clinical psychology at Columbia University which educated psychologists in the psychoanalytic tradition and by 1943 Ellis had started a part-time private practice while still working on his PhD. Ellis began publishing innovative articles even before receiving his PhD.

He also pursued additional training in psychoanalysis and in 1947 began a personal analysis. His psychoanalyst Horney would be the single greatest influence in his thinking, although the writings of Alfred Adler, Erich Fromm and Harry Stack Sullivan were also influential in developing his own perspective.

The more he knew about psychoanalysis, the more he doubted the efficacy of this approach. In 1950 he expressed his reservations, suggesting the need for scientific evidence, and considered that psychoanalysis was after all over a half century old and despite its long history still lacked a comprehensive formulation of its scientific principles. He pondered that such a formulation would surely strip from analytic theory and practices all frills of dogmatism, unverified speculation, bias and cultism, and thus nothing would remain but those principles and procedures which seemed well on their way to becoming clinically validated.

His task of building a full-time practice was aided by his growing reputation as a sexologist, especially from his books *The Folklore of Sex* (1951), *The American Sexual Tragedy* (1954) and *Sex without Guilt* (1958). Many psychology departments, even after he had achieved national prominence as a psychologist, banned or cancelled presentations by Ellis because of his over-liberal perception of sexuality. In 1951, Ellis became the American editor of the *International Journal of Sexology* and began publishing a number of articles advocating sexual liberation. He also wrote the introduction to Donald Webster Cory's controversial book, *The Homosexual in America*, and thereby became the first prominent psychologist to advocate gay liberation. He was married three times.

Effectiveness was extremely important to him and thus he began to explore new methods. The approach that became increasingly prominent was based on a pattern he found most clients had in common: a tendency to irrational and inflexible thinking. This insight, united with his studies of stoic philosophy (Marcus Aurelius and Epictetus), obliged him to move towards a new theory of psychotherapy. The notion that became his theoretical guideline was that disturbing emotions are a result of an individual's view of the situation, not the situation itself: 'If you are distressed by anything external, the pain is not due to the thing itself but to your own estimate of it; and this you have the power to revoke at any moment.'

By 1955 Ellis was advocating a new rational, more active and directive type of psychotherapy: rational-emotive therapy. He argued that he would attempt to help the client uncover his self-defeating beliefs and behaviours by demonstrating their irrationality or rigidity. Soon Ellis began teaching his new technique to other therapists. In 1959 Ellis published the book *How to Live with a Neurotic*, which explored his new method. His strong cognitive emphasis provoked most therapeutic schools with the possible exception of the followers of Alfred Adler. Consequently, he frequently experienced hostility from other therapists.

He founded the Institute for Rational-Emotive Therapy, a non-profit organization, in 1959, which was solely based on his new paradigm. 'Rational' Ellis claimed, in his mind, always meant 'self-helping' (Palmer et al. 1995: 12). Furthermore, therapy would only ever be successful if clients engaged in homework assignments in order to support the change that had been initiated in the therapy sessions. Only 'work and practice' would lead to lasting improvement of one's psychological state. The main difference to other CBT approaches was working through the 'absolute musts' clients cognitively adhered to. He had also come to the conclusion that giving clients too much warmth would make them feel good but not help them change. So he recommended 'good rapport' rather than 'warmth' added to tough handling of 'unhelpful thinking patterns'. He was a self-proclaimed 'passionate sceptic' and was on many occasions open to challenges. His basic message was that all people are born with a talent 'for crooked thinking', or distortions of perception that sabotage their innate desire for happiness. But he recognized that people also had the capacity to change themselves.

He was active until his death at 93 years of age; he was known and therefore had much more influence of how people perceived modern therapy than perhaps any other contemporary in his field. Let him speak for himself in a response to *The New Yorker*: 'Freud was a genius, but some of his psychoanalysis was as nutty as could be.' 'I don't damn any person, including Stalin, Hitler and President Bush.' Yes, but Green's article on me and Rational Emotive Behavior Therapy forgot to add, 'I do damn and actively work against many of their thoughts, feelings and *behaviors*.'

Reference

Palmer, S., Dryden, W., et al. (1995) *Rational Interviews*. London: Centre for REBT.

Annotated further reading

Palmer, S., Dryden, W., et al. (1995) *Rational Interviews*. London: Centre for REBT.

A very useful booklet containing ten interviews with Albert Ellis, which conveys his passion, his thinking and his humanity.

The following three internet resources are helpful in researching the details of Professor Ellis's life:

A Brief Biography of Dr Albert Ellis 1913–2007, by Dr Ellis and Mike Abrams PhD, www.rebt.ws/**albertellisbiography**.html (accessed 20 August 2011).

http://www.nytimes.com/2007/07/25/nyregion/25ellis.html?pagewanted=all (accessed 20 August 2011).

Letter to *The New Yorker*, from Dr Albert Ellis, 9 October 2003, http://www.rebt.ws/recentarticles.html (accessed 20 August 2011).

Empathy

See also: core conditions; integrative models; interpretation; paraphrasing; person-centred counselling; preferences; the therapeutic relationship

In everyday language, empathy is seeing from another's point of view, putting yourself in their shoes, being on their wavelength. In counselling, it is a prominent quality in most approaches, notably person-centred and psychodynamic, but with different emphases (at best) and with many subtle aspects (Elliott et al. 2011). Rogers (1980) defined it as 'entering into the private, perceptual world of the other . . . being sensitive, moment by moment to the changing felt meanings which flow in this other person . . . communicating your sensing of the person's world' (p. 142).

Rogers thus viewed empathy as a way of being with another person, leaving aside your own emotions, feelings, perceptions, values and needs as much as you can. He emphasized the 'as if' aspect of empathy, which is distinct from *identifying* with the other person or what has vividly been called 'fusing'. It is also evident from Rogers' definition (and he made numerous attempts) that empathy is an inference about the inner experience of another person, and that it is communicated to that person.

Empathy has proved difficult to measure, partly because of differences in definition, but recent work on neurophysiological measures may prove more useful (Decety and Ickes 2009). Generally however, the conclusion of a review published in 1996 still holds: that the different conceptions have led to 'theoretical confusions, methodological difficulties, inconsistent findings and neglected areas of research' (Duan and Hill 1996: 269).

Churchill and Bayne (1998) suggested a way of bringing some order to this confusion: that personality differences could underlie the different conceptions and explain why each is seen as the truth by its proponents. In support, they found some clear relationships; for example, experienced counsellors with a greater tendency to organize and plan their lives had a more active conception of counselling compared to those who tended to have a more receptive, 'let's see what happens' kind of personality.

However, the most obvious link between personality and conception of empathy – that people who are more logical and analytic tend to favour cognitive empathy while those who see feelings as more important than logic tend to emphasize emotional empathy – was not supported. The researchers explain this finding as an effect of counsellor training: the emphasis on emotions in most training may have obscured a real relationship. This explanation does of course need to be tested.

Three of the many subtle aspects of empathy in counselling are:

1   Emphasis on the aim of empathy as either (a) to collect information to inform a diagnosis and to help (the counsellor as expert) or (b) to help the client understand themselves (the client as expert). Mearns and Thorne (2007: 83) wrote that 'the counsellor's understanding is not the aim . . . the aim is to create the conditions where the client comes to understand himself'. Jung was almost as clear: 'It is relatively unimportant whether the psychotherapist understands or not, but everything hangs on the patient's doing so' (source unknown).

2   Many textbooks include examples of 'empathy' which are banal, and it is a difficult quality to illustrate, partly because it is a process and partly because it has significant nonverbal elements. I think there are good examples, i.e. not banal, in Mearns and Thorne (e.g. pp. 67–8) and Bayne et al. (2008: 77–8).

3   Empathy is most difficult when the other person's experience and background are very different from your own – particularly so if you don't agree with or like them. However, it is not necessary – or perhaps even desirable – to be empathic instantly (see the entry on **paraphrasing**).

Two questions about empathy are how important it is in everyday relationships and what are the best ways to become more empathic. On the first of these, Rogers suggested that in most relationships, congruence is 'probably the most important element' (1980: 160), whereas in counselling, or when the other person is in pain, confused or suffering in other ways, empathy is. On the second, good evidence is lacking but one suggestion is to read novels, presumably with understanding and feeling.

Overall, empathy is well supported as a vital element of the effective therapeutic relationship (Cooper 2008; Elliott et al. 2011) but the outcome literature also suggests that it is irritating for some people (Cooper 2008: 108). The greatest efficiency (and most clients will appreciate lower cost and greater speed) may be likely to result from empathy as a preparation for offering your client an interpretation or new perspective and as a continuing element in the therapeutic relationship.

References

Bayne, R., Jinks, G., Collard, P. and Horton, I. (2008) *The Counsellor's Handbook: A Practical A–Z Guide to Integrative Counselling and Psychotherapy*, 3rd edn. Cheltenham: Nelson Thornes.

Churchill, S. and Bayne, R. (1998) Psychological type and conceptions of empathy in experienced counsellors. *Counselling Psychology Quarterly*, 11: 379–90.

Cooper, M. (2008) *Essential Research Findings in Counselling and Psychotherapy*. London: Sage.

Decety, J. and Ickes, W. (eds) (2009) *The Social Neuroscience of Empathy*. Cambridge, MA: MIT Press.

Duan, C. and Hill, C.E. (1996) Theoretical confusions in the construct of empathy. *Journal of Counseling Psychology*, 43: 261–74.

Elliott, R., Bohart, A.C., Watson, J.C. and Greenberg, L.S. (2011) Empathy. *Psychotherapy*, 48(1): 43–9.

Mearns, D. and Thorne, B. (2007) *Person-centred Counselling in Action*, 3rd edn. London: Sage.

Rogers, C.R. (1980) *A Way of Being*. Boston, MA: Houghton Mifflin.

Annotated further reading

McLeod, J. (2009) *Introduction to Counselling*, 4th edn. Maidenhead: Open University Press.

For discussion of several conceptions of empathy.

Mearns, D. and Thorne, B. (2007) *Person-centred Counselling in Action*, 3rd edn. London: Sage.

Discusses empathy in the person-centred approach in depth.

Erikson, Erik (1902–1994)

See also: Eriksonian analysis

Erikson was born in Frankfurt, Germany in 1902 and died in the USA in 1994. His mother, Karla, was a Danish Jew married to, but separated from, a Jewish stockbroker in Copenhagen (Waldemar Salomonsen). Although Erik was originally registered under the name of Salomonsen, Karla had been estranged from her husband for some time suggesting that he was not Erik's biological father. There appears to be little information about Erikson's biological father, although speculation suggests he was a non-Jewish Danish man named Erik Erikson. Two years after Erik's birth Karla married Erik Homberger who adopted Erik and they raised him to be Jewish. Erikson always signed himself Erik Homberger Erikson. Erikson's focus on 'identity' (Erikson 1959/1980) is likely to have been shaped by his background and particularly because it seemed unlikely that he ever met his biological father so consequently part of his origins would have always remained a mystery to him.

Erikson trained in psychoanalysis in Vienna and qualified in 1933 just as the Nazis came to power. He left Vienna initially for Denmark and then for the USA (Boston) where he became the first psychoanalyst in the city. He worked as a clinical academic at Harvard and then Yale, where he did his study observing a Native American Sioux community. That work influenced his understanding of the influence of culture on development. He later reinforced his thinking on this with his comparison of the Sioux with his study of the Yurok tribe. He finally went to work as a teacher and academic clinician at the University of California at Berkeley.

Erikson believed that childhood was important and the longer the experience of childhood the greater the civilization of a group or society. His clinical and academic work was focused on anxiety in young children, apathy in Native Americans and Nazism among the young.

Erikson was identified as one of the first 'ego psychologists' and believed that culture and history were fundamental influences on identity.

Erikson's work, particularly his psychosocial developmental stages model (see **psychosocial development**), has sometimes been seen in opposition to Freud's model of psychosexual development (see **psychosexual development**). This is not the case though. Erikson himself always made it clear that his work was a complement and development of Freud's (Erikson 1950/1963) and based upon the assumption of the psychosexual developmental model.

References

Erikson, E. (1950/1963) *Childhood and Society*. New York: Norton.
Erikson, E. (1959/1980) *Identity, Youth and Crisis*. New York: Norton.

Annotated further reading

Erikson, E. (1950/1963) *Childhood and Society*. New York: Norton.
Erikson, E. (1959/1980) *Identity, Youth and Crisis*. New York: Norton.

Although somewhat old fashioned both these books written by Erikson himself cover the basic ideas and the clinical perquisites of his work.

Eriksonian analysis

Little is written to describe the particular approach that Erikson took towards his clinical work although much was with children and young people. Erikson himself used clinical case studies to underpin his developmental theory and his clinical work drew out the fact of developmental crises and the role of identity as a pivotal phase in development and analysis (Erikson 1950/1963; 1959/1980). He was known as an 'ego' psychologist, a fact which goes some way to defining his approach to psychoanalysis.

Erikson believed, in contrast to Freud, that the ego was more than just a mediator between the unconscious levels of the superego and the id. He saw the ego as a positive driving force in human development and personality so that the ego's main task was to develop and maintain a sense of identity. His analysis therefore was directed to supporting and developing a strong sense of identity from where growth and emotional development can take place. Erikson's understanding of the social and cultural context was also part of his approach to clinical work and he was particularly concerned that individuals gained a sense of belonging.

He considered that patients who had weaker egos and poorly developed identity would find it difficult to deal with difficulties in their life or in their community and might experience an identity crisis. An identity crisis occurs when a person lacks direction, feels unproductive, and does not have a clear sense of who they are or who they will become. He believed that we all have identity crises at one time or another in our lives and that these crises do not necessarily represent a negative state but can be a driving force toward positive resolution (see **psychosocial development**).

It is interesting that Erikson's model of psychosocial development has remained important particularly for social work and clinical psychology practitioners, probably because of his interest in the role of culture and community in shaping behaviour. However, his integration of Freud's ideas of development, including infantile sexuality, have been overlooked by most commentators.

References

Erikson, E. (1950/1963) *Childhood and Society*. New York: Norton.
Erikson, E. (1959/1980) *Identity, Youth and Crisis*. New York: Norton.

Annotated further reading

Erikson, E. (1950/1963) *Childhood and Society*. New York: Norton.
Erikson, E. (1959/1980) *Identity, Youth and Crisis*. New York: Norton.

Both books are the most useful ones for teasing out Erikson's approach to analysis as there is little written on it by Erikson or others per se. What becomes apparent in his books is the way he approaches analysis based on a Freudian model along with a more culturally aware take on the psyche.

Ethical concepts

See also: boundaries

Perhaps it is no accident that the growth of counselling has corresponded with the decline of organized religion, resulting in more people turning to professionals for help with the moral decisions that were previously the domain of religion. It is, of course, vital that counsellors are mindful of the moral dilemmas which their clients face, as well as their own moral and ethical assumptions, which may impact on their work with clients.

This section will focus on ethical principles and guidelines of value to counsellors rather than how to resolve ethical dilemmas in practice.

The counselling and psychotherapy professions have only come to realize the importance of ethical considerations since the 1980s. Rosenbaum (1982) wrote one of the first books to focus on the ethical aspects of therapy. Clearly relying on one's feeling or intuition about a particular moral judgement can be fraught with danger, particularly where the counsellor is inexperienced or the situation is an unusual or alien one. Clients from different cultures provide a good example of when one's feeling about what is right might be totally inappropriate for the client.

Bond (2010) identified a range of sources of ethics including personal ethics, the ethics implicit in different therapeutic approaches, organizational policy, professional codes or frameworks and the law.

Personal ethics

We all have some kind of moral or ethical code even if we find it difficult to describe it coherently. However, a counsellor may find that their personal ethics sometimes conflict with their professional ones. It may, for example, be appropriate to tell a friend if someone discovers their partner is taking heroine, but it would not be ethical to tell that friend if the information was disclosed in a therapy session.

Ethics implicit in different therapeutic approaches

A therapist's choice of theoretical approach will inevitably be influenced by their personal ethics, so that a strong belief in client autonomy may lead to an attraction to a humanistic approach. This is not a problem in itself, but it is crucial that therapists are aware of the inevitable ethical biases in their model of choice and of areas they may be ignoring by rejecting other approaches.

Organizational policy

Policies can vary a great deal, although most counselling organizations specify procedures to be followed in relation to many ethical dilemmas. For example, confidentiality is rarely absolute in cases where a client may self-harm. There may be a conflict between what the counsellor believes to be ethical based on the needs of the client and what the organizational procedures dictate. So, for example, an organization may require that a questionnaire to assess client progress is completed towards the end of every session, but the counsellor and client may regard this as intrusive and as distracting from the therapeutic work.

Professional codes and guidelines

Bond states that frameworks which outline shared understanding of ethical principles and provide guidance as to how to deal with ethical dilemmas (such as the British Association for Counselling and Psychotherapy (BACP) Ethical Framework 2010) tend to work better than rigid directives of what counsellors should be doing. There are occasions, according to Bond, when it may be more ethical to breach the code, though these are rare. The ethical principles for counselling and psychotherapy have developed out of those applied to medical ethics. It is important to consider broad ethical principles as well as more specific practical guidelines when considering ethical issues.

Legal issues

It is becoming increasingly important to consider how the law impacts on ethical decision making. It is also important to be aware that different types of organizations have different legal obligations. Bond (2010) advises that all therapists need a basic knowledge of the law in relation to contract, confidentiality, defamation, negligence, the protection and disclosure of records and acting as a witness in court.

As previously mentioned, professional organizations produce their own ethical guidelines in order to assist their members in dealing effectively with ethical dilemmas, but also to guard the reputation of the profession and to protect the clients from harm. The BACP and UKCP (United Kingdom Council for Psychotherapy) are two such organizations to which many counsellors and psychotherapists belong. Until 2002, members of BACP (then BAC) adhered to the Code of Ethics and Practice for Counselling. In 2002 this was replaced by the Ethical Framework for Good Practice in Counselling and Psychotherapy, which places more emphasis on the values, qualities and ethical principles seen as important with regard to ethical practice (Bayne and Jinks 2010). The ethical principles are as follows:

- being trustworthy (also referred to as fidelity): being reliable and trustworthy, including honouring confidentiality and any agreed contracts;
- autonomy: respecting the client's right to make his or her own decisions, which includes informed consent and choosing to participate in counselling;
- beneficence: acting in ways most likely to promote the client's welfare. This includes deciding, as far as is possible, which interventions are likely to be most helpful to a particular client;
- non-maleficence: behaving in ways which will do no harm. This includes ensuring that one's training and supervision ensures sufficient competence to practice and to work effectively with one's client group;
- justice: treating clients fairly and ensuring fair distribution of services. Legal requirements need to be taken into account;
- self-respect: ensuring one takes care of oneself as well as the client. This may include methods of avoiding stress and burnout.

Sometimes these principles may be in conflict with each other such that resolving an ethical dilemma involves giving priority to one over another. For example, non-maleficence and justice often have to take priority in a crisis situation (Bayne and Jinks 2010).

In conclusion, ethical principles and frameworks are not absolutes and can be perceived very differently by different cultures. While western cultures generally conceptualize moral codes in abstract terms, non-western cultures often invest moral virtues into qualities of persons (McLeod 2009).

References

Bayne, R. and Jinks, G. (2010) *How to Survive Counsellor Training: An A–Z Guide*. Basingstoke: Palgrave Macmillan.

Bond, T. (2010) *Standards and Ethics for Counselling in Action*, 2nd edn. London: Sage.

British Association for Counselling and Psychotherapy (BACP) (2010) *Ethical Framework for Good Practice in Counselling and Psychotherapy*. Lutterworth: BACP.

McLeod, J. (2009) *An Introduction to Counselling*. Maidenhead: Open University Press.

Rosenbaum, M. (ed.) (1982) *Ethics and Values in Psychotherapy: A Guidebook*. New York: Free Press.

Annotated further reading

Bond, T. (2010) *Standards and Ethics for Counselling in Action*, 2nd edn. London: Sage.

A core text for anyone studying or investigating ethical concepts.

Jones, C., Shillito-Clarke, C., Syme, G. et al. (2000) *Questions of Ethics in Counselling and Psychotherapy*. Buckingham: Open University Press.

An accessible book covering a wide range of ethical dilemmas written in a question and answer style format.

Existential counselling

See also: anxiety, existential; gestalt therapy; phenomenology; logotherapy

Perhaps a common perception of existentialism is the idea that everything – both an individual's internal and the external world – exists only in their consciousness, so that there is no existence apart from that which exists inside themselves. In other words, does that chair exist in reality or only in one's mind? According to Claringbull (2010: 92) 'our individual existences . . . depend on our own unique experiences and interpretations of those experiences'. The aim of existential philosophy is to understand the experience of being human;

it is a search for some core dimensions of meaning (such as choice, freedom, isolation, death) and ultimately about living more authentically.

Historical perspective

Existential philosophy grew out of a rejection of many of the traditional sources of meaning including religion and community, resulting in a search for new meanings. Nietzsche and Sartre were well known figures in the development of this philosophy. Others were also involved in its early development. Kierkgaard, as well as Nietzsche, was an initiator in this new way of thinking and introduced the idea that truth could only be discovered subjectively by facing up to the inherent contradictions in living, rather than by avoiding the anxiety this evoked by adhering to religious dogma or 'objective' science. Husserl and Heidegger were forerunners in the introduction of the phenomenological method as a means of exploring existential concepts in a rigorous way. The focus was on describing and understanding the essential aspects of life rather than analysing and explaining them. Sartre wrote from an existential perspective, focusing particularly on emotions, imagination and people's relationship to the social and political spheres (van Deurzen 2002).

Theoretical assumptions

Existential philosophy assumes that there is no such thing as an essential self. People define themselves in relation to the environment, including other people and are in a constant state of flux. Wartenberg (2008, in McLeod 2009) cites a number of key themes: being alone and with others (the individual versus the collective); self- multiplicity (the self being made up of various often conflicting parts); living in time (having a sense of the past, present and future and of how one's own death fits into this); agency and intentionality (a balance between being powerful and powerless and how much responsibility do we have for our own life); embodiment (the challenges of living within a body and what our body tells us) and truth (what does truth mean to us? Is it personal experience or scientific knowledge that informs our search for truth?).

Emmy van Deurzen (2002), a key writer on existential counselling, outlines the four basic dimensions of existence which are central to existential philosophy: the physical, the psychological, the social and the spiritual. It is the way we make sense of these various dimensions which determines what we aspire to and what we fear (van Deurzen 2002). The physical relates to our attitude to our body and its needs, our response to illness and to mortality. It also includes response to surroundings, to possessions and to other bodies. The conflicts here centre around attempts to control nature through keeping fit or use of medical procedures, or seeking temporary respite through health or wealth versus acceptance of one's bodily limitations. The social aspect concerns the ways we relate to the social world, including to our own and others' class, race and culture. Conflicts focus on belonging and acceptance versus isolation and rejection. The psychological dimension concerns how we relate to ourselves internally and includes our views about our personality, past and present experiences and future possibilities. Polarities include affirming or berating the self and being active or passive. The spiritual dimension concerns how we relate to the unknown and the ways we create a philosophical outlook. While some people find meaning through an established religious perspective, others create meaning in a more individual way. The conflict focuses around purpose and meaninglessness; hope and despair. People often search for something worth dying for or a way of overcoming or dealing with the anxiety-provoking issue of mortality.

Another central concern is anxiety or angst. This is seen as an inevitable consequence of caring about others and the world around us. A lack of this anxiety could in itself be problematic as it may reflect a sense of emptiness. Claringbull (2010) explains angst as resulting from the conflict between what is meaningful in our world and actual experience. We can reduce this conflict by recreating, or perceiving differently, ourselves or our worlds.

Existential therapy

Existential therapy regards psychological distress not as something within the client which needs to be addressed and worked through via therapy, but as the result of avoiding life's truths or being unable to cope with them. Many people cope with life by adopting certain roles and accepted beliefs which act as a buffer to the more terrifying aspects of existence. However, it is often a crisis such as a bereavement or loss of a job which shocks someone into becoming aware of their difficulties with facing life's realities. Boredom, as manifested in a sense of the futility of day-to-day routines, can also generate disturbance (van Deurzen 2002).

Social support networks are essential in helping people deal with the difficulties faced in life and particularly when crises occur. However, these networks are less available as communities disperse and society becomes more complex and demanding. Another issue, though, is whether the support that is available aims only to comfort rather than to also help the individual to face the difficulty and deal with it (van Deurzen 2002). Existential therapy is one way of working through the issues which arise out of the crisis and is particularly well suited to dealing with life crises.

The process of therapy

Part of the process of this type of therapy is becoming more aware of our mental state so that, rather than allowing it to function automatically, we can reflect upon it, make more considered choices and avoid making the same mistakes again and again. When someone experiences a crisis, they can be propelled into changing their habitual ways of thinking, which often results in growth. This type of therapy tends to be exploratory and to focus on a search for meaning and understanding. As with person-centred counselling there are no techniques as such, although phenomenological enquiry is used to get at the essential truth of an experience or feeling.

Some limitations

Since existential counselling is based on a complex philosophical framework, the key principles can be difficult to define, particularly as there is not one specific form of existential philosophy. There are also few specific techniques so applying the ideas to practice can be a confusing business. Often therapists find themselves borrowing techniques from other approaches (Corey 2009).

As a result of the above issues it is very difficult to undertake systematic research on existential counselling; indeed many existential counsellors, because of their philosophical outlook, are unlikely to value evidence-based practice and research.

Van-Deurzen (2002) emphasizes the importance of high levels of maturity, 'wisdom' and extensive training in order to be an effective existential counsellor. These requirements may be unrealistic for many people.

References

Claringbull, N. (2010) *What is Counselling and Psychotherapy?* Exeter: Learning Matters.

Corey, G. (2009) *Theory and Practice of Counselling and Psychotherapy*, 8th edn. Belmont, CA: Thompson Brooks-Cole.

Deurzen, E. van (2002) Existential therapy. In W. Dryden (ed.) *Handbook of Individual Therapy*, 4th edn. London: Sage.

McLeod, J. (2009) *An Introduction to Counselling*, 4th edn. Maidenhead: Open University Press.

Annotated further reading

Cooper, M. (2003) *Existential Therapies*. London: Sage.

A really good introduction to a range of existential approaches.

Yalom, I.D. (1989) *Love's Executioner and Other Tales of Psychotherapy*. Harmondsworth: Penguin.

An engaging and thought-provoking book which gives an insight into how a therapist might work with a range of clients facing existential dilemmas.

Eye movement desensitization and reprocessing (EMDR)

EMDR is a form of psychotherapy that was developed by Francine Shapiro to reduce trauma-related disorders caused by exposure to distressing events such as rape or war. The goal of EMDR is to process distressed memories, reducing their influence and allowing the patient to develop more adaptive coping mechanisms.

EMDR is now recommended as one of the two treatments of choice for post-traumatic stress disorders (PTSD) by the National Institute for Health and Clinical Excellence (NICE) in the UK. It is an innovative therapy that is useful for any condition where a specific memory or memories act as triggers for current and ongoing distress (childhood abuse and neglect, phobias, current anxieties, life events, obsessive compulsive disorder (OCD), eating disorders and others).

In 1989 the *Journal of Traumatic Stress* published a paper by a then unknown psychologist, Shapiro. Here she describes a new method (EMDR) which claims to totally change or at least improve long-term trauma that had led to OCD in a single treatment session.

As was to be expected her publication did not only lead to extreme interest in the world of trauma treatment but equally to severe scepticism. Joseph Wolpe, one of the founders of behaviour therapy, for example, had been convinced by the research that Shapiro had carried out and by the results he could see in large numbers of individuals. To this date he has edited and published over 30 papers in his *Journal of Behavioural Therapy and Experimental Psychiatry*.

There are significant communalities between EMDR and CBT, as for example the formulation of negative and positive beliefs in connection with post-traumatic stress disorder (PTSD), as well as cognitive restructuring. EMDR further integrates elements of various other approaches including psycho-dynamic, imaginal exposure, inter-personal, experiential, physiological and somatic therapies.

Neuropsychology and research into PTSD have shown that clients suffering from PTSD show a clear activation of the amygdala and the surrounding regions when being examined in a PET scanner. All the participants needed to do was to listen to a recording of 'their' trauma and their centre of fear was 'on fire', while at the same time their left prefrontal cortex – the part of the brain responsible for the expression of language – seemed completely 'frozen'.

Their ability to find words for the terror they had experienced was literally deactivated and inaccessible. This proves that when a traumatic or distressing experience occurs, it can overwhelm usual coping mechanisms, both neurological and cognitive.

Shapiro discovered that making people move their eyes back and forth, thus imitating rapid eye movements (REM) as experienced while dreaming, and also using tapping and tones, known as bilateral stimulation, can somehow rewire 'free floating' memories of the traumatic experience to such an extent that they can thereafter be 'filed' and stored as it were, no longer causing distress. Once filed and stored the clients could still remember the incident, but looked at it more like an observer, staying emotionally distant. After treatment cessation, the individual is no longer distressed, when the memory is accessed. Instead they recall the incident with a new perspective, new insight, resolution of the cognitive distortions, elimination of emotional distress, and relief of related physiological arousal.

In 1995 a study published in the *Journal of Consulting and Clinical Psychology* demonstrated that 80 per cent of participants experienced release from their traumatic symptoms within three 90-minute sessions. Fifteen months later the same benefits still continued!

EMDR attempts to bring to mind traumatic memory in all its varying components: ocular, emotional, cognitive and sensory (body memory) and then the client follows the therapist's hand moving rapidly back and forth. This process activates the 'adaptive information-processing system' in order to effectively metabolize the dysfunctional anxiety provoking memory. It facilitates quick access to all channels of association to the trauma and the past and as they are evoked, they seemingly connect with the cognitive networks that contain more appropriate information grounded in the 'now' (Servan-Schreiber 2004: 92).

Research for EMDR primarily focused on disorders coming from distressing life experiences; as mentioned above, post-traumatic stress disorder. But it remains controversial because research tends to question the methods and theoretical foundations of EMDR.

The therapy process and procedures are as follows:

Phase I starts with a discussion of the patient's history and a treatment plan. The therapist can attempt to identify targets and maladaptive beliefs. Phase II helps the client to discover a safe place or an image that elicits comfortable feelings. This safe place can be used to bring closure to a session that is incomplete, or to help a client tolerate any aspects of the session that are particularly upsetting.

Phase III attempts to create a snapshot image that represents the target and the disturbance associated with it. The image helps the client focus, and a positive and a negative cognition is identified.

Phase IV asks the client to focus on the image, the negative cognition, and the disturbing emotion. Then as described above, the client is also invited to follow a moving object with their eyes at the same time and is asked about what has come up during this process, anything from a thought to a memory.

Phase V is referred to as the installation phase and the client is asked about the positive cognition. Then the snapshot and the positive cognition are held together, again with eye movement monitored.

Phase VI contains a body scan, in which the client is asked if any pain or discomfort are still present, and if so, to focus on it. More eye movement is used to reduce these.

Phase VII, the debriefing session, refers to the therapist giving information and support and to help find inner balance by means of relaxation practices.

Phase VIII finally establishes a re-evaluation to see whether the trauma has been released. If not more sessions are arranged.

Three meta-analysis were carried out in the late 1990s and early 2000 which resulted in the outcome that EMDR was at least as effective as any other proven trauma treatment. Not only that, but it also proved to be the quickest and best tolerated intervention.

Reference

Servan-Schreiber, D. (2004) *Healing without Freud or Prozac*. London: Rodale.

Annotated further reading

Servan-Schreiber, D. (2004) *Healing without Freud or Prozac*. London: Rodale.

This very readable account by a psychiatrist who previously only prescribed medication and was by coincidence 'converted' to including broader spectrum therapies, offers two chapters on EMDR. It is a fluently written account and among the most useful self-help books on the market. The main difference is however that Schreiber includes an abundance of references that prove any of his hypotheses. In the year of its publication it reached No.1 international bestseller level!

Shapiro, F. (2001) *EMDR: Eye Movement Desensitization of Reprocessing: Basic Principles, Protocols and Procedures*, 2nd edn. New York: Guilford Press.

A short but helpful introduction to EMDR.

F

Feminist counselling

See also: assertiveness; integrative models; multicultural counselling

Feminist counselling has existed since the 1970s and has developed in tandem with the Women's Movement. There is no single school of feminist counselling, nor is there a single theoretical position or set of techniques. However, the central common premise upon which this approach to counselling is based is that most cultures are to some extent patriarchal resulting in the oppression of women by men. In addition, many of women's problems are not internally caused but result from, or are exacerbated by, the inequalities arising from living in a patriarchal society.

Examples of these inequalities include the fact that women have less power than men in many areas of society, including the work situation. Far more managers and bosses are men, while women are more prevalent in junior and menial roles. Women, unlike men, are expected to be supportive and nurturing and as a result often find it difficult to get their own needs met. Traditional concepts of female sexuality regard women as passive and sexually undemanding, so that women not adhering to this stereotype may be seen as deviant. There is intense pressure to conform to the sexualized and idealized images of women's bodies which are heavily used in advertising and the media. These and other inequalities inevitably impact on women's perceptions of themselves, often in a negative way.

Feminist counselling places emphasis on social and cultural factors as well as intra- and interpersonal ones. Jocelyn Chaplin (1999) described this approach as a different way of being and one which recognizes 'the deep interconnectedness of our "internal" psychological worlds with the "external" social and material worlds' (Chaplin 1999: 5). It not only considers male/female inequalities, but also those such as race, disability and sexuality as these too can result in discrimination.

Many feminist counsellors are integrative or eclectic in their approach, drawing on a range of theoretical perspectives. A brief discussion follows of how feminist counsellors have both developed and rejected aspects of the some of the main theoretical perspectives.

Psychoanalysis

Some of Freud's psychoanalytic ideas such as penis envy and his interpretation of children's disclosure of sexual abuse as fantasies are now regarded as outdated and, in the case of the latter, unethical. Indeed there has been a forceful feminist critique of psychoanalytic and psychodynamic psychotherapy. Having said this, followers of Freud such as Karen Horney (1924, cited in Chaplin 1999) recognized that women's envy was more about men's dominant position in society than about physical differences, so identifying social factors as having an influence on women's mental health. The Women's Therapy Centre in London was established by Eichenbaum and Orbach, two feminist object relations therapists, who focused on issues such as eating disorders, and who developed the premise that personal problems need to be understood, at least in part, as methods of coping with societal inequalities, rather than as individual dysfunctions.

Humanistic approaches

Humanistic concepts such as personal empowerment, growth and relative equality between counsellor and client sit comfortably with many feminist counsellors. Principles such as empathy, genuineness and, more controversially, self-disclosure are cited by Irene Bruna Seu (2006) as being used by some feminist counsellors to create a more equal counselling relationship than existed in some previous approaches to counselling.

Cognitive-behavioural approaches

Techniques such as assertiveness training, role-play and behavioural experiments can be used to assist clients in challenging existing inequalities. The development of certain skills can serve to empower clients in their day-to-day lives.

Goals of feminist counselling

One of the main aims of feminist counselling is to help women to break free of restricting sex-role stereotypes and to define themselves in other ways. This may include identifying their own needs and values which may have been buried beneath social expectations. More radical feminist counselling has a highly politicized agenda and places strong emphasis on social action to fight discrimination. Violence or the threat of it is seen as central to women's lives (Burstow, 1992 in McLeod 2009)

According to Bruna Seu (2006) work with clients is likely to include: helping them to find social or personal solutions to their problems rather than pathologizing the person; enhancing the self-reliance of the client by discussing the process and direction of the counselling and by recognizing and focusing on strategies to address the power imbalance between client and counsellor; developing the client's awareness of their oppression and focusing on ways to combat this; encouraging feelings and behaviour which a client may find difficult due to sex-role stereotyping (for example meeting their own needs or expressing anger).

Research findings

There is, as yet, little research evidence to demonstrate the effectiveness of feminist counselling. This may result in this approach being excluded from settings which will increasingly only support 'evidence-based' approaches (McLeod 2009).

Critical perspectives

There are inevitably potential difficulties with perceiving women's psychological problems as resulting predominantly from external factors, just as there are with seeing them as originating entirely from within the individual. The emphasis on the former in feminist counselling may lead to a failure to focus on important psychological factors.

Another criticism levelled at feminist counselling is that practitioners could use their position and influence over vulnerable clients to promote their feminist viewpoint. Also the emphasis sometimes placed on equality in the therapeutic relationship and on the value of self-disclosure by the counsellor could result in a blurring of the professional boundaries.

References

Bruna Seu, I. (2006) Feminist psychotherapy. In C. Feltham and I. Horton (eds) *The SAGE Handbook of Counselling and Psychotherapy*. London: Sage.

Chaplin, J. (1999) *Feminist Counselling in Action*, 2nd edn. London: Sage.

McLeod, J. (2009) *An Introduction to Counselling*. Maidenhead: Open University Press.

Annotated further reading

Chaplin, J. (1999) *Feminist Counselling in Action*. London: Sage.

Still relevant in that it explores feminist themes and issues in a practical way, effectively relating them to case examples.

Ross, L.R. (ed.) (2010) *Feminist Counselling: Theory, Issues and Practice*, 2nd edn. London: Sage.

An informative collection of articles on a wide range of issues.

Free association

See also: psychoanalysis; psychodynamic therapy; interpretation; dream analysis

Free association is a technique most commonly associated with psychoanalysis and psychodynamic therapy, although it may also be used in other approaches which draw on psychodynamic methods. In brief, the client is encouraged to talk about anything that springs to mind without any need to consider whether it is meaningful or logically presented. The reason for free association being so central to the psychodynamic approach even to this day, is that it is seen to facilitate access to the client's unconscious mind. As the client talks in this unstructured and relatively uninhibited way, their fears, hopes and fantasies are far more likely to be revealed than if the therapist posed a series of questions or imposed a structure on the session in some other way. The underlying assumption here is that thoughts and images in the client's conscious mind, which are expressed when free associating, often originate from the client's unconscious mind which is trying to find a form of expression. This unconscious material may not be immediately clear to either client or therapist, but if the therapist succeeds in skilfully interpreting and making links between what the client is saying, the client can become more aware of their unconscious processes. For example, the therapist might pick up signs of repression in a client's hesitation or resistance to their interpretations.

The use of the couch is an important tool in facilitating free association. Although rarely used in once-weekly sessions, it is common in more frequent sessions where the work is of greater intensity and depth. The lack of face-to-face contact is aimed at reducing the need to demonstrate and respond to social cues, thus enabling the client to get in touch with whatever comes into their mind. The therapist is also enabled to engage in free floating attention (Jacobs 2005) so as to focus on the client's associations and to identify reasons for the client's defences and resistance. The other important area that the therapist will explore is how the therapeutic relationship (the relationship between the therapist and client) reflects the client's other relationships, both past and present. Use of the 'rule of abstinence' or holding back, if done sensitively rather than punitively, can also assist the client in free associating (Jacobs 2010).

Free association is not limited to use with adults. Melanie Klein believed that it was possible to analyse children from the age of 2 years. Kleinian analysts who work with children may interpret the therapeutic relationship using free association as well as the use of play (Cooper 2002).

A range of eclectic and integrative approaches use free association as one of a range of techniques. For example, cognitive analytic therapy (CAT), an integrative approach which also employs role-play, active emotional expression, word association and CBT exercises, may encourage client free association to assist with freeing up emotional or cognitive expression (Dunn 2002).

There is very little empirical evidence to support the effectiveness of free association, just as there is very little to support much of the psychodynamic approach. This does not necessarily mean that it is not effective with some clients. (See Cooper 2008 for a detailed discussion of the quantity and value of the research evidence for a wide range of therapeutic approaches and techniques.) However, there is some evidence which suggests that interpretation, which therapists use to highlight patterns or links between past and present experiences, relationships or thoughts, feelings and behaviours in the material generated via free association, can be effective (Cooper 2008).

There are inevitably potential problems with the use and interpretation of free association by therapists, particularly if they are not well trained in the use of the technique. For example, therapists may interpret a client's hesitancy as evidence of resistance, when it may be that their interpretation is inaccurate. This may be damaging to clients who are already emotionally vulnerable. That said, clients, therapists and observers have consistently rated interpretations as one of the most helpful therapist responses (Elliot et al. 1982; Hill et al. 1988, in Cooper 2008).

References

Cooper, C. (2002) Psychodynamic therapy: the Kleinian approach. In W. Dryden (ed.) *Handbook of Individual Therapy*, 4th edn. London: Sage.

Cooper, M. (2008) *Essential Research Findings in Counselling and Psychotherapy: The Facts are Friendly*. London: Sage.

Dunn, M. (2002) Cognitive analytic therapy. In W. Dryden (ed.) *Handbook of Individual Therapy*, 4th edn. London: Sage.

Jacobs, M. (2005) *The Presenting Past: The Core of Psychodynamic Counselling and Psychotherapy*. Maidenhead: McGraw-Hill.

Jacobs, M. (2010) *Psychodynamic Counselling in Action*, 4th edn. London: Sage.

Annotated further reading

Jacobs, M. (2010) *Psychodynamic Counselling in Action*, 4th edn. London: Sage.

An excellent introduction to this and other psychodynamic concepts from a practical perspective.

Klein, M. (2001) *Psychodynamic Counselling Primer*. Ross-on-Wye: PCCS Books.

A concise introduction to the main concepts, which is particularly suitable for those new to the subject.

Freud, Sigmund (1856–1939)

See also: Freudian analysis; free association; structural model of mind; psychosexual development; defence mechanisms

Freud, along with Charles Darwin, Albert Einstein and Karl Marx, has been acknowledged as one of the foremost thinkers and person of influence of the nineteenth/twentieth centuries. Freud's work on the unconscious and psychoanalysis continue to be inextricably integrated into twenty-first-century popular culture (Bocock 1983; Gay 1995; Horrocks 2001) with his concepts and ideas frequently used in everyday conversation by people, perhaps only minimally aware of their origins.

Sigmund Freud was born in Freiberg, Moravia (then part of the Austro-Hungarian Empire now the Czech Republic) in 1856 but died in London aged 83, having left Vienna where he had spent most of his working life, fleeing from Nazi persecution.

He was born into a Jewish family, but although well versed in Jewish culture, his father influenced his family away from their religious roots. Freud's Jewishness nevertheless had a major influence on him throughout his life. He was raised as a Jewish 'atheist' as were many Austrian and German middle-class Jews in the late nineteenth century, but despite rejection of his religion he was subjected to anti-semitism in a number of forms that impacted both on his personal and family life as well as his career (Frosh 2005; Geller 2007).

Freud's background however was probably the inspiration for everything that followed and perhaps even influenced the progress and evolution of the psychoanalytic movement.

Freud's professional background

Freud trained in medicine, being particularly interested in neurology, which led him to work with Charcot in Paris (in the mid-1880s) to examine hypnosis and hysteria. On his return to Vienna, Freud advocated the clinical use of hypnotism but was pilloried for that and also for publicly representing some of Charcot's other 'radical' ideas, one of which was that men, as well as women, could suffer from hysteria. Building on from theoretical and clinical work on hypnosis and hysteria, Freud developed the technique of **free association** which he saw as more successful than hypnosis for treating hysteria. Free association was an effective way of overcoming a patient's **resistance** to psycho-analytic inquiry. So instead of focusing the patient upon a particular issue of concern (such as their headache or anxiety), Freud suggested they say anything that came into their head. This ensured there was no *conscious* direction to their thoughts. Freud argued that it was essential for the patient to report liter-ally everything and not censor material brought into the analytic situation. The overall aim was to bring repressed material into consciousness rather than hold back anything by resistances – see **defence mechanisms**). If the patient applied what Freud saw as the fundamental rule of psychoanalysis, engaging in free association, then unconscious material would be available to the analytic situation (see Gay 1995: 24–6) (see **Freudian analysis**).

The unconscious

Although the concept of the unconscious was familiar to some extent before Freud (e.g. in literature as with Wordsworth, Shakespeare and Goethe) and philosophy (e.g. Neitzsche, Schopenhauer and Feuerbach) (Bocock 1983) there is a sense that 'no one knew the insights were there in the early writers *before* a thinker like Freud' (Bocock 1983: 18). Freud's innovation though was to refine the idea and build it into the centre of a systematic psychological theory, which included being one of the three levels of the psyche (mind) conscious, preconscious and unconscious (Craib 2001) (see **structural model of the mind**). The unconscious was for Freud the most important part of the psychic dynamic as it was the most primitive and contained both repressed and potentially unacceptable material that was inaccessible and the source of neurotic and psychotic behaviours. Material in the unconscious, for Freud, was sexual.

Despite the many scientists among Freud's contemporaries who chal-lenged the notion of the unconscious he firmly believed that the unconscious is both 'necessary' and 'legitimate' and he claimed to hold numerous proofs of its existence. He argued that it was *necessary* because the data of consciousness have a very large number of gaps and there is often no evidence for psychical acts in healthy, neurotic or mentally disturbed people in consciousness. Conscious acts are connected and intelligible. However, sometimes acts are only rendered intelligible if the related unconscious processes are revealed. Freud said that he could go further in support of an unconscious state in that at any given moment consciousness occupies only a small part of our mind, so our knowledge and thoughts about other things must exist unconsciously. He felt he had made the point so plainly that he failed to see how the existence and activity of the unconscious could be denied (even though for many, including many academic psychologists, it is denied).

The assumption that the existence of an unconscious is *legitimate*, he proposed, is argued thus: that we are aware of our own consciousness and make the valid assumption that others too have such a consciousness and from this we draw inference about them and their motives. Freud argued that if we apply to ourselves the same inference, i.e. that there is another, second consciousness 'which is united in oneself in the consciousness one knows', then we might also assume a third and fourth level of consciousness and that with psychoanalysis the internal objects are less unknowable then the external world (see Gay 1995: 572–7). Thus for Freud the human struggle is to make sense of what is happening externally (in reality) and relating that to what is going on at every level of our internal world (see **Freudian analysis**).

In the twenty-first century such convoluted arguments are no longer necessary. Popular understanding of Freud's model of the unconscious is well known as an everyday concept and among social scientists it is a useful mechanism for explaining a range of contradictions in human individual and social behaviours. Horrocks (2001) describes Freud's propositions as postulating a fundamental incoherence between the surface and what lies underneath, i.e. the unconscious (Horrocks 2001: 1) confirming that Freud once and for all shattered the idea that human beings are homogeneous and rational. Freud went on to publish several influential papers based on his early work, about his 'talking cure' and the role of the unconscious as central to the psychoanalytic process.

Infantile sexuality and fantasies of sexual abuse

Freud saw sexuality as 'sensuality' with both pleasure and pain. Pain is the increase in tension within the organism (he tended to employ biological terms to elucidate his theory) and pleasure is the removal or relief from the pain and tension. He considered that a degree of tension is central to life but beyond a certain threshold the organism needs relief from the pain and tension.

In 1914 (although not published until 1918) Freud wrote his case history of 'Wolf Man', which reintroduced the idea of infantile sexuality that was still not 'acceptable' to the prestigious Viennese medical circle, who once again castigated Freud for these ideas. The case study began with questions about the Wolf Man's observation of his parents' sexual intercourse which may or may not have been a dream but ultimately after several years in analysis was at the root of his anxieties, depression and emotional disturbances.

Freud's thinking and its developments are well documented and he wrote and lectured copiously about his work almost until his death in 1939.

Major works

Perhaps his most important works include in 1900 *The Interpretation of Dreams* (Freud 1900), *Totem and Taboo* (Freud 1914), *Introductory Lectures* (Freud 1917) and *Group Psychology and the Analysis of the Ego* (Freud 1921) (see **groups**).

Freud's structural model of mind is dealt with elsewhere, as is his model of **psychosexual development**.

Psychoanalytic theory, thinking and practice have evolved since his work and ideas. However, many theorists and psychoanalysts still identify with classic Freudian thinking (see **psychoanalysis**).

Research and evaluation

Does psychoanalysis (Freudian or any other version) lend itself to research (Emde and Fonagy 1997)? It has been a problem in the past to measure outcome and effectiveness of psychoanalysis by its nature and because there has been resistance among clinicians who have held a general mistrust of the research methods available (Busch and Milrod 2010). Certainly there have been several attempts to evaluate the outcome of psychoanalytic and psychodynamic therapies particularly in comparison to other methods of counselling and psychotherapy (Leichsenring and Leibing 2007; Shapiro et al. 2003). There is a tendency in the literature, and for political and economic reasons, to support the effectiveness of brief psychotherapies (e.g. cognitive behavioural therapy or cognitive analytic psychotherapy) over the longer-lasting psychoanalysis or psychoanalytic psychotherapy, although now there is a growing evidence base suggesting the effectiveness of psychoanalysis for neurotic and some psychotic conditions. One recent study suggests the competence of the therapist is a crucial factor (over and above the method of therapy provided). Controlled quasi-experimental effectiveness studies provide evidence that psychoanalytic therapy is (1) more effective than no treatment or treatment as usual, and (2) more effective than shorter forms of psychodynamic therapy (Leichsenring 2005).

References

Bocock, R. (1983) *Sigmund Freud*. London: Tavistock.

Busch, F.N. and Milrod, B.L. (2010) The ongoing struggle for psychoanalytic research: some steps forward. *Psychoanalytic Psychotherapy*, 24(4): 306–14.

Craib, I. (2001) *Psychoanalysis: A Critical Introduction*. Cambridge: Polity.

Emde, R.N. and Fonagy, P. (1997) An emerging culture for psychoanalytic research? *The International Journal of Psychoanalysis*, 78: 643–51.

Freud, S. (1900) *The Interpretation of Dreams* (Vol. S.E. 4, 1953). London: Hogarth Press.

Freud, S. (1914) *Totem and Taboo* (Vol. S.E. 13, 1–161, 1955). London: Hogarth Press.

Freud, S. (1917) *Introductory Lectures on Psychoanalysis* (Vol. S.E. 15, 1953). London: Hogarth Press.

Freud, S. (1921) *Group Psychology and the Analysis of the Ego* (Vol. S.E. 13, 1955). London: Hogarth Press.

Frosh, S. (2005) *Hate and the 'Jewish Science': Anti-seminitism, Nazism and Psychoanalysis*. Basingstoke: Palgrave.

Gay, P. (1995) *The Freud Reader*. London: Vintage.

Geller, J. (2007) *On Freud's Jewish Body: Mitigating Circumcisions*. New York: Fordham University Press.

Horrocks, R. (2001) *Freud Revisited: Psychoanalytic Themes in the Postmodern Age*. Basingstoke: Palgrave.

Leichsenring, F. (2005) Are psychodynamic and psychoanalytic therapies effective?: a review of empirical data. *The International Journal of Psychoanalysis*, 86(3): 841–68.

Leichsenring, F. and Leibing, E. (2007) Psychodynamic psychotherapy: a systematic review of techniques, indications and empirical evidence. *Psychology and Psychotherapy: Theory, Research and Practice*, 80(2): 217–28.

Shapiro, D.A., Barkham, M., Stiles, W.B. et al. (2003) Time is of the essence: a selective review of the fall and rise of brief therapy research. *Psychology and Psychotherapy: Theory, Research and Practice*, 76(3): 211–35.

Wright, E. (1992) *Feminism and Psychoanalysis: A Critical Dictionary*. Oxford: Blackwell.

Annotated further reading

Peter Gay's book, *The Freud Reader*, contains over 830 pages of extracts from Freud's most important works including some of his autobiographical writing. Craib, Geller, Frosh and Horrocks below provide different but interconnected accounts of his life and work which are insightful and easy to read.

Craib, I. (2001). *Psychoanalysis: A Critical Introduction*. Cambridge: Polity.

Craib provides a helpful overview of Freud's work from a critical perspective.

Frosh, S. (2005) *Hate and the 'Jewish Science': Anti-seminitism, Nazism and psychoanalysis*. Basingstoke: Palgrave.

This book shows the political context in which psychoanalytic thinking emerged and particularly how Freud became positioned within the subsequent psychoanalytic movement.

Gay, P. (1995) *The Freud Reader*. London: Vintage.

Peter Gay's book *The Freud Reader* contains over 830 pages of extracts from Freud's most important works including some of his autobiographical writing. Part One includes his early ideas (including the case of Anna O), Part Two onwards provides classic theories, extracts about therapies and techniques (including the case of the Wolf Man) as well as his papers which revise his early ideas and some of his later considerations including **negation** and the dissolution of the **Oedipus complex**.

Geller, J. (2007) *On Freud's Jewish Body: Mitigating Circumcisions*. New York: Fordham University Press.

Geller discussed the influence of Freud's Jewish background (which is complex and about which Freud is ambivalent) on his life and work.

Freudian analysis

See also: Freud, Sigmund; defence mechanisms; dream analysis; free association

Freudian psychoanalysis was based upon the work of Sigmund Freud (see **Freud, Sigmund**) particularly his theory of the unconscious and the use of *free association* as the method. As one psychoanalyst put it: 'Psychoanalysis cannot be taught . . . Because it can occur only through a personal act of understanding' (Symington 1986: 15). The aim is to investigate the unconscious to understand the individual's external behaviour and thus reach some 'truth' about reality.

The setting

Psychoanalysis takes place between two people – the analyst and analysand/patient – over several years (at least three) and either four of five times a week for around 42 weeks each year. Thus it is both intensive and extensive. The focus is upon the analysand's inner world and reaching a greater understanding or link between external reality and that inner world. The analytic training is equally (if not more) long and intensive. It is vital within Freudian (and Kleinian) analysis that the analyst has their own psychoanalysis and continues to have psychoanalytic supervision to work with the unconscious issues between the patient/analysand and themselves.

The ritual is important. The analysand lies on a couch with the analyst sitting behind them. The analysis takes place in the neutral space of the consulting room in which, apart from the necessary furniture (and perhaps a clock and tissues), there should be no identity or character. However, as every analyst in one collection of analytical and critical anecdotes have proposed (Raphael-Leff 2002), this space has an atmosphere, 'inhabited by the analyst's soul' (or energy) and by the invisible presence of the patients who visit daily. No analytic rule or strict analytic setting can avoid the primary fact that there is an encounter between two people and that unavoidable events develop in a session triggered by expressions, gestures, movements and voice.

The process

Two people are in a room together for 50 minutes and during that time interactions occur on conscious and unconscious levels and these interactions relate to the present (i.e. what is going on in the room) and to the past (i.e. events that are in the patient's conscious memory and in primitive form in their unconscious). This is also true for the psychoanalyst. In the 'ideal' version the patient talks using free association and at some junctures the analyst makes an interpretation verbally (although it is likely that the analyst will also begin to develop thinking about interpretations without verbalizing them). While the aim is to investigate the patient's unconscious the process involves the analysis of the relationship in the room.

Transference is the unconscious transfer of feelings for one person (e.g. the patient's mother) to another – in this case the analyst. This happens naturally between people who meet each other in everyday circumstances. So for example we may take an instant dislike to someone although we cannot immediately say why. However, we behave towards them *as if* there is a reason for that dislike transferring feelings that in reality belong to someone else to this new person.

In the psychoanalytic context, the patient knows nothing much about their psychoanalyst and thus the material that emerges from acting on and discussing their relationship enables insights into unconscious motivation and repressed feelings (see **defence mechanisms**). Initially Freud believed that transference in analysis was a barrier to treatment but came to believe that the transference was central to the analytic process.

Countertransference occurs when the analyst has a logically inexplicable feeling when with a particular analysand/patient. For instance they may feel as if they want to scream with frustration or feel drained of energy. One example was that an analyst felt fat even though neither she nor the patient was overweight. However, she eventually discovered that this had been a fear of the patient's who had once been very overweight (Orbach 2000) and this insight opened further therapeutic opportunities. As with transference, Freud initially identified countertransference as a barrier, describing it as a neurotic disturbance in the psychoanalyst that got in the way of taking an objective view of the patient. However, it is now increasingly recognized to be 'the most important source of information about the patient as well as a major element of the interaction between patient and analyst' (Segal 1993: 13). It was Paula Heimann who particularly drew attention to the importance of countertransference (see **Kleinian analysis**) while classical Freudian analysis pays it less attention.

Projection, as with other defence mechanisms, is a means of reducing anxiety. Projection is a defensive process whereby an individual denies their own feelings (often unacceptable ones) and attributes them to another. In psychoanalysis a patient may unconsciously feel that the analyst is hostile to them for example, when in fact the patient themselves feels hostile to the analyst and to others. Once this is identified, the analyst and the patient can explore the origins and the expression of those feelings. (See **projective identification** and **Kleinian analysis**.)

Dreams

Freud considered dreams to be a vital source of unconscious information and central to the material available to the analytic couple (Freud 1900). He used the same method of free association with dreams as with other analytic material and in the context of his own dreams would write them down without trying to censor or make any sense of them at the time of writing. He then made associations to the people and actions in his dreams. Similarly he expected his patients to report dream material in a similar way and then to make associations with the analyst.

Freud suggests dreams are about wish fulfillment. The content is disguised (or 'censored') through representation of repressed material via different symbols such as familiar places and people (Freud 1952/1989: 65). He considered that far from dreams being disturbances of sleep they were the guardians of sleep and the dream symbolization was a way to defend ourselves against primitive desires (Freud 1900).

References

Freud, S. (1900) *The Interpretation of Dreams* (Vol. S.E. 4, 1953). London: Hogarth Press.
Freud, S. (1952/1989) *On Dreams*. London: W.W. Norton and Co.
Orbach, S. (2000) *The Impossibility of Sex*. Harmondsworth: Penguin.

Raphael-Leff, J. (2002) *Between Sessions and Beyond the Couch*. Colchester: Centre for Psychoanalytic Studies, University of Essex.

Sayers, J. (1997) *Freudian Tales: About Imagined Men*. London: Vintage.

Segal, H. (1993) Countertransference. In A. Alexandris and G. Vaslamatzis (eds) London: Karnac.

Symington, N. (1986) *The Analytic Experience: Lectures from the Tavistock*. London: Free Association Books.

Annotated further reading

Raphael-Leff's book makes good reading. It is a series of accounts by psycho-analysts about their feelings between sessions with their patients although not all the analysts are Freudian. Kleinian analysis is more common in the UK than Freudian, although nevertheless some of the processes and concepts overlap. Horrocks is easy to read and brings in clinical examples with a new interpretation of Freud's work. Janet Sayers' *Freudian Tales* (Sayers 1997) using case studies of women and patriarchy is also a good and informative read.

G

Games

See also: assertiveness; drama triangle; life scripts; transactional analysis

Games is a central concept in transactional analysis (TA), most famously described in *Games People Play* (Berne 1964). A game in TA is an interaction between two or more people who have hidden motives and which leads to a pay off such as feeling depressed or hurt or confirming a view of the world as 'Not OK' in some way. They are therefore not fun and can be very serious indeed. They are essentially dishonest.

For example – and Berne gave his games catchy names which some people find appealing and others unprofessional – in 'Why don't you – yes but' (YDYB) one person complains, the other suggests a solution and the first person says 'Yes but . . .'. The first person knows at some level of their awareness that they won't act on any of the suggestions made, and the second person knows the first will reject each suggestion yet continues to offer them. A possible pay-off for each of them is that one wants to feel helpless and the other to show that they care and that they want to help.

YDYB was the first game detected by Berne and led to him and others finding or creating many more. For example, UGMIT is 'You Got Me Into This' and NIGYSOB is 'Now I've Got You, You Son of a Bitch'.

Berne saw it as possible and desirable to be free of games and therefore more capable of the 'real living of real intimacy' (1964: 17). To escape from a game, first observe it perhaps through noticing that something is 'going on', then assertively decline to play. For example, in another game called 'Ain't it awful' one person wants to complain and be agreed with and perhaps escalate the complaining. The other person can decline to play, for example by saying 'It sounds as if you've decided things are hopeless' (an empathic response) or 'I see things differently' (a challenging response) or 'You sound really unhappy about this. I wonder if it's worth looking for some solutions' (empathy plus challenging).

References

Berne, E. (1964) *Games People Play*. Harmondsworth: Penguin.

Annotated further reading

Berne, E. (1964) *Games People Play*. Harmondsworth: Penguin.

> Analyses the idea of games, describes numerous games and has a final
> section on 'Beyond games'. It was reissued in 2010.

Gestalt therapy

See also: humanistic approaches; person-centred counselling; existential
counselling

Developed by Fritz and Laura Perls and Paul Goodman in the 1950s, Gestalt
therapy, like person-centred counselling and transactional analysis, is founded
in the humanistic tradition. It is similar to these other approaches in a number
of ways. The focus is on individual freedom, authenticity and responsibility,
on the natural tendency of the human organism towards growth and on the
central importance and validity of an individual's perception of their experience. It differs from the person-centred approach in its focus on conflict
between different parts of the self and on its use of active, experiential work
within sessions, which could include enacting issues in a dramatic way.
Although a relatively small number of therapists would describe their main
theoretical orientation as Gestalt, this approach has had a significant influence
on the development of humanistic therapy.

Gestalt psychology proposes that human beings strive to create meaning in
their lives and that it is the whole pattern or shape of an individual's sensory
experience, rather than the individual elements, which they use to arrive at that
meaning. So it is a piece of music as a whole, its tune or harmony, which we
hear and which is meaningful rather than all the separate notes (Hough 2010).
The word 'gestalt' is German for 'pattern', 'shape' or 'form'. Another central
premise is that people develop self-awareness through direct experience rather
than, for example, focusing on the past or on mainly thoughts or feelings.

Perls, for the purposes of Gestalt therapy, proposed that in order to be
psychologically healthy, people need to be aware of all aspects of themselves,
including their physical, emotional, cognitive and spiritual elements. Health is
about all these parts being integrated within ourselves. He also focused upon
how people become aware of their own needs in relation to the external environment, which includes other people, as it is the satisfactory fulfilment of these
continually emerging needs which keeps people in a state of equilibrium. When
Gestalt therapists refer to figure and ground, the figure is the individual's needs

at any particular moment and the ground is the background of awareness against which they see their needs. If the most important need at the time is met it will fade into the (back)ground, enabling other needs to emerge. This is known as the formation and destruction of Gestalts. The emphasis is on there being an interdependent relationship between an individual and their environment (Hough 2010).

Other important aspects of the theoretical framework include self actual-ization/developing the individual's potential, and the central significance of the present. Although significant childhood relationships may have affected someone's ability to recognize their needs and to meet them, any issues from the past are dealt with in the present by experiencing the past in the present as part of the therapy. So a client may, for example, be helped to get in touch with strong feelings from the past which may no longer be within their awareness, but which may be preventing other needs from being met.

Like many other theoretical approaches to counselling or therapy, the Gestalt model is a complex one, so that only some of the key aspects can be covered here. Ellis and Smith (2006) outline the links between this approach and existentialism, including the focus on an individual's responsibility for their own existence and the importance of exploring their existence from a phenomenological perspective. There are also links with eastern philosophy and religion with a shift from over-reliance on thinking to an awareness of the importance of the present moment and on allowing things to emerge.

In terms of techniques, clients are encouraged to get in touch with aspects of themselves which they may be ignoring. For example, if someone seems very out of touch with their bodily sensations, the therapist will focus on the body and what it conveys. Similarly, the 'empty chair technique' can be used to encourage a client to talk to conflicting aspects of the self or to someone else in the past or present with whom they are in conflict. It is crucial that the therapist is able to establish a counselling relationship based on authentic contact and trust.

Research findings

There has not been a great deal of research into this approach. However, what has been undertaken has tended to focus on the 'empty chair technique'. This has been shown to be effective in situations such as imaginary conversations with abusive parents or carers (Paivio et al. 2001, in Cooper 2008).

Limitations

This approach not only demands a high level of participation and creativity from the counsellor but also from the client. As such it will not appeal to all, including those who do not see the value in making links between physical and emotional parts of themselves. Clients from some eastern cultures may not find it appropriate to focus on bodily sensations, expression of strong feelings or role-play with others including with the deceased (Hough 2010).

References

Cooper, M. (2008) *Essential Research Findings in Counselling and Psychotherapy: The Facts are Friendly*. London: Sage.

Ellis, M. and Smith, J. (2006) Gestalt therapy. In C. Feltham and I. Horton (eds) *The SAGE Handbook of Counselling and Psychotherapy*, 2nd edn. London: Sage.

Hough, M. (2010) *Counselling Skills and Theory*. London: Hodder Education.

Annotated further reading

Clarkson, P. (2004) *Gestalt Counselling in Action*, 3rd edn. London: Sage.

Clearly demonstrates how the theory works in practice.

Hough, M. (2010) *Counselling Skills and Theory*. London: Hodder Education.

The chapter on Gestalt therapy and psychodrama contains one of the clearest descriptions of the key concepts and techniques of Gestalt therapy. For readers wanting a little more detail than is included here, but who are also new to the approach, it is an excellent introduction.

Joyce, P. and Sills, C. (2009) *Skills in Gestalt Counselling and Psychotherapy*. London: Sage.

Covers both the theory and process of Gestalt counselling really well.

Goal consensus

See also: client feedback, collecting; collaborative empiricism; integrative models; personality; the therapeutic relationship

Early in counselling, counsellors and clients generally discuss what the client hopes to achieve from their time together. This aspect of counselling can include numerous elements, for example how much the goals are discussed, how much agreement there is about them, how much the counsellor explains the nature of counselling and how committed the client is to their goals. Tryon and Winograd (2011), whose formal definition includes the elements above and others, concluded on the basis of a meta-analysis of 15 studies that 'better outcomes can be expected when patient and therapist agree on therapeutic goals and the processes to achieve those goals' (p. 50). Like collecting feedback from clients, goal consensus is a concept that can apply in all schools of counselling and psychotherapy.

Tryon and Winograd (2011) also carried out a meta-analysis of 19 studies on the closely related concept of collaboration, and concluded that 'outcome appears to be considerably enhanced when patient and therapist are actively involved in a cooperative relationship' (p. 50). Collaboration means working together in an active and assertive way rather than a passive or submissive one.

One problem with research into both goal consensus and collaboration is the variety of measures used, which is partly the result of different definitions used. Another is that the relationships with therapeutic outcome are correlational and thus it may be quality of relationship leading to greater consensus and collaboration, or both processes may be involved.

Reference

Tryon, G.S. and Winograd, G. (2011) Goal consensus and collaboration. *Psychotherapy*, 48(1): 50–7.

Annotated further reading

Tryon, G.S. and Winograd, G. (2011) Goal consensus and collaboration. *Psychotherapy*, 48(1): 50–7.

The authors make several recommendations for therapeutic practice, for example to encourage clients to be active participants, though their tone may seem somewhat paternalistic. However, their final recommendation is an adventurous one: 'modify your treatment methods and relational stance, if ethically and clinically appropriate in response to patient feedback' (p. 56). This concept is discussed in the entry for **preferences** as the 'authentic chameleon issue'.

Groups

See also: basic assumption groups; Bion, Wilfred R.

What is a group?

There are inconsistencies across the disciplines of psychology, psychodynamic theory and social science generally about the meaning of the 'group'. Typically definitions of the group relate to its function, the nature of its membership (i.e. why people join and whether membership is voluntary), its goals and eventual purpose. For example a group has been described as an aggregate of individuals standing in relation(s) to each other (Cartwright and Zander 1968). Similarly 'a plurality of persons who interact with one another in a given context more than they interact with anyone else' (Sprott 1977: 9). Also 'a number of persons who communicate with one another often over a span of time, and who are few enough so that each person is able to communicate with all the others, not at secondhand, through other people, but face-to-face' (Homans 1975: 1). These classic definitions and descriptions are typically reductionist, stripping richness from the 'group' for the purpose of 'measuring' and predicting behaviours.

Groups such as those described above are referred to as *primary groups* and include the family and the therapeutic group. However a 'virtual' group, such as Facebook, may also be defined as a primary group. There are also *secondary groups* which do not necessarily come face-to-face, although potential members have characteristics in common, e.g. members of an organization.

Why is the 'group' important for understanding human experience? There are alternative traditions from which theories of group dynamics have emerged. These are psychoanalysis and (to a lesser extent) early social psychology.

Psychoanalysis and the group

From the beginning of life we are faced with relating to the 'other' from whom we gain our sense of 'self', physically, emotionally and intra-psychically (Bowlby 1977; Klein 1959/1993; Winnicott 1965). The boundary between 'self' and 'other' does not correspond to the boundary of the physical body as our mental life, from the start, involves the introjection and projection of objects and part objects (Spillius 2007). Bion had clear views on the importance of this work as it relates to groups: 'I consider that group mental life is essential to the full life of the individual, quite apart from any temporary or specific need, and that satisfaction of this need has to be sought through membership of a group' (Bion 1961/1983: 54).

The first significant attempt at an analysis of group behaviour was made at the start of the twentieth century by Le Bon (1920) whose book *The Crowd* (1895/2009) illustrated his observation that individuals in a large group demonstrate behaviour that does not constitute the total of their behaviour as individuals. He considered that a 'collective mind' emerges when people are bound together in some way and that in addition, forces of contagion and suggestibility are at work so that the group acts as if it were hypnotized.

In the same year McDougall's book *The Group Mind* (1922/2005) was published and in *Group Psychology and the Analysis of the Ego* (1921/1922), Freud developed Le Bon's and McDougall's ideas in the context of psychodynamic theory, arguing that the binding force of the group derives from the *emotional* ties of the members, which are expressions of their libido.

Studies of group psychology developed quickly during and after the Second World War. In Britain the work of Wilfred Bion, Tom Maine, Maxwell Jones and others led to innovations in group psychotherapy and the study of organizations through psychoanalytic theory. One important outcome was the therapeutic community (e.g. Whiteley 1970). Another was Bion's work which led to the Group Relations Training Programme (GRTP) at the Tavistock Institute in 1957. This evolved into the Leicester Conferences with other organizations using this model across the world (Miller 1999).

In the USA during the 1950s, social psychologists began to study group dynamics and demonstrated how the *presence of others*, either face to face or in the mind, has an impact on how we behave, particularly but not only, under stress (Asch 1956; Darley and Latané 1968; Milgram 1963; Zajonc 1965).

During this period Kurt Lewin (1947) established the Research Center for Group Dynamics at the Massachusetts Institute of Technology, and the National Training Laboratories in Bethel, Maine where groups were used to develop interpersonal sensitivity training.

Bion's theory of group processes

The group then is particularly important both for the influence it has on individuals, the ways people behave when they are in groups and through an intrinsic need for each of us to seek group membership of some kind. A group operates on both conscious and unconscious levels and as Bion suggests, each of us is an individual but we also each have 'a group self' within us (Grotstein 2007: 180).

Wilfred Bion (1961/1986) who arguably made one of the greatest contributions to understanding group dynamics, informing both group psychotherapy and the study of the unconscious life of organizations, initially worked with small therapeutic groups based on the 'Northfield Experiments' with ex-prisoners of the Second World War and then other service personnel who required rehabilitation.

As with any long and influential career his thinking developed and changed. He was particularly influenced by undergoing psychoanalysis with Melanie Klein and later by the work of Lacan. To understand Bion it is important to take account of his claim (see extract above from p. 54 of Bion 1961/1983) which is qualitatively different from many other explanations of the group, in that he recognized that the group is *inside* the individual. Grotstein (2007) who was analysed by Bion and subsequently read the full corpus of his work, claimed that Bion's ideas were difficult to understand and required linking of both text *and* experience. Grotstein also demonstrated that Bion's work on groups at the beginning of his career led to his considerations of the processes of 'thinking' (Bion 1962a) and the 'container-contained' (Bion 1962b).

Bion's initial ideas came from his therapeutic work and observations that a group can be deflected from its main task (i.e. the work it is supposed to be doing whether cleaning or therapy). A 'group mentality' emerges from the development of a group over time as it continues to meet, because individual contributions conform to this mentality. Group mentality is a complex concept. Thus:

> no real idea can be obtained outside the group itself. . . . In the group mentality the individual finds a means of expressing contributions which he wishes to make anonymously, and, at the same time, his greatest obstacle to the fulfillment of the aims he wishes to achieve by membership of the group.
>
> (Bion 1961/1986: 52–3)

A 'group culture' therefore forms which unconsciously constrains individual members (see also Sherwood 1964). Bion's experience of being analysed by Klein developed his ideas about this observation which progressed to give greater expression to the concept of the *basic assumption groups* which grew from his ideas about group culture (see Gould 1997).

The group is a complex concept and one which has not been served well by positivist experimental psychology in recent years (Brown 2000). Groups are not simply individuals communicating face to face in a manner that can be observed and measured objectively, although there is no doubt that some things might be learned that way. There is a powerful emotional/unconscious content in all meetings and groups that mirrors the model of the 'rational' ego and the 'irrational' unconscious individual mind.

Since early accounts of crowd behaviour it has been clear there is *something* unconscious at the heart of the group. Bion's theory of basic assumptions, instinct, emotion and learning from experience remain pertinent to organizational life (Armstrong 1992; 2007). What is sometimes hard to grasp is the skill to pick up the nuances in the group that mark the shift from work/primary task groups to basic assumption groups. What Bion and his successors have shown is how making sense of group culture in this way assists mental health and well-being in individuals, groups and organizations.

References

Armstrong, D. (1992) Names, thoughts and lies: the relevance of Bion's later writing for understanding experiences in groups. *Free Associations*, 3B(2): 261–83.

Armstrong, D. (2007) Emotions in organizations: disturbance or intelligence. In C. Huffington, D. Armstrong, W. Halton, L. Hoyle and J. Pooley (eds) *Working Below the Surface*. London: Karnac.

Asch, S.E. (1956) *Studies of Independence and Conformity: I: A Minority of One Against a Unanimous Majority*. Washington: American Psychological Association.

Bion, W.R. (1961/1986) *Experiences in Groups, and Other Papers*. London: Tavistock.

Bion, W.R. (1962a) A theory of thinking. In W.R. Bion *Second Thoughts: Selected Papers on Psycho-analysis*. London: Heinemann. (Reprinted: London, Karnac Books, 1984.)

Bion, W.R. (1962b) *Learning from Experience*. London: Heinemann.

Bowlby, J. (1977) The making and breaking of affectional bonds. I. Aetiology and psychopathology in the light of attachment theory. An expanded version of the Fiftieth Maudsley Lecture, delivered before the Royal College of Psychiatrists, 19 November 1976. *British Journal of Psychiatry*, 130: 201–10.

Brown, R. (2000) *Group Processes*. Oxford: Blackwell.

Cartwright, D. and Zander, A.F. (1968) *Group Dynamics: Research and Theory*. Evanston, IL: Row, Peterson.

Darley, J.M. and Latané, B. (1968) Bystander intervention in emergencies: diffusion of responsibility. *Journal of Personality and Social Psychology*, 8: 377–83.

Freud, S. (1921/1922) *Group Psychology and the Analysis of the Ego*. New York: Boni and Liveright.

Gould, L.J. (1997) Correspondence between Bion's Basic Assumptions Theory and Klein's Developmental Positions: an outline. *Free Associations*, 41: 15–30.

Grotstein, J.S. (2007) *A Beam of Intense Darkness: Wilfred Bion's Legacy to Psychoanalysis*. London: Karnac.

Homans, G.C. (1975) *The Human Group*. London: Routledge and Kegan Paul.

Klein, M. (1959/1993) Our adult world and its roots in infancy. In M. Klein, *Envy and Gratitude and Other Works 1946–1963*, London: Virago.

Le Bon, G. (1895/2009) *The Crowd: A Study of the Popular Mind*, 5th edn. New Jersey: Transaction.

Lewin, K. (1947) Frontiers in group dynamics: concept, method and reality in social science; social equilibria and social change. In D. Cartwright (ed.) *Field Theory in Social Science: Selected Theoretical Papers*. New York: Harper and Brothers.

McDougall, W. (1922/2005) *The Group Mind: A Sketch of the Principles of Collective Psychology, With Some Attempt to Apply Them to the Interpretation of National Life and Character*. Whitefish, MT: Kessinger Publishing.

Milgram, S. (1963) Behavioral study of obedience. *Journal of Abnormal Psychology*, 67: 371–8.

Miller, E. (1999) Dependency, alienation, or partnership? The changing relatedness of the individual to the enterprise. In R. French and R. Vince (eds) *Group Relations, Management and Organisation*. Oxford: Oxford University Press.

Sherwood, M. (1964) Bion's experiences in groups: a critical evaluation. *Human Relations*, 17: 113–30.

Spillius, E. (2007) *Encounters with Melanie Klein: Selected Papers of Elizabeth Spillius*. London: Free Association Books.

Sprott, W.J.H. (1977) *Human Groups*. Harmondsworth: Pelican.

Whiteley, J.S. (1970) The response of psychopaths to a therapeutic community. *British Journal of Psychiatry*, 116(534): 517–29.

Winnicott, D.W. (1965) *The Maturational Process and the Facilitating Environment.* New York: International Universities Press.

Zajonc, R.B. (1965) Social facilitiation. *Science*, 149: 269–74.

Annotated further reading

Bettelheim, B. (1979) *The Informed Heart: Autonomy in a Mass Age.* New York: Avon Books.

This book includes some important real-life examples and analysis of group behaviour and observations by the author. It is easy to read albeit harrowing in places.

Bion, W.R. (1961/1986) *Experiences in Groups, and Other Papers.* London: Tavistock.

As with most of Bion's writing this is not an easy read, although because there are lots of mini-vignettes it is easier than some of his other work. It is however the classic psychotherapeutic/psychodynamic text on group behaviour.

Eisold, K. (2005) Using Bion. *Psychoanalytic Psychology*, 22(3): 357–70.

Eisold provides a clearly written paper talking of Bion's classical work on groups and the importance of group work in psychodynamic group therapy and understanding of organizations.

H

Humanistic approaches

See also: existential counselling, Gestalt therapy; person-centred counselling; phenomenology; self-actualization

Humanism is a philosophical perspective which views human beings in an essentially positive way. It is heavily influenced by existential and phenomenological philosophy as well as by Buddhism. The counselling approaches which sit most comfortably under this umbrella term are person-centred counselling, gestalt therapy and existential counselling, although transactional analysis also draws on humanistic ideas.

Humanism stresses human beings' capacity for creativity, free choice and self-fulfilment, while also recognizing that adverse circumstances can get in the way of these natural processes. It stands in sharp contrast to the more deterministic perspectives of psychoanalysis and behaviourism (Hough 2010).

A key figure in the humanistic tradition is Abraham Maslow (1908–1970) who turned from behaviourism as a way of explaining human behaviour to the idea that people are motivated by various needs, with the highest order need being self-actualization or self-fulfilment. He believed in the crucial role of care-givers in children's development, including the importance of being valued by those care-givers as well as by other people in later life (Hough 2010). He developed a theory of motivation which consists of a hierarchy of human needs. (See Figure 2.) According to his theory the needs lower down in the hierarchy, such as hunger or a safe environment, must be met before those higher up can be pursued. However, he argued, if people fail to fulfil their potential this can cause real mental anguish.

Humanistic approaches to counselling all adhere to the basic principles described above, together with the belief in focusing on the individual's perspective of their world and their issues, as it is by this means that they will be able to get in touch with and experience at a deep level what is hindering the process of self-actualization.

Like any approaches, humanistic models have their limitations as well as their strengths. They were developed from a western perspective and are less likely to be seen as relevant by those from eastern, collectivist cultures where esteem and self-actualizing needs are of little importance. Also they have limited applicability to those in third-world countries concerned with meeting

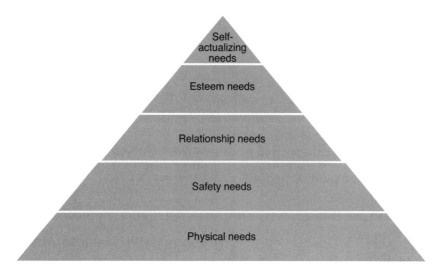

Figure 1 Maslow's hierarchy of needs

their basic needs for sustenance and shelter. Some clients from whatever culture who prefer more structured or directive forms of intervention may find these approaches 'wishy washy' and aimless. Psychodynamic approaches may be more effective where client problems are linked to deeply repressed unconscious traumas and clients with phobias or addictions may respond better to approaches such as CBT or REBT.

Reference

Hough, M. (2010) *Counselling Skills and Theory*. London: Hodder Education.

Annotated further reading

Plock du, S. (2010) Humanistic approaches. In S. Strawbridge, R. Woolfe and W. Dryden (eds) *Handbook of Counselling Psychology*, 3rd edn. London: Sage.

A really useful analysis of the common strands in the various humanistic approaches to counselling and of the differences between the American and European conceptions of humanistic thought.

I

Imagery, guided

See also: cognitive behavioural therapy; multimodal therapy

In the 1960s the majority of CBT approaches and in particular the behaviour division advocated to reduce 'theoretical and philosophical principles' and focused instead on empirical research. Thus the only way to conceptualize and understand CBT application truly is to look at some major CBT interventions. Here clients are guided in imagining a relaxing scene or series of experiences or objects.

Numerous clinical observations suggest that an individual visualizing an imagined scene reacts as though it was actually occurring; therefore, 'induced' images can have a deep effect on behaviour. Neuro-psychology also has deduced that the brain cannot really differentiate between 'real' or 'perceived' images. Thus learning to perceive helpful images can be used in a multitude of applications. Apart from CBT other therapy schools like NLP and MMT have integrated this approach into their repertoire.

Guided imagery techniques have been applied to – and found to be effective or at least helpful with – a variety of populations, including individuals with phobias (including agoraphobia, social phobia and specific phobias), mild to moderate depression, generalized anxiety disorders, post-traumatic stress disorder, obsessive-compulsive disorder, sexual deviation or difficulties, chronic fatigue syndrome, children's behavioural disorders and acute and chronic pain (and other physical disorders).

Guided imagery has also contributed to the achievement of skills and overcoming anxiety in normal life situations that include learning or improving motor skills, test taking and public speaking. In addition, visualization and imagery, along with other behavioural techniques, have been applied to the fields of business, industry, child rearing, education, behavioural medicine and sports.

Commonly used imagery techniques include anti-future shock imagery (preparing for a feared future event), positive imagery (using pleasant scenes for relaxation training), aversive imagery (using an unpleasant image to help eliminate or reduce undesirable behaviour), associated imagery (using imagery to track unpleasant feelings), coping imagery (using images rehearsing to reach a behavioural goal or manage a situation well including one or two little challenges that they visualize dealing with well), worst-case scenario technique (exaggerating a feared situation and using imagery to cope with it). Mastery imagery can assist clients to imagine doing anxiety-provoking tasks well. Coping imagery however is more realistic. The client still succeeds with her task, but has a little 'glitch' that she copes with, such as dropping her notes on the floor, calmly picking them up and asking the audience whether they remember where she needs to continue from.

Time-projection imagery helps the client who is presently very upset about a recent event (a break-up, loss of job) and is encouraged to see himself one month from now, then six months and finally a year. From past experience they may be able to realize that pain and disappointment tend to fade with time.

To increase visualization, it is important to involve all senses in addition to the visual sense. For example, if the client is to be walking down a quiet country lane, they are encouraged to imagine hearing bird song and other wildlife sounds – maybe a truck in the far background – smell the moist air and aromas from some trees and wild fruit, and observe body sensations, etc. It is emphasized to the client that the most important aspect of imagining is the feeling of actually experiencing the scene – of being in it rather than just seeing oneself in it.

Both the therapist and the client construct a relaxing scene by discussing exactly what the client finds pleasant. It is better if the client chooses all images and the therapist trains the client to visualize the selected images as vividly as possible. Unless the therapist consults with the client, an inappropriate image may even trigger re-traumatization (e.g. using 'the sea' or 'a lake' with some-body who had a drowning experience in the past).

Once a pleasant scene has been selected, the client is asked to assume a relaxed position and sits or lies with closed eyes, if this is acceptable, before being guided in visualization. A common beginning instruction may be: 'Imagine you are lying on a warm pebble beach'. The therapist continues to guide the relaxation by using phrases such as: 'Notice the texture of the shell you have just picked up and the colour of the sea. Focus on the sounds you hear and the smells you pick up . . .'. The client is asked to practise at home between sessions. A CD of the guided imagery in the recognizable voice of the therapist is useful to most clients for practising at home.

Guided imagery is not used in isolation but as a part of a therapeutic formulation and is appropriate for a range of problems and disorders.

Caution should be taken when using these techniques if clients have the following conditions: asthma attacks triggered by stress or anxiety, seizures triggered by stress or anxiety, cardiac conditions, hysteria and severe psychiatric disorders.

Annotated further reading

Mullin, R., PhD (2000) *The New Handbook of Cognitive Therapy Techniques.* New York: W.W. Norton and Co.

Albert Ellis once wrote that this volume includes more specific methods than does any other CBT book he knows about. It has a good 80 entries, many of which are very easy to follow.

Immediacy

See also: congruence; self-disclosure

Immediacy is a very useful counselling skill but one which can be difficult to use effectively. It involves discussing openly what is going on between the therapist and the client either at the present time or in the recent past. It is a form of genuineness and of self-disclosure. Egan (2007: 169) saw it as a useful tool for 'monitoring and managing the working alliance'. Rogers called it 'confrontation', which captures the fact that it can be a challenging intervention and, indeed, Egan categorizes it as a challenging skill.

An example of immediacy would be:

Therapist: I'm wondering if you are feeling angry at the moment. Your tone of voice seems to have changed and you seem tense. Does this fit at all with how you are feeling?
Client: I think I am feeling angry, but I'm not sure exactly why. It may be something to do with what you said earlier about my relationship with my mother . . .

The therapist and client are then able to discuss the client's feelings and, if appropriate, clarify any misunderstandings which may have arisen regarding what was said. As clients usually relate to their therapist in similar ways to how they relate to others, they can also gain insight into their style of relating.

Egan makes a distinction between immediacy, which focuses on the therapeutic relationship as a whole and that which concentrates on a specific event or interaction within the therapy (Egan 2007). The first could involve the therapist raising the issue of how the relationship may be helping or hindering progress. This type of discussion can provide the client with new perspectives on other relationships in the client's life and how they may be affecting those relationships by their behaviour. For example, a therapist might pick up that a client is very quick to agree with them and rarely puts forward a different viewpoint. She might therefore tentatively raise this as something she has noticed and ask the client for her perspective on it.

The second type of immediacy focuses on what is happening between client and therapist right now or very recently. For example the therapist might say: 'I'm getting a sense that things seem a bit strained between us at the moment and I'm wondering if you are feeling angry with me about something. Do you have any sense of this?'

The following are guidelines as to when immediacy might be an appropriate intervention:

- if there is a lack of progress in the therapy (there could be many reasons for this including resistance on the part of the client or some problem in the therapeutic alliance);
- if there is tension between therapist and client (which could result from many factors including sexual attraction or over-dependency);
- if trust seems to be an issue;
- if some kind of difference (such as interpersonal style, culture, class, race) seems to be getting in the way;
- if the therapist is confused by the client.

The reason for immediacy being an advanced skill is that it involves the use of a number of other skills and qualities, including attending, listening, empathy, self-disclosure, assertiveness, risk-taking, and an awareness of 'process', or in other words, what is going on within oneself, within the client and between both parties. It is also important not to overuse this skill or to use it inappropriately as this can unsettle the client or result in their withdrawal from the process. If used well its use can deepen the therapeutic relationship as well as encouraging the client to become more reflective about and open in their interactions with others.

Bayne et al. (2008) suggest that immediacy is more effective when the relationship is sufficiently well developed. They also advocate preparing the client for an immediacy intervention (e.g. 'I'd like to discuss something about what I think might be happening between us at the moment'); being descriptive not evaluative; owning the statement by using 'I' statements; using the present tense and asking for, and listening carefully to, the client's viewpoint.

References

Bayne, R., Jinks, G., Collard, P. and Horton, I. (2008) *The Counsellor's Handbook: A Practical A–Z Guide to Integrative Counselling and Psychotherapy*. Nelson Thornes.

Egan, G. (2007) *The Skilled Helper: A Problem-management and Opportunity-development Approach to Helping*, 8th edn. Belmont, CA: Thompson Brooks/Cole.

Annotated further reading

Milne, A. (2010) *Understanding Counselling*, 4th edn. Maidenhead: McGraw-Hill.

> Although this is a relatively brief discussion of the concept, it does include some specific examples which help to clarify the meaning of the term and its appropriate uses.

Individuation

See also: Jung, Carl

Individuation refers to the stabilization of the personality and the integration of the conscious with both the personal and collective unconscious. Individuation is a concept from the work of Carl Jung who describes the process as one through which a person becomes his/her 'true self'; one which is whole and distinct from the collective consciousness of their culture (Jung 1923).

Jung proposed that the pathway to psychological health, or individuation, demands a psychological wholeness integrating the good and the bad, the masculine and the feminine and other potentially conflicting parts of the human psyche that are in us all.

This is the focus of Jungian analysis. Individuation is a process informed by the archetypal ideal of wholeness, which in turn depends on a vital relationship between the ego and unconscious (Jung and Franz 1964). The aim is not to overcome one's personal psychology, to become perfect, but to become familiar with it. Thus individuation involves an increasing awareness of one's unique psychological reality, including personal strengths and limitations, and at the same time a deeper appreciation of humanity in general.

Without this integration, a person's life remains one of inner conflict where the ego struggles to ignore, repress or deny a part of the psyche. A man, for instance, becomes overly 'macho' if he rejects his tender, feminine side, his 'anima'. A woman who tries too hard to be perfect ignores her 'shadow' side. Jung argued that these and other examples of unbalanced living never result in positive mental health because either the rejected elements of the psyche invade our dreams and give us nightmares, or they take over the ego, resulting in an inflation in which a person becomes a dangerous caricature of that which he hides. Alternatively the ego might project, pushing what is rejected in oneself onto others and seeing evil or negative behaviours where they are not (King and Nicol 1999).

Jung suggested that if an individual's ego becomes too one sided (too feminine for example) with the conscious personality fixated on the dominant characteristics, then the repressed unconscious aspects of the individual's personality are projected onto another person. It becomes possible in Jung's approach to develop an awareness of the unacknowledged, repressed parts of the self as they become actualized in relationships with others. Therefore if an individual experiences an extreme emotion such as love or hate, what they may be experiencing is the repressed parts of themselves that they have projected onto the other.

The most basic projection is the 'shadow' side – i.e. the dark side of the personality. If we deny the bad parts of ourselves by projecting onto others, we are able to reject it rather than take responsibility for it.

Jung also saw this process in relation to anima/animus. Men and women may reject their feminine and masculine sides, projecting them onto others. For example a woman who represses her masculine side might project it onto her male partner and put their relationship under pressure for him to be 'totally' masculine and a man might do something similar which might lead him to frustration and violence (or self-harm).

While throughout their careers both Jung and Freud had much in common, they split up – theoretically and personally. The story of this parting is long and complex. For the purposes of this entry what stands out is Jung's emphasis on 'harmony' and balance as well as the emphasis on a collective unconscious, versus Freud's (and other psychoanalysts such as Klein) focus on conflict and how conflict between the external reality and internal world can be integrated.

References

Jung, C.G. (1923) *Psychological Types: Or the Psychology of Individuation*. Oxford: Harcourt, Brace.

Jung, C.G. and Franz, M.L. (1964) *Man and His Symbols*. Garden City, NY: Doubleday.

King, S. and Nicol, D.M. (1999) *Journal of Organisational Change Managment*, 12(3): 234–42.

Annotated further reading

Jung, C.G. (1923) *Psychological Types: Or the Psychology of Individuation*. Oxford: Harcourt, Brace.

Jung's original book is the most relevant although as with others, it is old fashioned.

King, S. and Nicol, D.M. (1999) *Journal of Organisational Change Management*, 12(3): 234–42.

King and Nicol's paper on the other hand is easy and informative to read with a practical element to it.

Integrative models

See also: Egan's skilled helper model

Prior to the 1960s, distinct, 'pure' theoretical approaches, such as psychodynamic and person-centred approaches, were generally preferred. However, there has been a shift in more recent years towards integrative and eclectic perspectives.

Although there have been attempts to make clear distinctions between integrative and eclectic approaches, there seems to be a movement towards viewing the approaches on a continuum rather than as distinct perspectives (Woskett 2006). Where distinctions have been made, these have tended to view eclecticism as drawing on different skills and strategies depending on particular client need, and integration as providing an overarching framework which incorporates and integrates more than one theoretical perspective. A perspective which seems to be holding its ground at the moment regards integration as 'a useful umbrella term to accommodate a range of approaches that extend beyond purist forms of therapy' (Woskett 2006: 6) and which include eclecticism.

Feltham and Horton (2006) put forward the view that most practitioners inevitably develop their own personal way of working once they have completed their initial training and start to work more independently with clients. In this sense they become, to some extent, integrative – although this view would be passionately contested by some purist practitioners!

Many attempts have been made to categorize different forms of integration. According to Feltham and Horton (2006) there are two main types: fixed systems and open systems. Fixed systems aim to combine aspects of different 'pure' theories such as cognitive analytic therapy (CAT). Open systems have an overarching framework which is fixed, but which enables concepts and methods from other approaches to be incorporated and synthesized within the framework. Examples of this type of system include Egan's 'skilled helper' model and Andrews' 'self-confirmation' model.

McLeod (2009) identifies a number of different ways of achieving integration which can be defined as either technical or theoretical forms of integration. The former focuses on integration at the level of clinical theory or techniques while the latter takes place at a more abstract, theoretical level. Some of the main types of integration he identifies are as follows:

1 Technical eclecticism

This type of eclecticism adopts a systematic approach to choice of techniques based on, for example, a structured formal assessment and categorization of a client's presenting problems or by considering what research findings indicate will be appropriate interventions. As it is mainly atheoretical it does not encounter problems with attempting to integrate potentially incompatible theories. One criticism, however, is that its lack of theory means that it does not have the guiding principles which theory tends to provide.

2 Common factors approach

This approach identifies a number of factors such as the therapeutic relationship, having hope and clear structure which have been consistently shown to have a positive impact on therapeutic progress. However, it is also important to consider what the client believes will work for them and to obtain ongoing feedback on how the therapy is progressing from their point of view.

3 Theoretical integration

As mentioned earlier, this approach provides a central framework or concept into which ideas and methods from other approaches can be incorporated or integrated. These can be open or fixed systems and include Egan's model and CAT. A positive feature of theoretical integration is that research can be carried out into its effectiveness as it is a complete approach to therapeutic practice. A possible criticism is that it can result in yet another new theory (McLeod 2009).

4 Assimilative integration

This is based around the idea that individual practitioners develop their own personal way of working over a number of years by initially training in one approach, then incorporating or assimilating aspects of other approaches into their original theoretical framework. Unlike technical eclecticism, it is not restricted to techniques, but covers theory too.

5 Collaborative pluralism

Developed by Cooper and McLeod (2007), this approach aims to devise an individualized therapy for each client based on collaboration and discussion with the client. The client plays an active role in defining the problem(s), developing the goals of what they want to achieve in the therapy and arriving at how they are going to do that. While collaborative pluralism is able to draw on the strengths of the integrative approaches which have preceded it, it is so new as to have very little research evidence to support its effectiveness. It could also be problematic to gather this evidence as the therapeutic work will be different with each client.

While there is a definite movement towards increased use of integrative approaches in the counselling and psychotherapy world, there are also a significant number of therapists who adhere strongly to one theoretical perspective. Psychodynamic and person-centred perspectives tend to be more problematic to integrate with other approaches than are CBT or TA for example.

Possible limitations

Successful integration is not an easy process and there can be a danger of creating a haphazard mix of theories and concepts which do not form a coherent whole and lose the essential nature of all of the approaches. For example, approaches with significantly different theories of human development or concepts of the counselling relationship are unlikely to integrate effectively. The empirical research demonstrating the effectiveness of open integrative systems is particularly limited due to the difficulties of measuring such individualized counselling models (Feltham and Horton 2006).

References

Cooper, M. and McLeod, J. (2007) A pluralistic framework for counselling and psychotherapy: implications for research. *Counselling and Psychotherapy Research*, 7: 135–43.

Feltham, C. and Horton, I. (eds) (2006) *The SAGE Handbook of Counselling and Psychotherapy*, 2nd edn. London: Sage.

McLeod, J. (2009) *An Introduction to Counselling*, 4th edn. Maidenhead: Open University Press.

Woskett, V. (2006) *Egan's Skilled Helper Model: Developments and Applications in Counselling*. London: Routledge.

Annotated further reading

Corey, G. (2009) *The Art of Integrative Counseling*, 2nd edn. Belmont, CA: Thompson Brooks Cole.

Corey outlines his personal approach to integration using a single client case.

Norcross, J.C. and Goldfried, M.R. (eds) (2005) *Handbook of Psychotherapy Integration*. New York: Oxford University Press.

This book provides a comprehensive guide to integrative perspectives and includes a summary of the arguments supporting integration.

Interpretation

See also: counter-transference; dream analysis; free association; psychoanalysis; psychodynamic counselling; transference

Interpretation is a technique used in psychoanalysis and psychodynamic counselling in which the counsellor makes 'statements which go beyond what the client has overtly recognised to suggest new understandings of experiences' (Cooper 2008: 122). Dreams, the transference relationship and material arising during free association can all provide rich material to interpret. Links might be made between past and present relationships outside the counselling room, or certain patterns in the way a client thinks or feels may be suggested. For example, the counsellor might suggest that the client tends to experience strong negative feelings towards dominant men in the way she did with her own father. The main purpose here is to help the client to become more aware of and to understand the origins of their difficulties so as to have more control over them and a greater capacity to respond differently. Interpretation is a difficult technique to use effectively, for the reasons given below, but it can lead to positive insights for the client if clear and accurate.

Interpretations are likely to be more effective if they are offered tentatively rather than dogmatically. Timing is another crucial factor, in that they need to raise something which is close to the client's awareness, and are generally better received when the therapeutic relationship is sufficiently well developed. Accuracy is more likely if sufficient evidence has been acquired to support the interpretation and clarity of expression will increase the likelihood of the client understanding what is meant (Cooper 2008).

Yet from another perspective, it could be argued that interpretations can at times be an abuse of a counsellor's power. The client is often vulnerable and could take on board interpretations which are not meaningful to them because they trust the counsellor's judgement more than their own. Transference interpretations may sometimes be used when it might be more appropriate for the counsellor to acknowledge their own part in an alliance rupture rather than placing all the responsibility on the client. Listening to the client's response is a vital part of effective interpretation as is deciding on whether to pursue the interpretation or whether to put it on hold or abandon it altogether.

Research evidence

Unlike many other psychoanalytic techniques, there is a substantial body of research supporting the value of this particular skill. Research suggests that accuracy of interpretations (both transference and other relational ones) tend to be related to better counselling outcomes. However, frequent use of transference interpretations is linked to poorer outcomes, which suggests that it is more effective to limit the use of this technique. In addition, transference interpretations tend to be more effective when the therapeutic relationship is strong (Cooper 2008).

Reference

Cooper, M. (2008) *Essential Research Findings in Counselling and Psychotherapy: The Facts are Friendly*. London: Sage.

Annotated further reading

Jacobs, M. (2010) *Psychodynamic Counselling in Action*, 4th edn. London: Sage.

An excellent introduction to this and other psychodynamic concepts from a practical perspective.

Klein, M. (2001) *Psychodynamic Counselling Primer*. Ross-on-Wye: PCCS Books.

A concise introduction to the main concepts which is particularly suitable for those new to the subject.

Introjection

See also: depressive position; object relations theory; paranoid-schizoid position; projective identification

Introjection is the theoretically important, unconscious phantasy that occurs in the paranoid-schizoid position when parts of others are 'taken into' the self.

In the paranoid-schizoid position the parts taken in will be split and idealized – either wonderful and larger than life or denigrated – excessively persecuting and dangerous (Segal 1993). The boundary between self and other is denied so that the self may be felt to be attached to, or identical with, a very powerful idealized other who can do no wrong.

Introjection is the foremost mechanism in the depressive position (Symington 1986). As well as feeling bad and sad about having damaged the mother, the baby is perceiving the mother as a person with feelings and introjects her as a whole (rather than part) object. If the caring and feeding is good, the infant will introject this, and will therefore have a good sense of what things are like outside.

References

Segal, J. (1993) *Melanie Klein*. London: Sage.
Symington, N. (1986) *The Analytic Experience: Lectures from the Tavistock*. London: Free Association Books.

Annotated further reading

Segal, J. (1993) *Melanie Klein*. London: Sage.

Julia Segal's book provides an excellent introduction to Klein's life and theories including introjection.

Symington, N. (1986) *The Analytic Experience: Lectures from the Tavistock*. London: Free Association Books.

Symington provides a contextualized application of introjection in his published lectures aimed at his psychoanalysis students. This makes an informative, lively and clear read.

Irrational beliefs (IBs)

See also: rational emotive behaviour therapy; Ellis, Albert

Irrational beliefs are attitudes, beliefs, values, etc. that a person strongly holds despite objective evidence, generally available and understood, to the contrary.

There are many different interpretations of irrational beliefs in psychotherapy. However, we do know that such beliefs feed and keep alive disorders such as panic attacks, agoraphobia, anger and more. It is believed that we develop our own belief system as we grow up. We are nevertheless not always rationally choosing IBs because people's assumptions are often based on both logical and illogical as well as unconscious input (http://panicdisorder.about.com/od/understandingpanic/a/IrrationalBelie.htm).

Albert Ellis identified three basic IBs that lead to self-defeat:

- 'I must do well and win the approval of others or else I am no good.'
- 'Other people must treat me considerately and fairly, or else they are not good and deserve to be condemned and punished.'
- 'I must get what I want, when I want it. If I don't get what I want, it's terrible and intolerable.'

For example if a person believes that they are likely to have a panic attack at social functions, they may avoid such events. In their unconscious automatic reasoning just beneath the level of awareness they may have IBs like this arising: 'People will think I'm crazy' or 'people will think less of me' or 'I would be so embarrassed if people noticed.'

Thus it can be said that the person's underlying belief about failure or rejection is the cause of the worry. In order to try and change IBs, you must first discover what they are and bring them into the level of conscious awareness, as they are frequently internalized, which is a process of making something an integral part of one's beliefs (http://panicdisorder.about.com/od/glossaryip/g/Internalization.htm). You must go through a process of detecting and debating to be able to free yourself from such unhelpful thinking patterns.

Detecting involves understanding the boundaries of the various belief systems. Those are usually held in the form of 'must', 'should' or 'ought', and those are usually placed on themselves or other people. 'I must be successful' is an example of that.

Debating is the process after you have detected the beliefs. You have to ask yourself, are they realistic? Are they logical? And last but not least, how would it help anybody to continue believing them, as they mostly cause distress? Furthermore your absolutist goals would need to be questioned such as whether you really 'must' have to be successful in order to be happy or content.

Effective changes of IBs can lead to a new way of thinking about oneself, others and one's environment and allow one to reach a level of acceptance of those imperfections that were once so troubling and that are actually part of the human condition (Corey 2009).

Reference

Corey, G. (2009) *Theory and Practice of Counseling and Psychotherapy.* Belmont, CA: Thomson Brooks/Cole.

Annotated further reading

Corey, G. (2009) *Theory and Practice of Counseling and Psychotherapy*. Belmont, CA: Thomson Brooks/Cole.

A very useful, straightforward book with clear information and logical explanations – easy to read, even the most difficult theory. The book offers a wealth of information from different approaches to ethical issues.

Kazantzis, N., Reinecke, M.A. and Freeman, A. (eds) (2010) *Cognitive and Behavioral Theories in Clinical Practice*. New York: Guilford Press.

This publication contains in-depth chapters on the rich approaches that CBT contains. Leading experts come together and describe with insight how each approach differs from the other. Recent research is given a prominent place.

J

Jung, Carl (1875–1961)

See also: archetypes; collective unconscious; word association

In his autobiography, Jung (1961) described a childhood of solitary play and some terrifying religious visions, which he came to see as signs from God that he should not hold to the traditional religious conventions of his time (his father was a pastor). He was also aware of having two very distinct selves: the insecure pastor's son and a wise old man who was remote from the human world in a timeless and boundless universe. He thought everyone contained both these personalities but that most people were not aware of their inner wisdom.

Jung had an 'absolute craving' (1961: 30) to read everything and chose to study medicine and then psychiatry because they combined the humanities and the sciences. After graduating, he set up an experimental laboratory in a psychiatric clinic in Zurich and developed the word association test as a method of diagnosing psychological problems. Like sentence stems, this test has the virtue of being very cheap and fairly quick but is not generally regarded as valid today. Essentially, the person being tested is asked to respond as quickly as they can to a set of words (the standard list was 100) and their responses and length of time before each response are noted. Blocks in expression or unusual responses are interpreted as indicating 'complexes' – one of several Jungian words that became part of everyday language.

Then, in 1906, Jung met Freud who he described as 'the first man of real importance I had encountered' (1961: 149). They are said to have talked for 13 hours at their first meeting and Freud came to see Jung as his successor. However, they disagreed fundamentally on some aspects of psychoanalytic theory – put simply, Jung saw Freud's views as too narrow, while Freud saw Jung's as too spiritual and occult (Jung had continued to read very widely, investigating palmistry, astrology, alchemy, etc.). The two men ended their relationship in 1912 and Jung continued to develop his own theories. He wrote extensively too, in a style which has been called abstruse – both profound and obscure.

Jung's most ambitious and controversial concept is probably archetypes and therefore the 'collective unconscious', and his most useful concept is psychological types, the theory of personality clarified and developed by Myers (see **preferences**).

Reference

Jung, C. (1961) *Memories, Dreams, Reflections*. New York: Random House.

Annotated further reading

Jung, C.G. (1968) *Analytical Psychology in Theory and Practice*. New York: Pantheon Books.

This book includes transcripts of a series of lectures by Jung in which he is personal and relatively clear about his main ideas.

Kabat-Zinn, Jon (1944–)

See also: being mindful; mindfulness-based cognitive behavioural coaching; mindfulness-based cognitive therapy; mindfulness-based stress reduction

It is thanks to the vision of the molecular biologist Jon Kabat-Zinn that the application of mindfulness in the secular environment of medicine and psychotherapy was made possible. He developed mindfulness-based stress reduction (MBSR) in the 1970s at the Centre for Mindfulness in Massachusetts.

He had been a keen practitioner of yoga, martial arts and insight meditation since his youth and was inspired by the benefits these traditions had brought to his personal life. He was convinced that others too could improve their own well-being by adopting practices from these Eastern traditions into their own lives.

He made a conscious decision to give up his original training in order to 'prepare' the way for mindfulness. His goal was to make it available as a life enhancing skill for the average person and to 'translate' parts of Buddhist wisdom and philosophy to reduce suffering where it was mainly caused by unhelpful thinking, expectations and behaviours. He tried to wrap the wisdom of the East into a digestible form of learning for people in the West. He saw it as his calling to connect meditation and medicine. He believes that this work is his Karma, a way through which he can express both his love for the Dharma (Insight, Truth) and for human beings. The main learning he tries to bring across is to reconnect to a life that includes the simple act of 'being' and to let go of 'doing' for brief periods every day and enjoy a simple breath, a simple moment of being alive! According to Buddhist teachings we are born with 'Buddha Nature' which simply means being aware and already being completely whole. By practising mindfulness we may realize that everything we need is already there, albeit seemingly dormant at times. When we gain insight into what we truly are: whole, complete and good enough, then we often experience a deep sense of freedom and healing. In short, if we learn to accept ourselves and our lot just as it is, we remove a lot of the causes of suffering. In an interview with C. Spannbauer (Spannbauer 2008: 29) Jon Kabat-Zinn refers to the Dalai Lama and quotes him: 'My religion is kindness'. Kabat-Zinn very much follows this notion in his teachings, books and engagement with others.

His eight-week MBSR course includes mental 'journeys through the body' (body scan), breathing and walking meditations and mindful movements, generally derived from Hatha yoga. Last but not least, the programme encourages participants to experience every single moment of their life as something special and as something almost miraculous, when life unfolds itself moment by moment; when you eat just eat or when you walk just walk.

The MBSR programme is much more widely practised since its small beginnings. For instance, it is now offered in more than 250 clinics across the USA to help patients heal from within. Many European countries have followed suit. The programme has shown to enable change in people who may have been unable to shift out of their chronic condition for decades. The only drawback is that you need to commit to an hour-long practice a day and this often requires a major change in how you use your time. People sometimes drop out before the eight weeks are over because they feel guilty or ashamed for not having found a way to integrate MBSR into their life.

MBSR research and practice outcomes have been scrutinized and many publications back up the positive effects the programme has on the general quality of life of participants who continue to implement mindfulness into their everyday life.

Reference

Spannbauer, C. (2008) *Im Haus der Weisheit. Spiritual Teachers Share their Visions for our Time.* Muenchen: Koesel.

Annotated further reading

Spannbauer, C. (2008) *Im Haus der Weisheit. Spiritual Teachers Share their Visions for our Time.* Muenchen: Koesel.

This book is a wonderful compilation of biographical chapters and interviews with people who have made a real difference to the world in the late twentieth century.

Klein, Melanie (1882–1960)

Melanie Klein was born Melanie Reizes in Vienna but moved to London in 1926 where she lived and worked for the rest of her life. Klein's father Moriz Reizes was a doctor, born into an orthodox Jewish family, although he himself eschewed religious dogma. Melanie was the youngest of four children whose birth was claimed to be 'unexpected' (Segal 1993) and it is sometimes reported as 'unwanted'. At the time of her birth the family were short of money and her mother (Libussa, more than 20 years younger than Moriz) opened a shop to help with the family finances. Melanie was fed by a wet-nurse and although she did not report lack of love from her parents she did report lack of attention.

In adulthood Melanie planned to study medicine and specialize in psychiatry. However, when she was 19 her father died and it is speculated that his death precipitated her agreement to marriage with Arthur Klein, which she soon recorded as a mistake. She apparently admitted to having affairs with other men fairly soon after her marriage. She had three children, Melitta, Hans and Erich, whom she would have had no means of supporting if she were to divorce Arthur (Segal 1993).

Klein was depressed for most of her early married life and with being at home caring for her young children, but in her 30s the family moved to Budapest and she went into analysis with Sandor Ferenzci. That experience, as well as reading Freud's *On Dreams* (Freud 1952/1989) (see **Freudian analysis**), led her to become committed to psychoanalysis.

Klein's detailed observations of her young son and encouragement from Ferenzci marked the beginning of her thinking and the development of her original ideas, which eventually led her away from the Freudian model.

Klein's life involved many losses, including her sister in childhood. Her brother Emmanuel died in 1902 just before she married Arthur Klein and her son Hans was killed while mountain walking in 1934.

In 1919 Klein became a member of the Budapest Psychoanalytic Society but was forced to leave Hungary because of an upsurge of anti-Semitism. She moved to Berlin (after a short stay with relatives in Slovakia where her children remained for a while). Arthur went to Sweden where he remained.

In Berlin she became a member of the Berlin Psychoanalytic Society in 1922. By 1924 she was in analysis with Karl Abraham until his death about two years later but she considered that her work with him was fundamental to her future work. Her interest was in the analysis of children and although Abraham supported her and helped her develop this work, after his death she felt professionally isolated in Berlin because of general fears about the analysis of children. She also wrote about the analysis of her own children (anonymized at the time).

Ernest Jones, the founder of the British Psychoanalytic Society, encouraged her to move to England which she did in 1926 aged 38 (Segal 1993).

Klein's writing

Klein's work cannot be understood without a basic grasp of classic Freudian psychoanalysis (see **Freudian analysis**) (Craib 2001; Hinshelwood 1994).

Although 'post' Kleinians and psychoanalysts from the Object Relations school added specifically to Klein's (more than Freud's) work she herself focused upon developing her thoughts and practices in relation to Freudian ideas. For example she built upon Freud's drive theory with her work on envy and unconscious phantasy (Klein 1984) and developed her concepts of 'position' (see **Kleinian analysis**) as a response to psychosexual development (see **psychosexual development**) and the Oedipus Complex (Klein 1928/1998; see **Oedipus complex**).

As Hinshelwood (1994) suggests although Klein's work emphasized the clinical, her writing was 'top-heavy with theory' (p. 1) as she drew theoretical inference from her psychoanalytic case studies – most frequently with children. For example in 1945 she provided a detailed example of clinical work with a 10-year-old boy discussing the early stages of Oedipal conflict (see **Oedipus complex**; Klein 1928/1998). This is rich in detail and observation but needs to be read several times in order to gain the sense of how she draws conclusions and develops her theoretical ideas from the anxieties he demonstrates. However, much of her writing (once the reader has a basic grasp of psychoanalytic perspectives) is clear to read.

Unlike Freud (see **Freud, Sigmund**) who had wanted his unpublished correspondence and notes destroyed, Klein left 12 boxes of clinical notes and nine boxes of lecture notes (Spillius 2007) although she appears to have destroyed her letters. In her unpublished lectures she writes at length about technique (see **Kleinian analysis**) and projective identification (see **defence mechanisms**) which later came to be seen as central to psychoanalysis although it was less significant for Klein during her career (Spillius 2007). She did write at length about envy and envious attacks (Klein 1984) and ways in which infancy influences adulthood (Klein 1962).

Her most significant publications are generally acknowledged to be *Notes on Some Schizoid Mechanisms* in 1946 (Klein 1946), *New Directions in Psychoanalysis* (Klein et al. 1955) and *Envy and Gratitude* her final (and controversial) work (Klein 1984).

Klein's central ideas

Klein held a different view from Freud's about the development of human psychology. Rather than following sequential stages of development, Klein thought that there was constant movement back and forth between mental *positions*, which she saw as a constellation of attitudes and mechanisms (Hinshelwood 1991; Segal 1993) that worked together and acted on preoccupations. She described the *paranoid-schizoid* position and the *depressive* position as being different ways of dealing with anxiety. Throughout life the paranoid-schizoid position may be used under stress.

References

Craib, I. (2001) *Psychoanalysis: A Critical Introduction*. Cambridge: Polity.

Freud, S. (1952/1989) *On Dreams*. London: W.W. Norton and Co.

Hinshelwood, R. (1991) *A Dictionary of Kleinian Thought*. London: Free Association Books.

Hinshelwood, R. (1994) *Clinical Klein*. London: Free Association Books.

Klein, M. (1928/1998) Early stages of the Oedipus conflict. In H. Segal and R.E. Money-Kyrle (eds) *Love, Guilt and Reparation and other Works 1921–1945*. London: Vintage.

Klein, M. (1946) Notes on some schizoid mechanisms. In H. Segal (ed.) *Envy and Gratitude and Other Works 1946–1963*. London: Virago.

Klein, M. (1962) *Our Adult World and its Roots in Infancy*, second impression. London: Virago.

Klein, M. (1984) *Envy and Gratitude: And Other Works, 1946–1963*: London: Hogarth Press.

Klein, M., Heimann, P. and Money-Kyrle, R.E. (1955) *New Directions in Psychoanalysis*. London: Tavistock.

Segal, J. (1993) *Melanie Klein*. London: Sage.

Spillius, E. (2007) *Encounters with Melanie Klein*. London: Routledge.

Annotated further reading

Much has been written about Melanie Klein and Kleinian analysis (see **Kleinian analysis**).

Hinshelwood, R. (1991) *A Dictionary of Kleinian Thought*. London: Free Association Books.

Hinshelwood, R. (1994) *Clinical Klein*. London: Free Association Books.

> Robert Hinshelwood's *Clinical Klein* and his *Dictionary of Kleinian Thought* contain almost all you might want to know about her ideas and clinical practice.

Segal, J. (1993) *Melanie Klein*. London: Sage.

> Julia Segal's book is an easy and engaging read about Klein's life and the detail of her work.

Spillius, E. (2007) *Encounters with Melanie Klein*. London: Routledge.

> Elizabeth Spillius's book reveals some of Klein's unpublished work as well as her lectures and for that and other reasons makes a fascinating read.

Kleinian analysis

See also: depressive position; Klein, Melanie; object relations theory; paranoid-schizoid position; projective identification

Klein did much of her work with children and her theory focused upon the very primitive elements of the human mind which were almost ungraspable. She considered that her patients' experiences were so remote from consciousness and verbal thought that they were difficult to communicate in a manner that is verifiable outside the particular analyst–patient relationship (Hinshelwood 1991). The emphasis in Kleinian therapy is taking the patient's subjective experience seriously and her writing about her clinical cases are very detailed and scrupulous. She was particularly influenced in her thinking and clinical practice by object relations which emerged from her experience and understanding of the transference relationship in therapy.

The key tenets of her clinical work were about the importance of content rather than instinctual origin, play therapy, unconscious phantasy, violence, sadism in phantasy relationships, envy, the death instinct and positions.

In that she was interested in the content of the mind rather than driving forces her clinical work was markedly different from classical (Freudian) analysts. She regarded children's play as the equivalent of free associations. She found in children (and thus adults) that interpretation modified anxieties and she worked particularly with the transference in the relationship with both children and adult patients. Kleinian analysis thus focused on the here and now rather than the past and the unconscious phantasies in the analyst–patient relationship.

Reference

Hinshelwood, R. (1991) *A Dictionary of Kleinian Thought*. London: Free Association Books.

Annotated further reading

Britton, R., Feldman, M. and O'Shaughnessy, E. (2007) *The Oedipus Complex Today: Clinical Implications*. London: Karnac.

This includes a detailed example of a clinical case study and provides evidence of her clear observation and understanding of primitive anxieties.

Orbach, S. (2000) *The Impossibility of Sex*. Harmondsworth: Penguin.

Susie Orbach's book provides a series of well-observed case studies particularly about the therapist's experience of the countertransference.

L

Lazarus, Arnold A. (1932–)

See also: multimodal therapy

Lazarus trained as a clinical psychologist and is an award winning, internationally acclaimed professor of psychology, therapist, author, lecturer and clinical innovator. Within the field of modern psychological therapy he is one of the pioneering figures, who first used the expression 'behaviour therapy' in the professional literature and went on to develop multimodal therapy (MMT). MMT has been perceived by many therapists in psycho-educational therapies as one of the most effective forms of cognitive behaviour therapy. He created his multimodal approach in response to certain constraints he considered traditional behavioural counselling to have.

Lazarus was born in Johannesburg, South Africa, in 1932 and is the author of 18 books and hundreds of scholarly and scientific publications, videos and sound recordings. He has received much recognition, such as the Distinguished Psychologist Award of the American Psychological Association (APA) in 1992. He is currently the Executive Director of the Lazarus Institute and has maintained an active psychotherapy practice since 1959.

In recent years, Lazarus has written popular psychology books such as: *Marital Myths: Two Dozen Mistaken Beliefs that Can Ruin a Marriage or Make a Bad One Worse* (Lazarus 1985). He refers to an incident that happened when he was 7 years old, as 'the seed from which his empathic response and helping ethos derived' (Dumont and Corsini 2000: 145). Several children had been harassing a little girl who seemed mentally impaired. She had been caught in the rain, was drenched, crying and frightened. He took her by the hand and at home his mother looked after her immediately: bathing her, feeding her and giving her dry clothes to wear. Lazarus describes both his own parents as kind and caring and says he inherited these traits from them.

In 1952 he set out to study English Literature at the University of Witwatersrand in Johannesburg, wanting to become a journalist after the completion of his degree. He was however so uninspired by the teaching that he switched to psychology and sociology. He initially studied Freudian, Rogerian and Sullivanian approaches, but had already encountered the 'conditioning therapy' of followers of Joseph Wolpe. For his PhD in clinical psychology (1960) he compared systematic desensitization and insight orientated methods for the treatment of phobias. In 1957 he spent three months in London as an intern in an Adlerian Institution (Marlborough Day Hospital).

In 1958, while still a graduate student, Lazarus published a paper in the *South African Medical Journal* describing a new form of psychotherapy that he called behaviour therapy. He began his private practice in psychotherapy in Johannesburg in 1959. In 1963 Lazarus spent a year as a visiting assistant professor of psychology at Stanford University, where he first became aware of the theories of Skinner. He returned to the University of Witwatersrand as a lecturer in psychiatry at the medical school. In 1966, he returned to the USA as director of the Behaviour Therapy Institute in Sausalito, California. That year he published *Behaviour Therapy Techniques* with Joseph Wolpe. The following year, he moved to Temple University Medical School in Philadelphia accepting a full professorship in the field of behavioural science.

Lazarus was the first psychologist to apply desensitization techniques for treating phobias in group therapy sessions. With Arnold Abramovitz, he was the first to use emotive imagery in treating children. He studied treatments for alcoholism and was one of the first to apply learning theory to the treatment of depression. By the 1960s, it was clear to Lazarus that the therapy movement he had initiated, utilizing the stimulus-response mechanisms of behaviourist psychology, was too limited for effective psychotherapy. His book, *Behaviour Therapy and Beyond* (1971) laid the foundations for what became known as cognitive behavioural therapy.

As Lazarus examined long-term results in patients who had undergone cognitive behavioural therapy, he found some inadequacies. For patients with anxiety and panic disorders, obsessive-compulsive problems, depression, and family and marital difficulties, the relapse rate following therapy remained very high. He therefore developed a multimodal therapy, which involves examining and treating seven different but interrelated modalities, or psychological parameters. These modalities are behaviour, physiology and lifestyle, cognition, interpersonal relationships, sensation, imagery and affect. Thus, multimodal therapy involves a complete assessment (BASIC ID) of the individual and treatments designed specifically for that individual. Lazarus developed his approach, in part, by questioning clients about the factors that had helped them in their therapy. In 1976, Lazarus founded the Multimodal Therapy Institute in Kingston, New Jersey, and he continues to direct that Institute. He established additional Multimodal Therapy Institutes in New York, Virginia, Pennsylvania, Illinois, Texas and Ohio. His book *Multimodal Behaviour Therapy* was published in 1976.

In 1975, Lazarus published his first popular self-help book, *I Can If I Want To*, with his colleague Allen Fay. His 1977 book, *In the Mind's Eye: The Power of Imagery for Personal Enrichment*, described the use of mental imagery for personal growth. His recent popular psychology writings include several books written with his son, the psychologist Clifford Neil Lazarus. Their 1993 book with Allen Fay, *Don't Believe it for a Minute! Forty Toxic Ideas That Are Driving You Crazy*, encouraged people to stop repeating the same mistakes. They argued that misconceptions, such as 'life should be fair', lead to depression, anxiety and feelings of guilt. During his career, Lazarus has treated thousands of clients, as individuals, couples, families and groups.

References

Dumont, F. and Corsini, R. (2000) *Six Therapists and One Client*. London: Free Association Books.

Lazarus, A. (1971) *Behaviour Therapy and Beyond*. New York: McGraw-Hill.

Lazarus, A. (1977) *In the Mind's Eye: The Power of Imagery for Personal Enrichment*. Rawson Associates.

Lazarus, A. (1985) *Marital Myths: Two Dozen Mistaken Beliefs that can Ruin a Marriage or Make a Bad One Worse*. Atascadero, CA: Impact Publishers.

Lazarus, A. and Fay, A. (1975) *I Can If I Want To*. Morrow.

Lazarus, A., Lazarus, C.N. and Fay, A. (1993) *Don't Believe it For a Minute! Forty Toxic Ideas That are Driving You Crazy*. Atascadero, CA: Impact Publishers.

Annotated further reading

Lazarus, A. (1971) *Behaviour Therapy and Beyond*. New York: McGraw-Hill.

This covers what has come to be called cognitive behavioural therapy. The book emphasizes personalistic variables, condemns dehumanization and describes a range of techniques that transcend the usual behavioural procedures.

Lazarus, A.A. (1981) *The Practice of Multimodal Therapy*. New York: McGraw-Hill.

Albert Ellis called this book one of 'the rare publications that beautifully encompass the art and science of psychotherapy'. It is recommended as the main source for integrating MMT into one's toolkit in advanced integrative psychotherapy.

Lazarus, A. and Fay, A. (1975) *I Can If I Want To*. Morrow.

The classic book of therapy, one of the best self-help books ever written (Albert Ellis). Based on the two significant assumptions that assertiveness is crucial in interpersonal relationships and that we are not victims of circumstance, but that the locus of control is in ourselves, this work shows how to change your thinking and your behaviour.

Lazarus, A., Lazarus, C.N. and Fay, A. (1994) *Don't Believe it For a Minute! Forty Toxic Ideas that are Driving You Crazy*. Atascadero, CA: Impact Publishers.

Two psychologists and a psychiatrist debunk 40 common misbeliefs that can lead to depression, anxiety and guilt. Examples of faulty beliefs include 'Life should be fair', 'Always strive for perfection' and 'Once a victim, always a victim'.

Life scripts

See also: archetypes; conditions of worth; drama triangle; games; self; self-actualization; transactional analysis

Eric Berne saw each of us as born without a script and with a basic trust that we and the world are OK. He called us princes and princesses. What happens next is that we learn a set of beliefs early in childhood about how the rest of our life is going to be. For example, someone who cares for an ill parent and has little time for other activities may see this as the meaning of their life and seek out caring roles as an adult in a compulsive, automatic way. Our script thus includes values, desires, beliefs and goals and it underlies behaviour.

The concept of life script is related to several other concepts on counselling and personality theory, for example conditions of worth, irrational beliefs and self-concept – how we see ourselves – but it is broader than self-concept because it includes beliefs about life and human nature too. Archetypes can be seen as one kind of script, though from a different source if Jung was right about the collective unconscious.

Script is fundamentally related to the idea of a real self, with scripts being obstacles to self-actualization. In Berne's view, we are ruled by our script and dutifully play a prescribed role. A script is learnt from repeated 'messages' from powerful sources, most obviously parents and guardians but also social class and culture. The messages can be from behaviour – a parent who is very driven by work, demonstrating that life is serious – or a direct comment made many times such as 'you're so clumsy', 'you're such a pretty little girl'. Some messages are positive and liberating, for example 'it's ok to express feelings'; others create scripts, which are restricting by definition.

Scripts can be uncovered through 'script analysis'. One approach is to use questions such as: What do your parents say when they criticize you? What could you do to make them happy? What words do you fear might appear in your epitaph? (the last question is moving into existential concerns but as a way of uncovering past influences). Others are: What were you told about your grandparents? How old do you expect to be when you die? (Steiner 1974 wrote that Berne's script told him that he'd die at 60, that Berne knew this, and that he died at 60 anyway). What did your parents/guardians pass on to you?

One or two of these questions may be enough to uncover significant aspects of a script, though not necessarily at once: memories may come up in the ensuing days and weeks, and your script (assuming this is a useful concept) gradually appears. It's not a magical or mystical process, and the values, beliefs and so on can be examined and replaced and a new set of decisions made about your life. Berne's aim in TA was to help clients reach a position of being OK (his term) – a prince or princess – again.

Reference

Steiner, C. (1974) *Scripts People Live*. New York: Bantam Books.

Annotated further reading

Berne, E. (1975) *What Do You Say After You Say Hello? The Psychology of Human Destiny*. New York: Grove Press.

This includes a script check list.

Steiner, C. (1974) *Scripts People Live*. New York: Bantam Books.

Most books on TA have a section on scripts but this is the most in-depth and provocative discussion by a writer who helped develop script theory.

Life traps

See also: schema therapy

When Jeffrey Young rewrote his schema therapy book for the general public and entitled it *Reinventing Your Life* (Young and Klosko 1994) he replaced the rather complex therapeutic term 'Early maladaptive schemas' by calling it 'life traps'.

On the first page of his self-help book he defines 'life traps' as 'patterns that start in childhood' and that seem to run like a thread through your whole life. They are considered to be unhelpful patterns of behaviour and beliefs, which create neuropathways. These thinking patterns came into existence due to deliberate or accidental treatments we received from significant elders prior to the age of approximately 10. 'We were abandoned, criticized, overprotected, abused, excluded or deprived – damaged in some way' (Young and Klosko 1994: 1)

We continue to run the behaviours based on those life traps long after having set up independent lives. They may have been useful in the past but now they are a hindrance to leading the life we wish to experience. The life traps are described below:

1   Abandonment This involves the sense that people we deeply care for will leave us or not provide emotional support. This life trap can lead to clingy relationships or to pushing loved others away. Another sign is anger that easily arises when you feel misunderstood or fear rejection.

2   Mistrust and abuse There is an 'expectation that others will hurt, abuse, humiliate, cheat, lie, manipulate, or take advantage' (Young and Klosko 1994: 18) of us. Usually you believe that all of this is done on purpose and thus you avoid close and trusting relationships.

3   Dependence You feel mostly that you are unable to handle your *everyday responsibilities* 'in a competent manner' (Young and Klosko 1994: 19). Others are seen as stronger and needed as a crutch and in a work context you hold back from moving into more responsible positions.

4   Defectiveness/shame (DS) You experience the feeling that one is defective, bad, unwanted, inferior or invalid in important respects; or that one would be unlovable to significant others if exposed. It may involve hypersensitivity to criticism, rejection and blame; self-consciousness, comparisons and insecurity around others; or a sense of shame regarding one's perceived flaws. These flaws may be *private* (e.g. selfishness, angry impulses, unacceptable sexual desires) or *public* (e.g. undesirable physical appearance, social awkwardness).

5   Vulnerability You constantly wait for some catastrophe to happen: disease, financial destruction ('having to live under a bridge'), becoming a victim of crime or natural catastrophes such as aeroplane crashes or earthquakes. Your existence is fear based and you may develop phobic avoidance or panic attacks.

6   Emotional deprivation You fear that you will never be truly loved by others and that no one actually cares for you deeply. Thus you tend to end up with emotionally cold friends or partners who also lack generosity. Thus you create your fear over and over again. Emotionally you feel angry or hurt and lonely. And often it is your anger that puts people off you.

7 Social exclusion You experience yourself as 'isolated from the rest of the world and different from other people'. This life trap can lead to social anxiety.

8 Failure You believe that you are not good or clever enough to achieve good outcomes at school, work or physical activities. It often includes ideas that you are stupid, inept, untalented, lower in status, less successful than others.

9 Subjugation You tend to exclusively want to serve others or please them and deny yourself your own needs and pleasures. You fear the wrath of others and enter relationships with domineering or needy others.

10 Unrelenting standards Only 100 per cent will ever be good enough; you place high expectations on yourself and others and material values are most important to you. You also look for the perfect partner.

11 Entitlement You believe that you are made of better 'stuff' than other people; you feel you are entitled to special rights and privileges; or not bound by the rules that guide normal social interaction. 'Often involves insistence that one should be able to do or have whatever one wants, regardless of what is realistic, what others consider reasonable, or the cost to others.' You usually act excessively competitively or dominate others. Self-discipline is an alien concept to you.

Reference

Young, J. and Klosko, J. (1994) *Reinventing Your Life: The Breakthrough Program to End Negative Behaviour and Feel Great Again*. New York: Plume Books.

Annotated further reading

Young, J. and Klosko, J. (1994) *Reinventing Your Life: The Breakthrough Program to End Negative Behaviour and Feel Great Again*. New York: Plume Books.

In this book, Young and Klosko describe some of the most common schemas, or life traps, and provide diagnostic tests for each with step-by-step suggestions on how to break free from them. The principles described are extremely useful in aiding the process of recognizing and changing negative thought patterns in a relatively short period of time and without the use of drugs.

Locus of evaluation

See also: conditions of worth; core conditions; person-centred counselling; self-actualization; self-concept

This section is best read in conjunction with the sections on self-concept, self-actualization and conditions of worth as they are all key concepts in the person-centred approach to counselling and are closely linked. If an individual has developed a relatively positive self-concept they are likely to evaluate issues and make decisions according to their own inner wisdom. Rogers (1961) believed that what 'feels right' is 'a trustworthy guide to behaviour' (1961: 190). The individual is then said to have developed an internal locus of evaluation. If, on the other hand, someone has a more negative self-concept, which results in their being estranged from their inner sense of what is right or wrong for them, they will find it difficult to trust their own thoughts and feelings in order to decide how to behave. Instead they will rely on the values and beliefs of significant others which have been internalized during the development of their self-concept. Such a person will have an external locus of evaluation and will very likely find it extremely difficult to make decisions independently as they will be out of touch with their true self and their actualizing tendency.

Reference

Rogers, C.R. (1961) *On Becoming a Person*. Boston, MA: Houghton Mifflin.

Annotated further reading

Casemore, R. (2006) *Person-centred Counselling in a Nutshell*. London: Sage.

A succinct guide to person-centred theoretical concepts and to the counselling relationship.

Cooper, M., O'Hara, M., Schmid, P.F. and Wyatt, G. (eds) (2007) *The Handbook of Person Centred Counselling and Psychotherapy*. Ross-on-Wye: PCCS Books.

An excellent, comprehensive overview of theory and practice.

Logotherapy

See also: existential counselling; anxiety, eristential

> Logotherapy is ultimately education toward responsibility.
> (Foreword to Frankl 1965)

Logotherapy was developed by the neurologist and psychiatrist Viktor Frankl. It is considered the 'Third Viennese School of Psychotherapy' (Allport 1959), Freud's psychoanalysis and Adler's individual psychology being the others. It focuses on a 'will to meaning' as opposed to Adler's doctrine of 'will of power' or Freud's 'will to pleasure' (Seidner 2009: 2). One could perceive it as an enhancement rather than a replacement for psychotherapy. 'Logo' derives from the Greek and expresses both 'meaning' and 'spirit' (without a religious connotation). Logotherapy is founded upon the belief that the most powerful driving force in humans is to find meaning in one's life (Seidner 2009: 3). The intent of logotherapy then is to assist seekers in their search.

Frankl was drawing on the ideas of existential philosophers Heidegger, Jaspers and Scheler and even before the Second World War he had started to develop logotherapy as his personal reaction against the apparent meaninglessness of an unreflected life. He founded Youth Advisement Centres in the late 1920s in Vienna and received his MD in 1930 from Vienna University. His first long-term employment was as a member of the Neuropsychiatric University Clinic.

Frankl's book, entitled *Man's Search for Meaning*, describes his theories and how they helped him survive his experience during the Holocaust when he was imprisoned in Auschwitz and Dachau. Here he was able to use some of his medical knowledge to help others without however having any medical tools available. He states that through the harrowing experience he nevertheless was able to further develop and reinforce his theories. He experienced human nature under the most extreme conditions and observed that most inmates chose to 'vegetate' but there were some who seemed to grow through this experience.

There are three basic principles of logotherapy, which Frankl also called 'existenzanalyse':

- Life has meaning under all circumstances, even the most despondent ones.
- Our main motivation for living is our will to find meaning in life.
- We have freedom to find meaning in what we do, and what we experience, or at least in the stand we take when faced with a situation of unalterable suffering.

The search for meaning doesn't necessarily mean the search for God or indeed any other supernatural being. It suffices to know why we live, which seems to help us overcome most obstacles.

According to Frankl: 'We can discover this meaning in life in three different ways: (a) by creating a work or doing a deed; (b) by experiencing something or encountering someone; and (c) by the attitude we take toward unavoidable suffering' and 'everything can be taken from a man but one thing: the last of the human freedoms – to choose one's attitude in any given set of circumstances' (Frankl 1959: 176).

On the meaning of the suffering, Frankl gives the following example: 'Once, an elderly general practitioner consulted me because of his severe depression. He could not overcome the loss of his wife who had died two years before and whom he had loved above all else. Now how could I help him? What should I tell him? I refrained from telling him anything, but instead confronted him with a question, "What would have happened, Doctor, if you had died first, and your wife would have had to survive you?" "Oh," he said, "for her this would have been terrible; how she would have suffered!" Whereupon I replied, "You see, Doctor, such a suffering has been spared her, and it is you who have spared her this suffering; but now, you have to pay for it by surviving and mourning her." He said no word but shook my hand and calmly left the office' (Frankl 1959: 178–9).

Logotherapy can be applied therapeutically in several different areas of destructive emotions, such as overcoming anxiety, as well as treating neurosis or depression. With anxiety, Frankl believed that the anxious individual doesn't understand that his anxiety is the result of dealing with a sense of 'unfulfilled responsibility' and ultimately a lack of meaning.

With a person who fears not getting a good night's sleep, which may be caused by them trying too hard to fall asleep, a logotherapist would suggest that the client go to bed and intentionally not go to sleep, thus relieving the anxiety which keeps them awake, and thereafter falling asleep eventually.

Logotherapy can also be used in the treatment of schizophrenia, as Frankl believed that any sufferers can first be taught to ignore voices and end persistent self-observation. Then during the same period, the client must be led toward meaningful activity as 'even for the schizophrenic there remains that residue of freedom toward fate and toward the disease which man always possesses, no matter how ill he may be, in all situations and at every moment of life, to the very last' (Frankl 1965: 207).

Some criticism of the approach is based on Frankl's philosophy being centre stage of the approach, not leaving much room for theoretical expansion and also a lacking in empirical research. The approach was never intended however to be a 'therapy' by itself but rather as an additional tool that could be added on to whatever therapy was being used. Lastly, Frankl was seen by many as the 'hero' which made it difficult for others to continue to develop the approach when Frankl was gone.

Frankl was interviewed at the Milton E. Erickson Foundation Conference entitled 'The Evolution of Psychotherapy' in 1985. This is held every five years and the speakers invited are those who have made significant contributions to psychotherapy, medicine and philosophy. Frankl was in his late 80s. He was asked by a member of the audience, why he decided to return to Vienna after his horrific experience during the Second World War, which ultimately also killed most of his family. His answer was brief and simple. He said: 'Why not!'

References

Allport, G.W. (1959) Preface, *Man's Search for Meaning*. Boston, MA: Beacon Press.

Frankl, V. (1959) *Man's Search for Meaning*. Boston, MA: Beacon Press.

Frankl, V. (1965) *The Doctor and the Soul: From Psychotherapy to Logotherapy*. New York: Vintage.

Seidner, S.S. (2009) A Trojan horse: logotherapeutic transcendence and its secular implications for theology. *Mater Dei Institute*.

Annotated further reading

Nelson-Jones, R. (1995) *The Theory and Practice of Counselling*. London: Cassell.

This book reviews many main psychological approaches and is particularly useful for counsellors who work integratively. However, it requires focus and attention. It contains very in-depth research of each topic and good guidance at the start of each chapter.

M

Mindfulness-based cognitive behavioural coaching (MBCBC)

See also: compassionate mind training; mindfulness-based cognitive therapy; mindfulness-based stress reduction

Currently there is a general interest in mindfulness-based interventions. Mindfulness-based stress reduction (MBSR) and mindfulness-based cognitive therapy (MBCT) (Baer 2005) are therapeutic interventions used in medical and mental health settings to help clients with a variety of physical and psychological problems. Research includes a vast spectrum of disease management such as pain (Kabat-Zinn et al. 1987); stress (Astin 1997); depression (Segal et al. 2002) and anxiety (Kabat-Zinn et al. 1992) and others.

The phenomenon of wanting to remain well in a culture that rarely permits enough time to recuperate from long working hours, commuting and less than healthy living environments is in itself a paradoxical desire.

The concepts of 'meaning and purpose' have been acknowledged as key factors for increasing psychological as well as physical resilience, something equally important whether related to work or to life in general (Morris 2008).

Mindfulness-based cognitive coaching (MBCC) is the latest development that draws upon the strategies of mindfulness-based therapies and the skills and methodology of cognitive-behavioural coaching (CBC). MBCC is applied to client groups who do not fall within the medical or therapeutic client arenas.

Being mindful, i.e. present in this moment where your life is actually happening, differs significantly from how the 24/7 life style has tended to shape twenty-first-century men's experience. The ability of connecting with what has been termed 'the here and now' stimulates a completely different physiological response as different parts of the nervous system become activated allowing the experience to take on new meaning (Collard and Walsh 2008).

There is significant evidence that learning to experience life from moment to moment can create calm and well-being, whereas over planning, ruminating and fretting triggers the so-called 'stress-response' which can lead to physical and mental illness (Palmer and Cooper 2007).

The research evidence

There is an increasing evidence base regarding the effectiveness of mindfulness based approaches such as the 2003 study by Rosenzweig et al., which demonstrated the lowering of psychological anguish among medical students. In 2003 the McCraty study demonstrated a reduction in blood pressure including an improvement of job satisfaction in hypertensive employees. The 2003 study undertaken by Davidson et al. highlighted improved changes in brain and immune function brought about through mindfulness meditation and the 2008 study by Collard and Walsh saw an improvement in the well-being of participants in all areas of their life.

References

Astin, J.A. (1997) Stress reduction through mindfulness meditation: effects on psychological symptomatology, sense of control, and spiritual experiences. *Psychotherapy and Psychosomatics*, 66(2): 97–106.

Baer, R.E. (ed.) (2005) *Mindfulness-based Treatment Approaches: Clinician's Guide to Evidence Base and Applications*. London: Academic Press, Elsevier.

Chaskalson, M. (2011) *The Mindful Workplace*. Chichester: John Wiley & Sons.

Collard, P. and Walsh, J. (2008) Sensory awareness mindfulness training in coaching: accepting life's challenges. *Journal of Rational-Emotive & Cognitive-Behavior Therapy*, 26(1): 30–7.

Davidson, R.J., Kabat-Zinn, J., Schmacher, J. et al. (2003) Alterations in brain and immune function produced by mindfulness meditation. *Psychosomatic Medicine*, 66: 148–52.

Kabat-Zinn, J., Lipworth, L., Burney, R. and Sellers, W. (1987) Four-year follow-up of a meditation-based program for the self-regulation of chronic pain: treatment outcomes and compliance. *Clinical Journal of Pain*, 2: 159–73.

Kabat-Zinn, J., Massion, A., Kristeller, J. and Peterson, L. (1992) Effectiveness of a meditation based stress reduction program in the treatment of anxiety disorders. *American Journal of Psychiatry*, 149: 936–43.

McCraty, R.M. (2003) Impact of a workplace stress reduction programme on blood pressure and emotional health in hypertensive employees. *Journal of Alternative and Complementary Medicine*, 9(3): 355–69.

McMahon, G. (2007) *Understanding Cognitive Behavioural Coaching*, training journal.

Morris, T. (2008) *What Do Buddhists Believe: Meaning and Mindfulness in Buddhist Philosophy*. New York: Walker & Company.

Palmer, S., and Cooper, C. (2007) *How to Deal with Stress*. London: Kogan Page.

Rosenzweig, S., Reibel, D.K., Greeson, J.M. and Brainard, G.C. (2003) Mindfulness-based stress reduction lowers psychological distress in medical students. *Teaching and Learning in Medicine*, 15(2): 88–92.

Segal, Z.V., Williams, J.M.G. and Teasdale, J.D. (2002) *Mindfulness Based Cognitive Therapy for Depression: A New Approach to Preventing Relapse*. New York: Guilford Press.

Annotated further reading

Kabat-Zinn, J. (2001) *Full Catastrophe Living: How to Cope with Stress, Pain and Illness Using Mindfulness Meditation*. London: Piatkus.

This is a comprehensive guide to the practice of mindfulness and how it can be applied to help in dealing with symptoms such as stress, anxiety, pain and illness. It includes straight-forward instructions on how to implement mindfulness meditation practices into your daily life and success stories of people who had attended Kabat-Zinn's mindfulness clinic. It also highlights the latest scientific research findings on the benefits of the practice.

Segal, Z.V., Williams, J.M.G. and Teasdale, J.D. (2002) *Mindfulness Based Cognitive Therapy for Depression: A New Approach to Preventing Relapse*. New York: Guilford Press.

This book presents an eight session programme called mindfulness-based cognitive therapy (MBCT). It provides the theoretical basis for the programme and a detailed structure of each of the group sessions, including useful reproducible materials such as session summaries and participant forms. It also provides guidance for clinicians on how to develop their own mindfulness practice. Furthermore, the guidance within the book is solidly grounded in current empirical research.

Mindfulness-based cognitive coaching (MBCC)

Teaching participants to become more *mindful* helps to assist clients to reconnect to the experience of 'being' rather than of 'doing'. In turn, this increases individual effectiveness and, as a by-product, personal productivity (Linley and Joseph 2004).

At the same time the skills associated with cognitive-behavioural coaching are interwoven with awareness training. Examples would be helping clients identify self-defeating core beliefs that lead to unhelpful emotional and behavioural consequences (McMahon and Leimon 2008).

The synthesis between mindfulness training and cognitive behavioural coaching that led to the birth of mindfulness based cognitive coaching provides the individual with the skills and strategies to devise new and healthier beliefs about self, others and the world in general with the ability to connect to the present.

MBCC can be used with individuals as well as with groups. The client needs to understand and be an active participant in his or her own coaching programme. The relevance and benefits of using a mindful approach to work and life are explored in relation to the client's presenting issue(s).

The coach and client decide on the best way of engaging in the MBCC process. *Commitment* is an essential requirement to ensure the best possible outcome and the client is made aware of this right from the start.

The client may opt for the complete MBCC (eight weeks) programme or have some of the concepts of MBCC introduced into an already existing coaching programme. Some practices may only take a few minutes but as Collard and Walsh (2008) found, clients can still reap the benefits even from such short periods of practice. The learning of mindful awareness increases with each and every application: 'A journey of a thousand miles starts with a single step!'

While there are a number of longer meditative 'journeys' such as the body scan (where an individual takes time to focus slowly on each part of their body for 45 minutes), benefits can be accrued from much shorter exercises (Kabat-Zinn 1994).

The client is encouraged to consider the way that a more realistic and compassionate (win-win) way of perceiving the world increases personal effectiveness and decreases negative emotional outcomes for everyone concerned. This process is used to assist the creation of the behavioural changes required to produce a more effective way of being (McMahon and Rosen 2008).

MBCC brings together two approaches into a model that provides the client with more control over and enjoyment of their daily life.

References

Collard, P. and Walsh, J. (2008) Sensory awareness mindfulness training in coaching: accepting life's challenges. *Journal of Rational-Emotive & Cognitive-Behavior Therapy*, 26(1): 30–7.

Kabat-Zinn, J. (1994) *Wherever You Go, There You Are: Mindfulness Meditation in Everyday Life*. London: Piatkus.

Linley, P.A. and Joseph, S. (2004) *Positive Psychology in Practice*. Hoboken, NJ: John Wiley & Sons.

McMahon, G. and Leimon, A. (2008) *Performance Coaching for Dummies*. Chichester: John Wiley & Sons.

McMahon, G. and Rosen, A. (2008), *Why Perfectionism at Work Does Not Pay* training journal http://www.mindfulnet.org/Mindful%20feelings%20at%20Work.pdf (accessed 26 December 2011).

Mindfulness-based cognitive therapy (MBCT)

See also: acceptance commitment therapy; cognitive behavioural therapy; dialectical behaviour therapy; Kabat-Zinn, Jon; mindfulness-based stress reduction

MBCT has traditionally been used as a group intervention to teach recovered recurrently depressed patients to disengage from depressogenic thinking that may lead to relapse. Segal et al. (2002) found out that even minor increases in sadness could reactivate depressive thinking neuro-pathways in formerly depressed client groups. CBT treatment had indeed been able to deactivate negative thinking however could not 'delete' it from the 'hard disk' of the mind.

Each new episode of depression hard-wired these depressive thinking patterns more and more and hence relapse tended to become more and more easily activated the more often a person had experienced a depressive episode.

MBCT thus was developed as a prevention tool and initially researched through a three-site randomized control trial (Segal et al. 2002). In a multi-centre RCT conducted in Toronto, Cambridge and Bangor, 145 participants were allocated to receive either treatment-as-usual (TAU), or, in addition to TAU, they received eight classes of MBCT. All the participants in the study had been symptom free for at least three months and off antidepressant medication when they entered the trial. They were known to be vulnerable to future depression because they had had at least two episodes in their past that met criteria for DSM Major Depression (the final episode having occurred within two years). The sample was stratified (arranged) on entry by the number of previous episodes (two only, or more than two). The researchers followed up the participants for 12 months after the eight weeks. Results showed that MBCT helped those who were most severe and substantially reduced the risk of relapse in those who had three or more previous episodes of depression (from 66 per cent to 37 per cent).

MBCT is based on an integration of CBT for depression with components of mindfulness practices. MBCT has didactic elements, which give the participants information about the particular difficulty they are dealing with. In the case of depression, participants are given information on the universal characteristics of depression to help them recognize their personal 'relapse signatures'. The pattern of mind which makes people vulnerable to depressive relapse is 'rumination', in which the mind repetitively reruns negative thoughts. The core skill that MBCT teaches is to intentionally 'shift mental gears'. There is little emphasis in MBCT, as in conventional CBT, on attempting to change unhelpful thoughts to more rational ones. The focus is on a *systematic* training to be more aware, moment by moment, of physical sensations and of thoughts and feelings as mental events. This facilitates a 'decentred' relationship to thoughts and feelings in which one can see them as aspects of experience which move through our awareness and which are not necessarily the reality in any given moment. 'We are not our thoughts!'

Key themes of MBCT include experiential learning (body scan, sitting meditation, mindful movement) and the development of an accepting, open attitude in which one intentionally faces problems and affective discomfort. Increased mindfulness assists early detection of relapse-related patterns of negative thinking, feelings and body sensations, allowing them to be addressed at a stage when this may be much easier than if such warning signs were not noticed or even ignored.

In Oxford, MBCT has been expanded to other treatment areas such as working with patients with chronic fatigue (Christina Surawy, Jill Roberts), eating disorders (Jill Roberts), and for patients who recurrently become suicidal as well as depressed (Mark Williams, Melanie Fennell).

MBCT is relatively cost and time effective and is now included in the NICE guidelines for prevention of recurrent depression.

Reference

Segal, Z.V., Williams, J.M.G. and Teasdale, J.D. (2002) *Mindfulness Based Cognitive Therapy for Depression: A New Approach to Preventing Relapse*. New York: Guilford Press.

Annotated further reading

Ma, S.H. and Teasdale, J.D. (2004) Mindfulness-based cognitive therapy for depression: replication and exploration of differential relapse prevention effects. *Journal of Consulting and Clinical Psychology*, 72: 31–40.

In this paper the randomized control trial which was the basis for *Mindfulness Based Cognitive Therapy for Depression* (2002) is repeated and finds very similar results. Not a bedtime read!

Segal, Z.V., Williams, J.M.G. and Teasdale, J.D. (2002) *Mindfulness Based Cognitive Therapy for Depression: A New Approach to Preventing Relapse*. New York: Guilford Press.

This book presents an eight session programme called mindfulness-based cognitive therapy (MBCT). It provides the theoretical basis for the programme and a detailed structure of each of the group sessions, including useful reproducible materials such as session summaries and participant forms. It also provides guidance for clinicians on how to develop their own mindfulness practice. Furthermore, the guidance within the book is solidly grounded in current empirical research.

Williams, M., Teasdale J., Segal Z. and Kabat-Zinn, J. (2007) *The Mindful Way Through Depression: Freeing Yourself from Chronic Unhappiness*. New York: Guilford Press.

This book explains how the use of mindfulness can help to break the cycle of chronic unhappiness and depression. It is a self-help book, which includes a CD on which Jon Kabat-Zinn talks you through the main practices.

www.mindfulnet.org
This is a recently developed secular website covering the diverse applications of mindfulness.

Mindfulness-based stress reduction (MBSR)

See also: Kabat-Zinn, Jon; mindfulness-based cognitive therapy

MBSR is a group-based programme which was designed and developed by Jon Kabat-Zinn and colleagues at the University of Massachusetts Medical Centre, Centre for Mindfulness (CFM) for populations with a wide range of physical and mental health problems. There has been extensive research looking at outcomes of this eight-week course since the late 1970s. CFM has offered and delivered MBSR to patients within a large traditional American hospital since 1979. In 1993 Bill Moyers, a well-known American journalist attended and filmed one of these courses. The result, *Healing from Within*, started a huge interest in the general and medical population who watched the TV programme.

By 1999 over 10,000 patients had completed the course. Kabat-Zinn and his co-trainers extended the teaching of MBSR into prisons, poor inner-city areas, schools, medical students, professional sport and into corporate environments. MBSR is now a recognized part in the field of integrative medicine within behavioural medicine and general health care. Its potential lies not only in treatment but also in prevention of 'dis-ease'.

The ancient tradition of mindfulness is adapted from its use as a spiritual practice and is delivered in an accessible, secular format. It helps participants to conquer the difficulties faced when suffering from a variety of physical and psychological illnesses. The training is not tailored to any particular diagnosis and MBSR research shows positive results for participants with chronic pain, fibromyalgia, multiple sclerosis, generalized anxiety disorder and panic attacks, psoriasis, some forms of cancer and others. The programme involves intensive training in mindfulness meditation, yoga movements and discussions on stress and life skills.

Annotated further reading

Kabat-Zinn, J. (1990) *Full Catastrophe Living*. New York: Dell Publishing.

This is a comprehensive guide to the practice of mindfulness and how it can be applied to help in dealing with symptoms such as stress, anxiety, pain and illness. It includes straightforward instructions on how to implement mindfulness meditation practices into your daily life and success stories of people who had attended his mindfulness clinic. It also highlights the latest scientific research findings on the benefits of the practice.

Kabat-Zinn, J. (1994) *Wherever You Go, There You Are*. New York: Hyperion.

This is a wonderful travel companion or bedtime read. Some of its short chapters are very easy to follow; others require more concentration and effort. It offers real insight into mindfulness as it can be used in everyday and meditative life.

Kabat-Zinn, J. (2005) *Coming to Our Senses*. New York: Hyperion.

How can we slow down? How can we get back in touch with all our senses? How can we become more playful and live truly in the NOW where our life is actually happening? Jon is a fabulous storyteller; follow him into the realm of being and sensing.

Toneatto, T. and Nguyen, L. (2007) Does mindfulness meditation improve anxiety and mood symptoms? A review of the controlled research. *The Canadian Journal of Psychiatry*, 52(4): 260–6.

About one-half (8/15) of the studies reported a statistically significant reduction in anxiety or depression after MBSR. Unfortunately, none of these studies included an active control group. Also, the durability of the outcomes is difficult to evaluate because only six studies reported follow-up data. Overall MBSR does not have a reliable effect on depression and anxiety.

Motivational interviewing (MI)

Motivational Interviewing (MI) is an individualistic approach that can be used in addition to CBT when treating alcohol dependency and other addictions, an approach that attempts to reinstate a person's lost self-esteem and self-control. MI has been described as 'one of the most important and innovative therapeutic intervention of the 1980s' (Whitehead 1992: 23).

MI represents one aspect of the larger topic of change: what motivates change in people struggling with personal problems? Miller and Rollnick (1991) state: 'What we hope to offer in . . . is a clear understanding of how people can be trapped by ambivalence, and how those who want to help them can strengthen their motivation for change' (Preface, p. ix).

MI moves towards helping clients build commitment and reach a decision to change. Included here are some historical and geographical perspectives that led Miller to develop MI.

In the mid-1970s William Miller began to develop MI. At first it was mere intuition, but when challenged by Norwegian psychologists on the nature of his seemingly successful techniques, he decided to attempt an interpretation and outline of his approach, and published it in 1983 under the title *Motivational Interviewing with Problem Drinkers*.

This first publication seemed rather long winded, and at times not specific enough in the actual practical application of the theory it presented. Miller seems to agree when he writes later: 'In the ensuing years, much progress has been made toward clarifying and specifying processes of motivational interviewing' (Miller and Rollnick 1991: 51).

Today MI is practised in many countries, particularly English-speaking ones, The Netherlands and Scandinavia. Three different aspects constitute the approach: background, practice and clinical application.

Background

This deals with questions such as 'motivation as a personality problem', 'search for an addictive personality' or 'Prochaska and Di Clemente's Stages of Change Model'. Miller tries to challenge the idea of the 'addictive personality' (he very much opposes 'labelling', just as CBT does) and the notion that people with addictive behaviours are constantly in denial.

Practice

This uncovers the principles of MI:

Motivation: here it is not defined as a personality trait but as an interpersonal process. In order to motivate a client to change, you attempt to encourage him to make the decisions that he deems necessary to improve his life. You avoid imposing change from without, as this might lead to rebellion, thus decreasing motivation.

Denial: Miller believes that it is not inherent in the person with addiction, but rather that it is a reaction to the counsellor's (therapist's) approach. That is, man tends to do the opposite of what he is told to do. Thus telling somebody that they have an alcohol problem might lead them to take the opposite point of view, traditionally labelled as denial.

Miller further explains that MI attempts to encourage people to take on responsibility for their own life and to deal with their problems themselves (as CBT attempts to do: psycho-education).

It acknowledges that unless people themselves see the need to change, no lasting change will ever be achieved. In order to create an openness to change the therapist has to be a good listener and interpreter, as they will feed back to the client in a structured and thus more potent form the reasons for change the client has given. At first the client may be very reluctant to come forward with such information. So it is of utmost importance to read between the lines, to remember the little dissatisfactions the client mentions and to tease out whether or not their importance has been undervalued.

The goal is to increase the client's *intrinsic motivation* and this is achieved by adhering to five general principles:

1. *Express empathy:* accept people as they are and where they are (based on C. Rogers). Ambivalence to change is seen as normal, consistent with reality. The therapist tries to elicit self-motivational statements.
2. *Develop discrepancy:* 'Motivation for change is created when people perceive a discrepancy between their present behaviour and important personal goals' (Miller and Rollnick 1991: 57).
3. *Avoid argumentation:* start with the client where he is. Avoid direct confrontation in order to avoid resistance and avoid labelling.
4. *Roll with resistance:* reframe statements of client to create a new momentum towards change. The therapist invites the client to consider new information and perspectives. The client is actively involved in finding solutions for his problem.

5   *Support self-efficacy:* the therapist is an enabler to help the client help himself. We are supposed to help the client to believe in himself and to have confidence that he can carry out the changes he has chosen (i.e. reduced drinking, occasional use or possibly abstinence).

The theoretical background of MI is contained in the principles of Egan (i.e. problem solving), Rogers (i.e. accurate empathy) and behavioural psychology (i.e. by changing what you do, you change what you think). Miller goes so far as to call it a non-directive approach (Miller and Rollnick 1991: 54), which it arguably is not. Miller's aim is to reach everyone (i.e. doctors, nurses, social workers, etc.) working with problems of addiction. MI puts large emphasis on personal choice and responsibility.

In creating a cognitive dissonance, however subtly or gently you may do that, you are inevitably directing the client to where, in many ways, you as the therapist want him to be, in other words to get him to be open to change. The therapeutic style is not truly reflective, as the client's comments are fed back in a modified form and are selected to create dissonance.

Clinical application of motivational interviewing

This introduces a wide selection of articles from all over the globe. Number 13, for example, explores MI within the context of Prochaska and DiClemente's model of change. This model describes a series of stages the individual may enter during the process of change (precontemplation, contemplation, decision, action, maintenance and relapse). Most treatment programmes have been concentrating on the action stage (i.e. how to overcome addiction) and might have been unsuccessful, for failing to recognize the client's lack of motivation to carry out the action. MI on the other hand intends to 'help the person move from pre-contemplation to action' (Miller 1983: 166). It tries to establish, first of all, whether the client is ready for change; if not, how to help him to decide whether change is desired in his case; what this change would entail and how to go about it.

One criticism of MI is that it is not really clear what proportion of people who overcome their addiction pass through the stages of change in an orderly or linear way. Might it be possible that just like in the stages of grief, participants in this therapeutic approach may get stuck in contemplation for a number of years and then fall back into relapse and never complete all the stages? How would such a scenario be dealt with?

The new approach points out a number of reasons for including MI in the treatment of addiction, such as:

- staff dissatisfaction with the confrontational style of management of 'addicts';
- users' dissatisfaction with traditional programmes;

- staff having attended an MI seminar finding it a lot more positive in its approach;
- growing concern about HIV infection indicated the need to attract more addicts to the programme;
- staff spend a lot of time arguing with clients rather than building a therapeutic relationship;
- clients seem much less eager than therapists to change their addicted lifestyle;
- large number of cases of burn-out among staff/drop out among clients.

It can be argued that services applying MI as part of their treatment programme seem to indicate an improvement in their service.

References

Miller, W.R. (1983) Motivational interviewing with problem drinkers. *Behavioural Psychotherapy*, 11: 147–72.

Miller, W.R. and Rollnick, S. (1991) *Motivational Interviewing*. New York, London: Guilford Press.

Van Bilsen, H. and Whitehead, B. (1991) Motivating selfcontrol. *Conference Report of the British Association for Behavioural Psychotherapy*, pp. 1–7.

Whitehead, B. (1992) Motivational interviewing. In: *Executive Summary*, published by: The Centre for Research on Drugs and Health Behaviour, 1992, No. 17.

Annotated further reading

Miller, W.R. and Rollnick, S. (1991) *Motivational Interviewing*. New York, London: Guilford Press.

The book under discussion is the only in-depth compilation of training material and analysis of MI available, and has been edited and partially written by its founder W.R. Miller. It offers an abundance of material (24 articles in all) contributed by no less than 19 practitioners.

It is an excellent manual for practitioners wanting to implement MI in their work. There remains however the problem that all contributors to the volume are supporters of MI, which must have led to a somewhat biased evaluation. There is, it seems, the need for comparative research so as to evaluate the effectiveness of MI in motivating clients to change.

Multicultural counselling

See also: collectivism – individualism dimension; integrative models; narrative therapy

The use of counselling and psychotherapy which places the client's cultural context at the centre of the therapeutic work is a relatively new phenomenon and one which has developed in tandem with a growing recognition that we live in a multicultural world. The main theoretical approaches to counselling were developed in western cultures and, it could be argued, have limited relevance to other cultures. Initially attempts were made to take a client's cultural background into account as an 'add-on' rather than as an integral part of the therapy. In multicultural counselling culture is regarded as central to the concept of self and an individual's problems are seen in the context of their culture as well as in relation to other aspects of their lives.

In simple terms, culture can be defined as 'the way people do things around here'. However, it is a complex term and includes the ways in which members of a particular group make sense of their world, which are embodied in a multitude of ways both in terms of underlying beliefs, such as how the self is conceptualized, and observable aspects of behaviour, such as use of language or non-verbal behaviour.

When working multiculturally Sue and Sue (2007) advocate the following:

- developing awareness of one's own biases in relation to culture;
- exploring and clarifying the client's world view;
- choosing strategies and techniques appropriate to the client's culture.

In terms of the first point, therapists need, as part of the personal development process, to develop an understanding of their own cultural identity and values in order to understand how this may affect how they work with clients. This includes an awareness of any prejudices and possible blind spots.

In order to understand the client's culture, Kleinman (1988, in McLeod 2009), a key writer in this area, suggested a series of questions that could help with establishing this. These included asking:

What do you call this problem?
What do you see as the cause of it?
What is it doing to you (to your body and mind)?
What fears do you have about the problem and the treatment?

Ridley and Lingle (1996, in McLeod 2009) stress the importance of demonstrating cultural empathy during this exploratory process. It is also important to be willing to discuss issues relating to culture and indeed to discrimination, as they arise. If a therapist does not do this for whatever reason, the client can feel ignored or silenced.

Regarding choosing culturally-appropriate techniques, these need to be chosen carefully and could include using techniques from other cultures. As an integrative approach, multicultural counselling lends itself to using different strategies and techniques in this way.

McLeod (2009) suggests a set of guidelines for practising multicultural counselling which include (1) an awareness of collectivism as opposed to individualism (which tends to be more highly valued in Eastern cultures); (2) the importance of recognizing and acknowledging the presence of discrimination in clients' lives; (3) an awareness of our own cultural biases and a willingness to employ other concepts of mental health, such as religious ones, as well as western concepts; also an openness to the client's cultural support systems such as traditional healing methods; and (4) a willingness to explore the client's cultural identity and to check things out with the client and to learn from them.

Research into multicultural counselling

There has not been a great deal of research into this type of counselling to date. McLeod (2009) identifies a number of research studies which suggest that black clients tend to prefer to work with counsellors from the same ethnic group and tend to drop out less often. However, he states that overall such studies do not produce definitive results. This area appears to be ripe for further research.

References

McLeod, J. (2009) *An Introduction to Counselling*. Maidenhead: Open University Press.

Sue, D.W. and Sue, D. (2007) *Counselling the Culturally Diverse: Theory and Practice*, 5th edn. New York: J. Wiley and Sons.

Annotated further reading

Palmer, S. (ed.) (2002) *Multicultural Counselling: A Reader*. London: Sage.

Discusses a range of central issues relating to theory and practice.

Pederson, P. (2010) *Counselling Across Cultures*. London: Sage.

This book contains a clear discussion of this particular cultural dimension together with a range of others. There is also information about the central aspects of different collective cultures.

Multimodal therapy (MMT)

See also: Lazarus, Arnold A.; social learning theory

Dr Arnold Lazarus designed multimodal therapy (MMT) in response to the constraints of traditional behavioural therapy. He emphasizes the need for systematic technical eclecticism as a basis for therapy. Techniques are chosen creatively for their effectiveness (based on published research evidence), without necessarily accepting the underlying theoretical principles.

The therapist is guided by one preferred theory (here Bandura's social and cognitive learning theory), but also uses techniques from other orientations. Misinformation (incorrect assumptions about life) and missing information (lack of life skills) are considered as the two major factors that cause emotional problems.

Lazarus chooses to access a client's problems by analysing seven distinct, yet interactive, modalities (BASIC ID); an idea which forms the 'bedrock' of multimodal therapy. This principle is the foundation on which assessment and treatment are based. He developed a questionnaire – the Multimodal Life History Inventory (MLHI) – which undoubtedly takes assessment to a deeper, concrete level than most other tools used at the start of therapy. The seven modalities are:

behaviour: people's actions
affect: people's emotions and feelings
sensation: sensory experiences (relating to taste, touch, pain, etc.)
imagery: fantasies, daydreaming, thinking in pictures
cognition: ability to think and analyse, beliefs
interpersonal: the social being in relationship to others
drugs/biology: health and physiology.

Once we understand how the seven modalities work, where the strengths and weaknesses of a person are, and which modalities may need therapeutic input, a programme of appropriate interventions is designed. Matching the correct interventions with the individual's needs is one of the great challenges in practising MMT. Palmer and Dryden (1995) point out how the modalities can be seen as linked together to produce an emotional (affective) response. Despite its breadth, MMT is brief, highly focused and problem solving in its approach. Whenever possible, empirically supported treatment methods are applied.

The therapist functions as a facilitator and educator, but the bulk of the work has to be done by the client. The MLHI is usually presented to the client after the first session (or even before start of therapy) to complete at home. The therapist can compare her personal notes with the MLHI and create the client's personal BASIC ID (see above) which highlights the areas the client wishes to improve. She also makes a list of the proposed interventions within each modality. They are explained to the client as change can only be achieved if the client can actually see the point in actively participating in them and putting them into practice. The ability to present techniques in ways that are acceptable to clients is a core skill in MMT (Palmer and Dryden 1995).

Lazarus expects the therapist to be an 'authentic chameleon' in style and approach (e.g. directive/non-directive; formal/informal, etc.), depending on the client's personal needs. There are no obvious drawbacks for the clients. It is important to note, however, that any therapist who wishes to work within this framework needs a wide variety of skills and ongoing continuous professional development.

Reference

Palmer, S. and Dryden, W. (1995) *Counselling for Stress Problems*. London: Sage.

Annotated further reading

Dryden, W. (1991) *The Essential Arnold Lazarus*. London: Whurr.

A very interesting collection of collated Lazarus publications from 1956 to 1990.

Lazarus, A. (1989) *The Practice of Multimodal Therapy*. Baltimore, MD: Johns Hopkins University Press.

This book is recommended as the main source for integrating MMT into one's toolkit for advanced integrative psychotherapy.

N

Narcissism

See also: depressive position; paranoid-schizoid position; psychosexual development

Narcissism as a general term has a place in popular language as meaning self-love. It can also be used to describe a person who is self centred and self obsessed, concepts that are somewhat negative (Kohut 1966).

The word narcissism came from the name of the mythological figure Narcissus – a handsome young man who, one day, when he was thirsty, drank from a pool of water in which he saw his reflection for the first time. As he had never previously seen what he looked like, he did not recognize the reflection and fell in love with it (i.e. himself). However, he was for ever afterwards pining for this love object whom he could never obtain.

Freud identified primary narcissism as the desire to survive based on the individual's sense of their 'self'. Narcissism, in the psychoanalytic sense, is the libidinal investment in the self (Kohut 1966). Freud, who originally took the term from Havelock Ellis (Hinshelwood 1994), identified early sexuality as involving autoeroticism (such as thumb sucking) in that the infant gains satisfaction through their own body and therefore is their own primary love object (Craib 2001). Freud considered this self-interest in infancy as a healthy and normal part of development. To be able to find oneself lovable, means the future ability to have successful relationships with others.

Melanie Klein (1959/1975), who substituted the notion of clear cut developmental stages with positions, proposed that the shift from concrete thinking characteristic of the paranoid-schizoid position, to working through the ambivalence and depressive anxieties of the depressive position, connects with the ability to mourn the loss of one's narcissistic omnipotence (Gyler 2010).

Secondary narcissism occurs when the libido withdraws from the external world and focuses its interest exclusively on the self which can occur when there is a particular problem the individual needs to confront such as chronic illness or pain or another form of extreme suffering such as bereavement.

The narcissist is self involved and the object of their greatest interest is their self. For the psychotic patient this means that the world around has been lost to them and Freud considered that the schizophrenic's withdrawal was the result of the libidinal energy invested in the self, alone.

Narcissistic personality disorder, subsequently identified by Kohut, refers to an individual who overestimates their attractiveness or desirability in some way regardless of the lack of outside affirmation and consequently needs a great deal of admiration from others. This type of individual has experienced a developmental arrest as the main caretakers may have withheld appropriate mirroring responses.

References

Craib, I. (2001) *Psychoanalysis: A Critical Introduction*. Cambridge: Polity.

Gyler, L. (2010) *The Gendered Unconscious: Can Gender Discourses Subvert Psychoanalysis?* London: Taylor and Francis.

Hinshelwood, R. (1994) *Clinical Klein*. London: Free Association Books.

Klein, M. (1959/1975) Our adult world and its roots on infancy. In *The Writings of Melanie Klein: Envy and Gratitude and Other Works 1946–1963* (Vol. 3, pp. 247–263). London: Hogarth Press.

Kohut, H. (1966) Forms and transformations of narcissism. *Journal of the American Psychoanalytical Association*, 14: 243–72.

Annotated further reading

Craib, I. (2001) *Psychoanalysis: A Critical Introduction*. Cambridge: Polity.

Craib's account of narcissism is clearly presented.

Narrative therapy

See also: multicultural counselling

This form of therapy is based on the idea that telling stories is the main way in which people make sense of, and communicate, their experience. These stories (which comprise much of our knowledge and understanding of ourselves and our worlds) are stories we have been told, ones we tell ourselves and ones we tell others. They are, therefore, heavily influenced by our family, social and cultural contexts. There are always alternative stories that can be told about a single event. Morgan (2000) captured the essence of narrative therapy when she described it as a way of talking about and understanding people's identities, their relationships, their problems and the effects of their problems on their lives. She also saw it as providing ways of understanding the ethics and politics of therapy.

Unlike the constructivist position which regards personal experience and meaning as being created by the individual, the narrative perspective is a form of social constructionism (McLeod 2009). It is a philosophical stance which proposes that meaning is instead shaped by a society or a culture. People create their personal identity by identifying with some of the stories which exist in their family and broader culture. For example, being unemployed is regarded as a sign of personal weakness in some cultures and this is likely to be incorporated into the personal identity of many in that position. Similarly some cultures may prescribe certain behaviours to those of a certain gender, race or sexuality so that dominant narratives can form a part of and prescribe how an individual should behave in a range of situations. People are regarded as being separate from their problems and there is an assumption, not dissimilar to that of the person-centred approach, that people do have the resources to reduce the effects of their problems.

In narrative therapy the focus is on the relationship between the client and the community rather than on the self. The aim is not to change internal psychological processes but to develop different, less restricting, versions of their stories. Clients are helped to see their problems as being outside themselves and to move away from the dominant narrative when there is a mismatch between this narrative and the life experience of the individual. McLeod (2009) outlines the process of therapy as follows: initially, the client is assisted in naming the problem as precisely as possible. This may involve using the client's terms rather than those of the dominant narrative. For example, the term 'depression' may be replaced by 'feeling hopeless'. This process of defining the problem assists the client with separating from the problem. A questioning approach is adopted by the therapist once the problem has been defined. White and Epston (1990) refer to this as 'relative influence questioning'. The idea is to help the client establish how the problem affects their life, as well as times when it had less effect. Clients often go through a period of confusion before they are able to start to create a new story and thus take on a new role in the world.

Therapeutic relationship

The counsellor adapts a facilitative role designed to help the client develop a more active role in creating their own story. McLeod (2009) emphasizes the importance of the 'not-knowing' therapist, who acts as editor and who suggests possible strategies (questions, writing) which the client could use to lessen the hold of the dominant narrative, replacing it with a different, less problem-focused one.

Use in other approaches or as a distinct approach

Narrative therapy can be used as a distinct approach as has been described above. Alternatively it can be used in, for example, psychodynamic approaches thus providing insight into the client's patterns of relating to others and assisting the client in developing more effective ways of telling their life story.

Research evidence

Perhaps because narrative therapy is a relatively new approach and because what research has been done has tended to focus on developing new methods for use in the therapy, there is little research evidence to support the effectiveness of this approach (McLeod 2006).

Limitations

A potential danger when using this approach is that there will be too little focus placed on the client's internal world and on changing their psychological processes. Well recognized terms such as depression and anxiety tend not to be used and yet these may be meaningful for some clients.

References

McLeod, J. (2006) Narrative Approaches to Therapy. In C. Feltham and I. Horton (eds), *The SAGE Handbook of Counselling and Psychotherapy*, 2nd edn. London: Sage.

McLeod, J. (2009) *An Introduction to Counselling*. Maidenhead: Open University Press.

Morgan, A. (2000) *What is Narrative Therapy? An Easy-to-read Introduction*. Adelaide: Dulwich Centre Publication.

White, M. and Epston, D. (1990) *Narrative Means to Therapeutic Ends*. New York: Norton.

Annotated further reading

Brown, C. and Augusta-Scott, T. (eds.) (2007) *Narrative Therapy: Making Meaning, Making Lives*. Thousand Oaks, CA: Sage.

This book covers the history of the approach as well as the theory and practice via discussion of a range of case studies.

Payne, M. (2006) *Narrative Therapy: An Introduction for Counsellors*, 2nd edn. London: Sage.

Payne provides a useful and personal introduction to narrative therapy, focusing particularly on the work of one of its founders, Michael White's, work.

Negation and disavowal

See also: blind eye; defence mechanisms; repression

The meaning of 'no' in the analytic setting was one of Freud's persistent pre-occupations (Gay 1995). Freud's description of 'negation' (Freud 1925) clarifies this in that 'the subject-matter of a repressed image or thought can make its way into consciousness on condition that it is denied. Negation is a way of taking account of what is repressed; indeed, it is actually a removal of the repression, though not, of course, an acceptance of what is repressed' (p. 367). In other words the analysand allows into the conscious material that she knows and does not know about at the same time. This is a similar mechanism to that of the blind eye, although that may be turning a blind eye to conscious as well as unconscious material.

Underlying the theory of negation are both Freud's and Klein's understandings of the intolerable, negative parts of the human psyche that are repressed, denied and expelled. Freud's (1920) *Death Instinct* (see **psychosexual development**) is essentially the drive towards a negativity, or negation of symbols or representations of outside 'reality', as a defence in part, but also as a creative, innovative function (Priel 2001). As a defence, the death instinct can be a rejection, by projection of something that has arisen in therapy (and thus by implication in other relationships) so that judgement about what is internal and what is external is confused (Priel 2001). Repressed concerns about, say the behaviour of someone you trust whom you think might betray you, both enter consciousness and are denied because you value the trust you have in that person.

We handle negative, intolerable information in that way. Freud (1925) clarified 'I should like to take this into me and keep that out of me' (p. 367). Close to negation is the mechanism of disavowal. That is the splitting between two attitudes – the one that fits in with the *wish*, i.e. that the crooked financier Bernard Madoff is as good as he says he is, and the one that fits with *reality*, i.e. that his claims and apparent successes cannot be true and at some point the fraud will be exposed (Freud 1927; Priel 2001).

Barrows (1995) drawing on Klein (1928/1998) (see **Klein, Melanie** and **Kleinian analysis**) suggests that infants/children both know and don't know about their position in relation to their parents' sexual relationship. 'Powerful defences are mobilised against this feeling of not knowing, all of which involve distortion of reality. In particular, these are omniscience, disavowal, and the denial of difference' (Barrows 1995: 87). Disavowal, as distinct from denial then, involves the vertical splitting of the ego so that one part knows and one part holds a contrary belief (Barrows 1995).

Britton (1994) following Klein (1975) and Steiner (1985) suggests that some clinical patients adopt or seek refuge in a *defensive organization* (of their relationship between internal and external realities). This is different from defences whereby the person engages with internal and external reality as they struggle with their guilt and self-hate. Defensive organization is a more pervasive syndrome (again described by Britton following Deutsch (1942) described by her as the 'As-if' personality who places *disavowal* at the centre of their mental life and characterizes their whole relationship with the world with a persistent sense of unreality and the apparent absence of inner experience or conflict. Sapochnik (2003), focusing specifically on corruption, cites Freud's term 'disavowal' to describe a mode of defence where an individual refuses to recognize the

> reality of a traumatic perception (LaPlanche and Pontalis 1985). Freud saw it as a psychotic mechanism and opposed it to repression. In effect, in response to the conflict between the ego and the id, the neurotic represses the id while, in psychosis, the individual deals with this conflict by disavowing reality – that is, the disavowal of a perception is turned towards external reality.
>
> (p. 188)

In other words (from Britton in relation to defensive organization) 'the flow of traffic between internal and external is stopped and something substituted for it . . . an artifact composed of aspects of the analyst and patient knitted together' (Britton 1994: 1).

Thus, as with Britton' and Deutsch's conceptualizations, this process is distinct from a 'normal' defence mechanism as conflict of the inner world – it is more like a *blockage of information and emotion* from the external world leaving the inner world (seemingly) 'untouched'. To take this clinical concept to the case of corruption in organizations such as Enron, the '"as-if" primary task is something like "being on the winning side". Put in terms of morality, the distinction is between "practicing morality" and "maintaining distance from immorality". But, since practicing morality must entail the uncovering of any immorality, the two are actually opposites' (Lenthall 1998).

References

Barrows, P. (1995) Oedipal Issues at 4 and 44. *Psychoanalytic Psychotherapy*, 9(1).

Britton, R. (1994) The blindness of the seeing eye: inverse symmetry as a defense against reality. *Psychoanalytic Inquiry: A Topical Journal for Mental Health Professionals*, 14(3): 365–78.

Deutsch, H. (1942) Some forms of emotional disturbance and their relationship to schizophrenia. *Psychoanalytic Quarterly*, 11.

Freud, S. (1920) *Beyond the Pleasure Principle* (Vol. 18). London: Hogarth.

Freud, S. (1925) Negation. *International Journal of Psycho-Analysis*, 6: 367–71.

Freud, S. (1927) *Fetishism*. London: Hogarth.

Gay, P. (1995) *The Freud Reader*. London: Vintage.

Klein, M. (1928/1998) Early stages of the Oedipus conflict. In H. Segal and R.E. Money-Kyrle (eds) *Love, Guilt and Reparation and Other Works, 1921–1945*. London: Vintage.

Klein, M. (1975) Our adult world and its roots on infancy (1959). In *The writings of Melanie Klein: Envy and Gratitude and Other Works 1946–1963* (Vol. 3, pp. 247–63). London: Hogarth Press.

LaPlanche, J. and Pontalis, J.B. (1985) Fantasy and the origins of sexuality. In V. Burgin, J. Donald and C. Kaplan (eds) *Formations of Fantasy*. London: Routledge.

Lenthall, A. (1998) 'Turning a blind eye': implications for organisations and consultancy. *Psychodynamic Counselling*, 4 (May).

Priel, B. (2001) Negation in Borges's 'The Secret Miracle'™: writing the Shoah. *International Journal of Psycho-Analysis*, 82(4): 785–94.

Sapochnik, C. (2003) Corruption: Oedipal configuration as social mechanism. *Organisational and Social Dynamics: An International Journal of Psychoanalytic, Systemic and Group Relations Perspectives*, 3(2): 177–90.

Steiner, J. (1985) Turning a blind eye: the cover up for Oedipus. *International Review of Psycho-Analysis*, 12: 161–72.

Annotated further reading

Freud, S. (1925) Negation. *International Journal of Psycho-Analysis*, 6(5): 367–71.

Freud's own account is useful as a base but needs careful consideration because this is a difficult concept to grasp.

Sapochnik, C. (2003) Corruption: Oedipal configuration as social mechanism. *Organisational and Social Dynamics: An International Journal of Psychoanalytic, Systemic and Group Relations Perspectives*, 3(2): 177–90.

This is a difficult but key concept in Freudian analysis and although it has sparked the interest and thoughts of some theorists and clinicians there is little reference to it in the more popular and accessible texts such as Craib. Sapochnik's paper provides interesting everyday examples.

Negative automatic thoughts

See also: cognitive behavioural therapy; cognitive distortions; irrational beliefs

The theoretical approach with which this concept is most closely associated is cognitive behavioural therapy (CBT). Aaron Beck first wrote about the relationship between thinking and depression in 1963, later formulating the 'negative cognitive triad', which postulated that those suffering from depression had a negative view of themselves, the world and the future. The emphasis in CBT is on cognition, while acknowledging the link between thoughts affect (feelings) and behaviours.

Negative automatic thoughts (NATs) need to be understood in the context of the CBT model and more specifically in relation to 'schemas', which are cognitive structures containing deep-seated concepts about oneself and the world. Certain events can act as triggers to these schemas which, in turn, give rise to negative automatic thoughts (or self-critical thoughts). We all have thoughts constantly flowing through our minds which we may not always be conscious of. These may be predominantly positive or negative in nature. However, people suffering from some form of mental illness usually have predominantly negative schema and NATs. For example, a man may be walking down the street and see someone they know on the opposite side of the road. The other person walks past them without acknowledging them, which may lead to the first individual thinking that the other person deliberately ignored them, perhaps because she dislikes him when, in fact, she may simply not have seen him. The schema triggering this thought may be about being unlikeable and not really deserving to have friends. The subsequent emotion may be anger or sadness. The resultant behaviour may be to ignore that person next time they meet. This example captures what Beck termed 'misinterpretations of situations, dysfunctional attitudes and self-defeating behaviour' (Beck et al. 1979: 148 in Loewenthal and House 2010).

Because negative automatic thoughts are closer to consciousness (usually regarded as being just below consciousness) than schemas, it is easier to identify and work on these initially as part of the therapy. The assumption is that emotional and behavioural problems are caused by the way in which someone makes sense of an event rather than by the event itself. So the focus in therapy needs to be on changing the thoughts and beliefs which give rise to the negative emotions and behaviour. The idea is to identify the thoughts – or internal monologue – to evaluate their appropriateness and replace them with more rational ones. Clients need to understand enough about the cognitive model, including the effect of thoughts on feelings and behaviour, for the aims of the therapy to be meaningful to them.

There is a substantial body of research evidence to support the effectiveness of CBT for a range of mental disorders which shows impressively low relapse rates for some disorders, including specific phobias and panic disorders (Cooper 2008). However, there have been a number of criticisms made about this approach, some of which can be specifically related to the concept of NATs. Spinelli (1994) raises the issue as to whether therapists can objectively decide what constitutes an irrational belief, which could similarly apply to a NAT. Clients are likely to accept the therapist's viewpoint as the expert (Corey

1991, in Spinelli 1994) without considering this thought or belief may actually be appropriate, bearing in mind a societal perspective. For example, if someone thinks that their life is tedious and meaningless because they spend much of it engaged in a repetitive job, this may be in part due to the huge societal pressure to live a rich and fulfilled life as well as to the individual's internalized belief in the meaninglessness of their occupation. If the emphasis is mainly on challenging and changing that thought or belief, the individual may never really start to explore the real issues behind their dissatisfaction, which may well be very real. It may well be more fruitful to accept some of the client's NATs and explore what it is that is at the heart of the difficulty for the client with a view to deciding on what lies behind the thoughts and the best possible way of dealing with the situation.

Another issue is the lack of focus on the client's feelings except in the way that they relate to their thoughts (Spinelli 1994). Some clients may be experiencing very intense emotions and may regard identifying and expressing these as far more important than working on their NATs. Clients need to accept the value of the cognitive model if they are to see the relevance of focusing on their thought processes. Not all clients will accept this model as right for them.

References

Beck, A.T. (1963) Thinking and depression. Idiosyncratic content and cognitive distortions. *Archives of General Psychiatry*, 9: 324–333.

Cooper, M. (2008) *Essential Research Findings in Counselling and Psychotherapy: The Facts are Friendly*. London: Sage.

Loewenthal, D. and House, R. (eds) (2010) *Critically Engaging CBT*. Maidenhead: Open University Press.

Spinelli, E. (1994) *Demystifying Therapy*. London: Constable.

Annotated further reading

Trower, P., Jones, J., Dryden, W. and Casey, A. (2011) *Cognitive-Behaviour Counselling in Action*, 2nd edn. London: Sage.

Clearly shows how this and other concepts work in practice using case study examples.

Westbrook, D., Kennerley, H. and Kirk, J. (2011) *An Introduction to Cognitive-Behaviour Therapy: Skills and Applications*, 2nd edn. London: Sage.

A very good introduction to the core concepts and skills of CBT.

Neuro linguistic programming (NLP)

Even though NLP is well grounded in psychological theory, in reality it mostly refers to 'action'. This idea was expressed thus: 'The greatest revolution of our generation is the discovery that human beings, by changing the inner attitudes of their minds, can change the outer aspects of their lives' (William James, American philosopher and psychologist, leader of the philosophical movement of Pragmatism, 1842–1910, http://thinkexist.com/quotation).

John Grinder, a linguistic professor, and Richard Bandler, a mathematician, both at the University of California developed NLP around 1975. At the time, Grinder and Bandler were students of Gregory Bateson, a British-born psychologist and anthropologist. Bateson and Milton Erickson, the influential hypnotherapist, are the two figures who provided the biggest influence on the birth and development of NLP.

Richard Bandler was then deeply involved in Gestalt therapy and adapted important aspects of Fritz Perls (the founder of Gestalt) attitude to therapy. NLP was born when Grinder and Bandler published their first book entitled *The Structure of Magic, 1* in 1975. They presented a set of explicit tools, by means of which others might be able to achieve excellent performance levels as therapeutic experts such as Perls, Erickson and Virginia Satir, an authority on family therapy, had done.

The terminology

'Neuro' refers to the brain and nervous system, in particular to the pathways of our five senses, by which we see, hear, taste, smell and feel, and how we organize our mental life. NLP is about increasing our awareness of these senses and learning how to use them consciously.

'Linguistic' refers to our ability to use language and how the specific words and phrases we choose to communicate mirror and affect the way we think. It also refers to our inner beliefs, habits and self-talk. The language patterns we use are a reflection on who we are and how we think.

'Programming' suggests that our thoughts, feelings and actions are simply habitual programmes that can be changed if we decide that they no longer serve us. A programme is a series of steps designed to achieve a specific result. In this particular aspect NLP is very similar to CBT.

Through awareness of the programmes you can alter your own and other people's experiences.

Some of the principles and assumptions of NLP

NLP starts with yourself. It is only by learning how to manage yourself that you can facilitate change in others. The unconscious mind is considerably more powerful than the conscious mind. NLP employs techniques that harness both and once we understand how we create our inner thoughts we can change them.

The map is not the territory: our mental maps are not the outside reality. We react to the world with our internal maps and inner filters rather than with pure, sensory-based input.

Our behaviour and experiences have a structure and result from how we use the representational systems, i.e. how we internally represent or store the information that is processed by our five senses.

Mind and body are part of one system. External behaviour is the result of internal behaviour.

People already have all the resources they need even if they do not currently have access to them.

People always make the best choice with the resources currently available to them. People are not their behaviours (this is once again in line with CBT). Underlying every behaviour is a positive intention. Even hurtful or harmful behaviour originally has a positive intention, wanting to be acknowledged. Separating the intention from the behaviour allows for changes to be made. We can redefine mistakes as feedback. If what we are doing is not working, we can change the approach. In any interaction the person with the greatest behavioural flexibility has the most influence on the outcome. The meaning of your communication is the response you get. Always add choices, never take them away.

There is a solution to every problem and 'the learning is the doing' (O'Connor and McDermott 2001: 167). McDonald (2001) even states that neuro-linguistic psychotherapy, derived from NLP, was accepted as a new form of constructivist psychotherapy by the UKCP (pp. 297–302). A critical Peter Schuetz (2006), on the other hand brings to light that there does not seem to be a fixed minimal length of training and that it can vary from 2–3 days to 35–40 days over at least nine months to achieve a professional level of competence. He says the multiplicity and general lack of controls has led to difficulty discerning the comparative level of competence.

References

Knight, S. (2000) *NLP at Work*. London: N. Brealey.

McDonald, L. (2001) Neurolinguistic programming in mental health. In J. France and S. Krame (eds) *Communication and Mental Illness: Theoretical and Practical Approaches*. London: Jessica Kingsley.

O'Connor, J. and McDermott, I. (2001) *Ways of NLP*. London: Thorsons.

Schuetz, P. (2006) A consumer guide through the multiplicity of NLP certification training: a European perspective. http://www.nlpzentrum.at/institutsvgl-english.htm (accessed 14 August 2011).

Annotated further reading

O'Connor, J. and McDermott, I. (2001) *Ways of NLP*. London: Thorsons.

A very readable book explaining the how and why of NLP. It is also a very positive book that focuses on the goodness of humanity.

O

Object relations theory

See also: Klein, Melanie; transitional objects; Winnicott, D.W.

Object relations theory is distinct from classical Freudian psychoanalysis in that instead of emphasizing drives at the centre of mental life, the emphasis is upon the relational context of development. Early relationships with other 'objects' (maternal object for instance) lay down the basic psychic structures that provide the pattern for all other relationships.

Klein's work, in some ways, was the springboard for object-relations psychoanalysis and some critics include her work under this heading. Klein however did consider that there are instinctual drives, especially the death instinct, and also that unconscious phantasies are crucial to psychological functioning. Those ideas separate her thinking from that of the object relations school. Consequently the development of object relations theory is more accurately attributed to the work of Fairbairn, Winnicott, Balint and Guntrip (Mendez et al. 1976) working in the UK within the British Psychoanalytic Society, where it has been particularly influential, although object relations thinking has become increasingly present in the USA since the 1980s (Frosh 1999; Hinshelwood 1991).

Klein's work was, notwithstanding, highly influential with object relations psychoanalysts, most particularly because using the play technique demonstrated that children's minds do have full and intense relationships with objects including toys, which are felt to have lived and died, as with a child's favourite teddy, small model animals or soldiers for instance. Winnicott was to develop this work on play as a key concept in object relations thinking (Winnicott 1971/2001).

Winnicott, challenging the primacy of classical psychoanalysis, proposes that the focus of analysis with children, and the basis for psychoanalytic thinking should focus on:

- the nature of the object;
- the infant's capacity to recognize the object as 'not me';
- the place of the object – outside, inside at the border;
- the initiation of an affective type of object relationship (see Winnicott 1971/2001: 2).

Winnicott argues that this approach is more important than thinking of the infant as at the 'oral stage'. He also argues that while psychoanalysis takes account of both inner reality and external reality it is also equally important to attend to an intermediate area of experience to which inner reality and external life both contribute. To this end he believed that the human task was to keep inner and outer reality separate while also interrelating them.

Balint was concerned about the emergence of the self/ego from the interpenetration of self and environment. Balint identifies the self as a separate concept from that of the ego. He sees the latter as similar to Freud's structure that is part conscious and part unconscious and defined by internal structures. He sees the self as being the sense (or lack of sense) of the self as an object understood by the self and thus closer to consciousness (Craib 2001).

Fairbairn, a Scottish psychiatrist and analyst, offered an alternative viewpoint regarding the libido. Whereas Freud assumed that the libido is pleasure seeking, Fairbairn thought of the libido as object seeking, i.e. the libido is focused on making relationships with others. The first connections a child makes are with the parents with whom a bond is formed. When the needs of the child are not met by the parents a pathological *turning away* from external reality takes place. Instead of actual exchange with others, fantasied, private presences are established, the so-called internal objects. To these internal objects the child relates in fantasied connections, the internal object relations.

Guntrip was a psychologist who studied the work of Klein and the object relations theorists such as Fairbairn and Winnicott (Guntrip 1952) and was particularly interested in working clinically with withdrawn individuals (Guntrip 1961). His own analysis had been with Fairbairn and then with Winnicott.

Frosh (1999) summarized object relations as having made some important contributions to psychoanalysis particularly in that it formulates its understanding of basic mental structures in social terms in that the mind comprises ego-object links which are internalized representations of external social relations. Thus individuality is an amalgam of personal/ego and social/objects. This is different from classical psychoanalysis which positions the individual in more biological and 'closed' terms (Frosh 1999). There are drawbacks to object relations in that the social vision is restricted to the mother-child network and the 'romanticisation' of the mother (Frosh 1999).

References

Craib, I. (2001) *Psychoanalysis: A Critical Introduction*. Cambridge: Polity.

Frosh, S. (1999) *The Politics of Psychoanalysis*, 2nd edn. Basingstoke: Palgrave.

Guntrip, H. (1952) A study of Fairbairn's theory of schizoid reactions. *British Journal of Medical Psychology*, 25(2–3): 86–103.

Guntrip, H. (1961) The schizoid problem, regression, and the struggle to preserve an ego. *British Journal of Medical Psychology*, 34, 223–44.

Hinshelwood, R. (1991) *A Dictionary of Kleinian Thought*. London: Free Association Books.

Mendez, A.M., Fine, H.J. and Guntrip, H. (1976) A short history of the British school of object relations and ego psychology. *Bulletin of the Menninger Clinic*, 40(4): 357–82.

Winnicott, D. (1971/2001) *Playing and Reality*. London: Brunner-Routledge.

Annotated further reading

Craib, I. (2001) *Psychoanalysis: A Critical Introduction*. Cambridge: Polity.

Craib provides a lucid version of object relations thinking and practice forming a good introduction.

Winnicott, D. (1971/2001) *Playing and Reality*. London: Brunner-Routledge.

Winnicott's book is accessible with clinical examples which bring the ideas to life.

Oedipus complex

See also: blind eye

> Ever since Freud discovered the Oedipus complex it has been recognized as the central conflict in the human psyche – the central cluster of conflicting impulses, phantasies, anxieties and defences. It has therefore become the centre of psychoanalytic work.
>
> (Segal 2007: 1)

Who was Oedipus?

The story of Oedipus Rex, as represented in Sophocles' play, has come to represent the core of much psychoanalytic theory and is central to Freudian analysis in particular. The play itself dates back to 429BC and its longevity is witness to the significance of the story for human relationships through the ages. Oedipus is the son of King Laius and Queen Jocasta of Thebes. The Oracle foretold that Laius would be killed by the hand of his son (who had just been born) and so he orders Jocasta to have the baby killed. She cannot face doing this herself so she hands Oedipus over to a servant who takes the baby to a mountain top to die of exposure and starvation. However, he is found by a shepherd who takes him to Corinth where he is raised by the childless King Polybus and Queen Merope. As he grows up Oedipus hears that he is not in fact Polybus's son and asks the Oracle about his true parentage. The Oracle tells him (instead of giving him the answer) that he will have a sexual relationship with his mother and murder his father. So because he then comes to believe that Polybus and Merope are his true parents he leaves Corinth to avoid harming them. He heads for Thebes where he meets Laius, they fight over the right of way and Laius is killed. He then arrives in Thebes where he meets and marries Jocasta (his real mother).

What is the Oedipus complex (crisis or oedipal situation)?

The myth and drama of this story was employed by Freud to describe a young boy's sexual desire towards his mother including both loving and hating her, and how this comes to be resolved. The guilt accompanying his desire makes him fear that his father will 'take way' the prized possession – his penis – because he recognizes that his mother has herself been 'castrated' and thus he experiences castration anxiety. By subsequently identifying with the father/masculinity/patriarchy, the Oedipal complex or crisis is resolved in that the boy gives up the desire for his mother and shares the desire for other women with other men. This process achieved core significance in Freudian theory and therapy because Freud himself considered the resolution of the Oedipus crisis to be a major developmental dynamic and the origin of the (inevitable perhaps) patriarchal structures to family and political life (Grosz 1990). The central significance of the Oedipus complex, the primal scene at the heart of 'family' life (the awareness of parental genital sexuality), is possibly one of the more difficult ideas for someone who is outside, or new to, psychoanalysis to grasp. However, Freud used this process conceptually to draw together the relationship between the 'ego' and the 'id' (see **psychosexual stages**) (Freud 1923/2007; Wright 1992).

Klein (1928/1998) considered that the Oedipal dynamic plays out in a different way from that proposed by Freud. From her work in analysing children she came to identify that the Oedipus complex occurred earlier than Freud suggested linking it to weaning and the aggressive and sadistic phantasies she observed in very young children (Spillius 2007).

But this is not the only point of contention among psychoanalysts. Despite Segal's assertion, above, that the Oedipus complex is the centre of psychoanalytic work, the significance of the Oedipus conflict has waned in psychoanalytic circles and (arguably) needs reviving (Loewald 2000). Even within psychoanalytic clinical circles the importance of the Oedipus complex has been disputed (O'Shaughnessy 2007).

Critiques of Freud's approach come from some very different perspectives. First there is the view that the Oedipal situation is not universal and cannot be typical beyond Western industrial cultures (Wright 1992) a view proposed and held by anthropologists.

The Lacanian perspective challenges Freud's 'pseudo' biological account of the Oedipus complex arguing that it is not the mother's perceived lack of a penis that removes her from her position as the powerful phallic mother, but that the child perceives her powerlessness in relation to the father and other men (Grosz 1990).

The Oedipal situation does have symbolic implications for patriarchal organizational structures in the family and society.

Family life and death

> 'Our first experience of an organization occurs in the family'.
>
> (Shapiro and Carr 1991: 22)

The Oedipus complex, the 'psychic representation of a central, instinctually motivated, triangular constellation of child-parent relations' (Loewald 2000: 239), links with the metaphor of the 'organisation as family' (Brotheridge and Lee 2006) and the application of family *therapy* concepts to understanding other institutions such as the work place (Hirschhorn and Gilmore 1980). In applying the Oedipus complex to understanding organizations for example it is important to hold in mind Loewald's description that there is an instinctual motivation in the triangular constellation and in an organization, as in the family, all the participants are engaged in finding a place they find tolerable *within* the system.

The Oedipal complex today

The heart of the Oedipal configuration is about *difference* and experiencing the 'triangular situation' whereby conflicts about seduction, betrayal and defending against anxiety are preoccupations. The baby/child feels constantly at risk of being 'left out' because of the close parental couple and fearing that a sibling might be favoured. Mitchell (2008) evocatively refers to 'hidden' siblings suggesting that the presence of a sibling evokes the danger of the other's anni-hilation at least in part because a 'toddler appears partly to believe that the baby about to be born is another version of itself' (p. 29) and a potential replacement.

This dynamic, although simple and familiar to social and developmental psychologists (Dunn 1988) as well as psychoanalysts, has a deeper meaning when played out consciously and unconsciously among adults (Klein 1959/1975). Where psychoanalytic thinking separates itself from traditional academic experimental developmental psychology (although not irreparably) is the extent to which the same patterns of anxiety, fear, rivalry, envy, competition and being left out displayed in infancy are played out unconsciously, and almost exactly as in infancy, in adulthood. Academic experimental psychologists typically recognize the impact of infant experiences on adulthood. However, their focus is on the long-term *consequences* of abuse or neglect in infancy or childhood for adult behaviours. Taking a psychoanalytic perspective however suggests that the ways in which adults unconsciously replay their experience of the primal scene have a compelling influence on relationships at work and provide a means of enabling both individual and systemic change.

A further note on gender and the Oedipus complex

Freud's account of the Oedipus complex, the 'classical' view, revolves around the phallic stage (around years 3 to 5) when the boy has phantasies of genital desire towards his mother. Through fearing his father's wrath and reprisals, which would lead to castration, he identifies with his father by taking in the patriarchal/parental authority (the phallus) to be his own internal monitor, represented in the development of the super-ego. The girl during the phallic stage comes to realize her own and her mother's 'lack' leading to her severing some of the close and exclusive attachment hitherto with the mother.

Freud himself saw this situation as 'complicated' and that the 'intricacy of the problem is due to two factors: the triangular character of the Oedipus situation and the constitutional bisexuality of each individual' (Freud 1923/2007). The triangular situation and the possibilities for being 'left out' or 'not having a place' in the family, team or organization is crucial to understanding power struggles (filled with competition, hatred, envy, narcissism and so on) which lie at the heart of organizational dynamics and family dynamics. Equally important, particularly for understanding the role of gender in such struggles, is the inherent bisexuality, through which girls/boys/women/men have the potential to relate to each other in a number of ways including through both love and hate.

In adulthood then the boy, recognizing his difference from his mother, has to leave her protection to make something of himself 'in the world' to become independent and also to rediscover her favour. He focuses therefore on work and the external world with an 'indifference' to its emotional connections with the intent that emotions are tied up in his relationship with his (eventual) female partner (Schwartz 2010).

A girl on the other hand (Chodorow 1978) has a continuing significant relationship with her mother. The classical position, that while boys react to their fear of castration girls experience penis envy, is played out by the girl seeing her mother as a sexual rival for her father. Consequently she feels hostility towards her mother. Chodorow argues that the Oedipus complex should not be seen as symmetrical for boys and girls. Girls may idealize a father who is not there enough and there is evidence from social psychology research that fathers more than mothers may 'gender type' their children encouraging boys to be like them and girls to be more seductive (pp. 118–19).

These scenes are reinforced through Kleinian approaches to the Oedipus complex. For Klein, the mother was the first and most important 'other'/'object' in the infant's physical and mental life. Klein (1928/1998) considered the Oedipus complex as starting in the first year of life, connected with the baby's relationship to the breast. As Segal describes it: 'It is the frustration at the breast, and crucially the weaning, that makes the infant turn to the father's penis and become aware of the triangular situation' (Segal 2007: 2). Crucially, for understanding both the family and organizations, Klein focuses upon the importance of 'hatred' (as well as love and desire).

'The Oedipal situation begins with the child's recognition of the parents' relationship . . . The failure to internalize a recognizable Oedipal triangle results in a failure to integrate observation and experience' (Laufer 2007). Working through the Oedipus complex happens through a series of rivalries and relinquishments – with the child being able to give up the desire to annihilate one parent as the rival for total possession of the other one (Laufer 2007).

The power of the primal scene reflecting the Oedipus complex, as an explanatory framework for gender relations at work and in the 'family', involving seduction, fathers, mothers and daughters (in particular), sibling relationships and 'otherness' as well as a lens with which to observe the system, becomes increasingly clear as the organization is conceptualized as a family (system). Borrowing from Loewald (2000) words such as 'destruction', 'demolition' and 'parricide' and consequent associations of 'betrayal', 'seduction' and 'violation' of bonds that link parents and children need to be explored in organizational life. Linked closely is the 'blind eye' turned to abuse within the organization/ family in the ways in which the system fails to manage its boundaries particularly of time, place and power/authority relationships (Schwartz 1994; 2010).

References

Brotheridge, C.M. and Lee, R.T. (2006) We are family: congruity between organizational and family functioning constructs. *Human Relations*, 59(1): 141–61.

Chodorow, N. (1978) *The Reproduction of Mothering: Psychoanalysis and the Sociology of Gender*. London: University of California Press.

Dunn, J. (1988) *The Beginnings of Social Understanding*. Oxford: Basil Blackwell Ltd.

Freud, S. (1923/2007) The Ego and the Id. In P. Gay (ed.) *The Freud Reader*. London: Vintage.

Grosz, E. (1990) *Jaques Lacan: A Feminist Introduction*. London: Routledge.

Hirschhorn, L. and Gilmore, T. (1980) The application of family therapy concepts to influencing organizational behavior. *Administrative Science Quarterly*, 25(1): 18–37.

Klein, M. (1928/1998) Early stages of the Oedipus conflict. In H. Segal and R.E. Money-Kyrle (eds) *Love, Guilt and Reparation and Other Works 1921–1945*. London: Vintage.

Klein, M. (1959/1975) Our adult world and its roots on infancy. In *The Writings of Melanie Klein: Envy and Gratitude and Other Works 1946–1963* (Vol. 3, pp. 247–63). London: Hogarth Press.

Laufer, M.E. (2007) The female Oedipus complex and the relationship to the body. In D. Birkstead-Breen (ed.) *The Gender Conundrum: Contemporary Psychoanalytic Perspectives on Femininity and Masculinity*. London: Routledge.

Loewald, H.W. (2000) The waning of the Oedipus complex. *Journal of Psychotherapy Practice and Research*, 9(4): 239–49.

Mitchell, J. (2008) *Siblings*. Cambridge: Polity.

O'Shaughnessy, E. (2007) The invisible Oedipus complex. In R. Britton, M. Feldman and E. O'Shaughnessy (eds) *The Oedipus Complex Today: Clinical Implications*. London: Karnac.

Schwartz, H.S. (1994) Acknowledging the dark side of organizational life. In T.C. Pauchant (ed.) *In Search of Meaning: Managing for the Health of our Organizations, our Communities, and the Natural World*. San Francisco, CA: Jossey-Bass.

Schwartz, H.S. (2010) *Society Against Itself: Political Correctness and Organisational Self-Destruction*. London: Karnac.

Segal, H. (2007) Introduction. In R. Britton, M. Feldman, E. O'Shaughnessy and J. Steiner (eds) *The Oedipus Complex Today: Clinical Implications*. London: Karnac.

Shapiro, E.R. and Carr, A.W. (1991) *Lost in Familiar Places: Creating New Connections between the Individual and Society*. New Haven, CT and London: Yale University Press.

Spillius, E. (2007) *Encounters with Melanie Klein*. London: Routledge.

Wright, E. (1992) *Feminism and Psychoanalysis: A Critical Dictionary*. Oxford: Blackwell.

Annotated further reading

Britton, R., Feldman, M. and O'Shaughnessy, E. (eds) (2007) *The Oedipus Complex Today: Clinical Implications*. London: Karnac.

This book (including a classic chapter from Melanie Klein's clinical work with children) makes sense of how the Oedipus complex might be understood in context in the twenty-first century.

Mitchell, J. (2008) *Siblings*. Cambridge: Polity.

This takes an innovative stance on the Oedipus complex.

Open systems theory

Systemic thinking is a framework, or tool, for observing the way organizations and families (Carr 2000) behave (Campbell et al. 1994; Lewin 1947; Schein 1985) which evolved from General Systems Theory (Miller and Rice 1967; Von Bertalanffy 1956) and focuses upon concepts related to organizational structure particularly:

- system
- task
- role
- authority
- boundary.

Systems

An organization or family that evolves like an organism and adapts to its environment necessarily has porous boundaries so that it can 'take in' and 'put out' beyond itself. This kind of organism, an *open system*, is one that changes, develops and grows and is therefore healthy.

A *closed system* may feel more secure in that it may not have to accede to unwanted influence or demands, but without taking in and providing for the world outside it will atrophy as with any other closed (minded) system (Morgan 2006). Examples of both open and closed systems might be a small business that fails to take account of the political and economic environment. Similarly a family might close up the boundary between outside and inside worlds but this is likely to lead them to failure because while avoiding scrutiny and disturbance from the outside, as they might see it, they don't gain support or advice or other resources that might help them.

Task

The task refers to the work the organization and its staff are contracted to undertake or the work that parents and children are expected to undertake – for the parents, raising children (which involves providing human and material resources), the children being expected to undertake their education and other developmental tasks. The system has a primary task, the main goal for the organization. This is also the task that people in the organization *believe* they are carrying out. While this might be a useful starting point for reflecting on the organization it is also a simplistic umbrella to cover the multiple tasks that any organization offering, for example, social services to children, families, the mentally ill or other vulnerable adults, has to provide (Zagier Roberts 1994). There is also a concept of an 'anti-task'. This occurs when the anxieties are so high that defensive activities to alleviate the anxiety are employed. One department became engaged in a group grievance against the senior managers, supported by the union. This took up most of their time and energy and kept them from the acute anxiety about the primary task of assessment of children and families at risk.

Role

This means the activities that are contained within a particular job description. Essentially a parent's role is defined by the primary task of the culture/society – that is the care of children. A counsellor or therapist is primarily engaged in working with their client/patient to understand and to enable the client/patient to understand themselves. The social worker has a particular part to play which is to work with a client group, with particular service users on their case load, to take their turn at assessment duty and to keep records (as well as other defined activities). It is not within the counsellor or the social work role to meet with senior staff from other agencies to develop policy, unless they have been given a special role to do this work. Understanding the boundaries of your own role is helpful in making sense of where your work ends and enables you to say 'no'.

Authority

It is also important to reflect on the authority in the system (Obholzer and Roberts 1994). Authority refers to the right to take an ultimate decision, which is binding on others. Formal authority resides within certain roles but there is also the potential for informal authority based on knowledge and personality. In the course of a consultancy comprising a reflective group with child care social work managers (Nicolson 2010) the first few meetings focused on the way the middle managers (the group members) were abused by senior staff. They wre repeatedly asked to address the questions 'where does the authority lie?' and later 'what would it take for you to take up your own authority?' The group felt very oppressed and depressed but eventually, thinking and reflecting on the system they realized that it was not a group of individuals who were (it seemed) per-secuting them but that the lines of authority were being used to pass down unacceptable messages. Perhaps, they considered, they didn't have to take every 'order' without challenge or criticism. They had their own authority that could be used once they understood where its boundaries lay.

Boundary

'Boundary' is the term used in open systems theory to describe the interface between different parts of the organization and the organization and the outside world. In the case of a school teacher this is the physical boundary to the school building, the classrooms, the website, the reception desk, the telephones, email and so on and also between the different roles such as teaching, support/manager and so on. Most leaders in organizations have the knowledge and abilities by definition to manage and negotiate those boundaries. For example, the senior managers relate to government/local authorities in ways that classroom teachers do not, but the senior staff are charged with having to manage the boundaries using knowledge and influence across the boundaries – inside with the staff and school pupils and outside with government and education authorities. Moreover, the porosity or opacity of the boundaries between the different organizations that have come together are central to functioning at most levels.

References

Campbell, D., Caldicott, D. and Kinsella, K. (1994) Key concepts of systemic thinking. In D. Campbell (ed.) *Systemic Work with Organisations*. London: Karnac Books, pp. 9–27.

Carr, A. (2000) Evidence-based practice in family therapy and systemic consultation. *Journal of Family Therapy*, 22(1): 29–60.

Lewin, K. (1947) Frontiers in group dynamics: concept, method and reality in social science; social equilibria and social change. In D. Cartwright (ed.) *Field Theory in Social Science: Selected Theoretical Papers* (Vol. 1). New York: Harper and Brothers.

Miller, E.J. and Rice, A.K. (1967) *Systems of Organisation: The Control of Task and Sentient Boundaries*. London: Tavistock.

Morgan, G. (2006) *Images of Organization*. London: Sage.

Nicolson, P. (2010) Alice in Wonderland: lost in (un)familiar places. Unpublished MA dissertation. Tavistock and Portman NHS Foundations Trust/University of East London.

Obholzer, A. and Roberts, V.Z. (1994) *The Unconscious at Work: Individual and Organizational Stress in the Human Services*. London: Routledge.

Schein, E. (1985) *Organizational Culture and Leadership*. San Francisco, CA: Jossey-Bass.

Von Bertalanffy, I. (1956) *General Systems Theory*. New York: George Braziller.

Zagier Roberts, V. (1994) The organisation of work: contributions from open systems theory. In A. Obholzer and V.Z. Roberts (eds) *The Unconscious at Work*. London: Routledge.

Annotated further reading

Obholzer, A. and Roberts, V.Z. (1994) *The Unconscious at Work: Individual and Organizational Stress in the Human Services*. London: Routledge.

Vega-Roberts' chapter is clear, concise and exemplifies the relevant material. Other chapters in this same volume lend further information and examples.

Organismic valuing process (OVP)

See also: assertiveness; conditions of worth; humanistic approaches; self; self-actualization

Carl Rogers was struck by the way babies react to their experiences directly and naturally and how they decide quickly and accurately whether or not their needs and desires are being met. They see things as they are and make healthy choices. He called this the organismic valuing process (OVP; Rogers 1964) and considered that we tend to gradually lose touch with our OVPs in childhood through what he called 'conditions of worth', i.e. learning to behave in certain ways to please other people more than to be in tune with our OVP. In his view, our behaviour, in contrast to infants' behaviour, tends to be influenced too much by politeness, diplomacy and fear and too little by how we feel, by our OVP.

Davis (1928) reported a dramatic and to some people shocking study that may illustrate the OVP in action: three newly weaned infants were allowed to eat whatever they chose from a large selection from every meal. They were 8, 9 and 10 months old and for two of them the experiment lasted six months and for the other a year. All the foods were natural: no milk products, no canned food. The following results can be interpreted as supporting the concept of an OVP at least as far as food is concerned (cf. Galef 1991), with two other qualifications: there was no chocolate cake, ice cream, etc. available to them and the meals were at set times. Some of the findings were:

1   The infants spat some foods out early on but learnt to recognize the different foods quickly and to know what and how much they wanted at each meal.
2   They chose balanced diets but not balanced meals, for example one of them ate seven eggs at one meal, another four bananas.
3   They ate salt occasionally, spluttering and even crying, but often going back for more.
4   They did not suffer from stomach pains or constipation.
5   They gained height and weight well and were judged to be happy and active.

These results may show the OVP in action. In contrast, adults often eat for reasons other than hunger, e.g. for comfort, entertainment or out of habit.

Joseph and Linley (2006) reviewed several studies which they interpreted as indirectly supporting the idea of the OVP. For example, some studies show that people are less motivated by extrinsic rewards (for example money) than intrinsic ones. Joseph and Linley were so encouraged by this research, even though they saw it as at an early stage, that they suggested that the concept of OVP 'might be set central stage as the fundamental pillar of positive therapy' (p. 59).

Counselling can be seen as trying to undo the negative effects of conditions of worth, to put clients back in touch with their OVPs. However, an adult's OVP takes other people's needs into account as well as our own, and makes a clear distinction between desires and behaviour. The mature OVP weighs lots of factors very quickly and well, in what Rogers called an 'exquisitely rational' way (1969: 29). The person rediscovers their clear inner sense of what is right or wrong for them.

References

Davis, L.M. (1928) Self-selection of diet by newly weaned infants. *American Journal of Diseases of Children*, 36: 651–79.

Galef, B.G. (1991) A contrarian view of the wisdom of the body as it relates to dietary self-selection. *Psychological Review*, 98: 218–22.

Joseph, S. and Linley, A.P. (2006) *Positive Therapy: A Meta-theory for Positive Psychological Practice*. London: Routledge.

Rogers, C.R. (1964) Toward a modern approach to values: the valuing process in the mature person. *Journal of Abnormal and Social Psychology*, 68: 160–7.

Rogers, C.R. (1969) *Freedom to Learn*. Columbus, OH: Merrill.

Annotated further reading

Davis, L.M. (1928) Self-selection of diet by newly weaned infants. *American Journal of Diseases of Children*, 36: 651–79.

Galef refers to this as a classic study and, like some other 'old' studies, it is worth seeking out.

Organizational dynamics

See also: blind eye; open systems theory; psychic prison

'Organizational dynamics' refers to the psychoanalytic and systemic analysis of organizational behaviour that takes account of both conscious and unconscious processes intrinsic to the organization itself as well as among the individual members. Thus the conscious part of the organization needs to operate defence mechanisms to protect itself from some of the unpalatable actions operating at an unconscious level. Recent, numerous cases of corruption provide examples of how defences (probably) unconsciously in place prevented key staff from recognizing what was really going on (Long 2002; 2008)

Organizations are like families in that individuals working in organizations relate to other people, consciously and unconsciously, in ways that reflect their early life experiences. They use the same defence mechanisms in managing their relationships at home, socially and at work.

Social defences against anxiety in organizations

Research in the 1960s at the Tavistock Centre in North London demonstrated that organizations themselves operate *social* defence mechanisms that can be both protective and dysfunctional as with those of individual organizational defence mechanisms. Following from the work of Elliot Jaques (1953) and Isobel Menzies (1984) both of whom took a (mostly) Kleinian view of psychoanalysis, the emphasis was on how organizations protected themselves against the anxieties inherent in their work. Menzies work on trainee nurses and how the system defended the nursing hierarchy from anxiety was decisive in the development of a psychoanalytic study of organizations. This was eventually linked to systemic work and has become associated with the organizational consultancy work of the Tavistock Centre and the Tavistock Consultancy Service.

Menzies (1984) describes the social defence systems operated in the training hospital as

> helping the individual avoid the experience of anxiety, guilt, doubt and uncertainty. As far as possible this is done by eliminating situations, events, tasks, activities and relationships that cause anxiety or, more correctly, evoke anxieties connected with primitive psychological remnants in the personality.
>
> (1984: 63)

The organization in the mind

The concept of the 'organization in the mind' was a model developed originally in the early 1990s by organizational and group relations consultants working at the Grubb Institute, the Tavistock Centre and the Tavistock Institute of Human Relations, to refer to what an individual perceives mentally about how organizations, relations in the organizations and the structures are connected. 'It is a model internal to oneself . . . which gives rise to images, emotions, values and responses in me, which may consequently be influencing my own management and leadership, positively or adversely' (Hutton et al. 1997: 114, quoted in Armstrong 2005: 4).

In other words, when we talk about our colleagues, guess what the senior management are doing/going to do and have fantasies about how well we fit, or don't fit, into the structure or system we do so in the context of the organization we 'hold' in our mind which may or may not relate to that which other members of the organization hold (Pols 2005).

Organizations are experienced cognitively and emotionally by their members when they think about how their organizations work and are structured. As Stokes (1994) explains it, everyone carries a sense of the organization in their mind but members from different parts of the same organizations may have 'different pictures and these may be in contradiction to one another. Although often partly unconscious, these pictures nevertheless inform and influence the behaviour and feelings of members' (p. 121).

Hutton (2000: 2) talks about it as 'a conscious or pre-conscious construct focused around emotional experiences of tasks, roles, purposes, rituals, accountability, competence, failure, success'. Morgan (2006) suggests that an organization may serve as a 'psychic prison' (see **psychic prison**) in that the:

> patterns and meanings that shape corporate culture and subculture may also have unconscious significance. The common values that bind an organisation often have their origin in shared concerns that lurk below the surface of conscious awareness. For example, in organisations that project a team image, various kinds of splitting mechanisms are often in operation, idealising the qualities of team members while projecting fears, anger, envy, and other bad impulses onto persons and objects that are not part of the team.
>
> (Morgan 2006: 226).

Organization under the surface

Gabriel and Schwartz (2004: 1) propose 'what goes on at the surface of an organisation is not all that there is, and . . . understanding organisations often means comprehending matters that lie beneath the surface'.

Although not necessarily (in fact mostly not) made explicit, even the most clear-thinking senior members of organizations hold an image of the organization in mind, expressing their fantasy/belief/perception of the organization based on conscious and unconscious knowledge (Halton 2007; James and Arroba 2005).

Structure in the mind

Most recently Laughlin and Sher (2010) take up a version of this concept which they name the 'structure-in-the-mind' in their analysis of developing leadership in social care. They reassert, in their model, that not only the local stakeholders (staff and service users) have a sense of the organization in the mind when considering, for instance, a particular Trust, but the range of stakeholders includes government bodies and service commissioners (in the round). They propose an inter-relationship between perceptions of communications from services (e.g. 'that you [management] don't listen and/or understand') and perceived communications from 'Head Office (or government or other bodies that control resources and practices) which include for example "just do it", "we know better" and "be rational" ' (p. 9).

What is significant here is that the organization and/or structure *in the mind* is where the leader and followers 'meet' emotionally as, similarly, do the various levels of leadership and governance bodies. It is a kind of 'virtual' space.

An example of this structure in the mind might be seen through the increase in stress for NHS employees detailed in a recent report by NICE where it was revealed that staff absence caused by work-related stress costs the UK over £28 billion. It was proposed that a poor working environment characterized by bullying and poor management was at the heart of this problem (Edwards and O'Connell 2007). In a context where there is distributed leadership and a highly trained professional, multidisciplinary workforce, such mismatches in how to run organizations and departments that lead to staff stress in these ways (e.g. being bullied and bullying) evoke questions about what is happening in the space between those who plan, govern and resource NHS Trusts and those who carry out the work.

References

Armstrong, D. (2005) *Organisation in the Mind: Psychoanalysis, Group Relations and Organisational Consultancy*. London: Karnac.

Edwards, S.L. and O'Connell, C.F. (2007) Exploring bullying: implications for nurse educators. *Nurse Education in Practice*, 7(1): 26–35.

Gabriel, Y. and Schwartz, H.S. (2004) Introduction: psychoanalysis and organization. In Y. Gabriel (ed.) *Organizationals in Depth*. London: Sage.

Halton, W. (2007) By what authority? Psychoanalytic reflections on creativity and change in relation to organisational life. In C. Huffington, D. Armstrong, W. Halton, L. Hoyle and J. Pooley (eds) *Working Below the Surface: The Emotional Life of Contemporary Organisations*. London: Tavistock.

Hutton, J. (2000) Working with the concept of Organisation-in-the-mind. Paper presented at the Inscape Conference, Coesfeld, Germany, 15 September. http://

www.grubb.org.uk/attachments/028_working%20with%20the%20concept%20 of%20Organisation%20in%20the%20mind.pdf (accessed).

James, K.T. and Arroba, T. (2005) Reading and carrying: a framework for learning about emotion and emotionality in organizational systems as a core aspect of leadership development. *Management Learning*, 36(3): 299–316.

Jaques, E. (1953) On the dynamics of social structure: a contribution to the psychoanalytic study of social phenomena deriving from the views of Melanie Klein. *Human Relations*, 6.

Laughlin, R. and Sher, M. (2010) Developing leadership in a social care enterprise: managing organisational and individual boundaries and anxiety. *Organisational and Social Dynamics*, 10(1): 1–21.

Long, S. (2002) Organisational destructivity and the perverse state of mind. *Organisational and Social Dynamics: An International Journal of Psychoanalytic, Systemic and Group Relations Perspectives*, 2(2): 179–207.

Long, S. (2008) *The Perverse Organisation and its Deadly Sins*. London: Karnac.

Menzies, I.E.P. (1984) *The Functioning of Social Systems as a Defence Against Anxiety: A Report on a Study of the Nursing Service of a General Hospital*. London: Tavistock Institute of Human Relations.

Morgan, G. (2006) *Images of Organization*. London: Sage.

Pols, J. (2005) Enacting appreciations: beyond the patient perspective. *Health Care Analysis*, 13(3): 203–21.

Stokes, J. (1994) Institutional chaos and personal stress. In A. Obholzer and V. Zagier-Roberts (eds) *The Unconscious at Work: Individual and Organisational Stress in the Human Services*. London: Routledge.

Annotated further reading

Armstrong, D. (2005) *Organisation in the Mind: Psychoanalysis, Group Relations and Organisational Consultancy*. London: Karanac.

Armstrong provides illustrated theoretical accounts of authority in organizations and the importance of making sense of the dynamics.

Halton, W. (2007) By what authority? Psychoanalytic reflections on creativity and change in relation to organisational life. In C. Huffington, D. Armstrong, W. Halton, L. Hoyle and J. Pooley (eds) *Working Below the Surface: The Emotional Life of Contemporary Organisations*. London: Tavistock.

Halton's chapter makes fascinating reading and clarifies some of the more difficult concepts about organizational dynamics from a down-to-earth perspective.

Paranoid-schizoid position

See also: depressive position; Klein, Melanie; projective identification; splitting

The paranoid-schizoid position from the start of life is a reaction to frightening phantasies of annihilation in which life itself is under threat, and to cope with it the infant separates the good from the bad. Thus the breast, which fulfils the infant's needs (food, comfort), is experienced separately from the one that is not available and denies the infant food and comfort thus placing her in danger of annihilation.

This was recognized by Klein as the process of 'splitting' to defend the ego from (the phantasy) danger (Klein 1959/1975).

Of course there *are* good and bad external objects but (more likely) some people only *behave* badly towards others *sometimes*. Therefore splitting is ultimately a distortion of reality. So as Spillius (2007) summarizes, for Klein unconscious phantasy accompanies gratification as well as frustration and both hate and love are innate and not particularly dependent on the external world.

An infant has innate unconscious knowledge (although hazy) of the physicality of her parents (and thus later of herself). As the infant feels the mother's body to be the source of all good and bad things the infant/child attacks the mother's body (in phantasy) out of frustration and in order to get possession of her mother's riches. These sadistic attacks arouse anxiety in the infant, which can be a spur to development although also induce a feeling in the infant that her own body is dangerous (Spillius 2007). Thus if you 'attack' someone they become dangerous objects. If anxiety about attacking the mother's body becomes excessive it leads to neurosis (or even psychosis in extreme cases).

For Klein, the first three months of infancy allow a 'normal' paranoid-schizoid position characterized by persecutory anxiety about good and bad or dangerous objects. The baby splits these objects in phantasy as 'totally' good and bad. Without this splitting the baby may not grow up to be able to understand that there *are* good and bad objects (people and situations) to which they will have to relate. Thus splitting is a developmental benefit if the infant receives good enough care.

In adulthood however a person may still split the good from the bad in ways that do not enhance development and are potentially harmful to the person themselves and the other people they relate to – this may well be a problem in the workplace. So for example the individual might see colleagues as all bad or all good and behave in ways that 'demonize' or 'idealize' others, which will have a detrimental impact on their judgement and could play out across the system (Klein 1959/1975).

References

Klein, M. (1959/1975) Our adult world and its roots on infancy. In *The writings of Melanie Klein: Envy and Gratitude and Other Works 1946–1963* (Vol. 3, pp. 247–63). London: Hogarth Press.
Spillius, E. (2007) *Encounters with Melanie Klein*. London: Routledge.

Annotated further reading

Segal, J. (1993) *Melanie Klein*. London: Sage.

Julia Segal's work is clear and comprehensive and a good place to start.

Spillius, E. (2007) *Encounters with Melanie Klein*. London: Routledge.

For greater detail and depth Spillius makes a valuable contribution to the literature.

Paraphrasing

See also: acceptance commitment therapy; empathy; interpretation

Paraphrasing is another term, like counselling itself, which is used in a variety of ways and given different names, which can be confusing. Kennedy-Moore and Watson (1999) – though they use the term 'empathic reflection' – define a paraphrase as an 'attempt to distil the essence of what clients are saying and to give form to the unstated feelings or perceptions that lie *immediately below the surface* of clients' remarks . . . they are sophisticated attempts to uncover buried thoughts and feelings' (p. 212, my emphasis). Thus, mmhs and other attentive behaviours are *not* empathy, though they are usually a helpful context for it. Rather, counsellors empathize when they say to a client the essence of what the client has said, or clearly implied, to them. It is therefore much more than saying 'I see what you mean', 'Tell me more about X' or 'I know how you feel'.

Tony Merry (personal communication, 2002) wrote after he'd marked some students' tapes (and the students concerned were in their first year and later developed their skills and passed the course):

There is little evidence of what it means to stay with a client, or to enter a client's frame of reference i.e. little appreciation of what empathic attending is all about. Students think they have to move a client on, make connections, see patterns, provide explanations, look for reasons etc. There doesn't seem to be an appreciation that patterns will emerge, connections will be made etc. once a client feels empathically understood in a non-judgmental atmosphere . . .

This statement illustrates very well the 'pure' person-centred position (Mearns and Thorne 2007; Merry 1999) on empathy and therefore paraphrasing, although Merry in the quotation above uses the term 'empathic attending'.

The artistic, warm, perceptive element of paraphrasing lies in part on deciding on the 'essence' of what a client says – the part that is most 'alive' for them, which has most emotional power – and on when to speak, and then speaking freshly and concisely, and in a way which allows the client to reflect on your paraphrase, and correct, refine or add to it if they wish. Rogers himself did not use the term 'paraphrasing' and disliked attempts to reduce the quality of empathy to techniques. However, analyses of some of his interviews (e.g. Gundrum et al. 1999; and others cited in Elliott et al. 2011) show that to a large extent he did indeed restate his clients' words in a fresh way etc. and that this tended to encourage an inward focus, acceptance of self (because the counsellor seeks to help the client understand and does not make judgements), insight and other self-challenges/new perspectives, and therefore possible actions.

References

Elliott, R., Bohart, A.C., Watson, J.C. and Greenberg, L.S. (2011) Empathy. *Psychotherapy*, 48(1): 43–9.

Gundrum, M., Lietaer, G. and Van Hees-Matthijssen, C. (1999) Carl Rogers' responses in the 17th session with Miss Mun: comments from a process-experiential and psychoanalytic perspective. *British Journal of Guidance and Counselling*, 27: 461–82.

Kennedy-Moore, E. and Watson, J.C. (1999) *Expressing Emotion: Myths, Realities, and Therapeutic Strategies*. London: The Guilford Press.

Mearns, D. and Thorne, B. (2007) *Person Centred Counselling in Action*, 3rd edn. London: Sage.

Merry, T. (1999) *Learning and Being in Person-Centred Counselling*. Ross-on-Wye: PCCS Books.

Annotated further reading

Hill, C.E. (2009) *Helping Skills: Facilitating, Exploration, Insight, and Action*, 3rd edn. Washington, DC, American Psychological Association.

Bayne, R., Jinks, G., Collard, P. and Horton, I. (2008) *The Counsellor's Handbook: A Practical A–Z Guide to Integrative Counselling and Psychotherapy*, 3rd edn. Cheltenham: Nelson Thornes.

Hill (pp. 147–62) and Bayne et al. (pp. 134–6) give detailed guidelines on paraphrasing as a skill, though Hill uses the term 'reflection of feeling'.

Gundrum, M., Lietaer, G. and Van Hees-Matthijssen, C. (1999) Carl Rogers' responses in the 17th session with Miss Mun: comments from a process-experiential and psychoanalytic perspective. *British Journal of Guidance and Counselling*, 27: 461–82.

Includes a transcript of an entire session with analysis by two person-centred counsellors and a psychoanalyst. Subtle and stimulating. For example, they comment that 'At times when the client has come to feel sufficiently her underlying experience of pain and anxiety, it is not necessary to reflect the feelings more sharply – it could even be quite disturbing' (p. 473).

Perls, Fritz (1893–1970)

See also: Gestalt therapy

Fritz Perls, who was born in Berlin into a Jewish, lower-middle-class family, is the best known of the co-founders of Gestalt therapy. He was the youngest of three siblings, having two elder sisters. His mother was the constant presence of his childhood as his father worked away for much of the time. Perls served in the German army as a medical officer in the First World War, which, like many of his contemporaries, left him somewhat traumatized. After the war he trained as a neuro-psychiatrist and a psychoanalyst. At the neurological insti-tute he was introduced to existentialism, phenomenology and 'holistic' thinking. During his psychoanalytic training and beyond he was analysed by several Freudians, followed by Wilhelm Reich (Parlett and Hemming 2002). In the 1920s he came into contact with the new ideas being developed within philosophy, art, politics and psychology.

Perhaps in part due to the fact that Perls was an excellent self-publicist, his is the name most commonly associated with Gestalt therapy. However, his wife Laura and Paul Goodman were also central players, with the latter contributing most in terms of the social and political dimensions of the theory (Feltham and Horton 2006). Laura was taught by some of the leading figures in the Gestalt School of Psychology, and her interest in dance and Eastern philosophy had a strong influence on the development of the approach.

As a result of his left wing views and his Jewish background, Perls left Germany for Holland in 1933 and from there moved to South Africa. His first book *Ego, Hunger and Aggression,* first published in 1942, was critical of psychoanalysis and outlined an alternative approach to therapy. After the war Perls moved to the USA and in the following decade the book *Gestalt Therapy: Excitement and Growth in the Human Personality* (Perl et al. 1951) was published. In 1952 the first Institute of Gestalt Therapy was established. Perls was a highly energetic promoter of this new approach to therapy, travelling round the country to disseminate his ideas to a wider audience. The approach gained popularity during this time with the Esalen Institute being established in California in the 1960s.

Clarkson and Mackewn (1993) present an interesting perspective on the extent to which Perls both helped and hindered the establishment of Gestalt therapy. They argue that he was very successful in bringing the approach to the attention of a wider audience via his workshops, the recordings of his work, his numerous interviews and appearances in the media; he enabled Gestalt therapy to be understood by the general public by working on the simplification of the key ideas; and he came up with some memorable phrases and 'sound bites' which stuck in the memory. From a more negative standpoint, they suggest that by popularizing the approach so successfully, Perls also detracted from the perception of it as a complex and serious approach. Some practitioners misinterpreted his methods, overemphasizing the confrontational and cathartic aspects and disregarding much of the theoretical component.

References

Clarkson, P. and Mackewn, J. (1993) *Key Figures in Counselling and Psychotherapy: Fritz Perls.* London: Sage.

Feltham, C. and Horton, I. (eds) (2006) *The SAGE Handbook of Counselling and Psychotherapy,* 2nd edn. London: Sage.

Parlett, M. and Hemming, J. (2002) Gestalt therapy. In W. Dryden (ed.) *Handbook of Individual Therapy,* 4th edn. London: Sage.

Perls, F.S. (1942) *Ego, Hunger and Aggression.* London: Allen & Unwin.

Perls, F.S., Hefferline, R.F. and Goodman, P. (1951) *Gestalt Therapy: Excitement and Growth in the Human Personality.* New York: Julian Press.

Annotated further reading

Clarkson, P. and Mackewn, J. (1993) *Key Figures in Counselling and Psychotherapy: Fritz Perls*. London: Sage.

A useful guide to Perls' life and ideas.

Person-centred counselling

See also: conditions of worth; core conditions; humanistic approaches; locus of evaluation; phenomenology; Rogers, Carl; self-actualization; self-concept

This section is intended to be read in association with the entries on the key concepts listed above to provide a sufficiently rounded summary of this model. As a theoretical framework, the person-centred approach sits very firmly within the humanistic tradition, presenting a very positive conceptualization of human nature. Human beings' main needs are to reach their full potential (or to self-actualize) and to be valued by others. The belief is that people have sufficient inner resources to deal effectively with whatever they face in life and the ability to reach their potential. These resources may at times struggle to surface due to challenging personal circumstances, but they are always present even if hidden or out of reach. People may seek counselling if they lose touch with these inner resources.

Another central aspect is the importance of phenomenology, in other words valuing how individuals experience the world and focusing on how they perceive and describe it, rather than attempting to interpret that individual perception. Hand in hand with this is the belief in the uniqueness of the individual, and in their being the expert on their inner experiencing. An individual's experiencing in seen, not as a static concept, but as an ever-changing process made up of thoughts, feelings and behaviours. 'Process' is a central term, with the emphasis in counselling being on process rather than content. In more concrete terms this means that the counsellor will aim to help the client, through the process of describing their here-and-now experience, to become more aware of their patterns of thinking, feeling and behaving and thus able to change them.

In terms of the approach to counselling, the relationship between counsellor and client is central, in fact it is sufficient in itself according to Rogers (1957). The counsellor is a facilitator who aims to establish a relationship with the client based on respect, empathy, transparency and equality as far as is possible.

The other key concepts of this approach, including those which relate to human development and to the core therapeutic qualities, or conditions, required in effective counselling are covered in separate entries.

Reference

Rogers, C.R. (1957) The necessary and sufficient conditions of therapeutic personality change, *Journal of Consulting Psychology*, 21: 95–103.

Annotated further reading

Casemore, R. (2006) *Person-centred Counselling in a Nutshell*. London: Sage.

A succinct guide to person-centred theoretical concepts and to the counselling relationship.

Cooper, M., O'Hara, M., Schmid, P.F. and Wyatt, G. (eds) (2007) *The Handbook of Person Centred Counselling and Psychotherapy*. Ross-on-Wye: PCCS Books.

An excellent, comprehensive overview of theory and practice.

Personal construct therapy

See also: constructivism

The first person to develop a methodical theory of psychotherapy along constructivist lines was the American clinical psychologist, therapist and educator George Kelly (1905–1967). Kelly was explaining that psychology tried to interpret the human condition and how to predict human reactions when confronted with novel experiences.

He seemed ahead of his time. Kelly very much implemented the point of view that each individual lives in their personal world, despite sharing the same cultures and families, for example. In contrast to Behaviourist theory Kelly believed that we respond to our world rather than just adopting behaviours without questioning them. We make sense of our experience by applying personal constructs we have created previously.

Kelly recommended we look at individuals and their behaviours as if we were a scientist. We might come up with theories as to why certain events had happened and then test our assumptions. 'We are active beings, form of motions' (Dryden et al. 2007: 175).

People create the various constructs to understand the world around them, which are based on observations and experiences. Kelly created the 'Repertory Grid', an interviewing technique which uses factor analysis to determine an idiographic measure of personality. The main point of the theory says: 'A person's unique psychological processes are channelled by the way s/he anticipates events. Every man is, in his own particular way a scientist' (Hogan et al. 1997: 657)

He proposes that throughout our lives we keep on creating constructs and theories about how the world works so that we can anticipate events. For example, at birth babies soon discover that if they cry for long enough, their mother will come. People eventually build and refine theories about other people, some of which could be turned into stereotypes, and they will frequently impose their theories onto others to be able to predict their actions better.

A construct has two extreme points, for example happy and sad, and we can place ourselves and other people at either extreme or somewhere in between. Kelly says that everyone's mind is filled with constructs at a low-level awareness. He believes that constructs are preverbal, often because they were developed before we had the use of words. Any person or group or circumstance can be characterized fairly precisely by the set of constructs we apply to it and the position of the thing within the range of each construct.

Kelly believed that rather than have the psychotherapist interpret the person's psyche, which would impose the construct onto the person, they should facilitate the patient finding his or her own constructs. To do this, Kelly created the Repertory Grid.

The Grid worked by Kelly asking the client to select about seven elements whose nature depended on what the client and therapist were trying to discover. For example: two special friends, two work-mates, two people you dislike, your mother and oneself. Then Kelly would select a few at random, and would ask something like: 'In relation to (whatever is of interest), in what sense would two of these people be alike or differ however from a third?' This would help indicate one of the extreme points of the client's constructs. As Kelly repeated this formula, he and the client would be able to reveal several constructs that the client might not have even been aware of. Several countries have adopted the use of the Repertory Grid, including the USA, Canada, the UK, Spain, Italy, Ireland, Australia and Germany. It is often used in the qualitative phase of market research, to identify the ways in which consumers see products and services.

Kelly was very much against the application of the medical (disease) model in the field of psychological treatment. He proposed to use a concept of functioning as a way of evaluating a person's well-being.

Clients were also 'coached' to act out fictional identities in their daily lives for a specified time-frame (usually for a few weeks), working from a 'self-characterization' developed by the client, the therapist and a consulting team. The client and therapist then practised this novel role in a series of thera-peutic enactments with the therapist acting out familiar people of the client's life. At the end of this period, the role was put aside and the therapist and client discussed the extent to which the client's sense of self and social world were non-fixed and provisional constructions, which may be perceived or experi-enced quite differently if viewed in alternative ways. Kelly's 'fixed role therapy' thus was the first form of brief therapy. In time he developed a complete 'psychology of personal constructs' that placed these procedures in a rigorous theoretical context, and suggested diagnostic, therapeutic and research methods targeting the unique meaning systems that individuals devised to make up and predict the themes of their lives.

One of the least developed aspects of personal construct area is group therapy. He advocated its use, albeit very little application has followed from Kelly's theories on group work.

Another restriction in PCT application may lie with the therapist, who may struggle with clients who are not fully cooperating. PCT uses a number of techniques from other schools such as dream material, guided fantasies and systematic desensitization. The UK Council for Psychotherapy, a regulatory body, classes personal construct theory under experiential constructivism.

References

Dryden, W. (ed.) (2007) *Handbook of Individual Therapy*. London: Sage.

Fransella, F. (1995) 'George Kelly' http://www.uk.sagepub.com/booksProdDesc.nav?prodId=Book203504& London: Sage (accessed 2 August 2011).

Hogan, R., Johnson, J. and Briggs, S. (1997) *Handbook of Personality Psychology*. San Diego, CA: Academic Press.

Annotated further reading

Fransella, F., Dalton, P. and Weselby, G. (2007) Personal construct therapy. In W. Dryden (ed.) *Handbook of Individual Therapy*. London: Sage.

This is a very helpful introduction to PCT, starting with its historical context, focusing on its development in the UK, and including impor-tant aspects such as goals, qualities of therapist and the therapeutic relationship. An interesting case study completes this chapter.

Jankowicz, A.D. (2003) *The Easy Guide to Repertory Grids*. Chichester: Wiley.

This publication provides a basic primer in repertory grid technique.

Personality

See also: life scripts; preferences; self; self-actualization

Personality differences are an important and practical topic for counsellors and psychotherapists, yet are generally ignored or only touched on in otherwise excellent textbooks (e.g. Egan 2010; McLeod 2009). Feltham and Dryden (2006) support this view indirectly, commenting that 'client temperament is an important area often overlooked or not well understood by counsellors' (p. 73). Here they are using temperament and personality interchangeably, for example including the characteristics of extraversion and introversion, formality and informality and hardness and softness in their discussion.

The relevance of contemporary personality theories to counselling has been particularly neglected, despite major advances (Singer 2005). Singer (2005) is the major exception to this neglect; he focuses on five factor or 'Big Five' theory, which is the most prominent theory in personality research since the early 2000s, as well as on two other levels of personality – motives and integrative life stories – and on one main area of application: helping counsellors understand their clients more deeply.

The most widely-used applied personality theory since the 1990s is closely related to the Big Five (so that most of the evidence for the validity of each of the two theories supports both of them) but differs markedly in tone and the central concept of preference (Bayne in press). This theory is psychological type theory in its Myers-Briggs Type Indicator (MBTI) sense.

Singer (2005) does not discuss psychological type theory or do more than touch on several applications of personality theory and research to counselling. These include counsellor self-awareness, improving communication during counselling (and therefore the counselling relationship itself), as a perspective on clients' problems in love, work, health, etc. and contextual aspects of counselling such as marketing, which some counsellors are very unenthusiastic about, the counselling room and its surroundings, and unjustly restricted ideas about the nature of 'good counsellors' (Bayne 2004; in press).

For example, psychological type theory suggests that people of each psychological type speak a different 'language' most comfortably and this raises questions about how flexible counsellors can be, or want to be (Lazarus, in a different context, called this the 'authentic chameleon' issue). Another example is helping counsellors and clients understand people of different types to their own as different rather than as deliberately irritating, immature or unreasonable. This can be a helpful reframing perspective in romantic, family and work relationships too.

Another application of personality theory to work is that people of different psychological types vary in their approaches to seeking work and enjoy particular kinds of work more. Similarly, personality theory predicts considerable variety in normal reactions to loss and to aspects of health such as diet, exercise and chronic illness. Thus, the standard approaches to helping clients lose weight of keeping a food diary, counting calories and so on work much more effectively with people with certain personality characteristics than with others.

Different strategies for coping with problems and how they are presented are also – at least in theory – likely to be more effective with each 'type'. A final example of a personality perspective on a client problem – though in this instance the true source of the problem may not be the client – is that some children of a particular personality type may be more likely to be misdiagnosed as having ADD or ADHD when the problem is that their school doesn't fit their kind of personality. Children (and adults) with these personality characteristics want action and to feel excited, and personality theory suggests several strategies to try before medication.

(Psychological type theory is outlined briefly in the section on **preferences**.)

References

Bayne, R. (2004) *Psychological Types at Work: An MBTI Perspective*. London: Thomson.

Bayne, R. (in press) *The Counsellor's Guide to Personality: Preferences, Motives and Lifestories*. Basingstoke: Palgrave Macmillan.

Egan, G. (2009) *The Skilled Helper: A Problem Management and Opportunity Development Approach to Helping*, 9th edn. Belmont, CA: Brooks/Cole.

Feltham, C. and Dryden, W. (2006) *Brief Counselling*, 2nd edn. Maidenhead: Open University Press.

McLeod, J. (2009) *An Introduction to Counselling*, 4th edn. Maidenhead: Open University Press.

Singer, J.A. (2005) *Personality and Psychotherapy: Treating the Whole Person*. London: The Guilford Press.

Annotated further reading

Bayne, R. (2004) *Psychological Types at Work: An MBTI Perspective*. London: Thomson.

Applies psychological-type theory to careers, time, communication, health, counselling and coaching, and leading and managing.

Funder, D. (2011) *The Personality Puzzle*, 5th edn. London: W.W. Norton.

A readable, stimulating and scholarly general textbook on personality theories.

Provost, J. (1993) *Applications of the Myers-Briggs Type Indicator in Counseling: A Casebook*, 2nd edn. Gainesville, FL: CAPT.

Brief case studies (two or three pages each) illustrating the author's work with clients of all the 16 psychological types.

Phenomenology

See also: existential counselling; gestalt therapy; humanistic approaches; person-centred counselling

Phenomenology, which was originally used in existential philosophy, is a form of philosophical enquiry developed by Husserl (1859–1938) and Heidegger (1889–1976). At a time when previous sources of meaning such as religion and community were being increasingly questioned, there was a growing interest in searching for new sources of meaning. A phenomenological approach to developing knowledge and understanding involves exploring individual personal experiences with a view to understanding the essential qualities of those experiences, rather than developing theories in order to make sense of experience. 'Experience' can be defined as 'a combination of bodily-sensed thoughts, feelings, actions and tendencies' which is constantly changing (McLeod 2009: 175).

Phenomenological enquiry stands in opposition to scientific 'objectivity' in that it requires that the researcher (or therapist) puts aside, as far as they are able, their own theoretical assumptions about whatever is being examined and describe it as fully as possible. This, in turn, leads to an understanding of the essential elements of that experience. According to McLeod (2009) there are three key facets to this type of enquiry:

1   It is about capturing experience as it is lived.
2   It involves capturing the details of experience, including the different aspects and how the experience changes over time.
3   It assumes that the concept of 'objective' reality does not exist; instead the individual constructs their own meaning.

Relevant counselling approaches

The following theoretical approaches to counselling share similar goals and assumptions. One of the main goals is to explore the meaning for the client of problematic areas of experience. Underlying these approaches is a basic assumption that we create our worlds and are ultimately responsible for our lives. The client, rather than the therapist, is the expert in their own internal world.

The person-centred approach aims to capture the 'felt experience' of the client in all its rich detail. Indeed, the concept of 'experiencing' is central to this approach. The emphasis is on the therapist supporting the client in describing the ongoing flow of experiences with a view to becoming more open to experience, including denied experience, and developing a greater trust in personal experience as a guide to values and behaviour.

Existential counselling uses phenomenological enquiry in order to get at the essential truth for the client of a situation or feeling. Although, like person-centred therapy, there are no specific techniques, Spinelli (1994) identifies three basic 'rules' which the therapist needs to observe:

- It is necessary to 'bracket' or separate any assumptions so that they can really hear what the client is saying.
- It is important to describe what is heard or observed rather than looking for a theoretical explanation.
- It is essential not to judge what is being described so that importance is only attached to certain areas when that will be helpful to the client. This is known as 'horizontalization'.

The Gestalt approach focuses on working with the client's immediate experience, the aim being to work through any 'unfinished business' in the client's past which prevents them from living authentically and taking responsibility for their actions. Phenomenological enquiry is relevant here in assisting the client to clarify their own personal truth.

According to Spinelli (1994: 361) the existential approach avoids the tendency to 'cure, change, help or promote growth' which results in the client experiencing acceptance of and by the self and of and by another. Thus the client can reach a true understanding of their issues and can challenge these where necessary, while the therapist is encouraged through the process of the therapy to continually challenge their beliefs.

However, because a phenomenological perspective focuses entirely on the client's individual point of view and places great trust in the client's lived experience, it is possible to inadvertently collude in a client's perception of events when presenting an alternative perspective may lead to greater insight.

References

McLeod, J. (2009) *An Introduction to Counselling*. Maidenhead: Open University Press.

Spinelli, E. (1994) *Demystifying Therapy*. London: Constable.

Annotated further reading

McLeod, J. (2011) *Qualitative Research in Counselling and Psychotherapy*, 2nd edn. London: Sage.

Includes an excellent chapter on how to undertake phenomenological research.

Spinelli, E. (2007) *Practising Existential Psychotherapy: The Relational World*. London: Sage.

Although the focus here is on a particular type of phenomenology, this book provides a valuable introduction to the theoretical assumptions underlying existential phenomenology as well as a way of putting the theory into practice.

Positive psychology (PP)

PP has been described as: 'the scientific study of ordinary human strengths and virtues' (Sheldon and King 2001: 216). When Martin Seligman gave a key note address to the American Philosophical Association in 1999, he emphasized that his new branch of psychology would not merely focus on the strength of human beings but back up its theories by studies involving thousand of participants.

Historically, when psychology was a new field it tended to focus on tasks such as curing mental disease, bettering life in general and supporting exceptional gifts in people. After the Second World War however the focus on improving mental illness (the disease model) became the main focus of psychology and the core interest of research and practice.

Positive psychology, despite its popular name, endeavours to use scientific research as originally intended; looking for how positive experiences, including joy, well-being, satisfaction, optimism, strength, flow and others actually prevent disease.

Humanistic psychology (Carl Rogers), which aimed at helping people to become 'fully functioning' and developmental psychology (Abraham Maslow), were early forerunners of PP. Maslow studied the most 'functioning and successful' people such as Einstein and Roosevelt in order to discover how they had reached their full potential.

So what PP left behind was the focus on destructive emotion and the disease model and refocused it on the advantages of positive affect and cognition.

In brief it was assumed and proven that positive emotions increase our ability to pay attention and think, basically because they cause our autonomic nervous system to stay within the parasympathetic response ('rest and digest'), which helps to create a healthy balance for the body. Positive emotions are responsible for the production of chemicals like serotonin and endorphins, which in turn create a sense of well-being and creative thinking.

Furthermore positive emotions reduce negative thinking pathways and thereby the stress response. They also enhance the experience of childlike enjoyment (moment to moment experience), contentment and the ability to experience love and compassion. The latter of course are the prerequisites for healthy relationships and encounters with others.

Already in 1906 the psychologist and philosopher William James had started exploring the concept of 'optimal human functioning'. Today (a century later) many of James' principles and research ideas are found in the work of Daniel Goleman and Martin Seligman. The former coined the concept 'emotional intelligence', which refers to managing and understanding our own and others' emotions. Martin Seligman developed the 'authentic happiness model' in the early years of this century. In a research he conducted with Diener they discovered that really happy people were characterized by having a rich social life, rarely spent time alone and were successful in their romantic relationships.

Seligman also emphasizes that we need to focus not merely on human strength as a general baseline for achieving positivity, but rather need to tune in with the individual's top five 'signature strengths' – abilities we are particularly good at.

The role of PP within the field of psychotherapy is to enlarge the therapist's skills and include the concept of healing and strengthening! Positive psychotherapy then actively 'elicits positive emotions and memories. It approaches transgressions, as well as acts of kindness; insults as well as compliments. Selfishness as well as compassion and kindness' (Rashid 2008: 12).

References

Rashid, T. (2008) Positive psychotherapy. *The Psychotherapist*, 39: 12–13.
Sheldon, K.M. and King, L. (2001) Why Positive Psychology is necessary. *American Psychologist*, 56: 216–17.

Annotated further reading

Boniwell, I. (2006) *Positive Psychology in a Nutshell*. London: Personal Well-Being Centre.

An excellent introduction with a good description of the why's and how's of positive psychology. A little brief on the historical perspective.

Preferences

See also: client feedback, collecting; personality; positive psychology; self; strengths

The concept of preference is at the heart of one theory of the main differences in personality (MBTI or psychological type theory, discussed briefly in the section on **personality**). Preference can be defined as 'feeling most natural and comfortable with a particular way of behaving and experiencing' and thus overlaps considerably with Linley's concept of **strengths** though he proposes hundreds of strengths and MBTI theory focuses on eight preferences. It states that some people are

More	*Whereas others are more*
outgoing and active	reflective and reserved
practical and interested in facts and details	interested in possibilities and an overview
logical and reasoned	agreeable and appreciative
planning and coming to firm conclusions	easy going and flexible

These descriptions are deliberately positive but most have negative variations, e.g. 'on a different planet' and 'flaky' for interested in possibilities, 'boring' and 'plodding' for practical. They also show that the psychological types aren't rigid 'boxes' but patterns of preferences – 16 types in all because there are 16 possible combinations (4 × 4).

Therapists can be irritated by clients whose preferences are very different from their own. They may also misjudge them as ineffective, immature, difficult or even suffering from a personality disorder, when they are just different. The preferences have several other implications for therapists and for counselling:

- as an approach to self-awareness;
- as an approach to being empathic more deeply and quickly;
- as a source of ideas and information on client's problems, for example with relationships and career choice;
- as an approach to the alluring but so far unrealized strategy for increasing counsellor effectiveness of matching therapists and clients.

Preference theory further suggests ways in which counsellors can adapt their communication style or 'language' with clients of different preferences to their own and for different stages of counselling. Provost (1993) put a subtle aspect of this application well. Her ideal is that counsellors can learn to 'talk sixteen types' (p. 24) but she appreciates that this may ask some (most?) counsellors to be too versatile so she also writes that 'although counsellors can build rapport by mirroring a client's type this does not mean that therapists should become a client's type' (p. 20).

Part of client feedback can be about preferences and 'languages', which raises the 'authentic chameleon' issue: how versatile can a counsellor be and still be congruent? For example, how comfortable would you be behaving formally with one client, then putting your feet on the desk with the next? And are you equally at ease with empathizing, challenging and goal-setting?

Finally, MBTI theory predicts that therapists with different preferences are most fulfilled, energized and skilled in different schools, styles and stages of counselling. Some consistent relationships between the preferences and schools of counselling have been found (some of the findings are reviewed in Bayne 2004) but the implications are not absolute or prescriptive. Rather, people with each of the preferences tend to have strengths in some settings and careers and corresponding weaknesses in others but it is possible to find or create a niche in an unusual career for your psychological type.

References

Bayne, R. (2004) *Psychological Types at Work: An MBTI Perspective*. London: Thompson.

Provost, J. (1993) *A Case Book: Applications of the Myers-Briggs Type Indicator in Counseling*, 2nd edn. Gainesville, FL: CAPT.

Annotated further reading

Bayne, R. (in press) *The Counsellors Guide to Personality: Preferences, Motives and Life Stories*. Basingstoke: Palgrave Macmillan.

Discusses all the ideas in this section in more detail as well as applications to health, love, education, etc. Also discusses the possibility, based on Nettle's (2007) review of Big Five Theory, that anxiety or worrying has sufficiently positive aspects to be treated as a fifth preference.

Provost, J. (1993) *A Case Book: Applications of the Myers-Briggs Type Indicator in Counseling*, 2nd edn. Gainesville, FL: CAPT.

Brief (two to three pages) and engaging case studies of the author's counselling with clients of each of the types.

Projection

See also: introjection; projective identification

Projection is used in different senses in psychoanalysis (Hinshelwood 1991):

1   perception
2   projection and expulsion
3   externalizing conflict
4   projection and identity
5   projection of parts of the self

1   In perception projection is part of the commonly understood psychology of perception in that on the basis of bodily sensations some are projected out beyond the body.
2   Projection and expulsion connected the expulsion of faeces with the phantasy of expelling an object that is repellent.
3   Klein found the mechanism of projection important in the externalizing of internal conflicts in children's play to external objects.
4   Projection helps the ego to deflect the death instinct and overcome anxiety by ridding the ego of bad objects and danger according to Klein.
5   Both Freud and Klein used the concept to project parts of the self onto others.

Projection is a defence mechanism which involves intrapsychically 'putting' something that is in oneself and unpalatable 'into' someone else (see also **projective identification**). If a person is always angry for instance, they may unconsciously and in phantasy expel anger that they find unacceptable in themselves by attributing it to another person (or people).

Freud, who identified repression as the most important defence mechanism, talked about repression and projection in the context of paranoia and self-reproach (Gay 1995: 95). The ego tries to assimilate the 'voices' that challenge the self so that where repression has failed, and the ego has been overwhelmed, the feelings that the ego tried to repress are expelled. The mechanism of projection thus involves the refusal of belief in the self-reproach.

Freud first wrote about projection in 1895 and the concept has gone through several iterations since then (Hinshelwood 1991). Klein for example found that projection enabled the externalization of internal conflict and therefore the externalization of guilt. However, both Freud and Klein (1946) used the concept to attribute certain states of mind to someone else. Thus hatred that someone might feel is attributed to another person and the feeling of hatefulness in oneself is alleviated.

References

Gay, P. (1995) *The Freud Reader*. London: Vintage.

Hinshelwood, R. (1991) *A Dictionary of Kleinian Thought*. London: Free Association Books.

Klein, M. (1946) Notes on some schizoid mechanisms. In H. Segal (ed.) *Envy and Gratitude and other Works 1946–1963*. London: Virago.

Annotated further reading

Hinshelwood, R. (1997) Primitive mental processes: psychoanalysis and the ethics of integration. *Philosophy, Psychiatry and Psychology*, 4(2): 121–43.

This is a challenging but rewarding read to be considered after reading earlier recommended articles and books on Klein and Freud (see entries for **defence mechanisms, Freudian analysis, Kleinian analysis**).

Projective identification

See also: introjection; paranoid-schizoid position; projection; splitting

One way in which we deal with emotional discomfort or intolerable feelings is by projective identification, which takes place while in the paranoid-schizoid position. Projective identification is a process by which an individual actively gets rid of intolerable feelings, which belong to themselves, by *pushing them into another person*.

While it can be a powerful way of communicating feelings it can also be a destructive attack unconsciously intended to destroy the comfort of the other by evoking the unbearable feelings a person has in the other person. Briefly the process involves deep splitting on the part of someone who needs to get rid of their hated parts although it has been suggested that Klein (and thus others) considered that it might be that good parts are also projected into a love object, which is equally unrealistic.

Projective identification was defined in 1946 by Klein as the prototype of the aggressive object-relationship representing an anal attack on an object by means of forcing parts of the ego into it in order to take over and control it. It is a phantasy remote from consciousness that entails a belief in certain aspects of the self being located elsewhere, the consequence being a depleted sense of self and poor sense of identity (Hinshelwood 1991). Projective identification relates to both projection and introjection and is a defence mechanism in the paranoid-schizoid position (Hinshelwood 1991; Klein 1984; H. Segal and Klein 1973; J. Segal 1993). The origin of Klein's thinking about this came from her work with disturbed young children which focused on the violent expulsion of excrements that she associated with disowned and harmful parts of the self. These harmful parts are expelled in hatred and represent split off parts of the ego that are projected *into* the mother. Klein made the point strongly that she meant 'into' (rather than 'onto' which distinguishes projective identification from projection) (Klein 1946). The phantasy in projective identification according to Klein is that by expelling harmful objects into the mother not only is the object/mother harmed, but the object can be controlled (violently) and possessed. The mother is felt to be *the* bad part of the self rather than a separate object and it is important to remember this because this is crucial for the mental state of people in the paranoid-schizoid position (see **paranoid-schizoid position**). She added the term projective identification a few years after first describing this process. The psychological results of this process are severe psychotic symptoms and a profound sense of a depleted, weakened ego (Hinshelwood 1991).

This concept has become increasingly important in the post-Kleinian developments of her work and underpins understanding of the depersonalization of borderline and psychotic conditions and is seen to be particularly relevant in understanding the externalization of the ego by schizophrenics.

Klein herself though (1962, 1984) suggested that envy was deeply implicated in projective identification thus representing 'forced entry' into another person in order to destroy them (or what they have).

Bion (Bion 1963; Hinshelwood 1991) later distinguished a 'normal' form of projective identification from the pathological one which has been elaborated subsequently by object-relations theorists and it has been suggested that it is a primitive form of communication as well as an attack in that a feeling of hatred or of inadequacy or confusion projected into another person is a communication. Analytically trained organizational consultants, counsellors and therapist/analysts can use this as a means of understanding the dynamics of the relationships.

References

Bion, W.R. (1963) *Elements of Psycho-Analysis*. London: William Heinemann.

Hinshelwood, R. (1991) *A Dictionary of Kleinian Thought*. London: Free Association Books.

Klein, M. (1946) Notes on some schizoid mechanisms. In H. Segal (ed.) *Envy and Gratitude and Other Works 1946–1963*. London: Virago.

Klein, M. (1962) *Our Adult World and its Roots in Infancy*. London: Sage.

Klein, M. (1984) *Envy and Gratitude: And Other Works, 1946–1963*: London: Hogarth Press.

Segal, H. and Klein, M. (1973) *Introduction to the Work of Melanie Klein*. London: Hogarth Press, (for) the Institute of Psycho-analysis.

Segal, J. (1993) *Melanie Klein*. London: Sage.

Annotated further reading

Orbach, S. (2000) *The Impossibility of Sex*. Harmondsworth: Penguin.

Orbach's experiences provide examples of projective identification as a form of communication and Julia Segal's introduction to Melanie Klein and her work provides a clear analysis.

Psychic prison

See also: organizational dynamics

'Psychic prison' is a metaphor, first used by Plato in *The Republic*, to develop the idea that those caught up in an organizational (or family) system share a vision of the world that is constrained by the unconscious phantasies of their own and their colleagues (or family members). They cannot escape this prison or way of thinking until they 'escape' from these psychic constraints after which they are unlikely to be able to convince those left that there is a world where different values and ways of being exist (Morgan 2006).

Morgan examines this metaphor by taking the reader back to Freud's notion of drive and repression in particular (see **defence mechanisms**; **repression**). In order to be able to work and live alongside others each individual needs to repress their innermost desires and thoughts in order to control their behaviour and Morgan considered the role of 'management scientists' in ensuring that organizations develop as psychic prisons to reinforce self-control/repressed desire.

Morgan examines organizational contexts as if they were patriarchal families following the Freudian model of development (see **psychosexual development**; **Oedipal complex**). He posits that organizations operate as if they were 'a man's world', not only dominated by men in senior positions but valuing the type of qualities that are attributed to the male, i.e. aggression and forthright behaviour. Conversely the value of behavioural characteristics typically attributed to females such as intuition, nurturance and empathetic support is downplayed.

Reference

Morgan, G. (2006) *Images of Organization*. London: Sage.

Annotated further reading

Morgan, G. (2006) *Images of Organization*. London: Sage.

Morgan's book is an excellent exposition of the emotional, social and structural elements of organizational life and his chapter on the psychic prison brings together the levels at which our image of the context in which we work is an interplay of conscious and unconscious material.

Psychoanalysis

See also: Eriksonian analysis; Freudian analysis; Kleinian analysis; structural model of the mind

Psychoanalysis is about both a means of understanding and explaining conscious and unconscious mental processes including personality, motivation and drives and a method of clinical treatment for people with psychological and mental health problems, including those with psychoses. It is known as a *depth psychology* and thus as a complex network of ideas and practices working in different ways and at different levels. It is about underlying structures of mind and the development of the psyche (Craib 2001: 9).

Sigmund Freud was its founding 'father', and although not the first to recognize the dynamic unconscious, he painstakingly, through his clinical and academic work as well as detailed self-reflection, developed a theoretical perspective on the role and importance of the unconscious that underpins both psychoanalysis and other psychodynamic approaches to mental health. His work was followed up by those who had worked with or been analysed by him, or those later influenced by him. The Nazi era had meant that many of the first group of analysts who were almost all Jewish (Frosh 2005), moved to other parts of Europe (mostly the UK, which included Freud himself) or to the USA (e.g. Erikson). Different schools have since developed on both sides of the Atlantic including object relations and Kleinian analysis (UK) and ego psychology (USA).

The overall aim of psychoanalysis is for patients to leave behind aspects of themselves and achieve new ones. It is a process of integration whereby the one-to-one 'talking' therapy between the analyst and the patient enables the patient to understand and own the parts of themselves they disowned (see

defence mechanisms) and experience a better balance between their internal worlds and external realities (Symington 1986).

What may be anathema to those who take a positivist view towards counselling and psychotherapies is that, as Symington states at the beginning of his lectures, 'psychoanalysis cannot be taught' and that 'psychoanalysis is not a thing' (p. 15). While he makes it clear that it is possible to talk about the topographical model of mind and concepts of resistance, repression, transference and describe the libido and death instincts, psychoanalysis itself is a complex reality which is both intrapsychic and interpersonal.

The process reflects both of these concepts. Patient and analyst meet four or five times a week and the patient is most probably lying on a couch while the analyst sits behind him/her. Thus the analyst can see the patient (although not the face) but the patient cannot see the analyst. This is intended to enhance the analytic process whereby the patient can freely associate and also unconsciously engage in transference towards the analyst. The analyst, when ready, makes interpretations to the patient about what is going on between them and sometimes about what they experience in the countertransference (see **counter-transference**) (Orbach 2000).

The process is one in which both analyst and patient have to focus as clearly as they can and work with the unconscious interpersonal and intrapsychic processes and many analysts suggest that they work very much between sessions with the unconscious residues of the analytic session (Raphael-Leff 2002).

The politics of psychoanalysis continues to intrigue social scientists (Frosh 1999). This includes where psychoanalytic ideas stand in society – for instance it is widely experienced as both elitist and patriarchal as well as being subject to criticism for not being a science and not subject to evaluation of its effectiveness (Craib 2001; Emde and Fonagy 1997).

However, there are also politics within psychoanalytic practice and thought including debates about the place of biology and drives (Frosh 1999) and how far psychoanalysis is connected to Judaism, or at least 'Jewishness' (Frosh 2005; Geller 2007).

References

Craib, I. (2001) *Psychoanalysis: A Critical Introduction*. Cambridge: Polity.

Emde, R.N. and Fonagy, P. (1997) An emerging culture for psychoanalytic research? *International Journal of Psychoanalysis*, 78: 643–51.

Frosh, S. (1999) *The Politics of Psychoanalysis*, 2nd edn. Basingstoke: Palgrave.

Frosh, S. (2005) *Hate and the 'Jewish Science': Anti-seminitism, Nazism and Psychoanalysis*. Basingstoke: Palgrave.

Geller, J. (2007) *On Freud's Jewish Body: Mitigating Circumcisions*. New York: Fordham University Press.

Orbach, S. (2000) *The Impossibility of Sex*. Harmondsworth: Penguin.
Raphael-Leff, J. (2002) *Between Sessions and Beyond the Couch*. Colchester: Centre for Psychoanalytic Studies, University of Essex.
Symington, N. (1986) *The Analytic Experience: Lectures from the Tavistock*. London: Free Association Books.

Annotated further reading

Craib, I. (2001) *Psychoanalysis: A Critical Introduction*. Cambridge: Polity.

This text is to be recommended as an introduction to psychoanalysis, albeit a challenging one. It is clear and informative particularly about Freud's and Klein's work. There is a critical component which is particularly helpful.

Frosh, S. (1999) *The Politics of Psychoanalysis*, 2nd edn. Basingstoke: Palgrave.

This book positions psychoanalysis in its historical and cultural contexts noting critiques of the discipline from various social and political positions. An informed and informative read but some prior knowledge is required.

Orbach, S. (2000) *The Impossibility of Sex*. Harmondsworth: Penguin.

An enjoyable account of countertransference and unconscious communications experienced by the therapist. The book is based on a series of detailed case studies.

Raphael-Leff, J. (2002) *Between Sessions and Beyond the Couch*. Colchester, Essex: Centre for Psychoanalytic Studies, University of Essex.

As with Orbach's work this book also provides insights into the experience of the therapist making it another intriguing read.

Symington, N. (1986) *The Analytic Experience: Lectures from the Tavistock*. London: Free Association Books.

This is a series of lectures to students of psychoanalysis at the Tavistock Centre providing a thought-provoking and clear outline of the major thinkers in British psychoanalysis and their contribution to the work of the Tavistock clinic and beyond.

Psychodynamic counselling

See also: psychoanalysis

Psychodynamic counselling emerged from psychoanalysis and is now considered to be one branch of a collection of therapeutic approaches that takes the importance of the unconscious and early life experience as its central tenets (Spurling 2004). These other approaches include psychoanalysis itself, psychoanalytic psychotherapy and psychodynamic psychotherapy (Jacobs 2006).

Psychodynamic counselling is sometimes also classified among 'psychological therapies' (Coren 2001; Spurling 2009) sitting alongside humanistic and behavioural approaches indicating perhaps that while the focus of psychodynamic counselling is upon the unconscious in common with psychoanalytic approaches, the relationship between the psychodynamic counsellor and the person consulting with them is more similar to that of other counselling approaches in that they are 'clients' (not patients) and the relationship with the counsellor is based upon acceptance and empathy and perhaps with less emphasis on defence mechanisms and interpretation (Wheeler 2006). However, there is a delicate balance to be held when trying to make distinctions between psychotherapy and counselling. It is, though, the case that while psychoanalytic therapies involve several years of work, counselling is more likely to focus on the resolution of a particular presenting problem (e.g. a traumatic event) and likely to take place over a shorter time span (perhaps between six months and a year).

It is in many other ways difficult to distinguish between psychodynamic counselling and other psychodynamic practices and it is worth noting that the academic journal *Psychodynamic Counselling* changed its name to *Psychodynamic Practice* in 2001.

There have been some evaluation studies of psychodynamic counselling (Archer et al. 2000; Simpson et al. 2003). There was evidence that psychodynamic counselling was seen in a positive way particularly by those counsellors who approved of psychodynamic concepts. Clients differed in how much they attributed positive change to the counselling process and the more positive they were at the start of the process, the more successful was the outcome likely to be. The Simpson et al. study also showed a significant improvement in depression and other mental health measures over time although this approach did not appear to be cost effective.

References

Archer, R., Forbes, Y., Metcalfe, C. and Winter, D. (2000) An investigation of the effectiveness of a voluntary sector psychodynamic counselling service. *British Journal of Medical Psychology*, 73(3): 401–12.

Coren, A. (2001) *Short-term Psychotherapy: A Psychodynamic Approach*. Basingstoke: Palgrave.

Jacobs, M. (2006) *The Presenting Past: The Core of Psychodynamic Counselling and Therapy*, 3rd edn. Maidenhead: Open University Press.

Simpson, S., Corney, R., Fitzgerald, P. and Beecham, J. (2003) A randomized controlled trial to evaluate the effectiveness and cost-effectiveness of psychodynamic counselling for general practice patients with chronic depression. *Psychological Medicine*, 33(2): 229–39.

Spurling, L. (2004) *An Introduction to Psychodynamic Counselling*. Basingstoke and New York: Palgrave Macmillan.

Spurling, L. (2009) *An Introduction to Psychodynamic Counselling*, 2nd edn. Basingstoke: Palgrave Macmillan.

Wheeler, S. (2006) *Difference and Diversity in Counselling: Contemporary Psychodynamic Perspectives*. Basingstoke: Palgrave Macmillan.

Annotated further reading

Spurling, L. (2009) *An Introduction to Psychodynamic Counselling*, 2nd edn. Basingstoke: Palgrave Macmillan.

This popular book now in its second edition is a useful introduction to psychodynamic counselling and provides information about the (subtle) differences between psychodynamic counselling and psychotherapy.

Psychosexual development

See also: structural model of the mind

In the course of development a child goes through a series of what Freud called psychosexual stages (Gay 1995). The **ego** and **superego** develop during the course of these stages (Freud 1923). Also the goals of gratification change according to the focus of the libido, which centres upon a particular part of the body, which he calls the erogenous zone, at each stage. These are the mouth, the anus and the genitals (Craib 2001).

Freud proposed five stages. From 0–1 years of age, the infant goes through the oral stage, when the libidinal focus is on the mouth, tongue and lips. The major source of pleasure surrounds this area, and attachment to the mother is related to her being a source of oral pleasure. The anal stage occurs at 1–3 years. During this stage the baby is sensitive to the anal region of its body, which corresponds to the parents' efforts in toilet training. If toilet training becomes fraught, which it often does, Freud considered that a child might suffer to some extent for the rest of its life. The phallic stage takes place between the ages of 3 and 5. It is characterized by a shift away from the anal region towards the genital erogenous zone. At this stage both boys and girls may begin quite naturally to masturbate.

Freud considered that an important event occurs during the phallic stage, which he calls the Oedipal conflict (see **Oedipus complex**). Freud put more emphasis on the events related to boys' development, but parallel occurrences, he believed, take place for girls. He suggested that the boy becomes intuitively aware of his mother's sexuality, and at about the age of 4 begins to have a (sort of) sexual attraction to his mother regarding his father as a sexual rival. He sees his father as having the ultimate power to castrate him as a punishment and thus the boy is caught between desire for his mother and fear of his father's power to achieve his revenge. The result of this conflict is anxiety, which he responds to with a process Freud calls *identification*. Thus he tries to make himself as much like his father as possible so that he is taking on some of his father's powers too.

The related process which, according to psychoanalytic theory, occurs for girls is not described very well by Freud, who asserts that the girl sees her mother as a rival for her father's sexual attentions although he argues she will not fear her mother's power so much as the boy fears his father's – perhaps because she assumes she has already been castrated. This means her anxiety is weaker and so is her identification (Brown 1975; Parens 1990).

Freud considered that successful resolution of the Oedipal crisis by identification with the appropriate parent is decisive for healthy development and disruption of the identification process is severely problematic. An example where a mother is more powerful than the father could create problems for boys in the family. However, for most of us the 'model' family as described by Freud is rare (Barrows 1995; Ogden 1987).

Between the ages of 5 and 12, Freud says that children go through a period of *latency* without any major developmental changes. During these years the child's friends are almost exclusively of the same sex and there is further development of the defence mechanisms, particularly those of denial (for instance, the child says that she/he is not tired when clearly unable to keep awake!), and repression, in which unacceptable thoughts and feelings are forced out of consciousness, particularly those about sexuality.

Between the ages of 12 and 18, and beyond, the adolescent's psychosexual stage corresponds with hormonal and biological changes, with the focus of interest on the genitals. The child is now interested in people of the other sex, according to Freud, with mature heterosexual love being the maturational goal (Berkovitz et al. 1966). Other psychoanalytic psychologists (e.g. (Mitchell 2008; Sayers 1997) have challenged Freud's developmental theory in this respect and shown gay relationships as one perspective on normal development.

Freud's work is a major attempt to explain human development, human relationships and emotions and explore the different ways in which we are (apparently) irrational. However, it is difficult to prove many of Freud's assertions which are value laden and partial.

Freud's studies of developmental psychology led him to believe that structural reorganization of the personality occurs at certain crucial points in development, and that these stages were universal features in the development of all human beings. Children want their wishes fulfilled immediately and flare up in anger if frustrated. They also show strong sexual passion. He considered that during socialization antisocial impulses were brought under control so that a process of internalization through which children moved from external behavioural controls (rewards and punishments) to internal self-controls occurred. This transition linked with children's feelings towards their parents. Parental pressure towards socialization makes children angry, and the thought of expressing this anger arouses their anxiety: partly because they might lose their parents if they were to express their anger too fervently. Children therefore repress their anger and turn it in on themselves. This is the foundation of 'guilt' – a powerful motivating force in development. The internalization of the parents' (and thus society's) rules are embodied in the superego which is a harsh, punitive and inflexible psychological mechanism.

References

Barrows, P. (1995) Oedipal issues at 4 and 44. *Psychoanalytic Psychotherapy*, 9(1): 85–96.

Berkovitz, I.H., Chikahisa, P., Lee, M.L. and Murasaki, E.M. (1966) Psychosexual development of latency-age children and adolescents in group therapy in a residential setting. *International Journal of Group Psychotherapy*, 16(3): 344–56.

Brown, F. (1975) Disturbances of psychosexual development of adolescent girls. *Mount Sinai Journal of Medicine*, 42(3): 216–22.

Craib, I. (2001) *Psychoanalysis: A Critical Introduction*. Cambridge: Polity.

Freud, S. (1923) *The Ego and the Id* (Standard Edition Vol. 19). London: The Hogarth Press.

Gay, P. (1995) *The Freud Reader*. London: Vintage.

Mitchell, J. (2008) *Siblings*. Cambridge: Polity.

Ogden, T.H. (1987) The transitional oedipal relationship in female development. *International Journal of Psychoanalysis*, 68 (Pt 4): 485–98.

Parens, H. (1990) On the girl's psychosexual development: reconsiderations suggested from direct observation. *Journal of the American Psychoanalysis Association*, 38(3): 743–72.

Sayers, J. (1997) *Freudian Tales: About Imagined Men*. London: Vintage.

Annotated further reading

Bee, H.L. and Mitchell, S.K. (1984) *The Developing Person: A Life Span Approach*, 2nd edn. New York: Harper and Row.

This textbook provides a simple and clear account of psychosexual development along with examples and relevant diagrams and photographs.

Nicolson, P., Bayne, R. and Owen, J. (2006) *Applied Psychology for Social Workers*. Basingstoke: Palgrave.

This textbook provides an account of psychosexual development with suggestions about application in social work practice.

Psychosocial development

See also: Erikson, Erik; Eriksonian analysis

Erikson was best known for his model of psychosocial development which proposed a version of development that combined biology, culture and psychology (Erikson 1950/1963). Within that model was the beginning of his focus on identity development in adolescence for which Erikson's work is still seen as decisive, although he himself was very much concerned with childhood as well (Erikson 1959/1980).

Psychosocial development focuses on the relationship between identity and the ability to cope with growing up and growing older in the context of the social world. He believed that over the life course an individual goes through a series of distinct developmental stages with a specific emotional task to accomplish at each stage. The stages are partly defined by cultural expectations, partly by biological stage and partly by the psychological context in which the child is growing. He also believed that any development task that is not successfully completed leaves a residue that interferes with later tasks.

The first year of life involves the infant in interacting with her caretaker, and it is the quality of that care that will give or deny the infant a sense of predictability or trust in the world. If the child's major experience leads to a sense of *trust* then the child is likely to go on to make successful relationships and have a positive sense of self.

The second stage, of *autonomy* versus *shame and doubt*, takes place when the child has developed basic skills of communication and physical dexterity and mobility. At this stage she has gained some control over her bladder and bowels. If she makes too many mistakes in the learning process then she will increasingly develop a sense of shame rather than a sense of accomplishment. Once again the quality of the care she receives will make a difference for better or ill.

Initiative versus *guilt* refers to the crisis around the child's ability to plan and take the initiative for some of her actions. She may also be interacting with other children during this stage. Again there is scope for a great many mistakes, and if the child is not supported by her caretakers she may experience too much of a sense of guilt about her failures.

Around the time of starting school, the emotional crisis is about *industry* versus *inferiority*. For the first time the child is put into competition with several other formerly unknown children. She is faced with the need for approval from strangers, and that is achieved via the quality of her work at school rather than her other personal qualities. If she doesn't do well, she risks feeling inferior to her peers.

The crisis for the adolescent is to resolve the battle between developing a sense of *identity* versus *role confusion*. There are so many opportunities and obligations that a teenager might be faced with, including those that surround sexual identity and the development of relationships. Successful resolution of this crisis is the development of an integrated sense of identity.

In young adulthood, during the crisis period of *intimacy* versus *isolation*, the task for the young woman is to manage to develop close relationships without losing her own identity.

The middle period of life, *generativity* versus *stagnation*, involves creativity and development of self and our talents. The generativity might involve career, hobbies or parenthood.

Ego integration versus *despair*, the final stage comprises the sum of life's parts. Did she manage to make sense of her life, achieve what she sought in the way that she wanted? If there are too many regrets, too many unresolved issues from earlier in life, then a sense of hopelessness may set in for the last stage of life.

A recent paper (Smith and Nicolson 2011), based on oral histories of older homeless men, identified the nuances in older age which the men employed trying to make sense of a life that for many would be seen as one of failure. This demonstrated both the strengths in Erikson's work (focus on the entire life cycle as a process of development) as well as the potential weakness (that positive outcomes at each stage indicate positive outcomes at earlier developmental phases).

Erikson and the 'woman' question

In apparent contrast to Freud's view that female development revolved around the 'penis envy' and what is *not* there, Erikson proposed that women's sense of their 'inner space' (womb) was crucial and that it was just as valuable, albeit different from, the possession of a penis (E.H. Erikson 1964). Erikson saw that girls aspired to the productivity of that space. Indeed the proposal of men's 'womb envy' has had currency in many circles. However, Erikson also made it clear that the inner space was also seen as potentially dangerous (to men).

Wolff (1979) proposed that Erikson's idea is on first glance more 'genial' than Freud's position on women although in fact Erikson was still bound to the view that anatomy was destiny and that women were different from men psychologically because of their biological differences.

References

Erikson, E. (1950/1963) *Childhood and Society*. New York: Norton.

Erikson, E. (1959/1980) *Identity, Youth and Crisis*. New York: Norton.

Erikson, E.H. (1964) Inner and outer space: reflections on womanhood. *Daedalus*, 93(2): 582–606.

Smith, G. and Nicolson, P. (2011) Despair? Older homeless men's accounts of their emotional trajectories. *Oral History*, 30–42.

Wolff, C.G. (1979) Erikson's 'inner space' reconsidered. *The Massachusetts Review*, 20(2): 355–68.

Annotated further reading

Bee, H. L. and Mitchell, S. K. (1984) *The Developing Person: A Life Span Approach*, 2nd edn. New York: Harper and Row.

Helen Bee's classic developmental textbook provides a simple account of the stages with examples.

Erikson, E. (1950/1963) *Childhood and Society*. New York: Norton.

This covers the 'eight ages of man'.

Questions

See also: brief therapy; paraphrasing; Socratic dialogue

Appropriate use of questions is a vital skill for any effective therapist. There are a number of different types of questions and ways of questioning, some of which are more effective in encouraging the client to feel safe and, therefore, to 'open up' than others. One way of categorizing questions is into 'open' and 'closed' questions.

In most situations open questions enable the therapist to actively listen and the client to explore their issues from their own perspective, for example, 'Can you say a bit more about how this incident with your sister has affected you?' Closed questions tend to be useful for collecting facts, such as, 'Have you seen a therapist before?' However, a series of closed questions can start to feel like being grilled, so they need to be used sparingly.

There are a number of dangers associated with asking questions, including open ones:

- Being asked a series of questions can start to feel like a diagnostic type of interview, similar to that employed by some medical practitioners.
- Clients can find themselves moving from their own frame of reference to that of the therapist so that they are responding to what the latter regards as important, rather than to their own concerns and meanings.
- A question and answer form of interaction can be established, resulting in the client waiting for the therapist to ask another question.

How to make questions more effective and less threatening

- Consider the reason for asking a particular question. Only ask it if it will aid the client in exploring an issue of importance to them. Questions which are asked out of curiosity or because the therapist is struggling to come up with how else to respond are best avoided.

- Open questions followed up with a paraphrase stand alone reflection often demonstrate a greater level of empathy than standalone questions.
- Stating the purpose of a question can reduce the possible threat of a question because the therapist's agenda is made more explicit.
- Questions which are expressed as statements can be experienced as more inclusive.
- 'Why' questions are best avoided as they are often difficult to answer and rarely allow the client to explore issues in a way that is helpful to them. Replacing 'why' with 'what', 'how' or 'in what way' can reduce the threatening feel of the question.
- Generally, it is not necessary to ask many questions in a therapy session. Paraphrasing and reflecting back usually contribute more to fostering an effective therapeutic relationship than do questions.

Responding to clients' questions

How a therapist responds to questions will to some extent depend on their theoretical approach. For example, a psychodynamic therapist is more likely not to answer the question, but to look for what might have led to the client asking it: 'I'm wondering what might lie behind your asking that question.' Other possible responses could be: (1) to briefly answer the question, following it up with a question to return the focus to the client (so, 'Have you had problems with alcohol?' 'No. Would you find it easier if I had?'); (2) to respond to what might be the underlying question. For example, in response to the previous question, a therapist might say: 'No, I haven't had alcohol problems, but I have found out quite a lot about it and I really want to understand what it's like for you' (Bayne et al. 2008).

Reference

Bayne, R., Jinks, G., Collard, P. and Horton, I. (2008) *The Counsellor's Handbook: A Practical A–Z Guide to Integrative Counselling and Psychotherapy*. Cheltenham: Nelson Thornes.

Annotated further reading

Culley, S. and Bond, T. (2011) *Integrative Counselling Skills in Action*, 3rd edn. London: Sage.

An accessible book covering a wide range of counselling skills including questions. A useful section outlining different types of questions and their uses.

Geldard, K. and Geldard, D. (2005) *Practical Counselling Skills*. Basingstoke: Palgrave Macmillan.

Includes an informative section on the use of questions.

R

Rational emotive behaviour therapy (REBT)

See also: Ellis, Albert; irrational beliefs

Rational emotive behaviour therapy was created by Dr Albert Ellis and is considered to be one of the first cognitive behaviour therapies. Ellis published and discussed RET (its original name) in published papers first in 1957, nearly a decade before Aaron Beck first set forth 'his' cognitive therapy.

There were precursors of certain fundamental aspects of REBT that have been identified in various ancient philosophical traditions, Stoicism being one of them. Ellis said, 'This principle, which I have inducted from many psycho-therapeutic sessions with scores of patients during the last several years, was originally discovered and stated by the ancient Stoic philosophers, especially Zeno of Citium (the founder of the school), Chrysippus (his most influential disciple), Panaetius of Rhodes (who introduced Stoicism into Rome), Cicero, Seneca, Epictetus and Marcus Aurelius. The truths of Stoicism were perhaps best set forth by Epictetus, who in the first century A.D. wrote in the Enchiridion: "Men are disturbed not by things, but by the views which they take of them".' The latter has often been cited as a cornerstone or the theoretical underpinning of REBT.

Shakespeare, many centuries later, rephrased this thought in *Hamlet*: 'There's nothing good or bad but thinking makes it so.'

This psychotherapeutic approach intends to teach clients how their belief systems may determine how they feel about and act towards challenges and life events. REBT focuses on four types of erroneous thinking that trigger the stress response:

- demandingness: rigid demands such as 'musts' and 'shoulds' towards self and others;
- awfulizing: also known as 'worst-case scenario thinking', with examples such as, 'Life is really awful' or 'This can only happen to me and I have been selected to suffer more than anybody else';
- low frustration tolerance (LFT): 'I can't stand the rudeness of young people today'; 'I will explode if another train is ever delayed'.

- global condemnation of human worth: damnation of self or others, e.g. 'As I failed my interview or in my last relationship, I am a real failure as a person'.

Emotional health and REBT

According to the ABC model of emotional disturbance, mental suffering does not directly stem from the problems we experience, but rather from the false or narrow notions we have about them.

It is irrational beliefs that seem to underlie most emotional disturbances such as expectations to be 'perfect', to be treated 'fairly' and to live in a world where we must experience pleasure rather than pain.

The way REBT helps clients to address these unhelpful beliefs, is to look at the client's basic assumptions about life and to help them adapt their views to a level where they no longer sabotage their feelings and actions.

While implementing the above we are however reminded that it is unhealthy to pursue only one's own interest and to disregard other people's needs. Therefore we try to promote 'enlightened self-interest' where everyone has rights. So we tend to offer a middle ground where everybody counts in order to create a world where at least at times we can live comfortably and happily.

Thus REBT may offer clients a 'new philosophy, a new outlook on life'.

Windy Dryden does however point out, that REBT is not suitable for clients with the following characteristics:

- A person feels opposed to the REBT view of psychological disturbance.
- A client disagrees with the therapeutic tasks outlined in REBT theory.
- The client is unable to carry out the assignments given.
- The client is at onset of therapy deeply disturbed.
- Client and therapist are a poor therapeutic match.
- The client's problems seem vague.

(See Dryden 2007: 365–6)

References

Dryden, W. (2007) *Dryden's Handbook of Individual Therapy*, 5th edn. London: Sage.
Ellis, A. (1957) Rational psychotherapy and individual psychology. *Journal of Individual Psychology*, 13: 38–44.

Annotated further reading

Kazantzis, N., Reinecke, M.A. and Freeman, A. (eds) (2010) *Cognitive and Behavioural Theories in Clinical Practice*. New York: Guilford Press.

This publication contains in-depth chapters on the rich approaches that CBT contains. Leading experts come together and describe with insight how each approach differs from the other. Recent research is given a prominent place. The REBT chapter places importance on clinical practice (pp. 134–7) and includes a typical case study (pp. 137–41).

Rationalization

Rationalization means just that – rationalizing an experience or action to show it in the light in which the person wishes it to be seen. Rationalization may also be used by a group, organization or society (Zaretsky 2000) to justify potentially unpalatable actions. Unconsciously repression evades self-understanding and in turn unconscious processes may be reinforced by a careful rationalization constructed to give the appearance of a good conscious reason (Hinshelwood 1997). Rationalization, according to Craib (2001), has the overtones of dishonesty in that it implies that the person is not giving the 'real' reason for their actions or motivations to others or to themselves. Rationalization can defend against threatening aspects of the outside world as well as internal impulses that the individual does not want to acknowledge.

References

Craib, I. (2001) *Psychoanalysis: A Critical Introduction.* Cambridge: Polity.
Hinshelwood, R. (1997) Primitive mental processes: psychoanalysis and the ethics of integration. *Philosophy, Psychiatry and Psychology,* 4(2): 121–43.
Zaretsky, E. (2000) Charisma or rationalization? Domesticity and psychoanalysis in the United States in the 1950s. *Critical Inquiry,* 26(2): 328–54.

Annotated further reading

Hinshelwood, R. (1997) Primitive mental processes: psychoanalysis and the ethics of integration. *Philosophy, Psychiatry and Psychology,* 4(2): 121–43.
Zaretsky, E. (2000) Charisma or rationalization? Domesticity and psychoanalysis in the United States in the 1950s. *Critical Inquiry,* 26(2): 328–54.

Both these articles indicate the complex and contradictory nature of thinking about the concept of 'rationalization' as a defence mechanism. These papers represent advanced reading material suggesting that rationalization hovers between conscious and unconscious levels of awareness for each of us.

Relational depth

See also: person-centred counselling; the therapeutic relationship

The concept of relational depth represents one of the ways in which person-centred counselling has developed since the early 2000s. While Rogers' core conditions have been regarded as the cornerstone of the therapeutic relationship in this approach to counselling for over half a century, relational depth constitutes a rather different way of viewing what a positive client/counsellor relationship comprises. McLeod (2009) captures its essence when he describes it as 'a state of profound engagement and contact in which each person is fully real with the other, and in which there is an enduring sense of contact and connectedness between client and therapist' (p. 200). It seems to occur when the client experiences a deep human response from the therapist, which is seen as something beyond professional interest, but which does not break ethical boundaries.

Although hard to define more precisely, Mearns and Cooper (2005) have outlined a range of strategies which they believe will assist in enabling relational depth to be experienced between client and counsellor: dispensing with expectations and agendas; encouraging deeper experiences; allowing oneself as the therapist to be deeply affected by the client; being transparent and working in the present.

McMillan and McLeod (2006) undertook some research into the client perspective on this issue and found that it was experienced quite rarely by clients but was felt to be meaningful when it did occur.

References

McLeod, J. (2009) *An Introduction to Counselling*. Maidenhead: Open University Press.

McMillan, M. and McLeod, J. (2006) Letting go: the client's experience of relational depth. *Person-centred and Experiential Psychotherapies*, 5: 277–92.

Mearns, D. and Cooper, M. (2005) *Working at Relational Depth*. London: Sage.

Annotated further reading

Mearns, D. and Cooper, M. (2005) *Working at Relational Depth*. London: Sage.

An excellent book which examines the crucial importance of the therapeutic relationship and which uses case study examples insightfully.

Repression

See also: narcissism; psychoanalysis

In Freud's concept of the structural model of mind, the superego acts as the conscience and a censor that forbids certain wishes, desires and drives to enter consciousness (where they might get expressed or acted upon) and these are particularly the drives (in his words) towards 'megalomania' which have roots in infantile narcissism (Gay 1995: 557). For Freud, repression was the first identified and most important defence mechanism.

Wright (1992), with a feminist take on repression, reasserts the Freudian position that repression must operate in two distinct stages – the first being the primal, or founding repression, whereby the unconscious is itself organized. Then there follow a series of repressions based on the images and wishes of the primal repression that Freud named 'after pressures' or repression proper (Wright 1992: 382). Freud's account of the resolution of the Oedipal crisis asserts that it is the boy's fear of castration that causes repression of his desire for his mother, with the establishment of the superego and identification with the father figure or patriarch. This caused Freud problems in relation to female development and he mostly failed to convince subsequent theorists, particularly those with a feminist position, with his version of the girl's weaker identification with the mother whom she continues to desire (Brennan 1992).

Craib (2001) advocated that repression is the most successful or 'healthy' way in which the ego defends itself. He warns of the difference between repression – where these thoughts and desires do not enter consciousness – and suppression – where people consciously avoid thinking about something that they find undesirable or distasteful in themselves. In the case of suppression the drive has reached consciousness and the person tries various means of 'returning' these thoughts to some place out of mind but this process eats up energy.

Billig (2006) proposed that discursive psychology, which focuses primarily on observable rather than inner phenomena, can nevertheless add to understanding the mechanism of repression in conversational analysis. He suggests that conversational interaction can have repressive functions in that people try to interact politely thus repressing the temptation of rudeness. However, repression itself occurs at an unconscious level during the interactional dialogue.

Fonagy (1999) in a controversial approach to psychoanalysis, challenged the traditional activity of bringing the buried and repressed past to the surface seeing the function of analysis as attending to the relationship between 'self and other' (the analyst). Blum (2003) counter-proposed that it was vital not to neglect the way in which childhood and psychoanalytic reconstruction uncover repressed anxieties.

Melanie Klein's work on repression is discussed in the entry on **splitting**.

References

Billig, M. (2006) A psychoanalytic discursive psychology: from consciousness to unconsciousness. *Discourse Studies*, 8(1): 17–24.

Blum, H.P. (2003) Repression, transference and reconstruction. *The International Journal of Psychoanalysis*, 84(3): 497–503.

Brennan, T. (1992) *The Interpretation of the Flesh: Freud and Femininity*. London: Routledge.

Craib, I. (2001) *Psychoanalysis: A Critical Introduction*. Cambridge: Polity.

Fonagy, P. (1999) Memory and therapeutic action. *International Journal of Psycho-Analysis*, 80: 215–23.

Gay, P. (1995) *The Freud Reader*. London: Vintage.

Wright, E. (1992) *Feminism and Psychoanalysis: A Critical Dictionary*. Oxford: Blackwell.

Annotated further reading

Craib, I. (2001) *Psychoanalysis: A Critical Introduction*. Cambridge: Polity.

Craib's book provides an introduction to this very important, but sometimes controversial, concept in psychoanalysis.

Fonagy, P. (1999) Memory and therapeutic action. *International Journal of Psycho-Analysis*, 80: 215–23.

Fonagy's research reported in this paper challenges the clinical value of dealing with repressed memories and emotions. This is for the 'advanced' reader who has got to grips with the concept of psychic defence mechanisms.

Resistance

See also: defence mechanisms; repression

Resistance is the propensity of a person in psychotherapy or psychoanalysis to fight against the insights of analysis (Freud 1925). The patient, undergoing the analytic process, does so ostensibly to liberate the forgotten material and feelings surrounding a repressed traumatic experience. However, some people engage in resistance against gaining insight into the unconscious repressed memories and in so doing maintain their neurotic defences against discovery and managing to work through the memories. Such resistance strives to keep the repression in place so that the original traumatic thoughts and feelings are not brought to the surface (Horrocks 2001).

Resistance is complex because, to understand it, it is necessary to see that some people have a vested interest in remaining neurotic which conflicts with their unconscious guilt and need to be punished, as well as other feelings including the desire to punish *other people* through exhibiting their misery and suffering to them. Thus there is an element of revenge characterized by the unspoken (mostly) statement 'look at what you have done to me' (Horrocks 2001).

Freud considered that the person in analysis who falls in love with their analyst and demands love in return is experiencing unconscious resistance to the progress of the analysis (Horrocks 2001).

References

Freud, S. (1925) The resistances to psycho-analysis. *The Standard Edition of the Complete Psychological Works of Sigmund Freud: The Ego and the Id and Other Works* (Vol. XIX, pp. 211–24).

Horrocks, R. (2001) *Freud Revisited: Psychoanalytic Themes in the Postmodern Age.* Basingstoke: Palgrave.

Annotated further reading

Horrocks, R. (2001) *Freud Revisited: Psychoanalytic Themes in the Postmodern Age.* Basingstoke: Palgrave.

Horrocks provides a fresh and thorough look at defence mechanisms including 'resistance' that is often overlooked in many texts.

Rogers, Carl (1902–1987)

See also: core conditions; locus of evaluation; person-centred counselling; self-actualization; self-concept; the therapeutic relationship

Carl Rogers is widely recognized as the founder of what has become known as person-centred therapy. He is also credited with being one of the founders (with Rollo May and Abraham Maslow) of humanistic psychology and a leading figure in the human potential movement (Masson 1988). Although his ideas were seen at the time as a departure from the two dominant approaches of psychoanalysis and behaviourism, his ideas and practice do sit within a particular humanistic tradition and a specific North American cultural context.

Carl Rogers was born into a strict Protestant family in the rural Midwest of America. His religious upbringing meant that leisure activities such as theatre and gambling were disapproved of. Rogers intended to become a church minister and, indeed, did start a course at a theological college. Having been exposed to other cultures and beliefs while on a conference in China, he decided to change direction and trained instead as a clinical psychologist. While studying he was exposed to the ideas of the progressive education movement, which emphasized the need to trust each child's inherent ability to learn and develop (McLeod 2009).

He began his career in 1928 as a psychologist for the Child Study department of the Society for the Prevention of Cruelty to Children in Rochester, New York. There he worked from an analytic perspective, making interpretations and helping people to gain insight into their thoughts, feelings and behaviours. It was while here that he started to become disillusioned with this approach and developed a growing belief that it was vital to listen to the client as it is they who will know what the real problems are.

In 1940 Rogers obtained his first professorship in psychology at Ohio State University. He started writing academic books, including *Counselling and Psychotherapy* in 1942. In 1945 he moved to the University of Chicago (where he wrote among other books *Client-Centered Therapy* in 1951), and in 1957 to the University of Wisconsin, as Professor of Psychology and Psychiatry where he stayed until 1963. While at Chicago, he clarified his ideas about his therapeutic approach which focused on the centrality of the therapeutic relationship and on a 'non-directive' approach to working with clients. The term 'client-centred therapy' was adopted around this time.

By 1963, Rogers had become disillusioned with the power politics within higher education and left to become involved in the Encounter Group movement. Claringbull (2010) argues that all his significant contributions to person-centred therapy were completed by the late 1970s.

Rogers' main ideas are discussed in more detail in the entry on **person-centred counselling**, so the focus here is on the relationship between his background and his ideas and his role in, and contribution to, the development of psychotherapy in the USA.

Certainly religion and science both had a strong influence on Rogers as a therapist. As a scientist he was one of the first people to develop methods by which to investigate therapy process and outcomes. He recorded and analysed client sessions, something which was new at the time. His religious background, though to some extent rejected, remained in his high moral principles and his belief in people needing to reach an individual understanding of their own destiny (McLeod 2009).

There is also much that is essentially embedded in American culture in Rogers' ideas. His distrust of experts, his focus on individual rather than collective or societal needs, his relative lack of focus on the past and his emphasis on autonomy and independence (Meadows 1964, in McLeod 2009). Rogers' approach to therapy was much more attuned than psychoanalysis or behaviourism to people living in the USA in the 1950s and 1960s. However, since the late 1980s, the influence of Rogers' ideas in the USA has declined rapidly, although Europe, South America and the Far East remain relative strongholds.

Although Rogers still has many followers, there are inevitably those who criticize and question his contribution to therapy. Masson (1988) refers to his form of therapy as 'a benevolent despotism' (1988: 229) rather than a malign one, arguing that he did not, for example, acknowledge or place much emphasis on the existence of abuse in his work and yet there was evidence of systematic abuse in some of the institutions he visited as part of his research. He also points out that the patients seen as part of Rogers' schizophrenic study were not volunteers, which seems to stand in opposition to his philosophy of free will and personal choice.

Overall though Rogers has had a profound influence on the development of therapy across the world and his ideas have been adapted for use in a wide range of settings such as staff development and organizational development. Courses which train person-centred counsellors continue to flourish in the UK and Roger's core conditions are frequently incorporated into a range of integrative and eclectic counselling models.

References

Claringbull, N. (2010) *What is Counselling and Psychotherapy?* Exeter: Learning Matters.

Masson, J. (1988) *Against Therapy: Emotional Tyranny and the Myth of Psychological Healing.* Glasgow: Collins.

McLeod, J. (2009) *An Introduction to Counselling.* Maidenhead: Open University Press.

Annotated further reading

Rogers, C. (1961) *On Becoming a Person.* Boston, MA: Houghton and Mifflin.

Rogers' own writings give a direct insight into his ideas and this book is the most widely read of all his work. It is made up of talks and articles produced between 1954 and 1957 when he was developing his model of the therapeutic relationship.

Thorne, B. (2003) *Carl Rogers.* London: Sage.

An accessible introduction to Rogers' life and to his main theoretical ideas.

Ruptures in the therapeutic alliance

See also: the therapeutic relationship

Alliance ruptures can be defined as a block or breakdown in the working relationship between client and therapist. These are inevitable in the therapeutic context, just as they are in any relationship, and can result from a range of factors, including errors on the therapist's part or misconceptions on the part of the client. Gelso and Carter (1994) have found that the alliance varies in its importance at different times in the therapeutic process, being, for example, of great importance at the beginning, then declining in importance as other issues emerge. However, the relationship may need to be focused upon when ruptures occur.

A leading figure in research into alliance ruptures is Safran (2000, 2001, in McLeod 2009) who, with colleagues in the USA, has undertaken some significant research in this area. Cooper (2008) points out that the rupture can relate to any one of the three main aspects of the therapeutic alliance: those of task, goals or the therapeutic bond. It is vital that the therapist can recognize when a rupture has occurred and is able to take steps to repair it. Safran et al. (2000, 2001, in McLeod 2009) outline a process whereby a therapist can deal effectively and constructively with such ruptures:

1   The first stage is to recognize the rupture, which is commonly expressed by the client either through anger or criticism (a confrontational approach), by non-participation (withdrawal) or a combination of the two.
2   It is then important to acknowledge the difficulty and to check it out with the client. This may be done by stating what one has noticed and asking the client to express any negative feelings they may be experiencing and to describe what the problem seems to be from their perspective. The therapist may want to acknowledge any responsibility she may feel at this point without being defensive.
3   The therapist can encourage the client to get in touch with any underlying feelings which are usually anger or sadness and to voice their needs or wishes.
4   How to resolve the issue can then be discussed, which may include whether and how these needs or wishes can be met.

One of the positive aspects of repairing ruptures in this way is the strengthening of the therapeutic alliance which usually results. Clients can also learn how to deal with relationship issues outside the therapy in a constructive way.

Cooper (2008) makes some important additional points regarding the process of dealing with ruptures. He stresses the need for the therapist to identify how they feel about the rupture, which will affect their decision as to how to discuss it with the client. For example, do they consider that the rupture relates to their own behaviour? He emphasizes the importance of the therapist taking responsibility for their part in the situation if appropriate. He also stresses the need to empathize with the client's experience and not to engage in transference interpretations which will serve to put all the responsibility onto the client. It is important to add to this, however, that such interpretations may be useful if well timed and if the client is likely to be receptive to them. If the issue relates to the goals or tasks of the alliance, then these may need to be renegotiated.

Research findings

There has been a focus on alliance rupture research in recent years giving rise to some interesting research findings. Having established with some certainty that a strong therapeutic alliance plays an important part in positive therapeutic outcomes, problems within this alliance and ways of resolving these have been seen as areas worthy of attention. That ruptures are frequent has been shown in a study by Safran et al. (2002, in Cooper 2008) which identified their existence in between 11 per cent and 38 per cent of sessions. There may be many reasons why ruptures occur, including therapist error, although transference issues may be responsible for some ruptures as well as client reactions to therapists' interventions and behaviours. Cooper (2008) in his informative summary of research evidence on a range of therapeutic factors states that there is little *direct* evidence to support the assertion that capacity to repair alliance ruptures is related to positive outcomes in therapy. However, there is some indirect evidence including a study be Safran et al. (2002, in Cooper 2008) showing that an emphasis on repairing alliance ruptures in brief relational therapy does have a significant impact on drop out rates (20 per cent) as compared to CBT (37 per cent) and psychodynamic therapy (46 per cent). An earlier study (Safran et al. 1990, in Cooper 2008) also showed that ruptures are more effectively resolved if therapists respond in a receptive way by, for example, apologizing or changing their behaviour.

References

Cooper, M. (2008) *Essential Research Findings in Counselling and Psychotherapy: The Facts are Friendly*. London: Sage.

Gelso, C.J. and Carter, J.A. (1994) Components of the psychotherapy relationship: their interaction and unfolding during treatment. *Journal of Counseling Psychology*, 41: 296–306.

McLeod, J. (2009) *An Introduction to Counselling*. Maidenhead: Open University Press.

Annotated further reading

Muran, J. C. and Barber, J.P. (eds) (2010) *The Therapeutic Alliance: An Evidence-Based Guide to Practice*. New York: Guilford Press.

Contains two very insightful chapters focusing on negative experiences/ alliance ruptures which include evidence-based guidelines on how to address these.

Sue, D. and Sue, D.M. (2008) *Foundations of Counseling and Psychotherapy: Evidence-Based Practice for a Diverse Society*. New York: J. Wiley and Sons.

Contains a section on preventing treatment failures/alliance ruptures.

S

Schema therapy

See also: cognitive behavioural therapy; life traps

Schemas are defined by Young et al. (2003) as patterns that frequently develop as consequences of 'toxic childhood experiences' (2003: 7) and are patterns that include memories, feelings, thoughts and sensations in the body which create dysfunctional behaviours with the outside world to a significant, alienating and destructive extent. For example 'dependence', which could be defined as the inability to deal with regular life issues without the help of others. (For more schemas see **life traps**.)

Jeffrey Young developed this integrative approach for long-term psychological problems and for treatment resistant clients. This means that schema therapy has been used for treating chronic rather than acute disorders.

Young stated in an interview with the author (Collard 2004) that he would personally need to have worked with a client for at least a year before he would use this approach in therapy. This may be seen as one of the drawbacks of schema therapy.

Schema therapy is particularly helpful for clients who recognize the existence of repetitive 'self-defeating' life patterns: 'People who are afraid of being alone, afraid of being controlled by other people, feel inadequate or people who have excessively high standards' (Collard 2004: 2).

Frequently, the clients treated with schema therapy are initially (according to DSM IV) labelled as suffering from 'personality disorders'. The problem with this label is that the therapist may discover a large variety of different symptoms which do not actually go together as a diagnosis, unlike 'depression' or 'anxiety' disorder. Hence, Young devised a list of categories of personality problems (see **life traps**), not disorders.

Schema therapy starts by the client completing a questionnaire. It enables both the client and the therapist to pinpoint which schemas/life traps are particularly significant and thus require treatment. Rather than talking of a 'disorder', insight is brought to patterns that recur again and again and make life unsatisfactory. An individual could have several of these life traps or only one or two. Young's intention has always been to make it really possible for therapist and client to access the interventions he developed with ease and confidence. He endeavours to avoid jargon whenever possible. His patients are people who may have experienced numerous therapies before, but were never truly helped to get 'unstuck'.

Specific therapeutic interventions (see http://www.schematherapy. com; e.g. cognitive interventions) are thus chosen to deal with those schemas that come up with a high score in the questionnaire. These interventions endeavour to work on breaking the recurrent and detrimental 'life traps' (schemas).

Schema-focused therapy proved to be effective in reducing borderline personality disorder-specific and general psychopathologic dysfunction and improved quality of life of participants even three years after therapy. Young suggests that the minimum time for treatment is 36 sessions (about nine months) (Collard 2004).

References

Collard, P. (2004) Reinventing your life through schema therapy: interview with Jeffrey Young. *Counselling Psychology Quarterly*, 17(1): 1–11.

Giesen-Bloo, J., van Dyck, R., Spinhoven, P. et al. (2006) Outpatient psychotherapy for borderline personality disorder: a randomized trial of schema focused therapy versus transference focused therapy. *Archives of General Psychiatry*, 63(6): 649–58.

Young, J., Klosko, J. and Weishaar, M.E. (2003) *Schema Therapy: A Practitioner's Guide*. New York: Guilford Press.

Annotated further reading

Young, J. and Klosko, J. (2003) *Reinventing Your Life: How to Break Free From Negative Life Patterns and Feel Good Again (A New Client's Guide to Schema Therapy)*. New York: Plume Books.

Reinventing your Life is perhaps one of the most useful self-help books ever published. It is a very helpful manual that complements one-to-one therapy.

Seduction

See also: Freud, Sigmund; Freudian analysis; psychosexual development

There is a close relationship between Freud's ideas about the theory of the unconscious and his seduction theory. Freud's ideas related to the seduction hypothesis were that hysteria was due to childhood sexual seduction or abuse. Freud considered that childhood memories are not consolidated until puberty and at that point are reconfigured to make sense to the adolescent her/himself. Freud's early hypothesis about seduction suggested that hysteria arose from the repression of early sexual trauma and in particular sexual abuse. Much of Freud's thinking and deliberations about sexuality, including seduction, took place in his intensive and frequent correspondence with Wilhelm Fliess (with whom he developed a close personal and professional relationship, which gradually distanced him from Josef Breuer).

In 1895 he published his first work with Breuer on hysteria, which he argued was the result of psychological conflict that could only be expressed through the physical body. This work, which was dominated by the two themes of the 'splitting of consciousness' and 'sexual frustrations', includes the well-known case of 'Anna O' who was eventually identified by his friend and colleague Josef Breuer as the first case describing 'psychoanalysis' (Gay 1995; Wright 1992). Both men wrote up her case history. Anna O was 21, with a previously 'normal' history, when she began living in a fantasy world but more significantly developed a squint, had problems of vision, and contractions in her upper and lower body that led to intermittent paralysis and following the death of her father, trauma and sleep walking. There were no apparent physical reasons for her condition. Her background was somewhat puritanical and the psychoanalysis (as it became known) eventually enabled her to gain a sense of her sexuality and sexual frustration, which she called her 'bad self'.

The case of 'Dora' was central to his hypothesis on seduction and its links to hysteria. Dora sought treatment for hysterical choking, withdrawal, depression, fainting spells and loss of her voice, symptoms diagnosed as being hysterical. It emerged during the analysis that Herr K., a friend of the family, had apparently made sexual advances to her while the two families were on holiday together. Herr K. denied anything on his part and put her accusation down to her imagination and also suggested that she had fantasized sexual intercourse with him. Her father sided with Herr K. that she had imagined his sexual advances. However, it was possible that Dora's father had a sexual relationship with Frau K. and Freud suggested that Dora had become an object of barter – that her father had 'handed her over' to his friend in exchange for his wife. He considered that this was unconscious.

In 1896 Freud addressed the Viennese Society for Psychiatry and Neurology advocating they take account of sexual aggression of adults towards children whether by subtle seduction or crude rape (see Gay 1995: 97).

Freud's original seduction theory was strictly confined to the realm of the psychoneuroses. The theory sought to explain the development of the unconscious by the repression, in the child, of memories of sexual scenes usually experienced while in the charge of an adult. It brought three interconnected levels into play:

1   a temporal dimension;
2   a topographical dimension;
3   a language-related dimension.

The temporal aspect of seduction was bound up with the concept of deferred action (or 'afterwardness' [Nachträglichkeit]). By this he meant that there was an interrelationship between at least two events separated by time but which after a period of time were experienced in mutated form by the individual. Left in suspense, the initial memory became pathogenic (potentially emotionally toxic) and traumatizing when revived by the occurrence of a second scene having some association or resonance with the first. Thus a person sexually abused in childhood might have 'forgotten' the experience until they began having consensual sexual relations or a related experience such as obstetric investigation. Then the early (half) memory would cause a trauma that may or may not come back into consciousness.

The topographical aspect involved the theory of an ego in the process of formation, armoured against attack from without but not against attack from within. Since what attacked it at the second moment was not an outside event but a memory, this ego was unprotected and could react only by repression (see **defence mechanisms**).

The linguistic aspect of the theory was suggested by Freud's analogy between the barrier separating the two moments of the psychical trauma and a translation, or a partial failure of translation (letter to Fliess of 6 December, 1896, *SE* 1, p. 235).

It is thus inappropriate to reduce the seduction theory to the simplistic assertion that the adult's seduction of the child brings on mental disturbance. At the close of 1897, Freud undertook a systematic critique of his theory that led him to abandon it, surrendering hysterics to their 'seduction fantasies'.

Seduction theory and infantile sexuality remain controversial among clinicians, scientists and the public and have become less influential in contemporary psychoanalytic thinking. Klein and Winnicott for example (see **Klein, Melanie**; **Kleinian analysis**; **object relations** and **Winnicott, D.W.**) focused their attention on aggression and envy rather than sexual drives. While therapists often attend exclusively to defences other than repression, it nevertheless persists as paternal and maternal fantasies which are forced back into the unconscious (Sayers 1997).

References

Gay, P. (1995) *The Freud Reader*. London: Vintage.
Sayers, J. (1997) *Freudian Tales: About Imagined Men*. London: Vintage.
Wright, E. (1992) *Feminism and Psychoanalysis: A Critical Dictionary*. Oxford: Blackwell.

Annotated further reading

http://www.answers.com/topic/general-theory-of-seduction#ixzz1V6pce9qN

This website is part of the 'Answers.com' series which is popular with students and with some justification because it is informative and provides links to other sources of valid information.

Self

See also: collectivism – individual dimension; constructurism; personality; preferences; self-actualization; strengths

The term 'self' is used in a wide variety of ways in the counselling, philosophy and personality literatures (e.g. Brown 2008; Funder 2011; McLeod 2009). Textbooks often avoid the problem of defining self, focusing instead on compound forms like self-acceptance and self-disclosure.

A key issue is whether 'self' is most usefully seen as a unified, coherent, autonomous system or as fragmented or conflicted: is there a real or core self, or multiple selves, or is the idea of a self, as in postmodernism, a philosophical error? Moreover, is the belief in an autonomous, separate self specific to Western culture? What about an emphasis on 'self-in-relation-to-others', on interdependence and collectivism rather than or as well as autonomy and individualism?

A relatively straightforward definition of 'self' that encompasses most of the divergent views touched on above is that it is a person's real emotions, thoughts, needs and feelings, etc. This meaning of self allows for individual variation: for multiple selves or a core self (or degrees of stability or fluidity), for change and development, and for some people finding fulfilment in autonomy, others in interdependence, and others in both.

The model of self and self-awareness depicted in Figure 2 suggests three senses of self, which each of us is accurately aware of to varying degrees. The first sense, inner fluid self-awareness, is self as defined earlier in this section. The second sense, inner and relatively stable self-awareness, is more arguable and indeed self theorists differ in how much stability they recognize (as discussed in the entry on **self-actualization**). Moreover, some traits for example may tend generally to be more stable than others. Similarly, some values are more likely to change with age or experience or 'phase' of life, and memories can be reconstructed dramatically. The third sense is outer self-awareness, awareness of our behaviour and appearance, and their impact on others.

More fluid inner self-awareness	Sensations Intuitions Thoughts Feelings Emotions Wishes Fantasies Wants/Intentions
More stable inner self-awareness	Preferences Traits Strengths Talents Values Attitudes Motives/Needs Memories Life stories
Outer self-awareness	Appearance Manner Actions

Figure 2 A model of self and self-awareness

Source: Modifed from Bayne et al. (2008)

References

Bayne, R., Jinks, G., Collard, P. and Horton, I. (2008) *The Counsellor's Handbook: A Practical A–Z Guide to Integrative Counselling and Psychotherapy*, 3rd edn. Cheltenham: Nelson Thornes.

Brown, G. (2008) *The Living End. Death, Aging and Immortality*. Basingstoke: Palgrave Macmillan.

Funder, D. (2011) *The Personality Puzzle*, 5th edn. London: W.W. Norton.

McLeod, J. (2009) *An Introduction to Counselling*, 4th edn. Maidenhead: Open University Press.

Annotated further reading

Bayne, R. and Jinks, G. (2010) *How to Survive Counsellor Training: An A–Z Guide*. Basingstoke: Palgrave Macmillan.

For more on several aspects of self development, including assertiveness, making decisions, strengths, critical thinking, expressive writing, value, stress, sleep, relaxation and time 'management'.

Self-acceptance

See also: cognitive behavioural therapy; rational emotive behaviour therapy; self-actualization

The ability to accept ourselves unconditionally is essential for being mentally balanced and for experiencing joy. Without self-acceptance we are much more prone to suffer from destructive emotions such as anxiety, depression, phobias, anger and unhealthy relationships.

If we get into the habit of evaluating ourselves negatively, rather than accepting ourselves (not our unhelpful behaviour patterns), it is possible to get caught up in 'self-aggrandizement' in order to overcompensate for perceived self-deficits.

The opposite of course can also be true, and we may become socially phobic and 'hide' from life if feeling inept and not good enough.

In CBT the two most common thinking errors that lead to damaged self-evaluation are beliefs about helplessness and worthlessness. Thus CBT interventions would endeavour to target those by applying cognitive restructuring and behaviour experiments.

Windy Dryden argues that unconditional self-acceptance can be learned by considering some of the following principles: you are equal to other humans in terms of shared humanity. Your essence, however, is fallible yet unique. Unconditional self-acceptance is closely linked with a flexible, preferential outlook and philosophy and promotes constructive actions rather than withdrawal from life (Dryden 1999: 19–29).

There is another notion that says that we can only accept ourselves fully if our parents have given us unconditional self-acceptance. According to psychological investigation humans cannot understand that they are separate entities from their parents or guardians prior to the age of 8. So we will only feel acceptable and worthy if this is the message we receive. This does not take into account that it is not necessarily us they reject but rather some unmanageable or destructive behaviour. We cannot comprehend that at times they are only doing what they think is right and part of their parenting duty when they reject some of our interactions and eventually (and particularly with highly critical parents) we may come to the conclusion that we as a whole entity are unacceptable – our behaviours, our minds and even all or parts of our bodies.

The psychologist L. Seltzer puts it like this:

> given how the human psyche operates, it's almost impossible *not* to parent ourselves as we were parented originally. If our caretakers dealt with us in a hurtful manner, as adults we'll find all sorts of ways to perpetuate that unresolved hurt onto ourselves. If we were frequently

ignored, accused, berated, blamed, taunted, chastised, or physically punished, we'll somehow contrive to carry on this indignity. So when (figuratively, at least) we 'beat ourselves up,' we're typically just following our parents' lead.

(Seltzer 2008)

In 2005 at a conference in Gothenburg entitled 'Meeting of Minds' the Dalai Lama and Aaron Beck (founder of CBT) met for a conversation about making sense of the twenty-first century. As the topic of 'lack of self-esteem and acceptance' was discussed, it took many attempts to translate the meaning of this term for the Dalai Lama, for Tibetan does not contain a word or concept for it. In this culture it is a given that you are totally worthy and acceptable because you are a living part of this universe. What must it be like to have this deeply ingrained notion that you are completely acceptable (even if some of your actions may not be) just because you are here?

References

Dryden, W. (1999) *How to Accept Yourself*. London: Sheldon Press.
Seltzer, L.F. (2008) The path to unconditional self-acceptance. http://www. psychologytoday.com/blog/evolution-the-self/200809/the-path-unconditional-self-acceptance (accessed 24 July 2011).

Annotated further reading

Dryden, W. (1999) *How to Accept Yourself*. London: Sheldon Press.

This book gets to the core of self-acceptance. The slim volume does look at the psychology of self-rejection, but its main purpose is to teach the reader how to walk towards change and acceptance. Self-acceptance, Dryden thinks, lies at the heart of happiness and contentment.

Self-actualization

See also: assertiveness; conditions of worth; congruence; death, fear of; organismic valuing process; self; strengths

Self-actualization is a term associated with several approaches to counselling, including person-centred (Rogers also used the closely related term 'fully-functioning') and Gestalt. For both these therapies, it is a therapeutic aim

(Joseph and Wood 2010). 'Finding one's real self', being true to oneself and authenticity are further similar or identical ideas, and just as vague and abstract.

However, Maslow, who wrote extensively about self-actualization (e.g. Maslow 1968), also defined it in terms of behaviour. For example, he suggested that one way a person self-actualizes is by experiencing fully, vividly and with total concentration. He suggested that most people, when asked their view of something, don't pause and look 'inside' to discover and express their true thoughts and feelings but try to impress or at least to fit in. He sees the consequence as widespread self-alienation. However, other personality theorists, for example Gordon Allport, have taken a radically different position: that most people are not self-alienated and that most self-report measures of personality are sufficiently valid to be useful as a result.

In Maslow's view there is a self to be actualized or to be alienated from, one that includes temperament and other potentials. In contrast, Rogers saw self as more fluid (see the entry on **self** which suggests that both views are true). Several theorists illustrate their conceptions of self and self-actualization by analogy with simpler life forms – oak trees, plants and tigers (Maslow), potatoes, seaweed, mice and lions (Rogers), lions and crocodiles (Jung), elephants and eagles (Perls).

For example, Perls (1969) argued that eagles actualize their real selves by roaming in the sky and building a particular kind of nest, and that they cannot *not* self-actualize. In contrast, people often don't self-actualize, in his view, because we have such a marked capacity to learn and pretend. He and the other theorists mentioned above further argue that when people's real selves are not actualized they persist 'underground' and press for expression. Presumably, the influential factors here (assuming the idea has some validity) are: (a) how robust the elements of self are; (b) how discouraging its early environment is; and (c) how discouraging it continues to be. Counselling of course may seek to counteract such influences. There may also be a general developmental tendency for older people to become 'more themselves'.

A potential source of confusion is that some person-centred theorists emphasize a distinction between actualizing and self-actualizing. In the terms used in this section and in the section on self, they use actualizing to mean the same as self-actualizing. More confusingly, they use self-actualizing to mean actualizing a person's **self-concept**, when self-concepts vary in how accurately or not they represent people's real selves. This is confusing! Apart from the semantic muddle, the basic practical problem remains: distinguishing between real and false aspects of themselves or others, which is something people are often concerned to do.

Five possible misinterpretations of the concept of self-actualization are that it means:

- doing what you like, regardless of other people;
- a morbid degree of introspection;
- being unflinchingly blunt;
- an idyllic state of mind;
- an elite way of life, for the rich and lucky only.

You may like to consider whether you agree with any of these views and if so, why.

References

Joseph, S. and Wood, A. (2010) Assessment of positive functioning in clinical psychology: theoretical and practical issues. *Clinical Psychology Review*, 30(7): 830–8.

Maslow, A.H. (1968) *Toward a Psychology of Being*, 2nd edn. New York: Van Nostrand Reinhold.

Perls, F. (1969) *In and Out the Garbage Pail*. Lafayette, CA: Real People Press.

Annotated further reading

Joseph, S. and Wood, A. (2010) Assessment of positive functioning in clinical psychology: theoretical and practical issues. *Clinical Psychology Review*, 30(7): 830–8.

This paper reviews attempts to measure self-actualization and other concepts of 'positive functioning', particularly the recently developed (2008) Authenticity Scale. They conclude that research is beginning to show such measures to be 'strong predictors of outcome', and that they can also change the meaning of therapy.

Vazire, S. (2010) 'Who knows what about a person?' The self-other knowledge asymmetry (SOKA) model. *Journal of Personality and Social Psychology*, 98: 281–300.

Whitsun, E.R. and Olczak, P.V. (1991) Criticisms and polemics surrounding the self-actualization construct: an evaluation. *Journal of Social Behaviour and Personality*, 6(5): 75–95.

Two wide-ranging and sophisticated reviews of many of the debates about self-actualization and self-awareness respectively.

Self-concept

See also: core conditions; locus of evaluation; person-centred counselling; self-actualization

The self-concept is a central aspect of the person-centred approach to counselling. It is basically how people define themselves, for example, 'I am caring, I am cheerful, I can sometimes be funny'. It is 'a fluid but consistent pattern of perceptions of the "I" or "me" in relation to the environment, personal values, goals and ideals' (Merry and Tudor 2006: 293). As well as a self as it exists in the present, people also have an 'ideal self' which is the self they ideally want to be. McLeod (2009) makes the interesting point that the self-concept might have been more accurately named the 'self process', as this term more precisely captures the fluid, ever changing nature of the self as conceived by Carl Rogers. The self-concept starts to develop during childhood and is heavily influenced by the responses of significant others during that time. If parents or carers are overly critical and punitive, the self-concept often becomes negative, false or what is known as 'conditioned'.

Thorne (2002) makes a clear link between the actualizing tendency (the natural tendency of all human beings towards the fulfilment of their potential) and the self-concept. The two are often not in harmony because the individual, in their desire to obtain approval from others, may disregard the promptings of the actualizing tendency and adapt the self-concept to fit with others' demands. If the resulting conflict is resolved reasonably effectively, major problems may not arise, though a person may still not reach their full potential. However, if the conflict is too great, an individual may become disturbed and alienated from their 'true' self. This disturbance can be maintained as the individual strives to defend the self-concept which gains the approval of others. A state of 'incongruence' is the result.

Individuals experiencing this 'conditioned' self might feel a sense of alienation, or may experience a heavy dependency on others' judgements, or may experience conflicts between their own values and externally imposed values. Often decision making is extremely difficult, because they have lost touch with their internal ability to get in touch with what is right for them.

For a better understanding of the process by which a client is helped to develop a more positive self-concept, which is in harmony with their actualizing tendency, this section needs to be read alongside the others above. In brief though, the client will, through the process of counselling, become more in touch with, and more accepting of, their own inner life, including those feelings which are regarded as less acceptable. Thus the client's self-concept starts to be defined more by themselves than by others.

A common criticism of this concept of the self is that the focus is entirely on the influence of significant others on development, with no consideration given to the potentially powerful influences of genetics and wider social influences. The very positive slant can seem to minimize the negative traits which people can exhibit.

References

McLeod, J. (2009) *An Introduction to Counselling*. Maidenhead: Open University Press.

Merry, T. and Tudor, K. (2006) Person-centred counselling and psychotherapy. In C. Feltham and I. Horton (eds) (2006) *The SAGE Handbook of Counselling and Psychotherapy*, 2nd edn. London: Sage.

Thorne, B. (2002) Person-centred therapy. In W. Dryden (ed.) *Handbook of Individual Therapy*, 4th edn. London: Sage.

Annotated further reading

Casemore, R. (2006) *Person-centred Counselling in a Nutshell*. Sage.

A succinct guide to person-centred theoretical concepts and to the counselling relationship.

Cooper, M., O'Hara, M., Schmid, P.F. and Wyatt, G. (eds) (2007) *The Handbook of Person-centred Counselling and Psychotherapy*. Ross-on-Wye: PCCS Books.

An excellent, comprehensive overview of theory and practice.

Self-disclosure

See also: Egan's skilled helper model

Therapist self-disclosure

Self-disclosure can be defined as any statement made by the therapist which reveals something personal about them. While some approaches (humanistic, existential) view self-disclosure by the therapist as an important skill, others, such as the psychodynamic approach, regard it as something which would hinder the therapeutic process by interfering with the transference process (Hill and Knox 2002, in Cooper 2008). According to Egan (2007) there are three types of self-disclosure: (1) non-verbal, which includes facial expressions and body language. Egan calls this 'indirect' self-disclosure as it is a natural and unavoidable part of communication; (2) historical revelation, such as, 'I've also experienced that', which Egan terms 'direct' self-disclosure; and (3) immediacy (such as 'I'm feeling confused', which is a distinct counselling skill. Historical revelation can be useful, but should not be used frequently, although both this and immediacy can be seen as a form of modelling, aimed at encouraging the client to talk more openly about themselves.

Egan (2007) provides some useful guidelines about effective self-disclosure which include the following:

- ensuring that any self-disclosure is appropriate, so the therapist needs to use it only if it is being used for a particular purpose;
- being mindful of the timing, so that it is not done prematurely before the client is ready for it;
- using it infrequently, otherwise clients may begin to regard the therapist as the one with the problems and could start to feel burdened by this;
- using it flexibly, adapting its use to the individual client;
- making sure it is used in a focused way, avoiding long, 'rambling' self-disclosures.

Hill and Knox (2002: 262, in Cooper 2008) also suggest:

- not disclosing material which is very intimate, such as sexual experiences or religious beliefs;
- using disclosures to validate the client's perspective, strengthen the therapeutic alliance or to offer a new perspective.

Research findings

There are no clear conclusions about the effectiveness of self-disclosure from the research undertaken so far. Some research suggests that it can frighten clients or cause them to see the therapist as having mental health problems. Other studies show that clients welcome it, regarding the therapist as open and down to earth (Bayne et al. 2008).

According to Cooper (2008) in his review of research findings, positive immediacy statements are viewed most positively by clients, certainly more than negative immediacy statements, and probably more than both positive and negative historical revelatory statements. There is also some evidence that clients prefer disclosure of less intimate material, such as professional issues, than more intimate details such as personal feelings.

Client self-disclosure

Clearly effective therapy involves in-depth self-disclosure from the client. At the same time, clients can avoid self-disclosing relevant material due to fear, shame or a lack of trust in the therapist. Therapists often need to focus on building trust with their client via a supportive and secure therapeutic relationship. If clients feel comfortable enough to be open about difficult thoughts and feelings, the therapeutic work is likely to be much more effective. On the other hand, it is important that clients do not feel pressurized to reveal more than they feel ready to disclose. Indeed, for those clients who find verbal self-disclosure problematic, writing can be an alternative to talking (Bayne et al. 2008).

References

Bayne, R., Jinks, G., Collard, P. and Horton, I. (2008) *The Counsellor's Handbook: A Practical A–Z Guide to Integrative Counselling and Psychotherapy*. Cheltenham: Nelson Thornes.

Cooper, M. (2008) *Essential Research Findings in Counselling and Psychotherapy: The Facts are Friendly*. London: Sage.

Egan, G. (2007) *The Skilled Helper: A Problem-Management and Opportunity-Development Approach to Helping*, 8th edn. Belmont, CA: Thompson Brooks/Cole.

Annotated further reading

Farber, B.A. (2006) *Self-Disclosure in Psychotherapy*. New York: Guilford.

This book focuses on issues surrounding client and therapist self-disclosure. The author draws on theory, practice (there are a range of diverse case studies) and empirical research. There is some valuable discussion as to how therapists can use self-disclosure effectively. Some readers may find the use of the word 'patient' rather than 'client' off-putting, but it is worth putting this to one side!

Feltham, C. (2010) *Critical Thinking in Counselling and Psychotherapy*. London: Sage.

A brief, but thought-provoking chapter on the issues associated with self-disclosure.

Social learning theory

See also: multimodal therapy

Social and cognitive processes are essential for comprehending human emotions, motivation and action.

Social learning theory is derived from the work of Albert Bandura, who is an academic psychologist and developed a number of theories that are usefully applied to psychotherapy, counselling and mentoring. His idea was an expansion of Julian Rotter's psychological research. Rotter is known for developing influential theories, including initially the 'social learning theory' and also the concept of 'locus of control'. Rotter's idea (1945) was based on people wanting to avoid negative consequences while wanting to have positive effects or results. If the person expects any sort of positive outcome from a particular behaviour, or thinks there is a high possibility of a positive outcome, then there is more chance that the individual would engage in that behaviour. As positive outcomes occur, the new behaviour becomes reinforced, which leads to the person repeating it again. Rotter's social learning theory suggests that behaviour is influenced by environmental factors or stimuli, and not psychological factors alone.

Bandura takes this idea and adds to it various aspects of behavioural and cognitive learning. He challenged Skinner's theory on reinforcement principles. Behavioural learning assumes that it is the environment you live in which causes people to behave in certain ways, while cognitive learning suggests that various psychological factors can influence how a person behaves. Human behaviour is mostly learned by observation and involves attention, retention, reproduction and motivation.

Bandura's assumption about human nature was that it is not developed due to inborn, genetic predispositions, but overall occurs by learning and experience. He consented that biological factors could however be responsible for limiting achievement through learning.

He assumed there to be five basic cognitive human abilities. One was the capability to symbolize. We are able to transform an experience into symbols. We are able to create ideas which go beyond the actual sensory experience. Two, we possess the ability of forethought and anticipation, which includes reflectivity. The third ability he calls vicarious capability, which suggests that we learn from observing others (modelling). The fourth factor is the capability to self-regulate, according to our own, personally developed standards of behaviour. Last of all he discusses self-reflection, which, as far as we know, is only developed in humans. This latter point however is only applicable if a person is able to self-reflect, i.e. has a functional prefrontal cortex and the willingness to self-reflect.

His work has actually affected the development of a number of psychotherapeutic approaches, in particular Arnold Lazarus' multimodal therapy. 'His work on observational learning . . . contributed to understanding how clients learn harmful and helpful ways of thinking and behaving' (Nelson-Jones 1995: 245).

Other approaches that drew insights from Bandura's theories were career counselling, educational settings where self-efficacy tools can be implemented into the curriculum and health awareness in health settings, where patients are assisted to implement good and eliminate bad health habits.

References

Nelson-Jones, R. (1995) *The Theory and Practice of Counselling*. London: Cassell.
Rotter, J.B. (1945) *Social Learning and Clinical Psychology*. Englewood Cliffs, NJ: Prentice-Hall.

Annotated further reading

Bandura, A. (1986) *Social Foundations of Thought and Action: A Social Cognitive Theory*. Englewod Cliffs, NJ: Prentice-Hall.

This is the definitive summary of Bandura's work. It is his 'bible'.

Nelson-Jones, R. (1995) *The Theory and Practice of Counselling*. London: Cassell.

This book reviews many main psychological approaches and is particularly useful for counsellors that work in an integrative fashion. However, it requires focus and attention. No bed-time reading!

Socratic dialogue

See also: Beck, Aaron T. cognitive behavioural therapy; collaborative empiricism

> A life unexamined is a life not worth living.
>
> Socrates

In cognitive behavioural therapy, Socratic questioning is recommended from the very beginning of treatment. Clients are again and again encouraged to consider, evaluate and test sources of information and reality versus their own beliefs. This process is facilitated by open-ended questioning, frequently referred to as 'guided discovery'.

The aim of this intervention is to help solve current problems and to bring new information into the client's awareness, thereby creating new neural pathways and thinking patterns for the future ('collaborative empiricism' – A. Beck). The therapist thus invites new insights to increase motivation for change.

The approach is based on the philosophical interactions Socrates had with his students. Like him the therapist asks the client informational questions in an empathic way, hoping to enable the client to find the answer within his own life experience or by looking at the behaviour of role models the client selected to be informed by. Questions are phrased in a manner to encourage thought and increase awareness rather than 'correct' answers. Clients are therefore able to discover for themselves their erroneous conclusions and behaviours. Whatever information the therapist receives is then collected and frequently summarized and once this has been done, the therapist follows up with synthesizing (analytical) questions: e.g. 'How do you see the problem now? What do you think you could use from our findings in order to respond differently when this problem occurs again?' Often the client comes up with their own better solutions. Socratic questioning creates a non-judgemental atmosphere and collaboration between the two parties (Beck 1993: 103).

Chris Allan argues that this philosophical intervention appears to be one of the most difficult ideas to learn in CBT. This is partly due to many textbooks recommending it, but insufficient guidance being offered to clarify exactly what skills the technique requires therapists to use. Socratic questioning is said to have been promoted by therapists such as Adler, Winnicott, Padesky and Beck. Allan says that Padesky argued in a paper: 'Socratic questioning: changing minds or guiding discovery', for example, that using Socratic questioning would best be introduced not to change a client's mind but to allow the client to explore and reflect on their thoughts and behaviours. In short the method uses four steps in order to guide the client to new insights:

- informational questions;
- empathy;
- frequent summaries (of what client or therapist have said);
- synthesizing (analytical) questions: e.g. 'What do you make of this?'

Beck refers to a source for Socratic questioning which is a publication by Overholser (1988), entitled *Clinical Utility of the Socratic Method*. Carey and Mullan reviewed the literature regarding the Socratic method in a paper published in 2004. Like Allan they too came to the conclusion, that

> despite being regarded as a fundamentally important psychothera-peutic procedure, a great deal of discrepancy exists concerning various

aspects of the method and incongruities. Discord occurs in the literature, for example, concerning the purpose of Socratic questioning and also what the components of the technique might be.

They seem to argue that striving towards transparency concerning Socratic dialogue would improve the practice of psychotherapy and get most benefits for the clients.

References

Beck, A., Wright, F., Newman, C. and Liese, B. (1993) *Cognitive Therapy of Substance Abuse*. New York: Guilford Press.

Carey, T.A. and Mullan, R.J. (2004) What is Socratic questioning? *Psychotherapy: Theory, Research, Practice, Training*, 41(3): 217–26.

Annotated further reading

Allan, C. In the room, blog. http://gandalwaven.typepad.com/intheroom/2006/11/one_of_the_diff.html (accessed 14 August 2011).

This is a very helpful blog that talks about real clients and sessions and ponders on the actual virtue and use of individual CBT interventions such as Socratic questioning.

Padesky, C. (1993) Socratic Questioning: Changing Minds or Guiding Discovery, Keynote address at European Congress of Behavioural and Cognitive Therapies, London, 24 September.

Padesky's definition and use seem to be the most commonly used ones. However, he also mentions possible alternative interpretations about Socratic dialogue. This is a stimulating and thought-provoking piece.

Splitting

See also: defence mechanisms; object relations theory; projection; projective identification

The concept of splitting was first proposed by Bleuler to designate a multiple splitting of thoughts by psychotic patients.

Freud called the integrity of the human mind into question by identifying the unconscious but did not consider the importance of splitting as a defence mechanism until late in his writing (Hinshelwood 1991). Freud, whose theories were characterized by the conflict present in the mind, proposed that the ego under pressure deals with anxiety by splitting the threat or by splitting the outside world into 'good' and 'bad' (Gay 1995). He held the view that the mind could hold more than one point of view so that the child might believe in Father Christmas and hold the excitement about that, but simultaneously know that it is only his father dressed up. This also reflected the prejudiced xenophobe who at the same time genuinely held that his best friends were foreigners (Hinshelwood 1991).

Klein and Kleinian and object relations theorists took the concept further and proposed that there were two types of splitting – the splitting of the ego (following Freud above) and the splitting of the object. Klein also proposed that for psychotic patients splitting was to defend the ego against the fear of annihilation.

The concept of splitting is the basis of other forms of defence mechanisms, particularly projection and underlies the work of Klein characterizing much of what takes place in the paranoid-schizoid position, and particularly projective identification. Klein's early work was about the splitting of the object, particularly how objects would be attributed with qualities that were very good or very bad. Infants and children would split the qualities and intentions of parents and others into wholly bad or good and the way this was handled came to be understood as a major feature of the personality development (H. Segal and Klein 1973; J. Segal 1993).

References

Gay, P. (1995) *The Freud Reader*. London: Vintage.

Hinshelwood, R. (1991) *A Dictionary of Kleinian Thought*. London: Free Association Books.

Segal, H. and Klein, M. (1973) *Introduction to the Work of Melanie Klein*. London: Hogarth Press, (for) the Institute of Psycho-analysis.

Segal, J. (1993) *Melanie Klein*. London: Sage.

Annotated further reading

Segal, J. (1993) *Melanie Klein*. London: Sage.

Segal's book is a particularly informative and clear exposition of Klein's theories.

Stages of change

See also: client feedback, collecting; the therapeutic relationship; death, fear of; integrative models

Stages of change is an integrative, transtheoretical concept which has been shown to predict therapy outcomes (e.g. Norcross et al. 2011). Five stages (sometimes four, omitting Preparation) are generally distinguished:

1   Precontemplation – the person is reluctant to be a client and usually doesn't see themselves as having any problems. They are at best doubtful about the value of counselling, at least for themselves. Other people may persuade them to try it.
2   Contemplation – the person recognizes that they have a problem or problems and have thought seriously about possible solutions.
3   Preparation – the person is intending to take action soon.
4   Action – the person is making changes and putting a lot of energy and time into doing so.
5   Maintenance – the person is working to prevent 'relapse' and, more, anticipating it as normal (though not inevitable) and manageable.

In counselling, stage of change for each problem – an important practical aspect of the concept – is assessed straightforwardly by asking: 'Would you say you are not ready to change in the next 6 months (precontemplation), thinking about changing in the next 6 months (contemplation), thinking about changing in the next month (preparation) or have you already made some progress (action)?' (Norcross et al. 2011: 151).

This may seem obvious in that it is merely saying (and finding in several studies) that counselling is more successful with clients who are ready to change. However, it does more. First, it counteracts the tendency for therapists to assume that clients are ready to change, i.e. are in stage 3. Indeed, Norcross et al. estimate that only 20 per cent of clients are in stage 3, with about 40 per cent in stage 1 and 40 per cent in stage 2. Second, it enables a focus on helping clients in stage 1 move forward. Third, it suggests treating problems in stage 2 gently, because clients tend to resist premature action. Thus, the general principle is a matching of stages and processes, for example awareness and stage 2, action and stage 3. Here, Norcross et al. suggest, crisply, 'a nurturing parent stance with a precontemplator, a Socratic teacher role with a contemplator, an experienced coach with a patient in action, and then a consultant once in maintenance' (Norcross et al. 2011: 152).

Reference

Norcross, J.C., Krebs, P.M. and Prochaska, J.D. (2011) Stages of change. *Journal of Clinical Psychology: In Session*, 67: 143–54.

Annotated further reading

Feltham, C. and Dryden, W. (2006) *Brief Counselling: A Practical Integrative Approach*. Maidenhead: Open University Press.

Includes several sections discussing aspects of using the Stages of Change model, complementing both the research findings reviewed by Norcross et al. (2011) and their excellent but concise guidelines for practice.

Strengths

See also: empathy; self

Linley (2008) has recently revived and refreshed the concepts of strengths. He defined strengths as ways of behaving, thinking or feeling that are 'authentic and energising to the user, and enable optimal functioning, development and performance' (p. 9). While this like most definitions is fairly dry, Linley is writing about how each of us can feel and be at our best.

His definition emphasizes enjoyment and energy as central to strengths: you can be good, even gifted, in a particular way but if you don't enjoy it, it's not a strength in his view. Moreover, 'we learn better in the areas where we are already strong' (p. 13). His ways of identifying strengths are based on the assumption about enjoyment, for example noticing what you or a client look forward to or miss.

Linley further suggests that there are many strengths that we don't have words for yet – he and other researchers are working on this. We do have over 100 words for different strengths so far with, he thinks, hundreds more to come. An example of a strength is 'lift' – improving other people's moods by being optimistic and encouraging.

Linley's conception of strengths has some far-reaching implications for therapy and more generally. For example, as with values, it can be very helpful to empathize with one or more of a client's strengths, while not of course neglecting their problems and the depth of their feelings about them. And when someone recognizes a strength in you, you probably feel understood and respected. At work, it implies an emphasis on employees developing their strengths as fully as they can rather than working on their weaknesses: for most people, aiming for excellence rather than all-round ability (cf. many appraisal and staff development interviews).

There are free questionnaire measures of strengths at the Centre for Applied Positive Psychology website (CAPP), at via.strengths.org and at authentichappiness.org, but bear in mind that there are many strengths still to be named.

Reference

Linley, A. (2008) *Average to A+ : Realising Strengths in Yourself and Others*. Coventry: CAPP Press.

Annotated further reading

Linley, A. (2008) *Average to A+ : Realising Strengths in Yourself and Others*. Coventry: CAPP Press.

Discusses many strengths and ways of identifying them, issues about them, for example whether a strength can be over-used, interactions between strengths to form new strengths, whether this conception of strengths means we can't be anything we want to be, and ways of dealing with weaknesses.

Structural model of the mind

See also: psychosexual development; psychosocial development; defence mechanisms

Freud argued that all behaviour and mental development is characterized by drives or motivating forces. Human development therefore involves the individual in the negotiation of both unconscious and conscious processes in the context of developing psychic structures. These negotiations are subject to defence mechanisms and structures that both link and separate the conscious and unconscious processes protecting the ego from innate drives and pain and anxiety arising from being alive. Craib (2001) describes this negotiation as finding a path through a dangerous forest albeit one with lots of animal tracks we can follow. We all have to find our own way, which depends on culture, social class, family history and our individual internal conscious and unconscious means of giving our journey its meaning (p. 47).

Instincts and drives

Craib proposed that the notion of 'instinct' (particularly the 'infamous' sexual instinct) led to relatively easy popular critiques of Freud's theories of psychic structures and processes, such as feminist ones whereby there was a view that 'anatomy' was equated with 'destiny' which potentially constrained women's experiences. 'No aspect of psychoanalytic theory has been, since the early years of the field, more problematic than the psychology of women. Freud himself admitted that his understanding of women was limited' (Winer et al. 2004: 1). So why has his theory survived the test of time theoretically and clinically?

'Instinct' suggests the reductionist and biological. Craib has thus suggested that a more accurate translation of Freud's position is 'drive' which is much more representative of what Freud intended as it applies directly to the psychic not the biological (p. 19) and thus describes a combination of physical energy and mental representations. This translation and the consequent conceptualization helps make sense of the psychoanalytic structural model of mind initially proposed by Freud more realistically without the diversion and anxiety of 'making excuses' for what have been attributed to him as misogynist beliefs.

These drives can be divided into the libido, which is the sexual drive, the life preserving drives, and the one that drives our psychological development (see **psychosexual development**).

In Freud's view the sexual drive was the most important and that within each of us, he believed, is the need to seek gratification, and this process occurs throughout life.

The other drive is the death instinct (Thanatos) which he proposed at a later stage in his career, not so much from his clinical work (as the sexual drive had been) but from observations of human experience particularly during the First World War about which he queried how the soldiers could have put themselves through so much misery and pain without rebelling (Craib 2001). He then divided the libido into Eros (drive towards pleasure) and Thanatos (the drive towards death). He proposed that these drives were from the same root and with the same aim – to release tension – although they have different ways of doing that. The life instinct does so through forming relationships with others, sexual activity, having children and the continuation of life (see also **Erikson, Erik** and **psychosocial development**). The death instinct chooses a more direct root – the release of tension for ever. However, it can be subordinated to the life instinct when it is directed against an external enemy, and Freud suggested the two are closely intertwined (see Craib 2001: 20). The co-existence of two contradictory drives is mirrored in the rest of the psychic structure proposed in all psychoanalysis – that is that the human psyche is structured as a series of many contradictions.

Psychic structures

Freud considered that there are three basic structures of personality that serve gratification of the drives. These are the id, ego and superego.

The id

The id is the original source of personality and contains everything that an individual inherits, the instinctual drives and the pleasure-seeking impulses as well as repressed material. Like a young child, the id can be seen to operate according to the pleasure principle, avoiding pain and obtaining pleasure, regardless of external considerations. This basic push for gratification remains part of the personality, but with the experience that gratification can often be achieved better by a more considered approach to the external world.

The id represents the deepest level of the unconscious mind and often individuals might experience feelings that make no obvious sense to them such as fear or anger or even 'nameless dread'. The id does not appear to have a structure itself but it is important to remember here that according to Freud and all other psychoanalytic thinkers the unconscious does not reflect chronological time and thus such feelings buried from infancy can reach up to the surface in adulthood at any time (Klein 1959/1975) and other than through psychoanalysis it is impossible to make full sense of them.

The ego

By planning and negotiating, the child gradually transfers energy from the id to the ego. This is the second structure to develop and mediates between the demands of the id and the realities of life. The ego also mediates between the id and the superego, known colloquially as the conscience. The ego lies between the unconscious and the conscious. The conscious part is what becomes our sense of who we are (e.g. what we call 'identity', see **psychosocial development**) or 'self', and has a coherence and chronological sense of time and place. However, the ego has an unconscious part that comprises internalized objects from infancy (see **object relations theory; Klein, Melanie**) and the mechanisms to defend the individual from unconscious anxieties through repression and other defence mechanisms. The ego also deals with anxieties arising from outside threats.

The superego

The superego, which enables individuals to decide between right and wrong, is the third structure to develop. Craib (2001) suggests that although the superego is involved with our conscious awareness of our behaviour Freud meant that it was also deeper with a more unconscious role than is frequently proposed. Thus Freud indicated that the greater the desire for an object the greater force is needed to repress that desire and that the superego is for the most part engaged in an internal struggle rather than one that is primarily concerned with the struggle between the ego and the outside world.

References

Craib, I. (2001) *Psychoanalysis: A Critical Introduction*. Cambridge: Polity.
Klein, M. (1959/1975) Our adult world and its roots on infancy. In *The writings of Melanie Klein: Envy and Gratitude and Other Works 1946–1963* (Vol. 3, pp. 247–63). London: Hogarth Press.
Winer, J.A., Anderson, J.W. and Kieffer, C.C. (2004) *Psychoanalysis and Women* (Vol. 32). London: The Analytic Press and the Chicago Institute for Psychoanalysis.

Annotated further reading

Bee, H.L. and Mitchell, S.K. (1984). *The Developing Person: A Life Span Approach*, 2nd edn. New York: Harper and Row.

This text provides a clear 'lay' version of the structural model of mind.

Craib, I. (2001) *Psychoanalysis: A Critical Introduction*. Cambridge: Polity.

Craib provides a critical analysis in his comprehensive and accessible book.

Sublimation

See also: defence mechanisms; repression

Sublimation is the transformation of harmful or undesirable impulses into something less potentially destructive or even positive and creative. Sublimation is frequently discussed along with repression as a crucial and healthy process through which the ego defends itself. Whereas repression keeps the threatening material away from consciousness, sublimation is an 'outcome' of a successful repression. So socially unacceptable feelings and potential actions will become sublimated into those that are acceptable and may lead the individual into successful areas of activity.

Freud, for example, focused on how erotic energy becomes sublimated into creative academic or artistic work and he considered that this was a critical component of civilization. Aggressive impulses may also be sublimated into sport.

There are problems however in seeing sublimation as overwhelmingly healthy. For example if the only way a manageable life becomes possible is through sublimating sexual or aggressive drives then the individual is likely to be less satisfied, or as Craib (2001) expressed it, the person can manage their life through a 'renunciation of satisfaction' (p. 39).

Freud believed (clearly in his own case) that work was the best way that a person can attach themselves to reality and what he called a secure place in a portion of reality. Work requires commitment to the particular task as well as the need to form and manage human relationships. Professional relationships, Freud in *Civilization and its Discontents* (1930) suggested, provide special satisfaction and can indeed be a path to happiness. He acknowledged of course that for the majority work was a financial necessity and individuals might have an aversion to work (Gay 1995).

References

Craib, I. (2001) *Psychoanalysis: A Critical Introduction*. Cambridge: Polity.

Freud, S. (1930) The future of an illusion, civilization and its discontents, and other works. *Civilization and its Discontents. The Standard Edition of the Complete Psychological Works of Sigmund Freud* (Vol. X X 1) pp. 57–146.

Gay, P. (1995) *The Freud Reader*. London: Vintage.

Annotated further reading

Craib, I. (2001) *Psychoanalysis: A Critical Introduction*. Cambridge: Polity.

Craib provides a clear introduction showing how defence mechanisms operate.

Systemic therapies

See also: open systems theory

Systemic psychotherapy is one in which the system is taken into account in formulation and clinical practice. Thus an individual's life and difficulties are seen in the context of their relationship with their parents, family, community and wider society. The approach to the analysis has ideas in common with a bioecological model of human development that takes all these levels into account when trying to conceptualize the developmental process

(Bronfenbrenner and Morris 2007). The origins of systemic thinking, as with open systems theory applied to organizations, comes from work on the evolution of organisims and how they adapt (or fail to adapt) to their environments (Miller and Rice 1967; Von Bertalanffy 1956).

There is also a clear link between systemic psychotherapy and the work of the British 'anti-psychiatrists' of the 1960s particularly Aaron Esterson and R.D. Laing who wrote about young women, diagnosed by the medical establishment as psychotic (schizophrenic) but when seen by the researcher/clinician in the context of their families, it was clear that their behaviours had elements of 'reality'. The pathology was consequently attributed to the family network (system) and the 'patient' was effectively their scapegoat on whom all the madness was dumped (Esterson 1970; Laing and Esterson 1964).

Systemic psychotherapy itself emerged from family therapy and particularly the work of, among others, Salvador Minuchin (Minuchin 1999) and Virginia Satir (Satir et al. 1975). The practice focuses upon the stories people tell about their lives and how they relate to the people, families, organizations and wider social networks, within them. Each person provides an account from their own perspective. This provides a sense to all involved of the system in which they live. What is relevant therefore is what goes on between people and their networks rather than the individual who is acting out the problems (Mandin 2007).

The conceptual difficulties involved in blending psychoanalytic and systemic thinking within psychotherapy are brought together by the *modus operandi* of the Tavistock Centre in London where systemic thinking is nuanced by Kleinian and post-Kleinian ideas and practice.

Systemic therapy is used widely in the UK and Europe to work with individuals, couples and families. Systemic therapists themselves might work individually or with another member of their (often multidisciplinary) team.

Systemic psychotherapy has become one the most important approaches taken towards family support in the British National Health Service with a popular journal (*Journal of Systemic Therapies*) devoted to exploring systemic therapy and there appears to be a particular and growing interest among social workers, for example in the *Journal of Social Work Practice* (Carr 2000; Mandin 2007) to take their place in this work particularly in relation to children.

The basic concepts have been 'updated' to become 'narrative' and 'reflective practice' since the 1980s and developments have taken place during that time which have adopted a relativist approach moving beyond the notion of 'objective reality' to take on board social constructionist ideas (Philp and Geldard 2011).

There are two main fields of application of systemic family therapy: the structural field (or constitutive) and the semantic field. Both belong to the large systemic system (Brasseur 1981).

References

Brasseur, F. (1981) About the systemic frame of psychotherapy. *Acta Psychiatrica Belgica*, 81(6): 542–79.

Bronfenbrenner, U. and Morris, P.A. (2007) *The Bioecological Model of Human Development*. Chichester: John Wiley & Sons.

Carr, A. (2000) Evidence-based practice in family therapy and systemic consultation. *Journal of Family Therapy*, 22(1): 29–60.

Esterson, A. (1970) *The Leaves of Spring: Schizophrenia, the Family and Sacrifice*. Harmondsworth: Pelican.

Laing, R.D. and Esterson, A. (1964) *Sanity, Madness and the Family*. Harmondsworth: Pelican.

Mandin, P. (2007) The contribution of systems and object-relation theories to an understanding of the therapeutic relationship in social work practice. *Journal of Social Work Practice: Psychotherapeutic Approaches in Health, Welfare and the Community*, 21: 149–62.

Miller, E.J. and Rice, A.K. (1967) *Systems of Organisation: The Control of Task and Sentient Boundaries*. London: Tavistock.

Minuchin, S. (1999) Retelling, reimagining, and re-searching: a continuing conversation. *Journal of Marital and Family Therapy*, 25(1): 9–14.

Philp, K. and Geldard, K. (2011) Moving beyond right and wrong: touchstones for teaching and learning constructionist therapy. *Journal of Systemic Therapies*, 30(2): 1–10.

Satir, V., Stachowiak, J. and Taschman, H.A. (1975) *Helping Families to Change*. New York: J. Aronson.

Von Bertalanffy, I. (1956) *General Systems Theory*. New York: George Braziller.

Annotated further reading

Laing, R.D. and Esterson, A. (1964) *Sanity, Madness and the Family*. Harmondsworth: Pelican.

One of the earliest expositions using case studies to demonstrate how we live in family and social systems and how systemic dysfunction allows for the scapegoating and labelling of family members. A 'must read' for all interested in family therapy.

Mandin, P. (2007) The contribution of systems and object-relation theories to an understanding of the therapeutic relationship in social work practice. *Journal of Social Work Practice: Psychotherapeutic Approaches in Health, Welfare and the Community*, 21: 149–62.

This article links psychotherapy and systemic therapy clearly and focuses on contemporary practice issues.

Miller, E.J. and Rice, A.K. (1967) *Systems of Organisation: The Control of Task and Sentient Boundaries*. London: Tavistock.

This is the classic text that led to thinking about the use of systemic approaches to organizations and eventually families and individuals.

T

Therapeutic relationship, the

See also: relational depth; ruptures in the therapeutic alliance

The relationship between therapist and client is a central component of all types of therapy, except perhaps online approaches and bibliotherapy. A huge amount of research has focused on this area and has consistently found a strong link between the quality of the relationship and the effectiveness of the therapy (Horvath and Bedi 2002; Cooper 2008). However, different theoretical approaches present very different perspectives on the nature of this relationship. Three of these perspectives – psychodynamic, cognitive-behavioural and person-centred – will be focused on here.

The psychodynamic perspective

One of the key aims is to create a relationship in which the client can re-experience feelings originally experienced in past relationships with childhood authority figures. This is known as a transference relationship. Since the 1950s, countertransference – the therapist's response to the client's material – has also been seen as important. It is via this re-experiencing of past hurts that the client can gain insight into, and work through, problematic past relationships which are impacting on their relationships in the present.

Another central concept in this approach is the therapist as 'container' (McLeod 2009). The therapist acts as vehicle to enable the client to express deeply buried hidden desires without having to consummate them. As psychodynamic therapy has developed, the relationship has become more of a collaborative process, although the therapist still refrains from sharing much about themselves, as this is seen to hinder the formation of the transference relationship. This type of neutrality is often referred to as presenting a 'blank screen', although 'being neutral' is probably a more accurate description.

The person-centred perspective

There are some similarities between the psychodynamic approach and the person-centred approach in that both encourage the client to share difficult thoughts and feelings within a relationship built on trust. However, the focus here is on the client's present reality and the therapist's role is to understand and accept the client's experiences, rather than to interpret them. The therapist needs to demonstrate certain 'core conditions' or qualities (empathy, acceptance and genuineness) in order to create the type of relationship which will facilitate change in the client. Carl Rogers believed that the relationship was the key to therapeutic change and that skills and techniques were unnecessary if the relationship was right. It is by fully acknowledging and experiencing their difficult thoughts and feelings that clients can get more in touch with their true selves and develop trust in their own perspective on the world. Autonomy of both client and therapist and a sense of equality between them are other important concepts. Mearns and Cooper (2005) highlight the idea of the 'authentic presence' of the therapist as having a vital role to play, so that the client can experience, sometimes for the first time, real and meaningful contact with another person. This in turn will enable to client to begin to develop their own capacity to form authentic relationships with others.

The cognitive-behavioural perspective

Whereas the relationship itself facilitates change in the approaches above, the relationship within CBT is not regarded as the central focus of the therapy, although it is still important. It is often conceptualized as similar to a teaching or coaching relationship, with the therapist supporting the client in learning new skills and challenging their irrational thoughts and beliefs. The collaborative nature of the relationship is key (McLeod 2009), with the emphasis being on focused interventions aimed at bringing about cognitive and behavioural change. Clients are often given homework tasks to complete between therapy sessions.

Although research suggests that no one approach is significantly more effective than any other, there is little doubt that different clients respond better to different types of counselling relationship (and overall approach). For example, some clients value the warm, supportive relationship offered by the person-centred practitioner, whereas others prefer the task-oriented, more directive approach of the cognitive-behavioural therapist. Ideally therapists would be able to adapt their relational approach to suit their clients, but in reality this rarely happens, particularly within 'purist' approaches.

References

Cooper, M. (2008) *Essential Research Findings in Counselling and Psychotherapy: The Facts are Friendly.* London: Sage.

Horvath, A.O. and Bedi, R.P. (2002) The alliance. In J.C. Norcross (ed.) *Psychotherapy Relationships That Work: Therapist Contributions and Responsiveness to Patient Needs.* New York: Oxford University Press.

McLeod, J. (2009) *An Introduction to Counselling*, 4th edn. Maidenhead: Open University Press.

Mearns, D. and Cooper, M. (2005) *Working at Relational Depth in Counselling and Psychotherapy*. London: Sage.

Annotated further reading

Feltham, C. (ed.) (1999) *Understanding the Counselling Relationship*. London: Sage.

Provides an excellent overview of the concept of the relationship in a range of theoretical approaches.

Stiles, W.B. (2006) The client–therapist relationship. In C. Feltham and I. Horton (eds) *SAGE Handbook of Counselling and Psychotherapy*, 2nd edn. London: Sage.

A succinct but informative chapter on the nature of the therapeutic relationship in three of the main theoretical approaches.

Transactional analysis (TA)

See also: humanistic approaches; phenomenology

Developed by Eric Berne in the 1960s, this approach has its roots in a number of philosophical and theoretical perspectives, including humanism, existentialism, psychoanalysis and phenomenology. Humanism is evident in the emphasis on individual autonomy and striving for growth and the importance of spontaneity and intimacy. Existentialism shows itself in responsibility for one's own actions and decisions and the idea that those decisions can be changed. Like the person-centred and Gestalt approaches, TA maintains that the best way to understand the world is through one's own experience. However, unlike those two approaches, early experience is seen to have a strong influence on the present, particularly in relation to the concept of ego states explained below.

A key factor of this approach is that it focuses on the patterns of communication between people, and as well as a therapeutic tool it can be used as a communication skills model (Hough 2010). It is therefore used in a range of group settings within areas such as education, management and the caring professions. Berne himself used it mainly in groups.

Figure 3

It consists of a unified theoretical model of psychological functioning both within the individual and between individuals. The key concepts are those of ego states, transactions, scripts and games or rackets. Ego states are 'ways of describing intra-psychic and inter-personal *processes* with regard to personality' (Tudor and Hobbes 2002: 245). They consist of three main states of mind which influence how an individual relates to others and which can lead to inflexible ways of relating. The three ego states are: Parent, Adult and Child which are diagrammatically represented in Figure 3.

Everyone moves between these ego states, which influence our thoughts, feelings and behaviour, though psychologically healthier individuals tend to use the different states more flexibly. The Parent state consists of messages and rules internalized from significant others. The Adult state is the rational part of the self which makes decisions; and the Child is the emotional, pre-verbal part. All states are affected by past influences. There are positive and negative aspects to each state so that the parent can be nurturing or critical and the Child can be free or spontaneous or conforming to parental expectations. The interactions, or transactions as they are known in TA, between our own and others' ego states can be explored to increase awareness as to where the inflexibility might lie. For example someone could be stuck in one ego state resulting in a failure to establish intimate relationships with others.

A life script is an ongoing psychological process, developed in early childhood, which governs an individual's behaviour through life. Script analysis in therapy enables the client to become more aware of and to challenge their script. If for example a client's script includes the idea that they must please others, they can be helped to recognize when they are applying this script and to develop alternative ways of behaving.

Games are

> repetitive sequences of transactions, between two or more people, which comprise a significant proportion of ... transactions ... conducted out of Adult awareness, incorporating a moment or moments of surprise and confusion, resulting in painful or inauthentic emotional states on the part of those who are involved.
>
> (McLeod 2009: 256–7)

These patterns of transactions, which act out the script beliefs, tend to maintain life scripts and hinder intimacy.

Limitations of the approach

Superficiality is a criticism which has been levelled at TA largely due to its use of everyday, colloquial terms such as 'games' and the concept of 'OKness'. Although it is, in fact, a complex and detailed theoretical framework, its instant appeal could result in it being applied simplistically. Other criticisms include the fact that it does not include any biological or spiritual dimensions which might influence human interaction (Tudor and Hobbs 2002). Like many other theoretical approaches developed before the 1980s it does not consider the issue of cultural diversity, so it may not be compatible with the beliefs of those from non-western cultural backgrounds who might not see the relevance of concepts such as life scripts or games. It also supports the medical model to some degree in its use of terms such as 'cure', 'treatment plan' and 'diagnosis'.

Research evidence

There has been very little research into the outcomes or processes of TA therapy. McLeod (2009) includes a brief review of some of the main TA research studies, but makes the point that none of these are sufficiently methodologically rigorous to be able to influence health care policy. This does not mean that TA is not effective, but more research is needed to demonstrate that it is.

References

Hough, M. (2010) *Counselling Skills and Theory*, 3rd edn. London: Hodder Education.

McLeod, J. (2009) *An Introduction to Counselling*. Maidenhead: Open University Press.

Tudor, K. and Hobbes, R. (2002) Transactional analysis. In W. Dryden (ed.) *Handbook of Individual Therapy*, 4th edn. London: Sage.

Annotated further reading

Stewart, I. (2000) *Transactional Analysis Counselling in Action*, 2nd edn. London: Sage.

This is a good introduction to how TA is used in practice.

Eric Berne's original texts are useful in order to get a sense of TA in its original form. For example, Berne, E. (1975) *What Do You Say After You Say Hello? The Psychology of Human Destiny*. London: Corgi.

Transference

See also: counter-transference; psychodynamic counselling; the therapeutic relationship

Transference is the process of transferring deeply held feelings originally experienced in childhood relationships to present relationships, including that with the therapist. This concept is a central one in psychoanalysis and psychodynamic therapy where the focus is on the therapeutic relationship. The idea is that the therapist presents themselves as a neutral, sharing very little of themselves with the client, thereby creating an environment where the client is encouraged to behave towards the therapist as they might towards other important figures in their life, both past and present.

One of the aims of transference is to enable clients to re-experience a range of feelings which might otherwise be inaccessible to them. This provides opportunities for the therapist to analyse conflicts which occurred in the client's past relationships, which may be still negatively affecting their present relationships. It is also a way of showing clients in a very direct, experiential way that they are repeating the patterns of their past (Etchegoyen 2005). Change is likely to occur as clients become more aware of old patterns of relating and, as a result, become freer to act in new ways (Luborsky et al. 2008, cited in Corey 2009). The ultimate aim of interpreting the transference relationship in psychoanalysis is personality change, although there is less emphasis on this process in less intensive psychodynamic therapy.

Transference is a key concept in psychodynamic therapy, and analysis of the transference is a central technique both in traditional psychoanalysis and more contemporary psychodynamic therapy. However, this concept has become so prevalent that therapists from other perspectives often use the technique in their own practice.

The analysis of the transference relationship can be a very powerful and insightful experience for clients, enabling them to behave towards the therapist in a more authentic way. Relationships with others are also likely to become less affected by conflicts from the clients' past relationships. Because the change occurs at a deep level of the psyche, supporters of this approach argue that the effects are likely to be profound and long-lasting.

One potential problem with analysing the transference in depth is that it often requires long-term, intensive psychotherapy for a successful outcome. Transference interpretations made too early on in the therapy can have a negative effect. Such long-term therapy will only be accessible to certain client groups and could be seen to support the claim that psychoanalysis is an elitist form of therapy. Clients also require a certain level of ego strength which many more disturbed clients may not possess (Luborsky et al. 2008, in Corey 2009).

Research findings relating to transference suggest that high levels of transference interpretations are not effective with clients who have poor relational abilities (Crits-Christoph and Gibbons 2002, in Cooper 2008). Indeed research undertaken since the early 1990s suggests that frequent transference interpretations are generally associated with poorer therapeutic outcomes (e.g. Høglend 1993, in Cooper 2008) and some researchers even conclude that transference interpretations in brief psychotherapy should be avoided altogether (Orlinsky et al. 2004, in Cooper 2008). However, if transference interpretations are accurate and made in the context of a strong and supportive therapeutic alliance, outcomes are much more favourable (Crits-Christoph et al. 1988 and 1993, in Cooper 2008).

Outside of the psychodynamic approach, transference is regarded from a rather different perspective. For example, Rogers saw tranference as something to get through before the serious work could start (Mearns 1994). Owen (1993, in Spinelli 1994) argued that the concept of transference gives therapists permission to disregard much of what is really going on between client and therapist at a conscious level. What might be interpreted by the therapist as transference on the part of the client could be a real and valid issue about the therapist's behaviour.

References

Cooper, M. (2008) *Essential Research Findings in Counselling and Psychotherapy: The Facts are Friendly*. London: Sage.

Corey, G. (ed.) (2009) *Theory and Practice of Counselling and Psychotherapy*, 8th edn. Belmont, CA: Thompson Brooks Cole.

Etchegoyen, H. (2005) *The Fundamentals of Psychoanalytic Technique*. London: Karnac Books.

Mearns, D. (1994) *Developing Person-centred Counselling.* London: Sage.
Spinelli, E. (1994) *Demystifying Therapy.* London: Constable.

Annotated further reading

Jacobs, M. (2010) *Psychodynamic Counselling in Action,* 4th edn. London: Sage.

Jacobs looks at aspects of theory, including tranference, as it occurs in practice.

Transitional objects

See also: Winnicott, D.W.

For Winnicott, the intermediate area between the inner and outer worlds are mediated by *experience* (see **Winnicott, D.W.**) (Dell'Orto and Caruso 2003). Accompanying the auto-erotic experience of the infant (e.g. thumb-sucking) there are often transitional phenomena such as part of a sheet or blanket that the baby takes into the mouth along with the fingers. This becomes the first 'not-me' object in the infant's experience.

These objects become vitally important for the infant as a defence against anxiety, particularly the depressive type (Winnicott 1971/2001: 4). If the infant has a particular favourite which they seek out and find it upsetting to separate from, this is the transitional object and the need for a transitional object may reappear later during times of stress or anxiety. Winnicott summarizes the qualities of the transitional object as follows:

a)   the infant assumes rights over the object;
b)   the object is affectively cuddled as well as excitedly loved and mutilated;
c)   it must survive instinctual loving and hating;
d)   it must seem to provide the infant with warmth or something that has a vitality of its own;
e)   it is not an hallucination but is outside the baby;
f)   over the course of years it becomes relegated to limbo rather than forgotten but does lose meaning.

Hence we find the characteristic family drama of an adult finding and remembering the details of his old teddy bear in the attic, or the cot blanket or teething ring that the person's mother couldn't bear to throw away (Castets 1966).

The analyst has been identified as a transitional object which also relates to Winnicott's concept of the holding relationship (Murray 1974). There has been wide adoption of the idea of the transitional relationship in the popular and more serious media dealing with couple relationships, particularly relationships that cover the transition following the end of a long-term one.

The transitional object has been subject of contemporary research into adolescent behaviour as well as food or the patient's own body in cases of bulimics binge-purge cycles (Sloate 2008) although the idea of the body as a transitional object had previously been considered for example in self-mutilation (Kafka 1969).

References

Castets, B. (1966) [The teddy-bear child. (The child as a transitional object. Remarks on mental retardations secondary to early psychoses in children)]. *Ann Med Psychol (Paris)*, 124(5): 649–76.

Dell'Orto, S. and Caruso, E. (2003) [W. D. Winnicott and the transitional object in infancy]. *Medical and Surgical Pediatrics*, 25(2): 106–12.

Kafka, J.S. (1969) The body as transitional object: a psychoanalytic study of a self-mutilating patient. *British Journal of Medical Psychology*, 42(3): 207–12.

Murray, M.E. (1974) The therapist as a transitional object. *American Journal of Psychoanalysis*, 34(2): 123–7.

Sloate, P.L. (2008) From fetish object to transitional object: the analysis of a chronically self-mutilating bulimic patient. *Journal of the American Academy of Psychoanalysis and Dynamic Psychiatry*, 36(1): 69–88.

Winnicott, D.W. (1971/2001) *Playing and Reality*. London: Brunner-Routledge.

Annotated further reading

Winnicott, D.W. (1971/2001) *Playing and Reality*. London: Brunner-Routledge.

This is the best account of transitional objects with a rationale for the ideas underpinning the concept.

There are several blogs focusing on transitional relationships (see for example http://www.singlemommyhood.com/2009/07/are-you-just-the-transition-relationship/#respond).

U

Unconditional positive regard

See also: congruence; core conditions; empathy; person-centred counselling

This concept is most commonly associated with Carl Rogers and the person-centred approach to counselling. It is an attitude, rather than a skill or technique, and comprises one of the core conditions developed by Rogers who defined it as 'the extent to which the therapist finds himself experiencing a warm acceptance of the client's experience as being a part of that client' (1957: 98). Mearns and Thorne describe it a 'fundamental attitude' of the therapist who 'deeply values the humanity of her client and is not deflected in that valuing by any particular client behaviours' (2007: 95). A range of other terms have since been used instead, including 'acceptance', 'respect', 'non-possessive warmth' and 'prizing'. This latter term was Rogers' own and fits more easily into an American context than a European one.

According to person-centred theory, unconditional positive regard is essential in order to create a safe, accepting relationship within which the client feels valued for who they are, including the parts of themselves which are less socially or personally acceptable. The client will then feel more able to explore their more difficult and unacceptable thoughts and feelings, thereby gaining greater insight into themselves and their issues.

This complete lack of judgement on the part of the therapist enables the client to break the self-defeating cycle of having to meet other people's expectations (see **conditions of worth**) in order to be valued (Mearns and Thorne 2007). Many clients can be locked into behaving in ways which protect the self (e.g. manipulative or aggressive behaviours) which also tend to alienate others and uphold the client's belief that they are unlovable. The therapist's attitude, assuming it is ongoing and consistent, challenges this belief. Ultimately the aim is to enable the client to become more accepting of themselves.

Students new to the concept sometimes struggle with the idea of being able to accept client behaviours which are morally or ethically repugnant to them such as child abuse or other criminal acts. The important distinction here is between accepting an individual and approving of certain aspects of their behaviour (or thoughts or feelings). Unconditional positive regard is also not the same as liking the client, nor is it about being nice to them (Mearns and

Thorne 2007). Indeed there can be an issue around being too warm and friendly with the client, who may then fear the therapist will withdraw this warmth if they say something 'inappropriate'.

Different therapists inevitably have different views on the most effective ways to convey unconditional positive regard to their clients. Rogers believed that a certain warmth was important, whereas Casemore (2006) argues that a certain clinical distance is vital. He also advocates noticing and describing aspects of the client such as body language (without interpretation) and discussing whether it means something to the client. Thorne (2002) believes that a smile can sometimes express this attitude more effectively than a statement and Mearns and Thorne (2007) advocate appropriate touch.

Many studies focusing on aspects of therapy found useful by clients indicate that unconditional positive regard is one of the most valued aspects of therapy (Conte et al. 1995, in Cooper 2008). However, when other aspects as well as client ratings are taken into consideration, a significant positive relationship between positive regard and positive outcomes are found in only about half of the studies (Farber and Lane 2002, in Cooper 2008). The conclusion of the largest ever review of empirical evidence relating to the therapeutic relationship (Norcross 2002) was that this quality was a 'promising and probably effective' aspect of the therapeutic relationship.

References

Casemore, R. (2006) *Person-centred Counselling in a Nutshell*. London: Sage.

Cooper, M. (2008) *Essential Research Findings in Counselling and Psychotherapy: The Facts are Friendly*. London: Sage.

Mearns, D. and Thorne, B. (2007) *Person-Centred Counselling in Action*. London: Sage.

Norcross, J.C. (ed.) (2002) *Psychotherapy Relationships that Work: Therapists' Contributions and Responsiveness to Patients*. New York: Oxford University Press.

Rogers, C.R. (1957) The necessary and sufficient conditions of therapeutic personality change. *Journal of Consulting Psychology*, 21: 95–103.

Thorne, B. (2002) Person-centred therapy. In W. Dryden (ed.) *Handbook of Individual Therapy*, 4th edn. London: Sage.

Annotated further reading

Casemore, R. (2006) *Person-centred Counselling in a Nutshell*. London: Sage.

A succinct guide to person-centred theoretical concepts and to the counselling relationship.

Cooper, M., O'Hara, M., Schmid, P.F. and Wyatt, G. (eds) (2007) *The Handbook of Person Centred Counselling and Psychotherapy*. Ross-on-Wye: PCCS Books.

An excellent, comprehensive overview of theory and practice.

Values

See also: assertiveness; empathy; death, fear of; organismic valuing process; self; strengths

Values are enduring beliefs about what matters and does not matter. They can therefore be crucial in making good decisions and in being assertive. Like emotions, they can also be clarifying and energizing. However, they may need exploring and examining before actions are taken: some values are based on irrational beliefs or express a prejudice or bias, however compelling one's 'gut reaction'.

Published lists of values are usually abstract, for example love, power, efficiency, but need not be, for example money, children, fishing. Indeed two ways of clarifying values, especially core values, are to press for greater specificity or greater abstractness. One variation of the technique of 'laddering' (Fransella and Dalton 2000) is to ask of each answer to a question 'What is it about X that is important to you?' Patrick (2003) gave this example. Her starting statement was 'I must have the beds made by ten'; this led via the laddering question to 'If not, someone might find out how untidy I am', then to 'I prefer people not to know how I really am; if they knew they wouldn't like me' and then to 'I wouldn't have any friends' and finally, at least on this occasion, to 'I'd have no social life'. Greater depth can therefore be reached quickly and in this particular example could have been pursued further: what is it about having no social life that is important to her? Laddering requires patience, trust and self-awareness, though it has the potential to increase these qualities too.

An assumption about values is that only a few (say five or so) can really be core, because time and energy are limited. This in turn implies that core values should be acted on. One application in counselling is to ask one or more of the following questions: can you identify where your values come from (as a way of distinguishing between authentic and false values)? Do you act on your values? Do you want to act more on your values? The implication might be that values are more likely to be authentic if you do act on them. However, some might say that it's how they feel after reflection that matters.

Apart from offering to help clients clarify, test, and perhaps change their values, therapists might also choose to disclose relevant values of their own, for example when seeking to repair an alliance rupture.

References

Fransella, F. and Dalton, P. (2000) *Personal Construct Counselling in Action*, 2nd edn. London: Sage.

Patrick, E. (2003) Values? Now where did I put them? *Counselling and Psychotherapy Journal*, August: 30–1.

Annotated further reading

Simon, S.B., Howell, L.W. and Kirschen Baum, H. (1995) *Values Clarification*. London: Little Brown and Company, revised edition.

Practical and varied selection of ways of exploring and identifying values.

Winnicott, D.W. (1896–1971)

See also: object relations theory; transitional objects

Donald Winnicott was a paediatrician and psychoanalyst and one of the founders of the object relations school and a leading contributor to the British Independent Group of Psychoanalysis. He spent his childhood in Plymouth and studied medicine at Cambridge, although he experienced a break in studies as he took part in the First World War as a probationer surgeon in the British Navy. He eventually worked at Paddington Green Hospital in London for around 40 years and gave over 20,000 consultations with the mother and child couple (Symington 1986).

Winnicott was in analysis with James Strachey (who translated the standard editions of Freud's writing). Winnicott was a child psychoanalyst who also worked with mothers, and one of his influential concepts was that of the 'good enough' mother in recognition that many mothers constantly worried and felt guilt because they were not perfect. Winnicott saw that provided enough love and good experiences were provided for the infant/child their experience would be one that would lead to health.

The good enough mother was able to provide what Winnicott named as a *holding environment* for their child, as did the therapist. The emphasis on the mother/baby relationship was on physically holding the baby so that the baby would be secure and feel the mother's body. The baby developed a sense of being held, fed, bathed and looked after and the baby would consequently feel that psychically. That experience would then develop to an understanding of the family and the outside world. Therefore the baby would have taken in a sense of how it was mothered and the feelings in response to that and face their future life with those objects internalized to make sense of their relationships. The holding environment can be compared with Bion's 'container-contained' and 'maternal reverie', both of which have direct implications for the analytic relationship as well as that of the mother/baby relationship.

Winnicott's interest was also in children's play and here he was concerned with the development of the self (Winnicott 1971/2001). He considered that it was important that children have opportunities for play early in life and that to mature too early (to have a sense of self that is based upon responsibility and others' expectations rather than maturing through play and thus self-discovery) means the development of a 'false' self. Therefore in common with some other analysts, particularly Freud and Erikson, Winnicott argued for maturational stages of development (Winnicott 1965). This contrasts in part with Klein's view of positions, although for Klein the early months are characterized by the paranoid-schizoid position and the infant/child needs to have had some maturational experience (biological and psychological) before they can take the depressive position.

Another of his important contributions was the **transitional object** (see separate entry) (Winnicott 1971/2001).

References

Symington, N. (1986) *The Analytic Experience: Lectures from the Tavistock*. London: Free Association Books.

Winnicott, D.W. (1965) *The Maturational Process and the Facilitating Environment*. New York: International Universities Press.

Winnicott, D.W. (1971/2001) *Playing and Reality*. London: Brunner-Routledge.

Annotated further reading

Winnicott, D.W. (1965) *The Maturational Process and the Facilitating Environment*. New York: International Universities Press.

Winnicott, D.W. (1971/2001) *Playing and Reality*. London: Brunner-Routledge.

These, like other books and papers by Winnicott, are classic texts which outline his work with children and the theories that came from this work, particularly object relations thinking.

Yalom, Irvin (1931–)

See also: anxiety, existential; death, fear of; existential counselling

Irvin Yalom is a leading figure in existential therapy. He says he was drawn to being a psychotherapist by an experience when he was about 13: his father had a severe coronary and when the doctor arrived 'everything changed. He assuaged my anxiety, let me listen to my father's heart to reinforce the idea it was going regularly. He was an angel of mercy that night and I think at that point I made the decision that I'd like to be able to pass that kind of relief to others' (interview in Kurtz 2008: 584).

Yalom says he chose psychiatry rather than medicine because he enjoyed the wisdom about human behaviour in novels by Tolstoy and Hemmingway. He recounts and analyses many of his own experiences and insights in *Staring at the Sun: Overcoming the Dread of Death* (Yalom 2008), including his father's death 20 years after the incident described above, the deaths of his mentors and vivid episodes from therapy sessions.

Yalom has also written major textbooks, e.g. *Existential Psychotherapy* (Yalom 1980), a book of 85 'tips for beginner therapists' (Yalom 2001) and novels. One of his novels, *Lying on the Couch* (Yalom 1997), is accurately described on the back cover as a 'dazzling psychiatric whodunnit'. The main character resembles Yalom in several respects – he's an eminent psychiatrist in his seventies – but the fictional psychiatrist has been accused of sexual misconduct with a 32-year-old patient. It has an intricate and engaging plot and it too includes numerous sharp and stimulating comments on therapy theories and techniques.

Reference

Kurtz, A. (2008) Staring at the sun. *The Psychologist*, 2(7): 584–5.
Yalom, I.D. (1980) *Existential Psychotherapy*. New York: Basic Books.
Yalom, I.D. (1997) *Lying on the Couch*. New York: HarperCollins.
Yalom, I.D. (2001) *The Gift of Therapy. Reflections on being a therapist*. London: Piatkus.
Yalom, I.D. (2008) *Staring at the Sun: Overcoming the Dread of Death*. London: Piatkus.

Annotated further reading

Yalom, I.D. (1979) *Love's Executioner*. Harmondsworth: Penguin.

> I think this is Yalom's best book, for both trainee and experienced therapists. It is 'tales' of ten clients, and written with striking grace and honesty. He intended the tales to teach existential therapy.

Index

abandonment, life traps 166
acceptance and commitment therapy
(ACT) 5–6
see also behaviour therapy; cognitive
behavioural therapy (CBT);
dialectical behaviour therapy (DBT);
mindfulness-based cognitive therapy
(MBCT)
vs cognitive behavioural therapy 5–6
Six Core Processes 6
ACT *see* acceptance and commitment
therapy
addiction *see* motivational interviewing
Adlerian therapy 7–8
encouragement 7–8
goals 7–8
inferiority complex 7
aim, this book's 1
Ainsworth, Mary, attachment theory 15
all-or-nothing thinking *see* cognitive
distortions (CD)
Allan, C., Socratic dialogue 283
Alpha (α) elements and Beta (β)
elements/functions, Bion, Wilfred
R. 32–3
anxiety 8–10
see also anxiety, existential; cognitive
behavioural therapy (CBT); schema
therapy
CBT interpretation 8–9
defence mechanisms 77
organizational dynamics 214
social defences 214
anxiety, existential 10–11
see also death, fear of; existential
counselling
apartheid, blind eye 36, 37
archetypes 11–13
see also collective unconscious; life scripts
defining 11
Neher, A. 56–7
assertiveness 13–14
see also self; self-actualization

defining 13
training 13
assimilative integration, integrative models
144
assumptions
existential counselling 104–5
neuro linguistic programming (NLP)
198–9
values 311
attachment theory 14–16
see also object relations theory;
psychoanalysis
Ainsworth, Mary 15
Bowlby, John 14–15
types of attachment 15
authority, open systems theory 210
auto-pilot *see* being mindful

Balint, M., object relations theory 202
Bandura, A., social learning theory
281–2
basic assumption groups 17–20
see also Bion, Wilfred R.; groups
dependency 18
fight-flight 18
pairing 18–19
safety in the mass 19–20
Bayne, R. *et al.*, immediacy 140
Beck, Aaron T. 21–3
see also cognitive behavioural therapy
(CBT); mindfulness-based cognitive
therapy (MBCT)
cognitive behavioural therapy (CBT)
49–50
cognitive therapy (CT) 21–2
Dalai Lama 22, 274
self-acceptance 274
behaviour therapy (BT) 23–5
see also cognitive behavioural therapy
(CBT); multimodal therapy
depression 25
team work 24
being mindful 26–8

see also Kabat-Zinn, Jon; mindfulness-based cognitive behavioural coaching; mindfulness-based cognitive therapy (MBCT); mindfulness-based stress reduction

beliefs *see* core beliefs; irrational beliefs

Berne, Eric 28–9
see also transactional analysis
Games People Play 26
life scripts 164–5
Sex in Human Loving 26

Bettelheim, Bruno, safety in the mass 19–20

bibliotherapy 29–31
see also cognitive behavioural therapy (CBT)
advantages 30
categories of books 29
limitations, potential 30
research findings 30

Billig, M., repression 259

Bion, Wilfred R. 31–4
see also basic assumption groups; container/contained; groups; projection; projective identification
Alpha (α) elements and Beta (β) elements/functions 32–3
projection 31–2
projective identification 31–2, 238
psychoanalytic thinking 32–3

Bion's theory of group processes 131–2

blind eye 34–9
see also Oedipus complex
apartheid 36, 37
concentration camps 36, 37
defence mechanisms 37
defending against external reality 37
'double agents' 35–7
examples 35–7
negation and disavowal 37
Steiner, J. 35

Bloom, William, compassionate mind training 58–9

borderline personality disorder (BPD), dialectical behaviour therapy (DBT) 80–1

boundaries 39–41
see also assertiveness; ethical concepts; games; psychoanalysis; psychodynamic counselling; self-disclosure
open systems theory 210–11

Bowlby, John, attachment theory 14–15

BPD *see* borderline personality disorder

brief therapy 42–4
see also cognitive behavioural therapy (CBT)
defining 42
limitations, potential 43
research evidence 43
suitability 42

BT *see* behaviour therapy

Buddhist influences
compassionate mind training 58–60
Kabat-Zinn, Jon 153–4

Buddhist psychology, cognitive behavioural therapy (CBT) 22

burnout, boundaries 41

CAPP *see* Centre for Applied Positive Psychology

Carey, T.A., Socratic dialogue 283–4

CAT *see* cognitive analytic therapy

catharsis 45–6
see also anxiety, existential; empathy

CB *see* core beliefs

CBT *see* cognitive behavioural therapy

CD *see* cognitive distortions

Centre for Applied Positive Psychology website (CAPP), strengths 288

chain analysis, dialectical behaviour therapy (DBT) 82

children
see also Winnicott, D.W.
free association 114–15
infantile sexuality 118–19, 203–8, 268–70
Oedipus complex 203–8
paranoid-schizoid position 219–20
psychosexual development 244–7
psychosocial development 247–9

Clarkson, P., Perls, Fritz 223

client-driven therapy, cognitive behavioural therapy (CBT) 50

client feedback, collecting 46–7
see also collaborative empiricism; goal consensus; integrative models; therapeutic relationship

client self-disclosure 280

cognitive analytic therapy (CAT) 47–9
see also personal construct therapy
free association 115

cognitive-behavioural approaches, feminist counselling 112

cognitive behavioural therapy (CBT) 49–52

see also mindfulness-based cognitive
  therapy (MBCT); multimodal therapy;
  rational emotive behaviour therapy;
  Socratic dialogue
Beck, Aaron T. 49–50
Buddhist psychology 22
client-driven therapy 50
defining 49–50
eye movement desensitization and
  reprocessing (EMDR) 107
funding 51
goals 50
Layard, Lord R. 51
National Institute for Health and Clinical
  Excellence (NICE) 49, 50
cognitive distortions (CD) 52–3
see also Beck, Aaron T.; cognitive
  behavioural therapy (CBT)
cognitive therapy (CT), Beck, Aaron T. 21–2
collaborative empiricism 54–5
see also cognitive behavioural therapy
  (CBT); negative automatic thoughts
  (NATs)
collaborative pluralism, integrative models
  144–5
collective unconscious 55–7
see also archetypes; dynamic unconscious;
  Jung, Carl
Neher, A. 56–7
synchronicity 56
collectivism – individualism dimension
  57–8
see also feminist counselling; multicultural
  counselling; narrative therapy
commitment, mindfulness-based cognitive
  coaching (MBCC) 176
common factors approach, integrative
  models 144
compassionate mind training 58–60
Bloom, William 58–9
Buddhist influences 58–60
Dalai Lama 59–60
Love/Enlightenment 58–9
meditation 59
self 59–60
concentration camps
blind eye 36, 37
safety in the mass 19–20
concepts, choice and focus 1–2
conditions of worth 61–2
see also core conditions; locus of

evaluation; person-centred counselling;
  self-actualization; self-concept;
  therapeutic relationship
unconditional positive regard 307
congruence 62–3
see also core conditions; empathy; person-
  centred counselling; Rogers, Carl;
  unconditional positive regard
defining 62
constructivism 64–5
see also personal construct therapy
narrative therapy 191
Piaget, J. 64
social constructivism 64
container/contained 65–7
see also Bion, Wilfred R.
object relations theory 66
projection 66
Cooper, M.
relational depth 258
ruptures in the therapeutic alliance 264–5
core beliefs (CB) 68–9
see also cognitive behavioural therapy
  (CBT); life traps; rational emotive
  behaviour therapy (REBT); schema
  therapy
core conditions 70–1
see also congruence; empathy; person-
  centred counselling; Rogers, Carl;
  therapeutic relationship; unconditional
  positive regard
research evidence 71
counselling theories, relevance of a range
  2–3
counter-transference 72–3
see also dynamic unconscious; Freudian
  analysis; psychoanalysis; psychodynamic
  counselling; transference
Freudian analysis 122–3
psychoanalysis 241
Craib, I.
repression 259
structural model of the mind 288–91
CT *see* cognitive therapy
culture
see also multicultural counselling
defining 185
narrative therapy 191

Dalai Lama 153
Beck, Aaron T. 22, 274

compassionate mind training 59–60
self-acceptance 274
Davis, L.M., organismic valuing process
  (OVP) 212–13
DBT *see* dialectical behaviour therapy
death, fear of 75–6
  see also anxiety, existential; self; Yalom,
    Irvin
The Death of Ivan Illych, death, fear of 75–6
defectiveness/shame (DS), life traps 166
defence mechanisms 76–8
  see also Freud, Sigmund; negation and
    disavowal; projection; projective
    identification; psychosocial
    development; splitting; structural
    model of the mind; sublimation
  anxiety 77
  blind eye 37
  denial 77
  psychoanalysis 240–1
  rationalization 77
  repression 77
  resistance 77
  seduction 270
defending against external reality, blind
  eye 37
denial 78–9
  defence mechanisms 77
  motivational interviewing (MI) 182
  reaction formation 78
dependency
  basic assumption groups 18
  life traps 166
depression
  behaviour therapy (BT) 25
  mindfulness-based cognitive therapy
    (MBCT) 177–8
depressive position 79–80
  see also Klein, Melanie; object relations
    theory; paranoid-schizoid position;
    projective identification; splitting
  narcissism 79
dialectical behaviour therapy (DBT) 80–2
  see also acceptance and commitment
    therapy (ACT); behaviour therapy (BT);
    cognitive behavioural therapy (CBT);
    mindfulness-based cognitive therapy
    (MBCT)
  borderline personality disorder (BPD)
    80–1
  chain analysis 82

dietary self-selection, organismic valuing
  process (OVP) 212–13
displacement 83–4
  see also defence mechanisms; dream
    analysis; sublimation
  dream analysis 83–4
  Freudian analysis 83–4
'double agents', blind eye 35–7
drama triangle 84–5
  see also assertiveness; games; life scripts
  Karpman drama triangle (KDT) 84–5
dream analysis 85–7
  see also dynamic unconscious;
    interpretation; Jung, Carl;
    psychoanalysis; psychodynamic
    counselling
  criticisms 86
  displacement 83–4
  Freudian analysis 83–4, 123
  Gestalt therapy 86
  Yalom, Irvin 86
Dryden, Windy
  rational emotive behaviour therapy
    (REBT) 256
  self-acceptance 273
DS *see* defectiveness/shame
dynamic unconscious 87–8
  see also archetypes; collective
    unconscious

eating disorders, cognitive distortions (CD)
  53
Egan, G., immediacy 139–40
Egan's skilled helper model 89–92
  see also integrative models
  criticisms 91
  principles 91
  research evidence 91–2
  stages 89–90
ego
  Eriksonian analysis 99
  psychosexual development 244
  structural model of the mind 290
ego states *see* transactional analysis
Ellis, Albert 92–5
  see also rational emotive behaviour
    therapy
  irrational beliefs (IBs) 148–9
EMDR *see* eye movement desensitization
  and reprocessing
emotional deprivation, life traps 166

emotional health, rational emotive
  behaviour therapy (REBT) 256
empathy 95–7
  see also core conditions; integrative
    models; interpretation; paraphrasing;
    person-centred counselling; preferences;
    therapeutic relationship
  defining 95
  measuring 96
encouragement, Adlerian therapy 7–8
Enlightenment/Love, compassionate mind
    training 58–9
entitlement, life traps 167
Erikson, Erik 98–9
  see also Eriksonian analysis; psychosexual
    development; psychosocial
    development
  structural model of the mind 289
Eriksonian analysis 99–100
  see also psychosocial development
  ego 99
ethical concepts 100–3
  see also boundaries
  ethical principles 102–3
  legal issues 102–3
  organizational policy 101
  personal ethics 101
  professional codes/guidelines 101
  therapeutic approaches 101
existential anxiety 10–11
  see also death, fear of; existential
    counselling
existential counselling 103–7
  see also anxiety, existential; Gestalt
    therapy; logotherapy; phenomenology
  existential therapy 105
  historical perspective 104
  limitations 106
  process of therapy 105–6
  social support networks 104–5
  theoretical assumptions 104–5
  van Deurzen, Emmy 104–5
existential therapy, existential counselling
    105
eye movement desensitization and
    reprocessing (EMDR) 107–9
  cognitive behavioural therapy (CBT) 107
  goals 107
  National Institute for Health and Clinical
    Excellence (NICE) 107
  obsessive compulsive disorder (OCD) 107

post-traumatic stress disorder (PTSD)
    107–8
  process of therapy 108–9
  rapid eye movements (REM) 108

failure, life traps 167
Fairbairn, W.R.D., object relations theory
    202
feedback, client *see* client feedback,
    collecting
feedback welcomed 3
feminist counselling 111–14
  see also assertiveness; integrative models;
    multicultural counselling
  cognitive-behavioural approaches 112
  critical perspectives 113
  goals 112–13
  humanistic approaches 112
  psychoanalysis 112
  research findings 113
fight-flight, basic assumption groups 18
Fonagy, P., repression 259
Frankl, Viktor, logotherapy 169–71
free association 114–16
  see also dream analysis; interpretation;
    psychoanalysis; psychodynamic
    counselling
  children 114–15
  cognitive analytic therapy (CAT) 115
  couch, use of 114
Freud, Sigmund 116–21
  see also defence mechanisms; free
    association; Freudian analysis;
    psychosexual development; structural
    model of the mind
  evaluation 119
  infantile sexuality 118–19, 203–8, 268–70
  major works 119
  professional background 116–17
  research 119
  unconscious 117–18
Freudian analysis 121–4
  see also defence mechanisms; dream
    analysis; free association; Freud,
    Sigmund; Oedipus complex
  counter-transference 122–3
  displacement 83–4
  dream analysis 83–4, 123
  ego 290
  id 290
  Kleinian analysis 123, 155

narcissism 189–90
negation and disavowal 193–4
process of therapy 122–3
projection 236
psychic structures 290–1
psychosexual development 244–6
repression 259
resistance 260–1
setting 121–2
splitting 284–5
structural model of the mind 288–91
sublimation 291–2
superego 246, 290–1
transference 122–3
funding, cognitive behavioural therapy
    (CBT) 51

games 125–6
    see also assertiveness; drama
    triangle; life scripts; transactional
    analysis
    McLeod, J. 301
Games People Play, Berne, Eric 26, 125–6
gender, Oedipus complex 206–7
Gestalt therapy 126–8
    see also existential counselling;
    humanistic approaches; person-
    centred counselling
    boundaries 40
    dream analysis 86
    limitations 127–8
    research findings 127
    self-actualization 127
goal consensus 128–9
    see also client feedback, collecting;
    collaborative empiricism; integrative
    models; personality; therapeutic
    relationship
    meta-analysis 129
goals
    Adlerian therapy 7–8
    cognitive behavioural therapy
    (CBT) 50
    eye movement desensitization and
    reprocessing (EMDR) 107
    feminist counselling 112–13
    motivational interviewing (MI) 182–3
groups 129–34
    see also basic assumption groups; Bion,
    Wilfred R.
    Bion's theory of group processes 131–2

defining 129–30
    psychoanalysis 130–1

Holocaust
    blind eye 36, 37
    safety in the mass 19–20
humanistic approaches 135–6
    see also existential counselling; Gestalt
    therapy; person-centred counselling;
    phenomenology; self-actualization
    boundaries 40
    feminist counselling 112
    limitations 135–6
    Maslow's hierarchy of needs 135–6

IBs see irrational beliefs
id
    negation and disavowal 194
    structural model of the mind 290
imagery, guided 137–9
    see also cognitive behavioural therapy;
    multimodal therapy
immediacy 139–41
    see also congruence; self-disclosure
    Bayne, R. *et al.* 140
    Egan, G. 139–40
    types 139–40
individualism see collectivism –
    individualism dimension
individuation 141–3
    see also Jung, Carl
    integration 141–2
infantile sexuality
    see also psychosexual development
    Freud, Sigmund 118–19, 203–8, 268–70
    seduction 268–70
inferiority complex, Adlerian therapy 7
integration
    see also integrative models
    individuation 141–2
integrative approach, cognitive analytic
    therapy (CAT) 47–8
integrative models 143–6
    see also Egan's skilled helper model;
    integration
    assimilative integration 144
    collaborative pluralism 144–5
    common factors approach 144
    limitations, potential 145
    technical eclecticism 144
    theoretical integration 144

interpretation 146–7
  see also counter-transference;
    dream analysis; free association;
    psychoanalysis; psychodynamic
    counselling; transference
  research evidence 147
interviewing, motivational *see* motivational
    interviewing
introjection 147–8
  see also depressive position; object
    relations theory; paranoid-schizoid
    position; projective identification
irrational beliefs (IBs) 148–50
  see also Ellis, Albert; rational emotive
    behaviour therapy

Joseph, S., organismic valuing process
    (OVP) 213
Jung, Carl 151–2
  see also archetypes; collective
    unconscious
  word association 151

Kabat-Zinn, Jon 153–4
  see also being mindful; mindfulness-based
    cognitive behavioural
    coaching; mindfulness-based cognitive
    therapy; mindfulness-based stress
    reduction
  Buddhist influences 153–4
Karpman drama triangle (KDT) 84–5
KDT *see* Karpman drama triangle
Kelly, George
  personal construct therapy 225–7
  Repertory Grid 226
Klein, Melanie 154–7
  central ideas 156
  narcissism 189
  structural model of the mind 290
  writings 155–6
Kleinian analysis 158–9
  see also depressive position; Klein, Melanie;
    object relations theory; paranoid-schizoid
    position; projective identification
  Freudian analysis 123, 155
  negation and disavowal 193
  Oedipus complex 204, 207
  projective identification 238
  splitting 285

labelling *see* cognitive distortions (CD)

Layard, Lord R., cognitive behavioural
    therapy (CBT) 51
Lazarus, Arnold A. 161–4
  see also multimodal therapy
legal issues, ethical concepts 102–3
life scripts 164–5
  see also archetypes; conditions of worth;
    drama triangle; games; self; self-
    actualization; transactional analysis
  Berne, Eric 164–5
life traps 165–7
  see also schema therapy
  Young, Jeffrey 165–7
limitations
  existential counselling 106
  Gestalt therapy 127–8
  humanistic approaches 135–6
  narrative therapy 192
  transactional analysis (TA) 301
limitations, potential
  bibliotherapy 30
  brief therapy 43
  integrative models 145
  transference 303
Linley, A.P.
  organismic valuing process (OVP) 213
  strengths 287–8
locus of evaluation 168
  see also conditions of worth; core
    conditions; person-centred counselling;
    self-actualization; self-concept
  Rogers, Carl 168
logotherapy 169–71
  see also existential counselling
  criticisms 170
  Frankl, Viktor 169–71
  meaning in life 169–71
  principles 169
  schizophrenia 170
  suffering 170
Love/Enlightenment, compassionate mind
    training 58–9

Mackewn, J., Perls, Fritz 223
magnification *see* cognitive
    distortions (CD)
Maslow, A.H., self-actualization 275
Maslow's hierarchy of needs, humanistic
    approaches 135–6
MBCBC *see* mindfulness-based cognitive
    behavioural coaching

MBCC *see* mindfulness-based cognitive coaching
MBCT *see* mindfulness-based cognitive therapy
MBSR *see* mindfulness-based stress reduction
MBTI *see* Myers-Briggs Type Indicator
McLeod, J.
  games 301
  phenomenology 230
  relational depth 258
  ruptures in the therapeutic alliance 264
  transactional analysis (TA) 301
McMillan, M., relational depth 258
meaning in life, logotherapy 169–71
Mearns, D., relational depth 258
meditation, compassionate mind training 59
Menzies, I.E.P., organizational dynamics 214
MI *see* motivational interviewing
mindful, being *see* being mindful
mindfulness-based cognitive behavioural coaching (MBCBC) 173–5
  see also compassionate mind training; mindfulness-based cognitive therapy; mindfulness-based stress reduction
  research evidence 174
mindfulness-based cognitive coaching (MBCC) 175–7
  commitment 176
mindfulness-based cognitive therapy (MBCT) 177–9
  see also acceptance and commitment therapy; cognitive behavioural therapy; dialectical behaviour therapy; Kabat-Zinn, Jon; mindfulness-based stress reduction
  depression 177–8
  key themes 178
  National Institute for Health and Clinical Excellence (NICE) 178
mindfulness-based stress reduction (MBSR) 179–81
  see also Kabat-Zinn, Jon; mindfulness-based cognitive therapy
mindlessness *see* being mindful
minimization *see* cognitive distortions (CD)
mistrust and abuse, life traps 166
MMT *see* multimodal therapy
Morgan, G.
  organizational dynamics 215

psychic prison 239–40
motivational interviewing (MI) 181–4
  background 181
  clinical application 183–4
  criticisms 183
  denial 182
  goals 182–3
  practice 182–3
  principles 182–3
  theoretical background 183
Mullan, R.J., Socratic dialogue 283–4
multicultural counselling 185–6
  see also collectivism – individualism dimension; integrative models; narrative therapy
  research 186
multimodal therapy (MMT) 187–8
  see also Lazarus, Arnold A.; social learning theory
Myers-Briggs Type Indicator (MBTI)
  personality 228
  preferences 234–5

narcissism 189–90
  see also depressive position; paranoid-schizoid position; psychosexual development
  depressive position 79
  Freudian analysis 189–90
  Klein, Melanie 189
  narcissistic personality disorder 190
narcissistic rage, cognitive distortions (CD) 53
narrative therapy 190–2
  see also multicultural counselling
  constructivism 191
  culture 191
  limitations 192
  other approaches 192
  research evidence 192
  therapeutic relationship 191
National Institute for Health and Clinical Excellence (NICE)
  cognitive behavioural therapy (CBT) 49, 50
  eye movement desensitization and reprocessing (EMDR) 107
  mindfulness-based cognitive therapy (MBCT) 178
NATs *see* negative automatic thoughts
negation and disavowal 193–5

see also blind eye; defence mechanisms;
  repression
blind eye 37
Freudian analysis 193–4
id 194
Kleinian analysis 193
psychosexual development 193
negative automatic thoughts (NATs) 195–7
  see also cognitive behavioural therapy;
  cognitive distortions; irrational beliefs
Neher, A.
  archetypes 56–7
  collective unconscious 56–7
neuro linguistic programming (NLP)
  198–200
  assumptions 198–9
  principles 198–9
  terminology 198
NICE *see* National Institute for Health and
  Clinical Excellence
NLP *see* neuro linguistic programming
Norcross, J.C. *et al.*, stages of change 286–7

object relations theory 201–3
  see also Klein, Melanie; transitional
  objects; Winnicott, D.W.
  Balint, M. 202
  container/contained 66
  Fairbairn, W.R.D. 202
  Frosh, S. 202
  Guntrip, H. 202
  structural model of the mind 290
obsessive compulsive disorder (OCD),
  eye movement desensitization and
  reprocessing (EMDR) 107
Oedipus complex 203–8, 245
  see also blind eye; Freudian analysis
  children 203–8
  criticisms 204–5
  gender 206–7
  Kleinian analysis 204, 207
  psychosexual development 245
  psychosexual stages 204
  Segal, H. 203
open systems theory 209–12
  authority 210
  boundaries 210–11
  role 210
  systems 209
  task 209–10
organismic valuing process (OVP) 212–13

see also assertiveness; conditions of worth;
  humanistic approaches; self; self-
  actualization
  Davis, L.M. 212–13
  Joseph, S. 213
  Linley, A.P. 213
  Rogers, Carl 212
organizational dynamics 213–17
  see also blind eye; open systems theory;
  psychic prison
  anxiety 214
  Menzies, I.E.P. 214
  Morgan, G. 215
  organization in the mind 215
  organization under the surface 215
  structure in the mind 216
organizational policy, ethical concepts 101
overgeneralization *see* cognitive distortions
  (CD)
OVP *see* organismic valuing process

pairing, basic assumption groups 18–19
paranoid-schizoid position 219–20
  see also depressive position; Klein,
  Melanie; projective identification;
  splitting
  children 219–20
  projective identification 238
paraphrasing 220–2
  see also acceptance and commitment
  therapy; empathy; interpretation
  defining 220
Perls, Fritz 222–4
  see also Gestalt therapy
  Clarkson, P. 223
  Mackewn, J. 223
  self-actualization 275
person-centred counselling 224–5
  see also conditions of worth; core
  conditions; humanistic approaches;
  locus of evaluation; phenomenology;
  Rogers, Carl; self-actualization; self-
  concept
personal construct therapy 225–7
  see also constructivism
  Kelly, George 225–7
  Repertory Grid 226
personal ethics, ethical concepts 101
personality 228–30
  see also life scripts; preferences; self; self-
  actualization

Myers-Briggs Type Indicator (MBTI)
228
psychological type theory 228–9
Singer, J.A. 228
personalization *see* cognitive distortions (CD)
phenomenology 230–2
see also existential counselling; Gestalt
therapy; humanistic approaches;
person-centred counselling
counselling approaches 230–1
McLeod, J. 230
Spinelli, E. 231
Piaget, J., constructivism 64
positive psychology (PP) 232–3
Seligman, Martin 232–3
post-traumatic stress disorder (PTSD),
eye movement desensitization and
reprocessing (EMDR) 107–8
PP *see* positive psychology
preferences 234–5
see also client feedback, collecting;
personality; positive psychology; self;
strengths
Myers-Briggs Type Indicator (MBTI)
234–5
professional codes/guidelines, ethical
concepts 101
projection 236–7
see also introjection; projective
identification
Bion, Wilfred R. 31–2
container/contained 66
Freudian analysis 236
uses 236
projective identification 237–9
see also introjection; paranoid-schizoid
position; projection; splitting
Bion, Wilfred R. 31–2, 238
defining 237
Kleinian analysis 238
paranoid-schizoid position 238
psychic prison 239–40
see also organizational dynamics
Morgan, G. 239–40
psychic structures, Freudian analysis 290–1
psychoanalysis 240–2
see also Eriksonian analysis; Freudian
analysis; Kleinian analysis; structural
model of the mind
counter-transference 241
defence mechanisms 240–1

feminist counselling 112
groups 130–1
psychodynamic counselling 243–4
see also psychoanalysis
psychological type theory, personality 228–9
psychosexual development 244–7
see also structural model of the mind
ego 244
Freudian analysis 244–6
negation and disavowal 193
Oedipus complex 245
seduction 268–70
superego 244, 246
psychosocial development 247–9
see also Erikson, Erik; Eriksonian analysis
PTSD *see* post-traumatic stress disorder

questions 251–3
see also brief therapy; paraphrasing;
Socratic dialogue
dangers 251
effective 251–2
responding to 252

range of counselling theories, relevance 2–3
rapid eye movements (REM), eye movement
desensitization and reprocessing
(EMDR) 108
rational emotive behaviour therapy (REBT)
255–7
see also Ellis, Albert; irrational beliefs
Dryden, Windy 256
emotional health 256
stress 255–6
rationalization 257
defence mechanisms 77
reaction formation, denial 78
REBT *see* rational emotive behaviour
therapy
reflection, catharsis 45
relational depth 258
see also person-centred counselling;
therapeutic relationship
Cooper, M. 258
McLeod, J. 258
McMillan, M. 258
Mearns, D. 258
REM *see* rapid eye movements
Repertory Grid
Kelly, George 226
personal construct therapy 226

repression 259–60
  see also narcissism; psychoanalysis
  Billig, M. 259
  Craib, I. 259
  defence mechanisms 77
  Fonagy, P. 259
  Freudian analysis 259
  superego 259
  Wright, E. 259
research, multicultural counselling 186
research evidence
  brief therapy 43
  Egan's skilled helper model 91–2
  interpretation 147
  mindfulness-based cognitive behavioural
    coaching (MBCBC) 174
  narrative therapy 192
  transactional analysis (TA) 301
research findings
  bibliotherapy 30
  feminist counselling 113
  Gestalt therapy 127
  ruptures in the therapeutic alliance 265
resistance 260–1
  see also defence mechanisms; repression
  defence mechanisms 77
  Freudian analysis 260–1
Rogers, Carl 261–3
  see also core conditions; locus of
    evaluation; person-centred counselling;
    self-actualization; self-concept;
    therapeutic relationship
  locus of evaluation 168
  organismic valuing process (OVP) 212
  unconditional positive regard 307, 308
role, open systems theory 210
Rotter, J.B., social learning theory 281
ruptures in the therapeutic alliance 264–6
  see also therapeutic relationship
  Cooper, M. 264–5
  McLeod, J. 264
  research findings 265

safety in the mass
  basic assumption groups 19–20
  Bettelheim, Bruno 19–20
schema therapy 267–8
  see also cognitive behavioural therapy;
    life traps
  Young, Jeffrey 267–8
schizophrenia, logotherapy 170

scripts, life *see* life scripts
seduction 268–71
  see also Freud, Sigmund; Freudian analysis;
    psychosexual development
  defence mechanisms 270
  infantile sexuality 268–70
Segal, H., Oedipus complex 203
self 271–2
  see also collectivism – individualism
    dimension; preferences; self-
    actualization; strengths
  compassionate mind training 59–60
self-acceptance 273–4
  see also cognitive behavioural therapy;
    rational emotive behaviour therapy;
    self-actualization
  Beck, Aaron T. 274
  Dalai Lama 274
  Dryden, Windy 273
  Seltzer, L. 273–4
self-actualization 274–6
  see also assertiveness; conditions of worth;
    congruence; death, fear of; organismic
    valuing process; self; strengths
  Gestalt therapy 127
  Maslow, A.H. 275
  misinterpretations 275–6
  Perls, Fritz 275
  self-concept 275
self-concept 277–8
  see also core conditions; locus of
    evaluation; person-centred counselling;
    self-actualization
  criticisms 277–8
  self-actualization 275
  Thorne, B. 277
self-disclosure 278–80
  see also Egan's skilled helper model;
    therapeutic relationship
  client self-disclosure 280
  research findings 279
  therapist self-disclosure 278–9
Seligman, Martin, positive psychology
  (PP) 232–3
Seltzer, L., self-acceptance 273–4
setting, Freudian analysis 121–2
Sex in Human Loving, Berne, Eric 26
sexuality, infantile
  see also psychosexual development
  Freud, Sigmund 118–19, 203–8, 268–70
short-term counselling *see* brief therapy

Singer, J.A., personality 228
Six Core Processes, acceptance and
    commitment therapy (ACT) 6
social constructivism 64
social defences, anxiety 214
social exclusion, life traps 167
social learning theory 281–2
    see also multimodal therapy
    Bandura, A. 281–2
    Rotter, J.B. 281
social support networks, existential
    counselling 104–5
Socratic dialogue 282–4
    see also Beck, Aaron T.; cognitive
    behavioural therapy; collaborative
    empiricism
    Allan, C. 283
    Carey, T.A. 283–4
    Mullan, R.J. 283–4
Spinelli, E., phenomenology 231
splitting 284–5
    see also defence mechanisms; object
    relations theory; projection; projective
    identification
    Freudian analysis 284–5
    Kleinian analysis 285
stages of change 286–7
    see also client feedback, collecting; death,
    fear of; integrative models; therapeutic
    relationship
    Norcross, J.C. *et al.* 286–7
Steiner, J., blind eye 35
strengths 287–8
    see also empathy; self
    Centre for Applied Positive Psychology
    website (CAPP) 288
    Linley, A.P. 287–8
stress
    see also mindfulness-based stress
    reduction
    rational emotive behaviour therapy
    (REBT) 255–6
structural model of the mind 288–91
    see also defence mechanisms;
    psychosexual development;
    psychosocial development
    Craib, I. 288–91
    ego 290
    Erikson, Erik 289
    Freudian analysis 288–91
    id 290

Klein, Melanie 290
    object relations theory 290
    superego 246, 290–1
structure in the mind, organizational
    dynamics 216
subjugation, life traps 167
sublimation 291–2
    see also defence mechanisms; repression
    Freudian analysis 291–2
suffering, logotherapy 170
superego
    psychosexual development 244, 246
    repression 259
    structural model of the mind 246, 290–1
synchronicity, collective unconscious 56
systemic therapies 292–5
    see also open systems theory
systems, open systems theory 209

TA *see* transactional analysis
task, open systems theory 209–10
team work, behaviour therapy (BT) 24
technical eclecticism, integrative models
    144
terminology notes 3
terror management theory (TMT), death,
    fear of 75
theoretical assumptions, existential
    counselling 104–5
theoretical integration, integrative models
    144
therapeutic approaches, ethical concepts
    101
therapeutic relationship 297–9
    see also relational depth; ruptures in the
    therapeutic alliance; self-disclosure
    cognitive-behavioural perspective 298
    narrative therapy 191
    person-centred perspective 297–8
    psychodynamic perspective 297
therapist self-disclosure 278–9
Thorne, B., self-concept 277
time-limited focus, cognitive analytic
    therapy (CAT) 47
TMT *see* terror management theory
transactional analysis (TA) 299–302
    see also humanistic approaches;
    phenomenology
    ego states 299–300
    games 300–1
    life scripts 300–1

limitations 301
McLeod, J. 301
research evidence 301
transference 302–4
  see also counter-transference;
    psychodynamic counselling;
    therapeutic relationship
  Freudian analysis 122–3
  limitations, potential 303
  problem, potential 303
transitional objects 304–5
  see also object relations theory; Winnicott,
    D.W.

unconditional positive regard 307–9
  see also congruence; core conditions;
    empathy; person-centred counselling
  conditions of worth 307
  defining 307
  Rogers, Carl 307, 308
unconscious, Freud, Sigmund 117–18
unconscious, dynamic *see* dynamic
  unconscious
unrelenting standards, life traps 167

values 311–12
  see also assertiveness; death, fear of;
    empathy; organismic valuing process;
    self; strengths
  assumptions 311
van Deurzen, Emmy, existential counselling
  104–5
venting emotions *see* catharsis
vulnerability, life traps 166

Winnicott, D.W. 313–14
  see also object relations theory;
    transitional objects
word association, Jung, Carl 151
worry *see* anxiety
Wright, E., repression 259

Yalom, Irvin 315–16
  see also anxiety, existential; death, fear of;
    existential counselling
  dream analysis 86
Young, Jeffrey
  life traps 165–7
  schema therapy 267–8